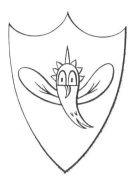

British Experimental Combat Aircraft of World War II

British Experimental Combat Aircraft of World War II

Prototypes, Research Aircraft and Failed Production Designs

Tony Buttler AMRAeS

Published in 2012 by Hikoki Publications

ISBN 9 781902 109244

Printed in China

Hikoki
1a Ringway Trading Estate, Shadowmoss Rd, Manchester M22 5LH
www.crecy.co.uk

Page 2: The first prototype Hawker Tornado P5219 with the original underwing radiator. *Chris-Sandham Bailey www.inkworm.com*

Contents

To my great friend Phil Butler who shares my passion for these fascinating aeroplanes.

Introduction

The idea of this book has been a pet subject for the author over many years, and my thanks to Crécy Publishing for bringing it to fruition. Over the last couple of decades several titles, and a mass of magazine articles, have been published describing British post-war experimental jet aircraft. Indeed, the author has recently added to the pile with *X-Planes of Europe* co-written for Hikoki with Jean-Louis Delezenne, but it is understood that no similar all-embracing publication has been produced which has looked at the equivalent experimental and one-off prototypes and failed production types produced during or for the war itself. *British Experimental Combat Aircraft* hopefully fills this gap, and is in many respects a companion volume to *X-Planes of Europe*.

The objective is to feature one-off aircraft, little known and unsuccessful designs from very roughly the decade that stretches from either side of the Second World War. Primarily we have aircraft that did not make it into service for various reasons, either because they were pure research aeroplanes or because they did not prove to be good enough for front line operations, or something better came along, or the war ended and they were no longer needed. If they are directly relevant to the conflict they are in, even if the aircraft appeared either before September 1939 or after May 1945. Included are production aircraft like the Bristol Buckingham and Westland Welkin. Neither of these reached service, but the Welkin broke new ground in that it flew at very high altitudes while the Buckingham was Britain's final attempt to produce a medium-size piston-powered bomber. Both are of interest and get little coverage and there are quite a few other types in here which were developed with the objective of putting them into service, but which came to nothing. Almost all of the aircraft covered are of course piston-powered but the first jet-powered research aircraft, the Gloster E.28/39, had to be included despite the fact that it has been described in many publications.

The book concentrates on fighter and bomber developments or powered research aircraft that had the objective of furthering the general knowledge for such types – even the little Hillson Bi-Mono was built with a follow-on fighter in mind. In addition, one-off modifications of production aeroplanes are brought together in an Appendix, but pure light aircraft and civil types (apart from the Napier-Heston Racer) do not qualify. This photo appendix reveals how numerous one-off variations of production types were flown to try out various changes to their airframes – a different powerplant, the addition of a gun turret, a different tailplane, or something else. The list in there is nothing like exhaustive but it is sufficient to give a feel for the type of work that was going on.

There are also some projects – generally unbuilt designs which were expected to have at least reached prototype status. This raised the problem of a demarcation line for the book – what to put in and what to leave out? Some types like the Supermarine 316 bomber were part built but never flown, which takes us into the territory covered by the author's earlier work *British Secret Projects: Fighters & Bombers 1935-1950* (Midland Publishing 2004). The solution was to set the parameters so that if military serials were allocated then a type gets in, but if such types had quite short lives and are covered in *British Secret Projects*, then they are covered again here only relatively briefly. However, the opportunity has been taken to include a few

new projects that still lay undiscovered when the 2004 volume was prepared. This is for interest and for the benefit of modellers.

Despite being designed and built well before the war started as part of the build-up for war, a few aircraft like the Gloster F.5/34 get a chapter because they were still flying when the conflict opened. Again, this brings in a grey area since direct rivals to Gloster's aeroplane (the Bristol 146 and Vickers Venom fighters) are omitted because their careers were over when war broke out (there is doubt whether the Martin-Baker M.B.2. ever flew after September 1939, but just in case it is in). Another disputed omission could be the Saunders-Roe A.33, rival to the Shorts Sunderland, the sole prototype of which was damaged beyond repair in 1938, but a line has to be drawn somewhere. The Napier-Heston Racer is here, however, despite being purely a civil aircraft with no military objective. This is because it would clearly have provided information and data that would have proved invaluable to the development of future fighter aircraft.

This new work makes an excellent complimentary volume to *British Secret Projects*. There is a wonderful variety of aircraft here, from huge flying boats to very small light aircraft. And during the war weird machines like the Miles M.39 Libellula could on occasion be seen by startled RAF aircrew who knew nothing of their existence (one would have loved to have heard their thoughts and observations about what they saw). Putting this volume together has been an especially enjoyable task with maybe a dozen of the author's most favourite aeroplanes involved, and finding previously unpublished information about the careers of the types covered never ceases to be a delight. Most of the subjects featured have had some magazine articles devoted to them but one hopes that extensive research, particularly in the British National Archives at Kew by the author and by other Air-Britain members, will provide a good deal of new information for the general enthusiast. Overall this book fills a gap in the literature by bringing together the lesser-known types of World War Two. There are some very impressive aeroplanes in these pages.

Tony Buttler, Bretforton, UK, December 2011

Acknowledgements

Great and sincere thanks must go to the following for their help in researching this book, and my sincere apologies if anyone has been left out.

Peter R Arnold; Robert Austin; David Birch (Rolls-Royce Heritage Trust); Joe Cherrie; Peter Green; Duncan Greenman (Bristol AIRchive); Harry Fraser-Mitchell (Handley Page Association); Peter Goulding; Tim Kershaw (Jet Age Museum); Paul Lawson and the staff of BAE SYSTEMS Brough Heritage; the late Eric Morgan; RAF Museum; The National Archives; Clive Richards; Brian Riddle (Royal Aeronautical Society); and Bill Taylor (de Havilland Support Ltd).

Extra special thanks must go to the following:

To Phil Butler of Air-Britain for supplying many photos, for making available the text of his articles in *Aeromilitaria*, and for reading through all of the chapters where he picked out some important inaccuracies and errors. And to Peter Amos (Miles Archive) and Les Whitehouse (Boulton Paul Archive) for checking through the chapters covering aircraft from their areas of expertise, and for supplying some additional information and text.

Finally, my great appreciation goes to Jeremy Pratt and Gill Richardson and the team at Crécy/Hikoki for all of their help. It has been a pleasure to work with you all.

1 Blackburn B.20 and B.40

Blackburn B.20

Type: Five-Seat Twin-Engine General Purpose Flying boat

Powerplant: Two 1,720hp (1,283kW) Rolls-Royce Vulture X liquid-cooled inline engines

Span: (floats retracted) 82ft 2in (25.04m), (floats extended) 76ft 0in (23.16m)

Length: 69ft 7.5in (21.22m)

Gross Wing Area: (including floats) 1,066sq.ft (99.14m^2)

Normal Loaded Weight: 35,000lb (15,876kg)

Rate of Climb: Not available

Maximum Speed: (Estimated) 306mph (492km/h) at 15,000ft (4,572m)

Service Ceiling: Probably never established

Armament (for production aircraft): 2 x 0.303in (7.7mm) machine-guns in nose and dorsal turrets, 4 x 0.303in (7.7mm) machine-guns in tail turret; 8 x 250lb (113kg) bombs

In March 1936 specification R.1/36 was raised to provide a relatively small general purpose Flying boat for the RAF with a maximum cruising speed of not less than 230mph (370km/h) and eventually two different types were ordered against it. The Saunders-Roe S.36 was put into production as the Lerwick but only twenty-one examples of this aeroplane were built and the type was not a success (in fact had the Lerwick not joined two squadrons for brief periods it would have qualified for this book). The rival Blackburn B.20 progressed no further than prototype status, but it was an unconventional and quite fascinating aircraft.

Until recent years most Flying boats had been biplanes which meant that there was usually somewhere to mount the engines at sufficient distance above the sea to keep the airscrews out of the water spray; the tail also needed to be kept clear of the water. The introduction of the monoplane made this more difficult and the RAF's superb Short Sunderland actually had a hull whose depth was several feet greater than would have been needed just to accommodate its crew and equipment. This also meant that the air-drag of the Sunderland hull was rather high.

The B.20 attempted to deal with this problem. In fact it was not a true Flying boat but rather a floatplane in that it was given a horizontally-spilt body with the lower portion a retractable 'float' or 'pontoon' which could be drawn up into the fuselage and faired with it. The bottom would extend to form what in effect was a single 'float' that pushed the upper fuselage and the wings upwards away from the water surface. With this retractable single pontoon both fuselage and pontoon could be made to the correct size and the resulting air-drag was about 75% of that of the corresponding boat hull. The appropriate airscrew diameter and water clearance could be provided by arranging the retracting structure to fit. When extended the pontoon's flat upper surface provided space for the crew to do all of the water handling, mooring, etc., and when lowered the aircraft could be taken into a hanger. In addition a damaged pontoon could be replaced, rather than requiring heavy repairs as per a normal Flying boat. In flight the B.20's 'lower' fuselage would retract into a 'notch' to form a solid streamlined fuselage

Three 'sail around' views taken by official photographers of V8914 afloat on the River Clyde in March or early April 1940. *All BAE Systems Brough Heritage*

while two smaller wingtip floats fitted under the outer wings for stability folded outwards to form the the wing tips. Blackburn's chief designer on this work was J.D. Rennie.

A single prototype, V8914 ordered under Contract 498571/36, was built by Blackburn's Clyde Division at Dumbarton, primarily to evaluate the concept of the retractable hull. It was powered by two Rolls-Royce Vultures and first flew on 27 March 1940, but on this flight the pilot experienced a problem with trimming the aileron. There were no trim tabs on the B.20's ailerons which meant any alterations had to be done on the ground, so it took another four or five flights to sort this problem out. Then on 7 April V8914 crashed into the sea during a test flight after the crew had experienced extreme vibration and been forced to bail out. The pilot Flt Lt Harry Bailey (Blackburn's chief test pilot) and two others died (Bailey because he was too low for his parachute to open) but two survivors were picked up by the armed merchant cruiser HMS *Transylvania*. This tragic loss brought an end to the B.20's development and the wreck survives as a designated War grave, but one of the engines was raised in 1998 after it had been caught in a fishing boat's nets. The cause of the loss was aileron flutter and had nothing to do with the retractable pontoon, which was simple and in operation had retracted well and given no trouble. Although the estimated maximum speed (with armament in place) was 306mph (492km/h) at 15,000ft (4,572m), accounts state that 345 mph (555km/h) was achieved on the first high-speed run to be made on 7 April before the unarmed prototype was lost. The B.20 was also expected to be able to cruise at 200mph (322km/h) for up to eight hours.

To those who worked on it the B.20 was nicknamed the 'nutcracker' – a name which referred to the fate of any individual who might still be on the central float when it was retracted. Although very little flying was completed with the single prototype the concept of the retracting float, and the aircraft itself, seems to have been very promising. It is a pity that the circumstances of the early war years prevented further work being done.

Detailed view of the B.20's pontoon and fuselage. Note the cabin access hatch and ladder. *The late Ray Sturtivant*

An image of the B.20 showing how the aircraft appeared in flight after the pontoon had been retracted. This illustration was created by retouching the photo of the B.20 on its beaching gear. *BAE Systems Brough Heritage*

Structure

Both hull and pontoon were both built in aluminium light alloy with a normal stressed skin structure employing transverse frames and longitudinal stringers. The 48ft 9in (14.86m) long pontoon had links so arranged that when it was extended it automatically provided the wing with the best angle of incidence required for take-off. The aircraft had a straight tapered wing with the Vulture engines mounted in nacelles quite close to the fuselage and the engines had three-blade propellers. A large single fin was fitted ahead of the tailplane and, on the prototype, the nose and tail turrets intended for the B.20 were replaced by rounded fairings. Bombs were to be carried in two cells on each side of the hull and in the wing centre section.

Blackburn B.40 Project

A drawing has recently come to light showing the Blackburn B.40 project to R.13/40 which, according to some sources, was intended to be a replacement for the Short Sunderland and was a proposed improvement of the B.20. However, a memo written by H.T. Tizard (later Sir Henry Tizard) in about late 1940/early 1941 described the B.40 as: "An experimental machine not of any great importance from the point of view of the war unless the war goes on a long while". Tizard added that he was in favour of this experiment being continued.

The B.40 was to be powered by two Bristol Centaurus radial engines, it had a defensive armament of one 20mm cannon in a power mounting, two turrets (including a retractable dorsal turret) each mounting a pair of 0.5in

Side view of the Blackburn B.20 set on its beaching gear and with the floats retracted. The image was taken at Blackburn's Dumbarton factory in March 1940. Note the notch in the lower fuselage roughly level with the wing leading edge where the float was attached, and the curved shape of the fin. The background has been removed, probably for security purposes. *BAE Systems Brough Heritage*

(12.7mm) machine-guns, plus four hand-held 0.303in (7.7mm) machine-guns. In early January 1941 another memo declared that the technical case for building the B.40 was a good one, and on 19 September two prototypes ES966 and ES979 were ordered under contract Acft/1474/C20b. However, by 20 December 1941 it was clear to the Air Staff that the aircraft's range, around 3,050 miles (4,907km) without a bomb, was not acceptable. In addition the B.40's single engine performance was not satisfactory either and so it was agreed that the project should be cancelled, which was done on 6 January 1942. The Sunderland of course proved to be an immensely capable and successful aircraft right through the war and for long afterwards, so the B.40's abandonment did not prove critical.

Drawing showing the Blackburn B.40 project. This had a span of 98ft 1in (29.89m), a gross wing area of 1,400sq.ft (130.20m²) and maximum weight 52,000lb (23,587kg) and it was to be powered by two 2,080hp (1,551kW) Bristol Centaurus radials, although the Napier Sabre was a possible alternative. It would have carried bombs and a single 20mm cannon plus four 0.5in (12.7mm) and four 0.303in (7.7mm) machine-guns.. *National Archives Avia 6/9595 via Phil Butler*

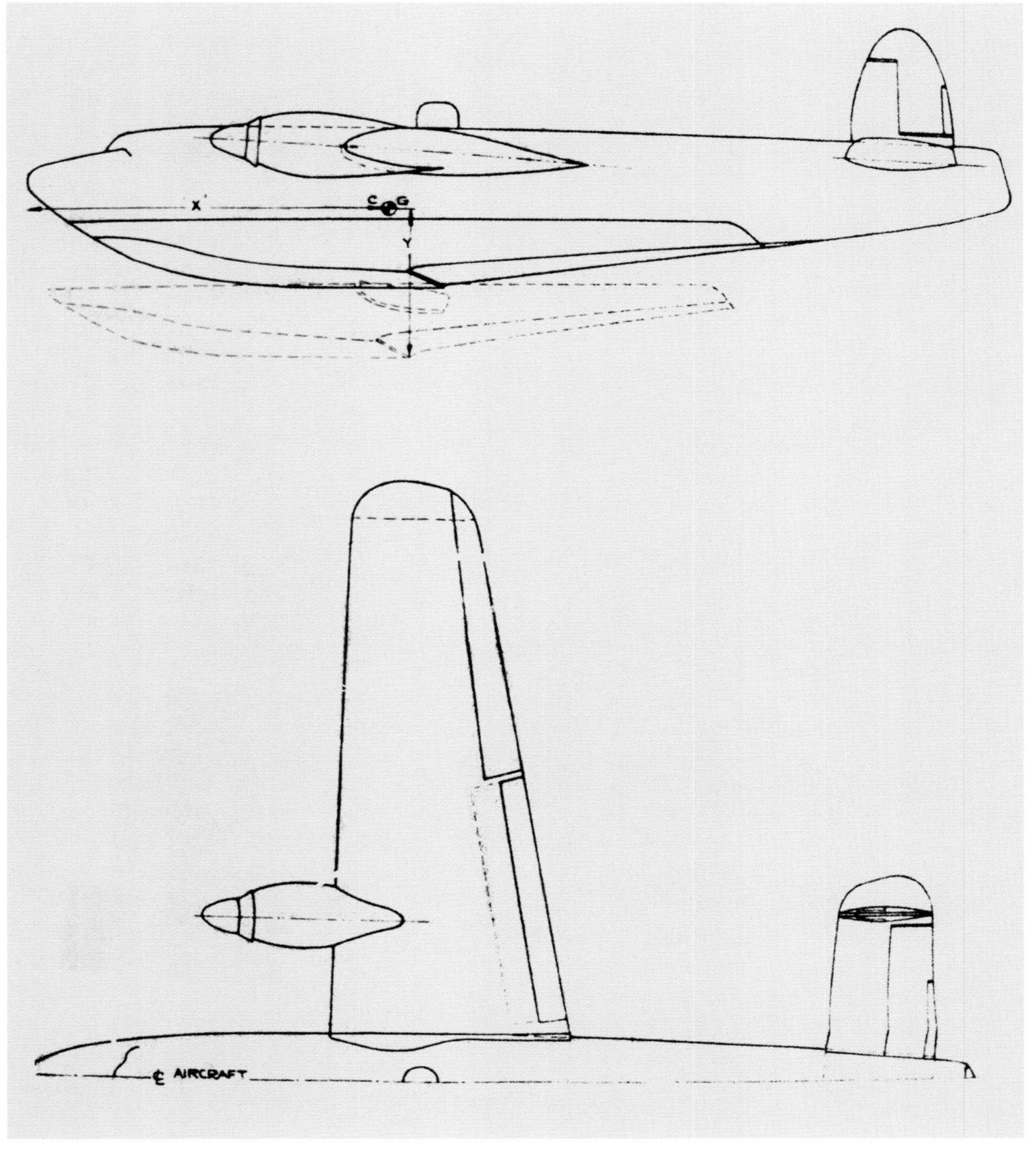

2 Blackburn B.44

Blackburn B.44

Type: Single-Seat Floatplane Fighter

Powerplant: One 2,240hp (1,670kW) Napier Sabre IV liquid-cooled inline engine

Span: 50ft 0in (15.24m)

Length: 39ft 4in (11.99m)

Gross Wing Area: 381sq.ft (35.43m^2)

All-Up Weight: 14,000lb (6,350kg)

Maximum Speed: 360mph (579km/h) at 25,000ft (7,620m)

Rate of Climb: 2,000ft/min (610m/min)

Service Ceiling: 38,000ft (11,582m)

Armament: 4 x 20mm cannon; 2 x 500lb (227kg) bombs

Blackburn's planing hull or 'pontoon' concept, carried on retracting struts and pioneered by the B.20 described in Chapter One, was also adopted for a single-seat fighter project, a design called the B.44 which is thought to have been under consideration from 1942 and into January 1943. Again created by J.D. Rennie, this aircraft was covered by Specification N.2/42 and Operational Requirement OR.114 of November 1942, the objective being to use sheltered water on austere island sites as a base or, when out of range of shore facilities, to fly them from escort carriers after hoisting them out over the water. RAF Coastal Command would use the B.44 to provide fighter cover for those areas of the Pacific and South-East Asia theatres where there was no suitable land base.

Like the first marks of Blackburn's equivalent land-based fighter, the Firebrand, the B.44 was to be powered by a Napier Sabre engine. It was to be capable of landing back on the water with its central float in the retracted position so, to ensure that there was sufficient clearance between the propellers and the water surface, the Sabre was to have contra-rotating propellers. Two prototypes were ordered to Contracts/Acft/2542 in October 1942 and these received the serials MZ275 and MZ277. A full-size mock-up was completed but both airframes were cancelled probably before any work had been done on them. In an assessment of the B.44 made by RAE Farnborough it was reported that the fighter would most likely suffer from porpoising during its take-off and that water spray would also damage the propeller. In addition, calculations indicated that even with a normal load it was doubtful if the B.44 would get into the air. A modified B.44 pontoon tested subsequently was judged to be satisfactory in terms of its stability, the formation of spray and water drag, but to keep the spray clear at low speeds would still require the pontoon to be modified a little more.

In the end the advent of large numbers of the smaller type of escort carrier, and the success in building ground-based airfields very swiftly following an amphibious landing, removed any need for a fighter like the B.44. Thanks to the security surrounding new developments in aviation during the Second World War, the existence of some of the types described in this book remained secret until well after the conflict was over. The B.44 was one such example and was not revealed to the public until a drawing appeared in *Flight* magazine in April 1947. It is understood that Blackburn's Sabre-powered B.43 project of 1942 was to be a Firebrand airframe fitted with two fixed floats and, as such, would have made an interesting comparison to the B.44.

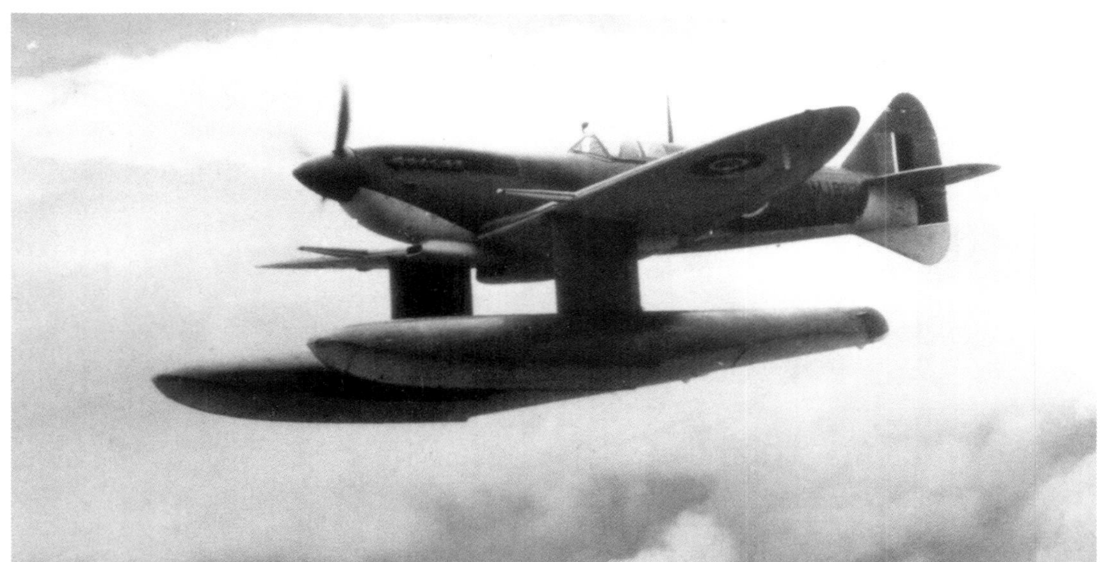

A different attempt to produce a flying boat fighter involved the fitting of floats to Supermarine Spitfires. Several examples, including this Mk IX, were thus tested in trials which took place in 1942-1944.

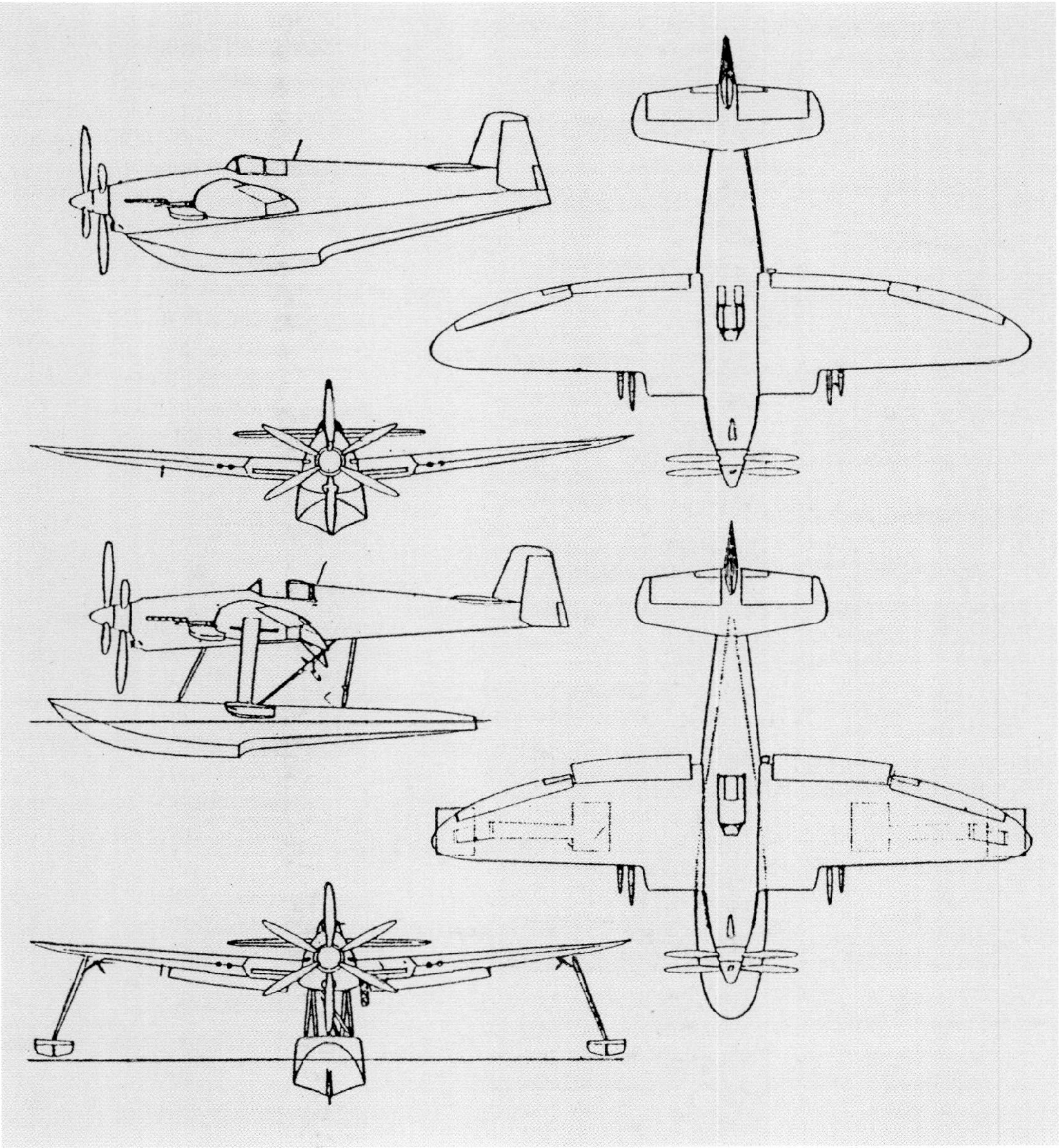

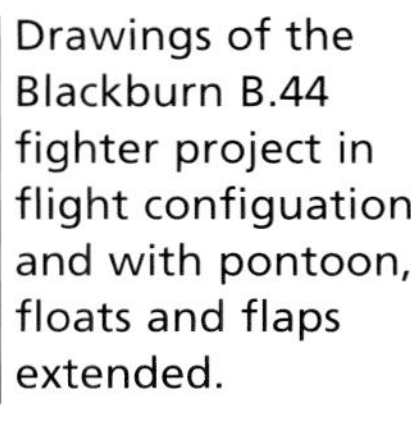

Drawings of the Blackburn B.44 fighter project in flight configuation and with pontoon, floats and flaps extended.

This photo of a wind tunnel model of the Blackburn B.44 is dated 4 January 1943. *BAE Systems Brough Heritage*

Structure

The retractable pontoon used by the B.20 also featured on the B.44, although in the fighter's case the stabilising wingtip floats used to provide stability while on the water would retract inwards into mainplane. The B.44's structure would presumably have been all metal, and specification N.2/42 stated that a fuel load of 157 gallons (714 litres) would be accepted. The four 20mm Hispano cannon were housed in the wings just outboard of the leading edge intakes and the fighter was to be adapted to carry two 500lb (227kg) bombs or two 90 gallon (409 litre) drop tanks under the wings. A trolley or beaching gear was to be made available to move the aircraft on the ground or on a carrier deck.

3 Blackburn B-48/Y.A.1 'Firecrest'

Blackburn B-48/Y.A.1 'Firecrest'

Type: Single-Seat Naval Fighter and Torpedo Bomber

Powerplant: One 2,825hp (2,107kW) Bristol Centaurus 59 radial engine

Span: 44ft 11.5in (13.70m), Span Folded: 18ft 0in (5.49m)

Length: 39ft 3.5in (11.98m)

Gross Wing Area: 361.5sq.ft (33.58m^2)

Maximum Take-Off Weight: 16,800lb (7,620kg)

Maximum Speed: 380mph (612km/h) at 19,000ft (5,791m)

Rate of Climb: 2,500ft/min (762m/min) at sea level

Service Ceiling: 31,600ft (9,632m)

Armament: 2 x fixed 0.5in (12.7mm) machine-guns in wings; 1 x 2,097lb (951kg) torpedo under fuselage, 2 x 500lb (227kg) bombs or 8 x 60lb (27kg) rocket projectiles or 2 x cannon under wings

When one considers the experiences of its own combat aircraft designs, it might be said that the Second World War was a difficult time for Blackburn Aircraft. At the start the Skua dive bomber did achieve some success but it was quickly outclassed by enemy aircraft, the Botha torpedo bomber proved to be underpowered and thus a failure, while the development of the Firebrand naval fighter was a struggle throughout and the type did not enter service until just after the war had ended. Eventually George Edward Petty's project team turned to a new aircraft which in fact turned out to be a full redesign of the Firebrand. It was labelled the B-48 and was unofficially named Firecrest by the firm, although not by the Ministry which always referred to it as the S.28/43 (its specification). In the text here, however, Y.A.1 (its designation under the post-war SBAC coding system) will be used throughout.

Work on the development of a new laminar flow wing began in September 1943. This was expected to increase the speed over the Firebrand by around 11-12 knots (20-22km/h) while at the same time reducing the wing weight. Specification S.28/43 was raised for the project (to meet Operational Requirement OR.150) and it was to have a Bristol Centaurus engine, two 20mm Mk.V guns and carry 1,800lb (816kg) of bombs or one Mk.XV torpedo. The design also featured a new fuselage with a raised cockpit placed closer to the nose to give a better view for the pilot. There was a simplified structure which saved yet more weight and some 70 gallons (318 litres) of additional fuel, and yet the estimated gross weight was still lower than the Firebrand's. A contra-rotating propeller and power wing folding were fitted and the decision to construct two prototypes was confirmed on 11 November 1943.

There were proposals for alternative powerplants including the E.122, the NS.79.SM version of Napier's Sabre engine, which offered a considerable improvement in performance, particularly at altitude. To a large extent this was due to the maximum power of the engine being achieved at a higher altitude than the Centaurus. For example, at an all-up weight of 15,763lb (7,150kg) for the Centaurus 77, and

Y.A.1 The first prototype photographed at Brough shortly after roll-out in the bitter weather of 18 February 1947.
BAE SYSTEMS Brough Heritage Centre

Almost the same angle showing the unusual but neat wing fold arrangement for storage aboard carriers.
BAE SYSTEMS Brough Heritage Centre

16,641lb (7,548kg) for the E.122, the estimated top speeds at 25,000ft (7,620m) were 305 knots (565km/h) and 367 knots (680km/h) respectively, and service ceilings 29,500ft (8,992m) and 34,500ft (10,516m). Consequently, on 14 March 1945 three Y.A.1 prototypes powered by the E.122 were authorised along with another Centaurus-powered machine. Specification S.10/45 was written around the Sabre Y.A.1, but in due course it was found that the balance of the later version had moved too far forward and the project would only work if the engine was switched to a position behind the pilot with a shaft drive to the propeller in the nose. Such a step would require a substantial redesign and so the E.122 project was cancelled following a Ministry meeting held on 8 October 1945. The three Y.A.1 Sabre prototypes were to have carried the serials VF254, VF257 and VF262 (Contract SB.84896); the three Centaurus aircraft were RT651, RT656 and VF172 (Contract SB.27216).

The roles envisaged for the Y.A.1 would put it into competition with both a design from Westland Aircraft (which eventually entered service as the Wyvern) and also a project submitted by Fairey in October 1944 which was known as the Fairey Strike Fighter. The latter was to be powered by two Rolls-Royce Merlin RM.17.SM engines buried within the fuselage and armed with four 20mm guns, but it was never ordered. The Wyvern went on to complete a modest service career in the 1950s, but by September 1946 it was clear that the Y.A.1 would need strengthening to make it acceptable to the Navy as a strike fighter. This would require some redesign just to produce a weight and performance that matched the Wyvern, so by the time the Y.A.1 was airborne it was not expected to enter production (despite the fact that no official decision on its future had yet been made).

In early 1946 when the Y.A.1 had reached final design the requirement for contra-rotating propellers was waived, necessitating the substitution of the Centaurus 77. In fact this engine was dropped at the same time from both the Y.A.1 and the Fairey Spearfish torpedo bomber (Chapter Eight), in each case the agreed substitute being the 2,825hp Centaurus 57 which would provide the required power. For the Y.A.1 it thus became necessary to redesign the fin and rudder and increase their combined area from 33 to 41sq.ft (3.1 to 3.8m^2). The new engine also needed special flexible engine mountings in which form it was renamed Centaurus 59. There were plenty of delays prior to the aircraft reaching flight test, at the start through manufacturing problems and then by the end of the war which removed much of the urgency behind the project. Then there was the appalling winter of 1947, but despite the severe snow and cold the first prototype RT651 was finally rolled out for engine tests on 18 February 1947. After being moved to RAF Leconfield not far from Beverley, the aircraft made its maiden flight on 1 April piloted by Blackburn chief test pilot Peter Lawrence.

By the end of September 1947 the three prototypes had been completed and enough spare parts were available to meet the demands of prototype flying. RT651 had accumulated 35 hours air time in 72 flights, but the other two had still not flown and in fact were redundant. Work on VF172 had been abandoned and on 10 November the MoS asked that Y.A.1 prototype flying should be brought to a halt altogether, and that any work on RT651 and RT656 should cease. However, just a week later VF172 was reinstated because of a decision to carry out an assessment of power-operated ailerons. Then in January 1948 Blackburn proposed that the redundant RT656 could be used for the purposes of strength-testing a complete airframe, a type of test for which there was little experience in Britain. RAE Farnborough agreed but it was December before the experiment was started (originally RT656 had been earmarked for the powered aileron work).

On 1 October 1947 Gp Capt Charles J.P. Flood, a Blackburn test pilot, reported on the test flying that had been completed with RT651. The work had mostly concentrated on the ailerons since these exhibited characteristics which masked the other controls. The main fault appeared to be the shape of the hinge moment curve which produced heavy ailerons at low speed, lighter ailerons in cruise, but heavy again at high speed. Considerable experimentation in balancing had failed to find an answer and it was concluded that the wing section and aileron shape were the problem. It was apparent that rate of roll would be very good if quick aileron could be applied, while the introduction of power assistance should give the aircraft excellent aileron control.

The Y.A.1 showed a measure of positive longitudinal stability, the large reserve making three-point landings difficult, particularly with the centre of gravity in the forward position. The elevator was sufficiently light and powerful to cover trim changes due to throttle over a large speed range without using the trimmer.

Little investigation of the rudder had been made but it had been found quite adequate for all manoeuvres performed so far and had exhibited no unpleasant features; all indications were that only detailed refinements were required on the rudder. Stalling with engine on and off, and flaps up and down, was in all cases very gentle, free from vice and with little tendency for wing drop. Flood considered that in some of its features the Y.A.1 showed major improvements over the Firebrand, in particular the pilot's view which he felt would make the aircraft an excellent rocket projectile platform and a capable dive-bomber. The landing was also much easier and the hydraulic wing folding and general cockpit layout were superior.

However, after deep discussions with RAE, Blackburn had been forced to conclude that the comparatively thick laminar flow section (17% at the inner fold joint, 15% at the wing tip) gave rise to non-linear hinge moments and variations with speed that were very difficult to surmount by aerodynamic balance alone. To improve lateral control the firm felt that satisfactory forces throughout the speed range could be achieved by power control with artificial feel, with manual reversion in the event of failure. Thus VF172 was adapted accordingly by the fitting of power operation components to the elevator and rudder, together with a new powered aileron system that comprised a single Lockheed Servodyne unit so installed that it would provide zero feed-back together with spring feel. Flight-testing had also shown that it would be beneficial to reduce the dihedral and consequently VF172 was modified with an outer-wing dihedral of only 3° (down from 9° on the first two aircraft).

Blackburn asked for permission to proceed with an intensive research programme on power control, explaining how it would be valuable to everyone and could be accelerated by converting another airframe to the same standard. In the event only VF172 was used, and although further testing was planned for RT651 in its original form, it is believed that the first prototype never flew again. VF172 had begun its MoS flight trials on or by 6 February 1948 (having presumably made its first flight a few days earlier), but by 30 November it had completed just 7 hours 40 minutes flying with 4 hours 15 minutes of that connected with demonstration flights at an Aeronautical Society garden party held at Brough, the SBAC show at Farnborough, and the Battle of Britain Day at Leconfield. By early February 1949 the effects of the reduced dihedral had still to be measured and, having at first pushed so strongly for this programme to go ahead, Blackburn was now criticised for

Close-up of the first Blackburn Y.A.1 prototype RT651 being flown by Peter Lawrence in July 1947. Lawrence made the type's first flight on 1 April.

The first two of three Firecrests including RT651 had 9° outer wing dihedral. *Tim Brown*

not putting enough effort into it. That got things moving. VF172 was flown by seven pilots of Aero Flight at RAE (three Navy and four RAF) in six hours of air time accumulated between 11 and 22 February. However, their opinions of the powered aileron system were generally unfavourable and some features of the cockpit layout were also criticised.

In the air the rate of control movement was considered satisfactory, as was the actual rate of roll, but the 'feel' of the aileron control was not; for example, the force required to hold on full aileron (about 25lb (11.3kg)) was much higher than the ideal. There also appeared to be a definite tendency for stick forces to fall off with increasing speed, being heavier on the approach than under cruising conditions. In certain areas an unpleasant 'lumpiness' caused jerky movements and aileron over-correction made the aircraft tiring and unpleasant to fly even in calm, clear air. Blind flying was difficult and lateral trimming to enable the pilot to fly level and stick free was impossible. Flights with elements of the artificial spring-feel removed

Similar view of the third Y.A.1 VF172 which shows the reduced dihedral on the outer wing. VF172 made its first flight in early 1948. It was broken up during 1950.

improved the situation in some areas (the 'lumpiness' disappeared when the powered control was switched out) but revealed more severe shortcomings. A few flights were made with the pre-load removed from the spring feel and in this condition there was an overbalancing tendency which, with the stick within an inch or two either side of the central position, felt as though it was balanced on a knife edge, slipping away to one side or the other on the slightest disturbance. In turbulent air it would move from side to side under the influence of the bumps. RAE suggested that this type of aileron 'feel' appeared identical to that of the Fairey Spearfish (Chapter Eight) and similar to late marks of Firebrand. The comparison between the Y.A.1 and Spearfish suggested that the cause may have been fundamental to power controls operated on these principles.

Wing Commander Maurice A. Smith flew VF172 for *Flight* magazine, his report appearing in the issue for 3 March 1949. He found the Y.A.1 was pleasant to taxi and, using about 15° of flap on the take-off, found that it gathered speed remarkably quickly, and with no appreciable tendency to swing. He reported the climb to be "good and steep" and in normal cruising found that all three controls were well harmonised. The elevators were reasonably light and the rudder sensitive, and directionally the Y.A.1 was not over-stable. With its present lack of feed-back the apparent weight of the ailerons was the same at all speeds. Smith had no hesitation in saying that "for high-speed rapid-roll operational work the powered ailerons would be excellent. With negligible effort the Y.A.1 can be made to roll at exceptional rate from one vertical bank to another [and] it completes a rapid full roll in about 3 seconds. Under these circumstances the powered control is felt at its best. The response is smooth and very positive."

A starboard side photo of VF172 taken during a test flight over the River Humber and its surrounding countryside. All of the air-to-air photographs of VF172 were taken on 2 February 1949.

Both photographs show VF172 in flight. The port side shot (above) gives a chance to look at the ailerons in operation, and the arrestor hook and large rudder.
BAE SYSTEMS Brough Heritage Centre

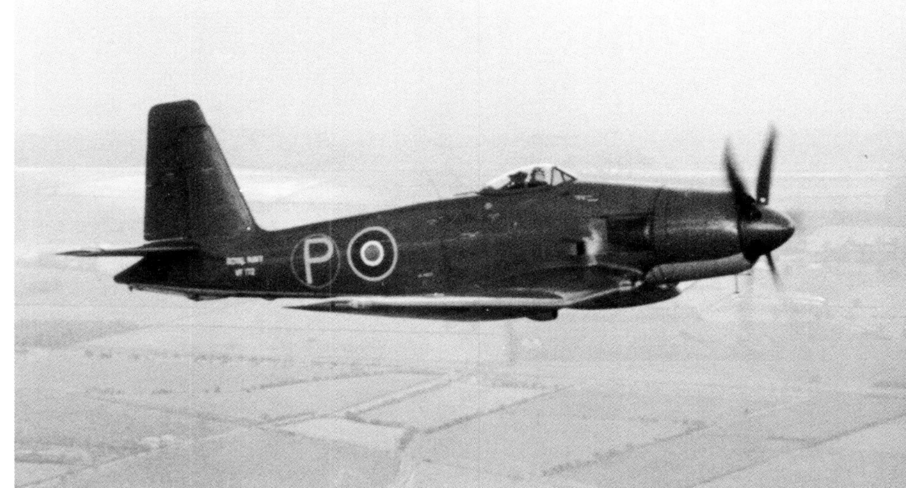

However, smooth use of bank, particularly at low speeds, would require practice because of a tendency to over-correct in response to rapid movement, and for general flying the powered ailerons (or elevators) would have been more pleasant to handle if the stick load was varied with speed and altitude. It was noted that the Centaurus' ability to operate at very low rpm while still providing sufficient power for the Y.A.1 to fly at 175-180 knots (324-334km/h) ASI at medium altitude accounted to a great extent for the aircraft's 400-mile (645km) radius of action when carrying a torpedo. For its size and weight the Y.A.1 had a most gentle stall and a low stalling speed – 80 knots (148km/h) all-up and 74 knots (137km/h) with wheels and flaps down and with good prior warning. The only aerobatics attempted were a couple of rolls, which the aircraft took effortlessly in its stride, and use of the trimmer was easy to get accustomed to. Landing was easy and the run following straight and short. Smith made one further take-off using full peacetime non-methanol take-off power with +9½lb boost and 2,700rpm, which gave: "...a most exhilarating performance and the Y.A.1 was airborne and climbing steeply almost before the throttle reached its open stop". To compare with Smith's report, one RAE pilot to fly VF172 was Capt Eric Brown who considered it to be even less manoeuvrable than the Firebrand Mk.VA. In the July 1978 issue of *AIR International* magazine he wrote that the aircraft often exhibited: "...a continuous lateral lurching motion, this being accentuated in turbulent air and quite unacceptable for instrument flying".

It is possible that in time these faults might have been rectified, but the performance gain wasn't worth the trouble and as stated already there were no plans to put the type into production. Some years ago Capt Brown explained to the author that the Y.A.1 had no real development potential as a torpedo bomber because, thanks to the new range of guided weapons coming into use, the operational role itself was diminishing. The suggestion that it might have done a similar job to the American Douglas AD Skyraider was countered by the comment that the latter was essentially a heavy lifter with wide versatility of operational roles. The Skyraider's performance came second to operational duties which gave a superb general purpose aircraft, but one that required an environment of air superiority to be successful. In no way could the Y.A.1 match the Skyraider.

RT651, carrying a torpedo, comes into land at Radlett in September 1947 during the SBAC Show. *Peter Green*

The power control trials undertaken with the Y.A.1 produced some valuable general information, but in March 1949 VF172 was placed in store along with the other two prototypes to await their disposal. Action was taken to remove them from CS(A) charge on 9 June but this was then delayed in the case of VF172 to allow Frank Bullen, Blackburn's production test pilot, to perform an aerobatic display with the aircraft at the Brough Air Pageant on 18 June. Earlier RT651 had been the first Y.A.1 to give public displays when in 1947 it appeared at both the SBAC show at Radlett and at an air day at Lee-on-Solent. At Radlett in September it carried a 'tin fish' on its Blackburn torpedo carrier, and although Charles Flood refrained from performing any advanced aerobatics the pilot did show off the type's excellent lateral control, a particularly desirable quality in a torpedo aircraft to enable it to take avoiding action. Those who had not seen the aircraft before were astonished by the speed at which the undercarriage retracted – between one to two seconds. Both RT651 and VF172 had been sold to Blackburn on 14 April 1950 and later that year they were broken up. The last recorded movement of RT656 shows that it was despatched to Culham on 25 March 1952.

Frustratingly for Blackburn the effort put into the Y.A.1, following so closely behind the difficult Firebrand programme, produced an unsuccessful aircraft and the Y.A.1 failed to progress beyond the three prototypes. No doubt this was a disappointment, but happily just a few years later things came together for the firm in a big way with the programme that produced the superb Buccaneer naval strike aircraft.

Near head-on view of the third prototype VF172. The reduced dihedral on this aircraft is again well shown. *BAE SYSTEMS Brough Heritage Centre*

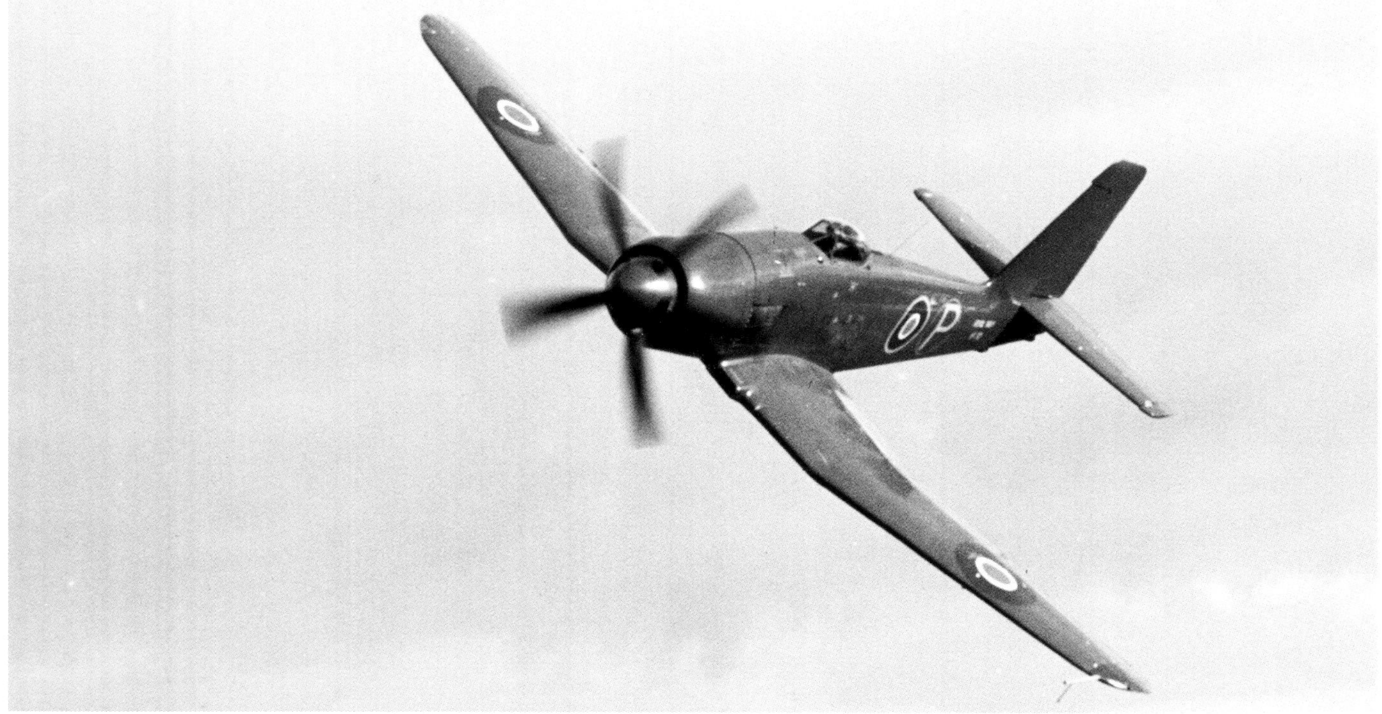

Starboard undercarriage leg of RT651 in a picture dated 26 September 1946. *BAE SYSTEMS Brough Heritage Centre*

Structure

The Y.A.1 had an all-metal low inverted gull-wing with stressed flush riveted skin. The centre-section had a two-spar structure (main and front spar, the latter giving support to the undercarriage legs) running through the fuselage and just over 6.5° of anhedral; the outer wing a single spar and on the first prototypes 9° of dihedral. The two outer wings were divided into inner and outer halves so that they could fold upwards and over, two hinge points allowed the wing to fold hydraulically into a very neat inverted 'V' above the centre-section. The inner part of the outer wing had a laminar-flow section and was built as a torsion box with ribs formed of simple pressed members. The wing centre section's box-type main spar had square section booms. High-lift slotted Fowler flaps were used on the centre-section and the inner portion of the outer wing (four in all), while the outer portion had ailerons with balance tabs. Dive-brakes were placed on the upper and lower surfaces of the middle wing and these and all of the control surfaces were hydraulically operated.

The fuselage was all metal and built in two sections, the front of tubular structure with detachable panels, the rear in stressed-skin monocoque. The fixed tail surfaces were stressed-skin, but the rudder and one-piece elevator were metal covered and had pressure-sealed internal and horned external balances. Balance and trimmer-tabs were also fitted to the elevator (port and starboard respectively)

The tubular structure of the front fuselage photographed on 18 July 1947 before panel fitting during the construction of what is almost certainly the third prototype, VF172. *BAE SYSTEMS Brough Heritage Centre*

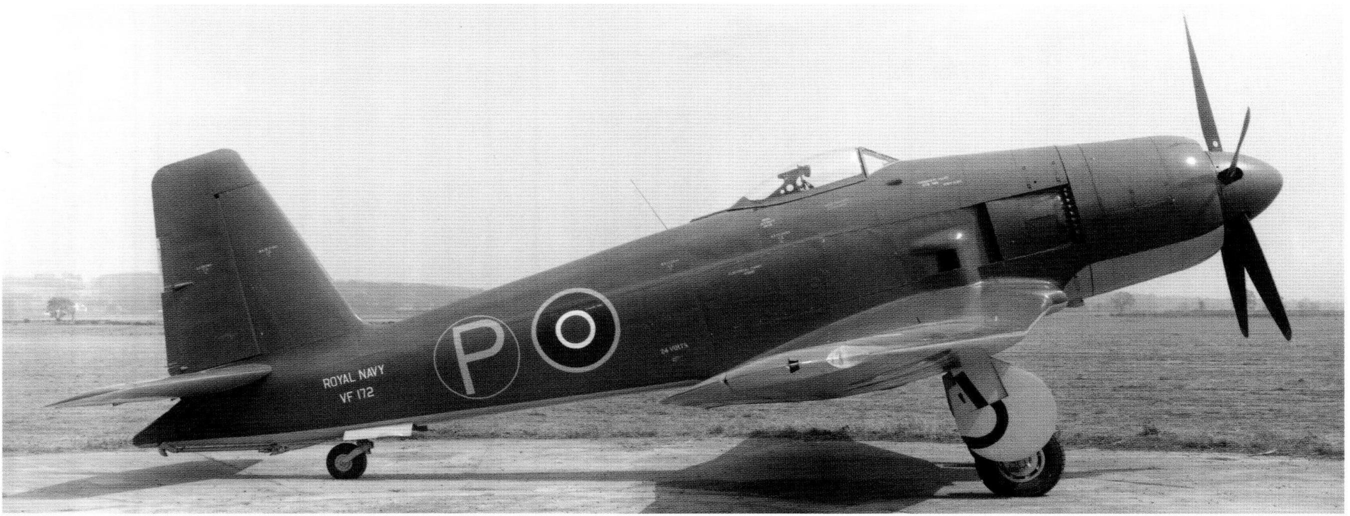

The Y.A.1's clean engine installation and fuselage are presented to advantage in this image of VF172 taken in June 1948.

and trim-tabs to the rudder. A short main undercarriage, made possible by the anhedral of the centre-wing, retracted inwards while the tail-wheel folded rearwards and an arrestor hook was placed directly behind the tailwheel. The Centaurus 59 had a Rotol five-blade constant-speed airscrew of 12ft 9in (3.89m) diameter and received air from intakes placed in the centre-wing leading edge.

No armament was ever fitted to the Y.A.1s, but the fixed 0.5in (12.7mm) machine-guns, would have been installed in the outermost part of the centre-wing, just inside the inner fold position. The torpedo was to go under the fuselage, and any rockets, bombs or additional guns were to be suspended beneath the outer wings. Internal fuel was carried in one 52 gallon (236 litre) fuselage and two 92 gallon (418 litre) wing tanks but, interchangeable with the weapon load, 45 or 90 gallon (205 or 409 litre) drop tanks could go under each wing and a 100 gallon (455 litre) tank on the fuselage centreline.

Three-view drawing of the Blackburn Y.A.1 in its original form with a contra-rotating propeller unit.

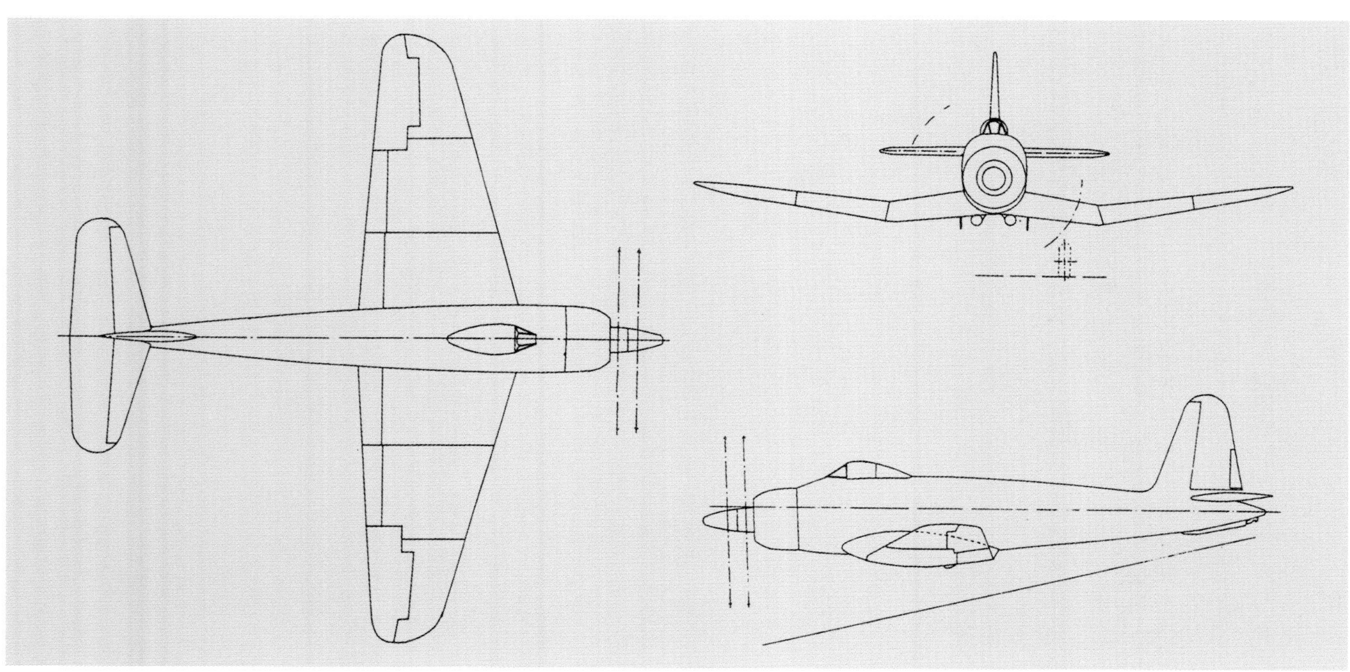

4 Boulton Paul P.92 and P.92/2

Boulton Paul P.92

(Air Staff Figures or Estimates as at 5 May 1939)

Type: Three-Seat Turret Fighter

Powerplant: Two 1,760hp (1,312kW) Rolls-Royce Vulture II liquid-cooled inline engines

Alternative (original plan): Two 2,055hp (1,532kW) Napier Sabre I liquid-cooled inline engines

Span: 62ft 6in (19.05m)

Length: 54ft 4in (16.56m)

Gross Wing Area: 650sq.ft (60.45m^2)

All-Up Weight: 22,000lb (9,979kg)

Rate of Climb: 3,220ft/min (981m/min) at 15,000ft (4,572m)

Maximum Speed: 384mph (618km/h) at 15,000ft (4,572m)

Service Ceiling: 38,000ft (11,582m)

Armament: 4 x 20mm cannon

Boulton Paul P.92/2

Type: Single-Seat Scale Model Test Aircraft

Powerplant: Two 135hp (101kW) de Havilland Gipsy Major II air-cooled inline engines

Span: 33ft 1.5in (10.09m)

Length: 27ft 6in (8.38m)

Gross Wing Area: 177sq.ft (16.46m^2)

Normal Loaded Weight: 2,778lb (1,260kg) (as tested by A&AEE)

Rate of Climb: Not available

Maximum Speed: 152mph (245km/h) at ground level

Service Ceiling: Not available

Armament: None fitted

At the start of the war in 1939 Boulton Paul Aircraft was a world leader in the development of turret-armed fighters, general manager and chief engineer and designer John Dudley North having already seen his company gain orders for the single-engined Defiant from the RAF. A second project for the firm came from Specification F.11/37 of 26 May 1937 which requested a twin-engine home defence day and night-fighter to attack enemy bombers. The speed of modern bombers was increasing, their defensive armament was also much stronger, and so to deal with them this new aircraft had to be capable of at least 370mph (595km/h) at 15,000ft (4,572m). Its primary armament was to be four 20mm cannon in a power-operated turret and proposals came in from Armstrong Whitworth, Boulton Paul, Bristol, Gloster and Hawker. Boulton Paul's P.92 project was declared the winner, but in the end this aircraft never flew. However, a half-scale model called the P.92/2 was flight-tested.

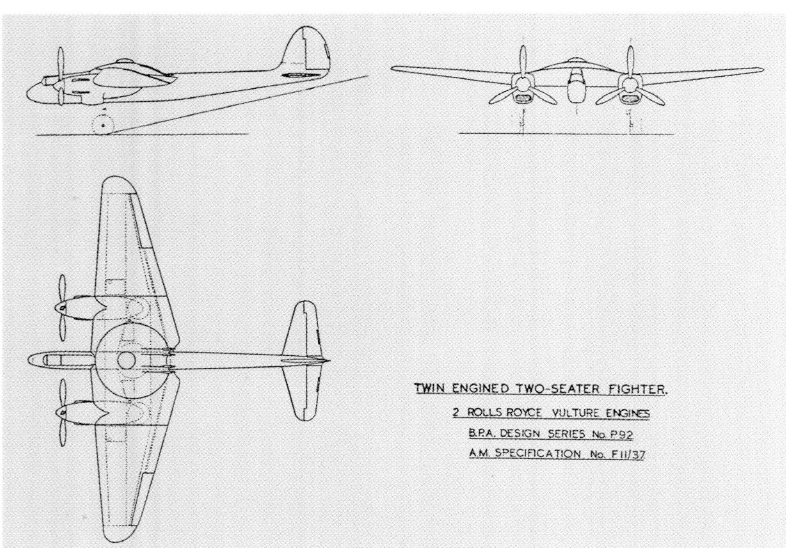

The Boulton Paul P.92 project as first proposed in July 1937. *Boulton Paul Association via Les Whitehouse*

Contract 708600/37 for two P.92 prototypes L9629 and L9632 was awarded on 2 March 1938, one of which was to be fitted with a pair of Rolls-Royce Vulture II engines and the other with Napier Sabre I power units. The specification when issued stated two crew were required, pilot and gunner, and this appears to have always been the case, despite many published sources stating that three were to be carried. The contract delivery date for the first machine was given as sometime between September 1939 and March 1940 with the second aircraft about four months behind the first. A mock-up was examined on 31 May 1938 and several points were raised, including a poor pilot's view out and that the operation of an aircraft of this type against a target in a lower hemisphere would be very difficult, but these problems were eventually sorted out. In the meantime a substantial wind tunnel programme was carried out to clear the P.92's aerodynamics, and in addition on 16 November 1938 it was recommended that both prototypes should be completed with the Vulture while a third airframe was to be ordered for the Sabre installation. This decision was prompted by the current state of development of the two engines and the third prototype was given the serial V9258. The manufacture of the first two aircraft is understood to have begun in mid-1939 and both of them were expected to be used for engine installation development. As 'built' the P.92's design differed from the original F.11/37 proposal mainly in its front fuselage, rear fuselage and fin shapes.

The outstanding feature of the P.92 was how the cupola of its saucer-shaped turret was merged into the high wing, with the guns almost completely within the body of the turret; this was well defined by tunnel work and was based upon patents filed by J.D. North in 1937 and 1938. However, because of aerodynamic problems with the turret housing involving air leakage around the periphery of the dome and through the gun apertures, by 7 January 1939 it was clear that L9629 would not fly before March 1940 (in addition the firm's drawing office staff had had to concentrate first on clearing work for the Defiant turret fighter). By then wind tunnel tests at RAE using a two-seventh scale model had also shown that when the guns were elevated to 45° and turned to 135° the level of drag would increase by as much as 35%, and it was problems like this that prompted the ordering of the P.92/2 scale model prototype. Tests with a single cannon turret mounted in the Defiant prototype and other examples also showed a similar drag problem during rotation, where the drag would increase by regular amounts until the existing turret motor stalled out at aft +/- 35°. There was a worry that there might be the same problem with the standard Defiant turret, but in fact the smaller 0.303in and 0.5in (7.7mm and 12.7mm) machine gun barrels brought no problems with drag.

Another problem that Boulton Paul had to solve was to be able to manufacture such a large turret ring while ensuring that it could stand up to the stresses of rotation under load, let alone the shock of having four cannons firing together. This was perhaps one of the earliest occasions where aeroelasticity in modern aircraft structures had to be taken into account since the ring had to encompass the upper wing and fuselage structures all moving in flight (or at least prevent their movement). Overall, progress with the P.92 airframes was very slow and then on 26 May 1940 the fighter was cancelled (published sources indicate that the prototype's structures were at the time still only around 5% complete). One reason behind the decision was the critical situation of the war itself (with the German advances in France) and the consequent need to standardise on the types of aircraft then being manufactured for the RAF. This move, pushed for and ratified by Minister of Aircraft Production Lord Beaverbrook, abandoned all cannon turret development and cut aircraft production in the immediate short term to five main types – Spitfire, Hurricane, Blenheim, Whitley and Wellington. However, published sources indicate that problems with the Vulture power unit (which suffered a troubled history) also contributed to the decision. In addition all work on cannon armed turrets was officially stopped by the Air Staff in 1940 with an order stating that the effort should concentrate on using rifle-calibre guns. The incomplete P.92/2, however, was allowed to continue.

The abandonment of the full-size fighter was incredulous to Boulton Paul until the full truth of the development difficulties being experienced with the new cannon guns was revealed to the firm in Sept 1940, when North was suddenly seconded by Beaverbrook to assist with sorting out the production and application problems associated with the weapon, which was limiting its use in cannon fighters. Up to this point Boulton Paul had only seen one-off weapons and minor snags, while information detailing the failure of feeds and parts on service fighters was not generally circulated.

The half-scale model aircraft V3142 was built to assess the full-size fighter's drag and aerodynamic qualities and was covered by Contract B.19037/39. Since Boulton Paul was busy with orders for its Defiant fighter (and no longer had the facility to build aircraft in wood) the airframe was constructed by Heston Aircraft as that company's J.A.8. It was powered by two de Havilland Gipsy Major II engines and made its first flight in the spring of 1941 piloted by Boulton Paul chief test pilot Flt Lt Cecil Feather. The exact date of the flight is unknown but the Boulton Paul log states that V3142 was allegedly moved to Wolverhampton from Heston Aircraft on 17 May (the aircraft was photographed there on the 17th presumably shortly after arrival). Once in Boulton Paul's hands at Wolverhampton (Pendeford) Airport, an assessment was begun on the effects the presence of the turret made on the aeroplane's aerodynamics and performance.

In July 1943, an incredibly long time after its first flight, V3142 was sent to Boscombe Down for handling trials. A&AEE's pilots found the cockpit long and narrow and rather cramped – the view ahead was good but was bad to the rear and side. In addition, for entry and exit the complete canopy had to be removed (with both engines stationary) while getting to the emergency exit hatch in the cockpit floor was also difficult – not a good situation for the pilot! The following comments A&AEE pilots relate to

An original manufacturer's model (in very poor condition) of the P.92 turret fighter.

Manufacturer's photo of the P.92/2. Note the enclosed undercarriage. *Boulton Paul Association via Les Whitehouse*

Lovely view of the P.92/2 scale model test aircraft which was possibly taken on 14 August 1943 during its period with A&AEE Boscombe Down. The turret was represented by a wooden hump, and note the pilot squashed into the tiny cockpit.

flights made at a take-off weight of 2,716lb (1,232kg). Taxying the aircraft was said to be fine and when the throttles were opened up for take-off there was a slight tendency to swing to the right, but this was easily checked with the rudder. Just slight backward pressure was enough to make the aircraft leave the ground cleanly and climb away at a steep angle. However, the main undercarriage wheels were badly out of balance and, while they were still rotating following the take-off, they set up a bad vibration throughout the airframe; the brakes had to be applied to stop this.

In the air the elevator was light and effective throughout the speed range, becoming heavier as speed increased but never excessively so. At all normal speeds the rudder was light and effective but there was a considerable falling off of effectiveness at the stall (but an adequate amount of control remained). The ailerons were very effective at all speeds, being light and responsive with no signs of any overbalance. The stick force increased very slightly with speed, but even at the maximum diving speed the ailerons were still light and positive. Under all conditions of flight with engines on there as sufficient elevator trim available, but when the engines were throttled back a large 'nose down' change of trim occurred, and in an engine off glide there was insufficient 'nose up' trimmer available to trim at speeds below 90mph (145km/h) ASI with flaps up or 85mph (137km/h) ASI with flaps down. With the flaps down the change of trim when the engines were throttled back was appreciably less, and when the flaps were lowered a slight 'nose down' change of trim occurred but this could be held easily on the control column.

From the point of view of stability, in general the longitudinal and directional characteristics were very satisfactory, but the lateral behaviour was a little unpleasant under rough air conditions. With engine off and flaps up the stalling speed was 59mph (95km/h) ASI, with flaps down 50mph (80km/h) ASI; with engines on the figures were 50mph (80km/h) and 42mph (66km/h) ASI respectively. With flaps up and engines running the aircraft exhibited a strong tendency to yaw to the right as the speed fell below 60mph (97km/h) ASI and considerable left rudder was required to hold a straight course. Flying on either engine singly proved easy and straightforward, the aircraft showing no tendency to bank, either as the engine was cut or in steady single-engine flight. Turns could be carried out with or against the running engine.

Rear view of the P.92/2. *Boulton Paul Association via Les Whitehouse*

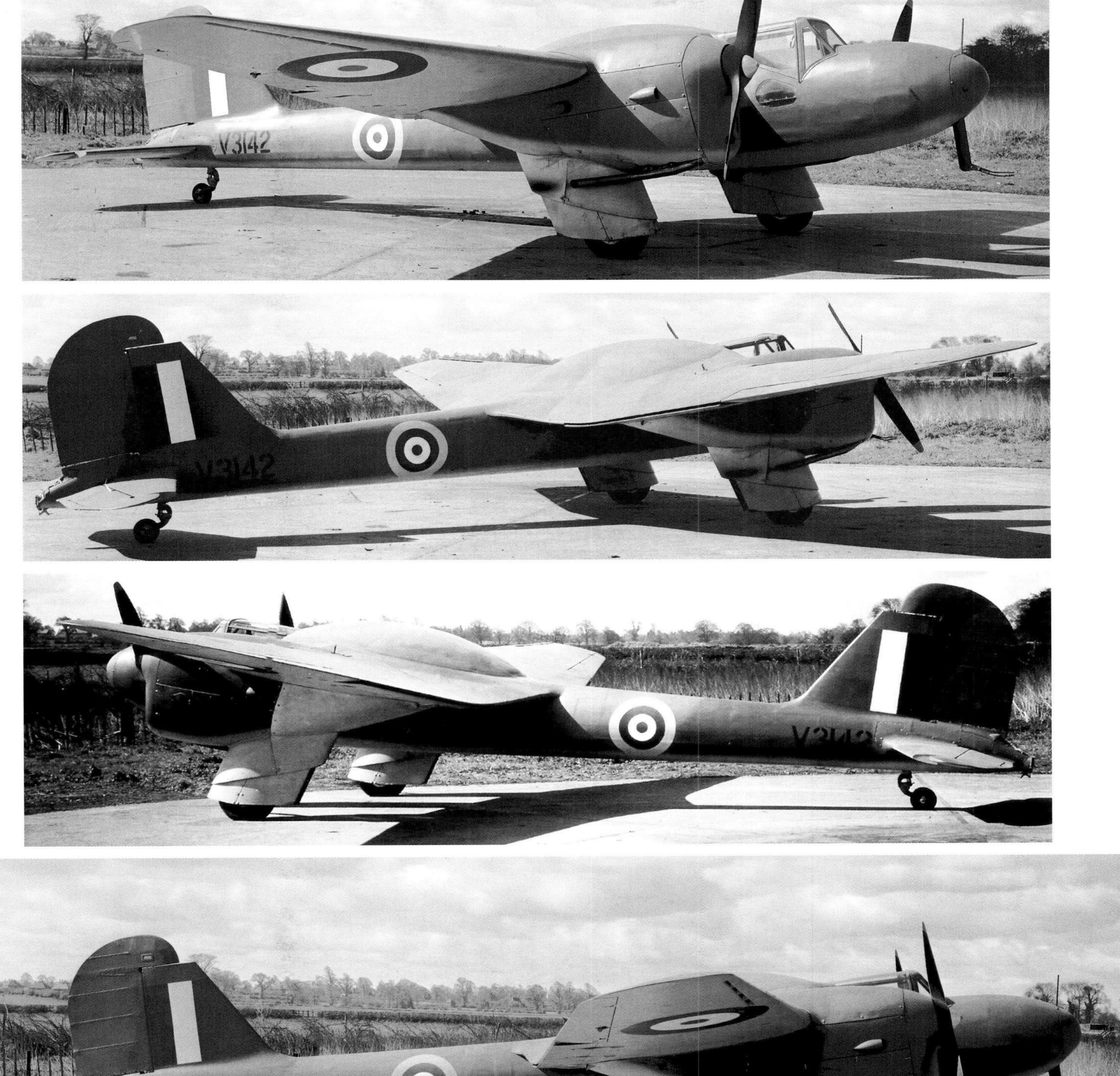

| Further walk-around views of V3142. *Boulton Paul Association via Les Whitehouse*

When diving at full throttle the speed had to be limited to 190mph (306km/h) ASI to avoid excessive engine rpm but the dive was quite steady and the stick force gradually increased. Recovery was quick when a light pull force was used. At 1/3 throttle the aircraft dived steadily and at the limiting speed (240mph (386km/h) ASI) only a moderate stick force was necessary to hold the aircraft in the dive. All controls were free from buffeting and overbalance, the ailerons remaining light and responsive while the rudder and elevators never became excessively heavy. When the control column was freed the P.92/2 recovered from the dive quite steadily. However, due to the shape of the undercarriage the wheels again rotated in flight, thus setting off more bad vibration. This was most marked in the dive and once again required the brakes to be applied. The landing run was quite short and the aircraft showed no tendency to swing. A higher maximum take-off weight of 2,778lb (1,260kg) made very little difference to the P.92/2's general handling qualities.

Afterwards, the stall performance was assessed with the leading edge slots sealed. For engine off the stalling characteristics were practically the same with the slots in the wings either open or sealed; however, with engines on the stalling characteristics were noticeably poorer with the slots sealed, the wing dropping relatively suddenly compared with the gentle fall that occurred with the slots open. Although stalling was the only condition under which the slots gave any noticeable benefit, their retention would help in the event of a stall following a bounce on landing and so appeared worthwhile. A&AEE's report concluded that the P.92/2 was very pleasant to handle. The aircraft possessed satisfactory longitudinal characteristics, but the lateral characteristics did require some improvement. The ailerons and rudder were satisfactory, but more upward elevator movement and trimmer 'nose up' range were required for gliding and landing. Overall the P.92/2 showed higher drag than previously predicted in RAE wind tunnel reports but, due to its lower engine power, its longitudinal stability was much better. Cecil Feather commented that it was a good report and that Boulton Paul had no serious disagreements with its findings, and that none of the findings

This A&AEE view of V3142 banking away from the camera provides particularly good detail of the fixed undercarriage.

were of a serious nature and all could be corrected (had the full P.92 been built).

Afterwards, V3142 may have been flown by Boulton Paul at times as a 'runabout', but in due course it was stored in a wooden hut about half way down the access track to Wolverhampton Airport. It survived there for a number of years before being dragged out and burnt on one Bonfire Night in the 1950's.

P.92 Structure

The P.92 was to have a slim fuselage of monocoque construction throughout with light alloy sheet skins stiffened by longitudinal corrugated stringers built on to a series of ring formers and built-up bulkheads. The thickened wing centre-section junction with the fuselage provided the room for a 13ft (3.96m) diameter turret in between the nacelles for the two Vulture engines (which were fitted with 13ft (3.96m) diameter variable-pitch propellers). Except when elevated above about 30° the turret had its four 20mm Hispano cannon in recessed slots, and the gunner was provided with a small offset transparent sighting hood. Each gun had 120 rounds of ammunition in four drums of 30 rounds each (when empty early Hispano cannon had to have their drums changed by the gunner). The turret was built in light alloy over braced ribs and had a faired shallow dome to reduce drag. The fuselage was to be built in five main units – nose portion including pilot's cockpit, centre section, rear section in two halves, tail section, and tail fairing piece. The wing had split flaps and Frise ailerons. The aircraft had a single fin and rudder and, in all, 349 gallons (1,587 litres) of fuel were to be carried. A 250lb (113kg) bomb container was also be carried by the prototypes as an alternative load, but the Air Staff became aware that this extra complication was unnecessary and almost certainly it would have

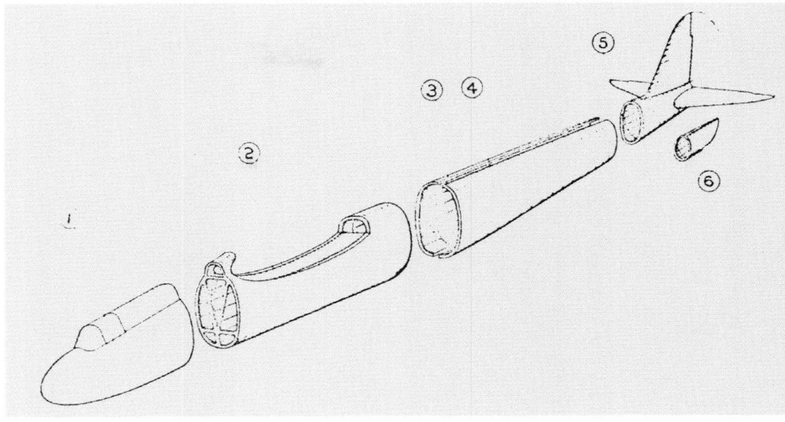

Plan showing the P.92's structure in five sections and with the rear fuselage also split into two. *Boulton Paul Association via Les Whitehouse*

been dropped from production aeroplanes. There was an ingenious device for the pilot to allow himself to be evacuated from the aircraft through a downward chute fitted in the rear of his seat.

P.92/2 Structure

The P.92/2 was a single-seat high-wing monoplane and its Gipsy Major IIs had two-blade fixed-pitch wooden propellers. Care had to be taken to ensure that the Gipsy's nacelles and cooling air ducting matched the P.92's. Plywood monocoque construction was used throughout and there was a dummy turret (with no dummy guns) placed above the centre section. Split trailing edge wing flaps were installed in three sections which extended from the wing root to the ailerons while (due to worries in regard to the wing's pronounced taper) permanent built-in slots were provided in the leading edges near the tips. The P.92/2 had a fixed undercarriage with the legs enclosed in large fairings, the cockpit roof was level with the wing upper surface, and an anti-spin parachute was fitted.

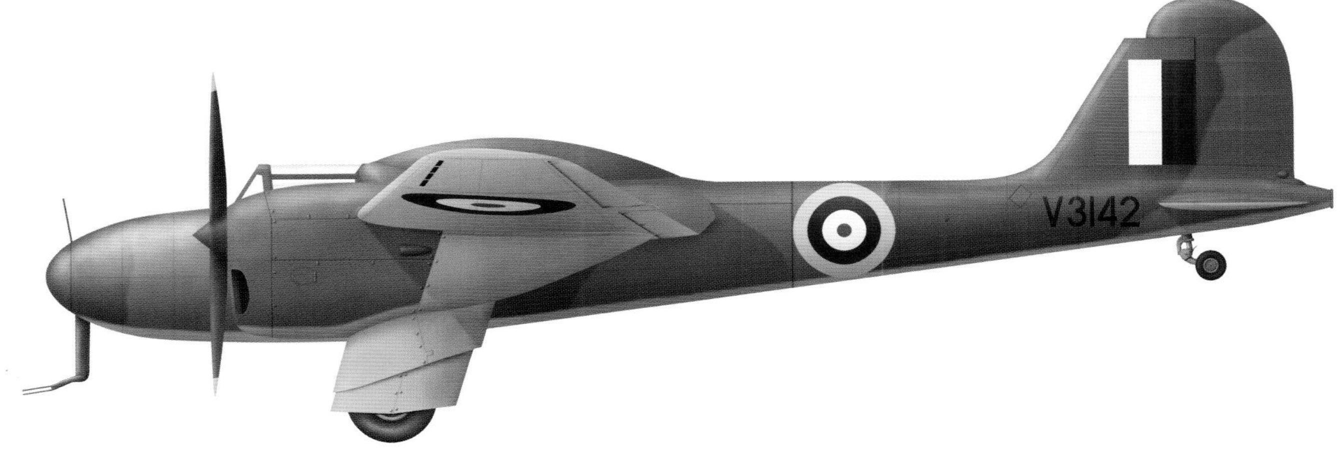

The P.92/2 was a sub-scale testbed for the proposed P.92 turret fighter. *Chris-Sandham Bailey www.inkworm.com*

5 Bristol and Handley-Page B.1/39 Bombers

Bristol 159

(1939 Brochure Figures or Air Staff Estimates)

Type: Seven-Seat Heavy Bomber

Powerplant: Four 1,550hp (1,156kW) Bristol Hercules HE.7.SM air-cooled radial engines

Alternative: Four Rolls-Royce Griffon liquid-cooled inline engines

Span: 114ft 6in (34.90m)

Length: 80ft 3in (24.46m)

Gross Wing Area: 1,800sq.ft (167.4m^2)

Maximum Weight: Hercules engines 77,860lb (35,317kg); Griffon 76,270lb (34,596kg)

Rate of Climb: Not available

Maximum Speed: Hercules 302mph (486km/h); Griffon 303mph (488km/h) both at 15,000ft (4,572m)

Service Ceiling: Hercules 25,300ft (7,711m), Griffon 23,700ft (7,224m)

Armament: 8 x 20mm cannon; 15,000lb (6,804kg) bombs

Handley Page HP.60

(1939 Brochure Figures or Air Staff Estimates)

Type: Seven-Seat Heavy Bomber

Powerplant: Four 1,550hp (1,156kW) Bristol Hercules HE.7.SM air-cooled radial engines

Alternative: Four Rolls-Royce Griffon liquid-cooled inline engines

Span: 115ft 0in (35.05m)

Length: 92ft 6in (28.19m)

Gross Wing Area: 1,815sq.ft (168.8m^2)

Maximum Weight: Hercules engines 77,090lb (34,968kg); Griffon 75,350lb (34,179kg)

Rate of Climb: Not available

Maximum Speed: Hercules 300mph (483km/h); Griffon 315mph (507km/h) both at 15,000ft(4,572m)

Service Ceiling: Hercules 23,500ft (7,163m); Griffon 25,700ft (7,833m)

Armament: 8 x 20mm cannon; bomb load unknown but well in excess of 9,000lb (4,082kg)

Maximum Speed: 152mph (245km/h) at ground level

The subjects of this chapter resulted from studies for what was initially termed the 'Ideal Bomber' for the RAF, a misleading term which in fact was later retitled 'Standard Bomber'. The story was a remarkable episode in pre-war RAF bomber design in that the object was to produce a bomber suitable as a replacement for the whole striking force of the RAF, both at home and abroad. But the concept was even more ambitious than that because the new machine would have to show an improvement on those designs already in hand – the Avro Manchester, Handley-Page Halifax and the Short Stirling. In other words it was hoped to design a successor to these three bombers before they themselves had come into use. There were many aspects to consider, not least the problem of putting too many eggs into one basket. An aeroplane of whatever size is still a fragile thing and if individual aircraft were to become too valuable there might have been a tendency to avoid risking them in the way that became apparent with capital warships during the 1914 War. Behind the scenes there was much argument and discussion but two different types were eventually ordered against the resulting requirements, although they were short lived.

By 1938 the British Air Ministry feared the performance and armament of the latest German fighters. No British bomber could outpace, outclimb or outmanoeuvre these aircraft, but if the bombers concealed themselves in cloud or darkness that would reduce their bombing accuracy and probably rob an attack of any decisive effect. Therefore, if the bomber was to reach its objective and get back home safely it must expect to fight its way through much of the outward and homeward trips. It was also clear that bombers could be used with much greater profit against German industrial and communications targets rather than directly against her armed forces and this placed increased premium on bomb load and range. Few targets could be destroyed with small bombs (canals, dams, bridges and railways would need large bombs) while operations against the Ruhr industrial complexes would entail a long flight from the UK, and such distances added immensely to the navigation load. It would be very difficult to put all of these changes into the pre-war Armstrong Whitworth Whitley and Vickers Wellington bombers.

Consequently, in March 1938 the Air Staff put together a paper that described an Ideal Bomber, and then a few months later Specification B.19/38 was produced which indicated that the bomber would have a strong defensive armament of eight 20mm "shell-firing guns" (cannon) mounted in two turrets amidships, one above and one below the fuselage, to provide protection above, below and to the aircraft's rear. On 28 December B.19/38 was revised as B.1/39 and the new document, issued in March 1939, outlined a cruise speed of 280mph (451km/h), a minimum range flying at 15,000ft (4,572m) with 9,000lb (4,082kg) of bombs aboard of 2,500 miles (4,023km), and (at that time) a gross weight of 50,000lb (22,680kg). The aircraft was to replace all current heavy and medium bomber types, fabric was not to be used as a wing covering (in other words all-

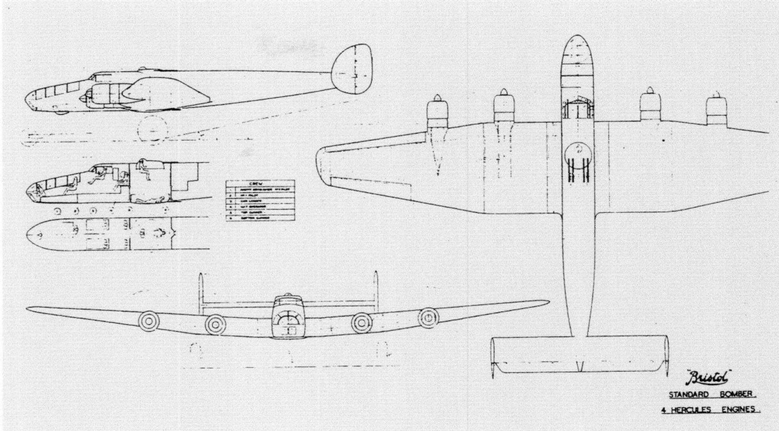

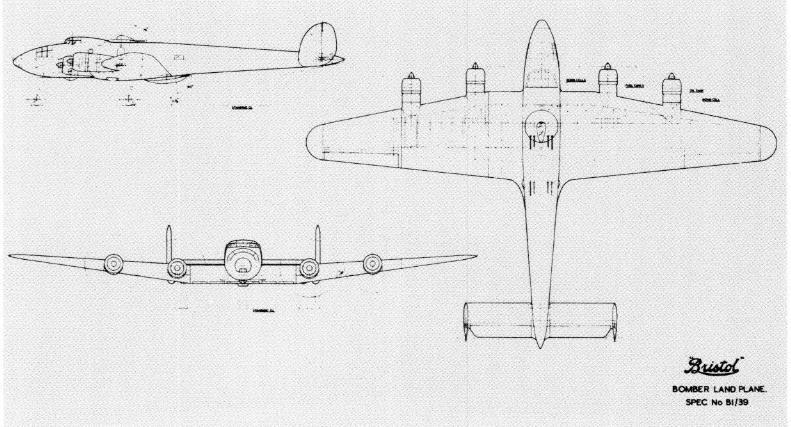

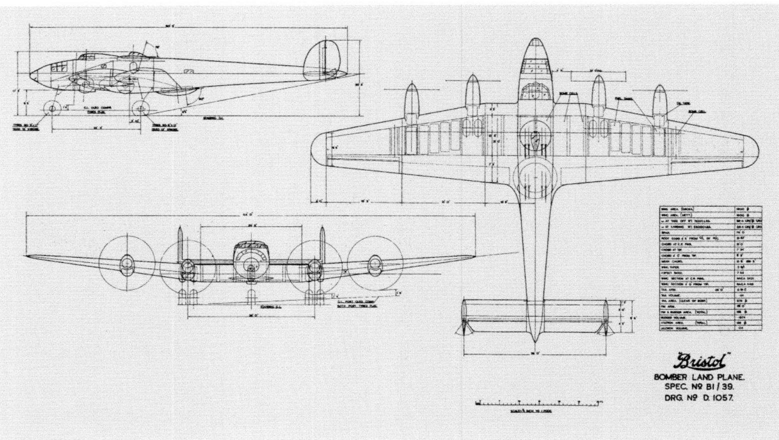

Top: Drawing showing the Bristol 159 'Standard Bomber'. This is thought to be a version of the 159 produced prior to the final layout being settled. *Duncan Greenman, Bristol AIRchive*

Middle: Bristol Type 159 'Beaubomber' is intended to be built. This was the version with Hercules engines. *Duncan Greenman, Bristol AIRchive*

Bottom: Bristol Type 159 'Beaubomber' variant with Griffon engines. *The late Jim Oughton Archive via Phil Butler*

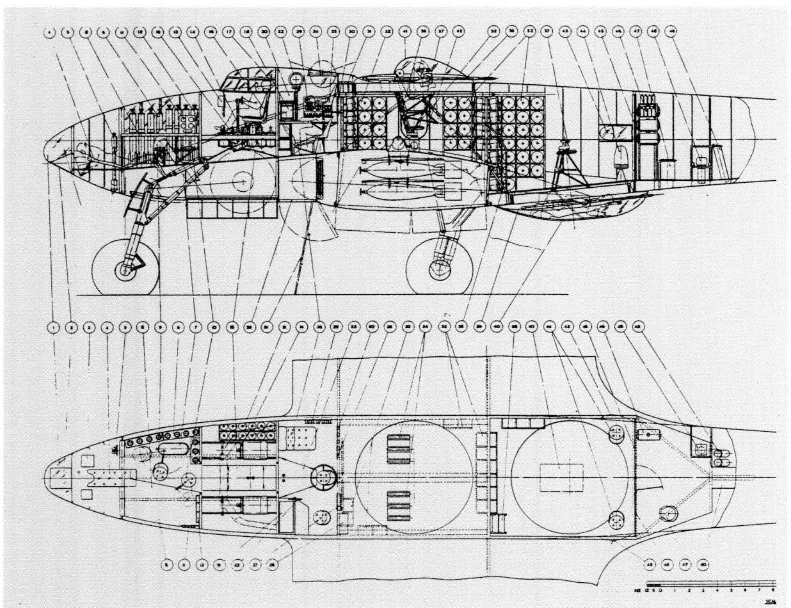

Drawing showing Type 159 interior detail. *Duncan Greenman, Bristol AIRchive*

metal structures were required) and it would be powered by four engines. From the design competition held in 1939 orders were placed for the aircraft proposed by Bristol (the Type 159) and Handley Page (the HP.60). In the meantime Boulton Paul (as part of its development programme for the P.92 turret fighter discussed in Chapter 4) demonstrated the mounting and firing of a single 20mm Hispano cannon in a powered gun turret, and so plans were made to use Boulton Paul turrets in the B.1/39. However, Frazer-Nash also developed a rival turret.

Known to the company as the 'Beaubomber', the Bristol 159 carried a maximum bomb load of 15,000lb (6,804kg), all of which were housed in the inner wing between the spars since putting the bombs here enabled the designers to install the heavy turrets near the aircraft's CofG. For its low wing the 159 employed orthodox wing construction and there was an armoured monocoque mid fuselage structure to hold the entire crew (except when the bomb aimer was in his nose position) and the 20mm cannon (not in Boulton Paul turrets, but in smaller streamlined Bristol-designed turrets). The favoured powerplant was the Bristol Hercules radial engine (the Rolls-Royce Griffon was an alternative) and the aircraft had a nosewheel undercarriage and eight internal fuel tanks which, for the 2,500 mile (4,023km) range requirement, would hold 2,580 gallons (11,731 litres). The 159 could carry a further four fuel tanks on the bomb racks while the maximum estimated range was 3,500 miles (5,632km) when flying at a speed of 280mph (451km/h). Wind tunnel tests with the design showed promise and indicated low drag and good stability, and by spring 1940 the process of structural design had reached an advanced stage.

No drawings or illustrations are known to exist for the Handley Page HP.60 but it was a development of the firm's Halifax and had a high wing position which helped the blending in of the upper Boulton Paul turret. The lower turret projected outside the fuselage, the wing was to be built using a wide box-spar construction and the aircraft had a long tricycle undercarriage and a twin fin. There was a difference in the quoted internal fuel for the 2,500 miles (4,023km) range for the two specified engines – 2,202 gallons (10,012 litres) with the Hercules and 2,104 gallons (9,567 litres) for the Griffon. It was specified that the undercarriages, wheels and tyres, and some other major components which required large metal forgings or castings, were to be interchangeable between the HP.60 and Type 159.

Two prototypes of each type were recommended in late in December 1939 and serials X2871 and X2875 were allocated to the Bristol 159, and X2880 and X2885 to the HP.60 under the respective Contracts B.62051/39 and B.62052/39, both of which were dated 7 May 1940. Back in August 1939 and preparatory to the construction of the B.1/39 prototypes, the Director of Technical Development had outlined a programme for both companies to build and flight test half-scale models, but by December

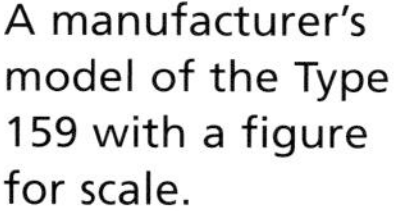

A manufacturer's model of the Type 159 with a figure for scale.

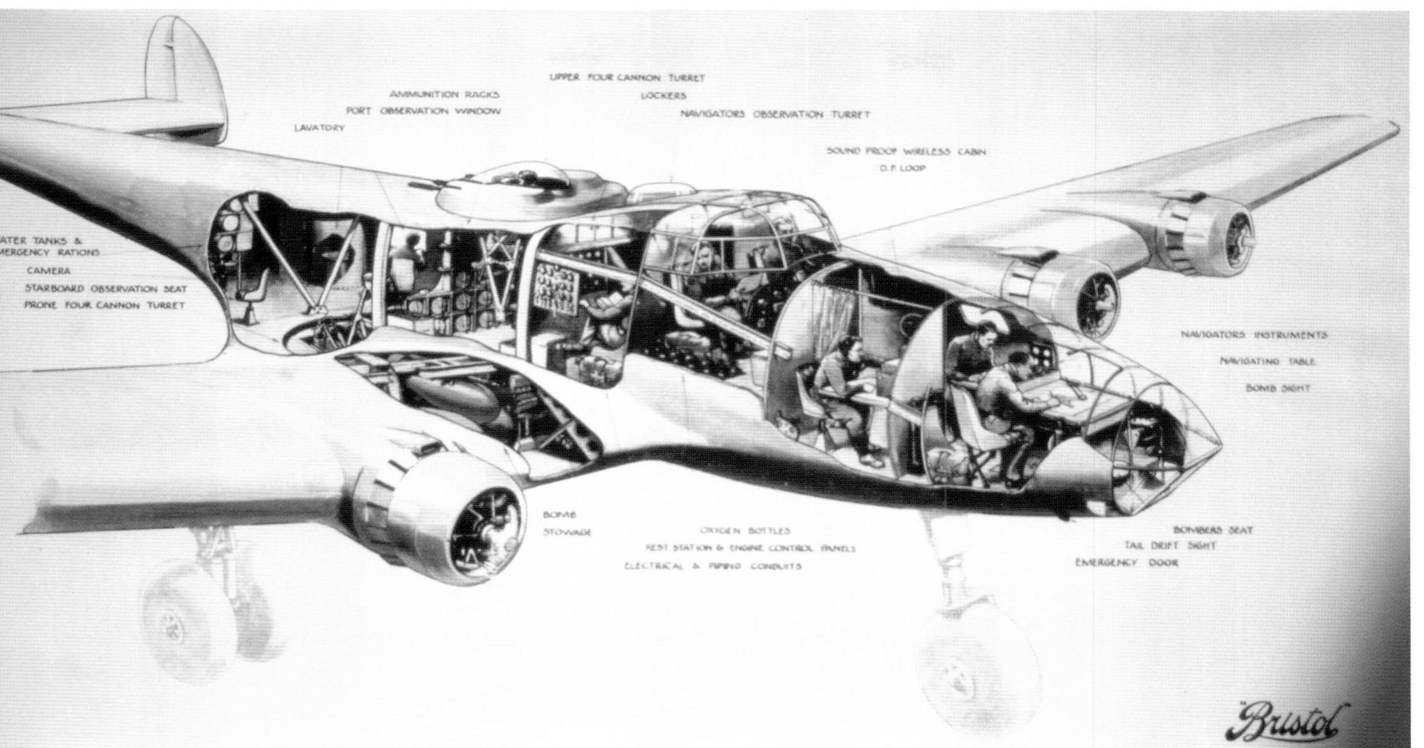

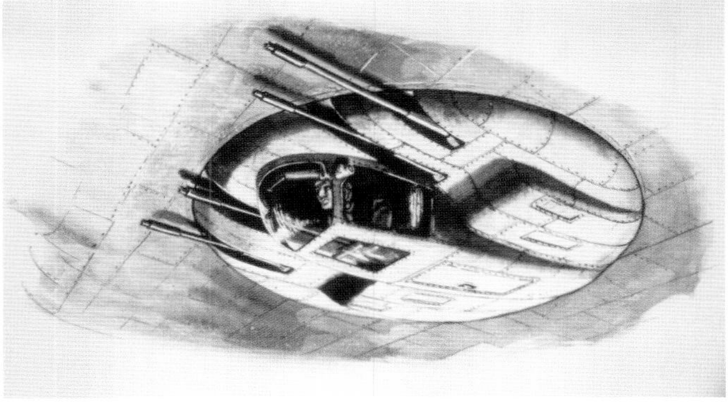

Top: Partial cutaway artwork giving further interior detail for the Bristol 159.

Above left: Artist's impression of the Type 159's multi-cannon upper dorsal 20mm turret, but it is not certain whether this is Bristol's own turret design or the rival from either Boulton Paul or Frazer-Nash.

Above right: Artwork showing the multi-cannon prone ventral 20mm turret. Each gun was to be fed by 30-round magazines, with twenty magazines in all allotted to each of the aircraft's turrets – quite a workload for the gunner to keep reloading.

the greater urgency introduced by the outbreak of war meant that the flying models were dropped. Instead the firms were to proceed direct to the design and construction of prototypes, and detailed mock-ups for each of the full-size bombers were completed. However, on 25 May 1940 Air Vice Marshal Tedder, the Deputy Air Member for Development and Production at the Ministry, concluded that work on the B.1/39 (and the Boulton Paul P.92 turret fighter in Chapter Four) should be suspended. Both firms were told of the decision on 18 June when all design work ended. The decision stemmed from the arrival of Lord Beaverbrook as the Minister of Aircraft Production and his desire, because of the critical situation with the German invasion of France, to increase the production of existing types of aeroplane only. Work on new projects like the cannon-armed B.1/39 and Boulton Paul P.92 (and also cannon turrets) was stopped. The mock-ups were cleared for dismantling in January 1941.

Mock-up of the forward fuselage of the Type 159 and (in the foreground) of the concurrent Bristol Type 162 light bomber project which was tentatively named Beaumont. These photographs are dated 14 January 1941 and may have been taken at this stage after instructions had been given to dismantle the Type 159 mock-up. *BAE Systems*

Thus the Ideal Bomber had a pretty short life. A post-war report noted that the most striking impression of the whole project was the extraordinary ambition behind it. Had either design reached fruition and proved successful in action then this would probably have been among the most outstanding achievements in the history of aircraft design to date. On the other hand it had it gone into mass production and proved inadequate or a total failure, the results would have been catastrophic. In the event those machines under development before the Ideal Bomber proved worthy successors to the Wellington and Whitley. The failed twin-Rolls-Royce Vulture-powered Avro Manchester was transformed with four Merlins into the triumphant Lancaster which performed feats that could scarcely have been contemplated in 1938 when the 'Ideal' discussions were underway, and the Handley-Page Halifax also achieved an outstanding career record. Nevertheless, the Ideal Bomber concept had much value in that it brought together what was known about the problems of bomber design at the time.

6 Bristol Buckingham

Bristol Buckingham B.Mk.I

Type: Four-Seat High Speed Day Bomber

Powerplant: Prototypes two 2,300hp [1,715kW] Centaurus IV radial engines; production two 2,400hp (1,790kW) Bristol Centaurus VII radial engines

Span: 71ft 10in (21.9m)

Length: 46ft 10in (14.3m)

Gross Wing Area: 708sq.ft (65.8m^2)

Empty Weight: 24,042lb (10,905kg)

Maximum Take-Off Weight: 38,920lb (17,654kg)

Rate of Climb: Approx. 1,700ft/min (518m/min) at sea level

Maximum Speed: 326mph (525km/h) at 1,000ft (305m) in MS gear; 345mph (555km/h) at 11,250ft (3,429m) in FS gear

Service Ceiling: 25,500ft (7,772m)

Armament: 4 x fixed 0.303in (7.7mm) Browning machine-guns in nose, 4 x 0.303in (7.7mm) machine-guns in dorsal turret, 2 x 0.303in (7.7mm) machine-guns in ventral position; 1 x 4,000lb (1,814kg), 2 x 2,000lb (907kg), 4 x 1,000lb (454kg), 2 x 1,000lb (454kg) + 4 x 500lb (227kg), or 6 x 500lb (227kg) bombs

This aircraft is one of two types in this book to reach series production and to be built in some quantity, but which then did not enter service. The failure of the relatively little known Bristol Buckingham is nevertheless an interesting story and shows how the capabilities of military aircraft moved forward during the war years, in the process leaving some aircraft like this bomber behind. The type deserves to be discussed a little more.

The origin of the Bristol Buckingham goes back to some company proposals made in January 1939 for a bomber version of the Bristol Beaufighter and powered by Bristol Hercules engines. Then in 1940 Specification B.7/40 was issued to provide a high speed light bomber for the RAF, although no suitable design was forthcoming. Separately, however, on 2 October 1940 Bristol proposed its Hercules-powered Type 162 which had evolved from the 1939 work and which the company had tentatively named Beaumont. This came close to B.7/40's limits and on 2 February 1941 plans were made to order three prototypes. However, had the Bristol team led by chief designer Leslie Frise (with Archibald Russell as his deputy – Russell became chief designer in 1944) realised how problems and design changes would interfere with the bomber's progress it would probably have been abandoned there and then. Very quickly increases in speed, bomb load and range necessitated a more powerful powerplant, and a subsequent re-design with a larger wing and two Bristol Centaurus radial engines was called the Type 163. This was accepted in March 1941 and the new type was named Buckingham and covered by specification B.2/41 of August 1941.

Construction in the Filton experimental workshop of the first of four Buckingham prototypes (serials DX249, DX255, DX259 and DX266 ordered under Contracts/Acft/236) got moving in November 1941, but a whole mix of troubles brought considerable delays to the aircraft's first flight, the placing of production orders (450 machines in all), and the manufacture of production aeroplanes. Much of the Buckingham story is a complex affair and affected many aspects associated with it. For example the introduction of the type into production would hit Bristol Bisley (Blenheim V),

Beaufighter and Beaufort manufacture and throughout the war MAP was loath to stop construction of in-service types, regardless of whether they were still up to date or not. MAP's primary brief was to get aircraft out of the door and when a new type was proposed, something would have to be cut back or dropped to make room for it. In addition, there were usually several new aeroplanes competing for any available capacity, and it was at one point agreed that producing 60 Buckinghams a month would displace capacity that could produce 35 Bisleys and 50 Beauforts or Beaufighters a month. The new aircraft would have its own development problems, and yet for some officials its existence created even more. For a period the Buckingham also had a rival in the form of the Napier Sabre-engined Hawker P.1005 to Specification B.11/41 (Chapter Seventeen).

early August when new ailerons were fitted. Also during August the longitudinal stability of the Buckingham was questioned for the first time. DX249 was tested by A&AEE Boscombe Down who reported that at a take-off weight of 30,500lb (13,835kg) the bomber showed no dangerous characteristics, but if the CofG was moved further back (as would be the case in service use) then longitudinal stability was lost; indeed the type was deficient in longitudinal and directional stability. Revisions to the tail unit were made during October and November, DX266 becoming the first aircraft to receive the larger tail unit that was introduced on production machines from the tenth or eleventh aircraft. The first production machine (KV301) flew on 12 February 1944 but these changes brought another problem, a loss of lateral stability brought about by the extra weight.

The first Buckingham prototype DX249, which was not fitted with armament, is pictured on 20 February 1943 immediately after roll-out and in its earliest configuration. *Phil Butler*

In this February 1943 view, it can be seen that the ventral cupola has not yet been fitted but a dummy dorsal turret is in place. Note the large rudder horn balances. *Phil Butler*

Nevertheless, on 4 February 1943 Bristol test pilot Cyril Uwins took DX249 on its maiden flight. Three of the Buckingham prototypes were fitted with the 2,300hp (1,715kW) high altitude-rated Centaurus IV while DX259 flew with the production engine, the moderate altitude 2,400hp (1,790kW) Centaurus VII. DX255 had a full fitting of equipment including working turrets. Flight testing, however, soon revealed problems, particularly with an unpleasant vibration which was not cured until

In the effort to find solutions both prototype and production Buckinghams were flown from Boscombe. Indeed, from April to November 1944 production aircraft KV304, KV306 and KV310 were employed by A&AEE on intensive flight trials but for long periods they were unserviceable. A report dated 26 June 1944 noted that the cockpit had not been well or even intelligently thought out, and practically without exception all of the essential knobs and taps were very awkward to access.

Two pilots who had flown the Buckingham for more than three hours described the aircraft as "heavy and sluggish at all speeds" and it had to be 'flown' the whole time. The controls were spring-tab operated which meant that it was impossible to 'feel' the aircraft and there was an appreciable time-lag between movement of the controls and the subsequent movement of the aircraft. These pilots felt that this aspect would make formation flying in the way it was done operationally (in tight boxes) almost impossible, but they were full of praise for the Centaurus engines which they considered to be the best part of the aircraft. A memo from Headquarters, No. 2 Group, dated 1 May 1944 described the Buckingham as: "...a retrograde step, rather than an advance on the [North American B-25] Mitchell. The Mitchell is pleasanter to fly, more stable (although slower) and seems infinitely better finished." In fact the Buckingham was about 30mph (48km/h) faster than the Mitchell (a similar medium bomber type) at 10,000ft (3,048m) at maximum weak mixture, but it was now over three years since the start of the Buckingham programme and the type was becoming out of date.

On 27 September 1944 Russell and Uwins met MAP's N.E. Rowe to discuss this persistent unserviceability and a series of modification actions was raised, the biggest involving the redesign and replacement of the undercarriage door closing mechanism (in mid-December 1943 DX255 had been lost in a crash due to undercarriage failure and in May 1944 a door failure had grounded all Buckinghams). In the end, after a great deal of testing, most of the Buckingham's flying weaknesses were solved or at least improved. KV324, an example representative of the final production version, was assessed by A&AEE between August and October 1944 at the maximum overload weight of 38,920lb (17,654kg) and in this condition the aircraft was considered to be acceptable for service use; however, no margin was available for any deterioration in the handling characteristics that would result from the addition of further equipment. The aeroplane featured the enlarged tailplane with a small chord elevators, spring tabs on the rudders, fin and rudder area increased by 20%, and the spring tabs on the ailerons had been replaced by balance tabs and a separate spring tab.

By September 1944 DX249 had been fitted with a dummy ventral cupola and 'production type' rudders. Note the shrouded exhaust. *Airbus Filton*

Side-on view of the second prototype DX255 taken on 6 November 1943 at Filton. During most of 1944 this aircraft was used by A&AEE Boscombe Down for a large volume of test flying. *Airbus Filton*

Three-quarter right side front view of DX255. It was the first aircraft to receive the full armament and was scrapped in November 1944. *Airbus Filton*

The Boscombe pilots who flew the aircraft with the new tail stated that it was more stable fore and aft, but was still tiring to fly. Laterally it was somewhat unstable – when a wing had dropped it could be raised easily with the rudder, but the latter was 'spongy' with the result that there was still a time lag before an even keel was regained. The Buckingham also had a pronounced tendency to swing on take off, but this was easily overcome. Plus points included the single engine performance which was good and could be maintained with a full load less bombs, the top turret permitted excellent all-round search and fire and the ventral position allowed reasonable search and fire in the rearward cone (60° traverse in azimuth and 45° depression), but it was extremely uncomfortable. The Buckingham's speed performance was also good.

However, it was too late. The end of the war was in view, the need for the Buckingham had passed and the type was destined never to enter service. In early 1944 it had been agreed that the type would operate overseas as a replacement for the Vickers Wellington and no examples would equip home-based squadrons (except for an operational trials unit). However, the development troubles and delays brought a decision in August 1944 that there was no operational use for the Buckingham in the RAF, and it was recommended that production should cease as soon as possible. Essentially, in its role as a tactical bomber the type was unusable, and alternative American types would be better suited to satisfy RAF needs (Mitchells eventually equipped half a dozen RAF squadrons during the second half of the war). The problem with this move, however, was that the Bristol labour force would then have no work until the forthcoming Bristol Brigand torpedo bomber programme had started. To fill the gap a minimum of 119 Buckinghams would have to be built even though they would be virtually useless. Every effort was made to find work in miscellaneous units for at least some of these airframes – and perhaps the most important step was a high speed courier aircraft conversion with the combat equipment removed and seating for four passengers. An extra 1,500 gallons (6,819 litres) of fuel was carried in long range tanks mounted in the bomb bay and KV338 served as a prototype, flying in this form on 21 October 1944.

Production Buckingham KV325. This aircraft is fully armed but the guns in the ventral cupola are only just visible. Note the access ladder alongside the ventral cupola and the larger fins. *Phil Butler*

Head-on shot taken at Boscombe Down of one of several Buckinghams tested by A&AEE to clear the type for operational service. It shows the open bomb bay doors to good effect, while the date of the picture should be familiar to most readers – 6 June 1944. *Crown Copyright*

There are very few photographs which show a Buckingham in flight and so the images shown here are well known. B.Mk.I KV335 was used for test purposes at Filton during the winter of 1944/45 and is fitted with the modified tail. *Airbus Filton*

KV335 in flight again. The Buckingham was a quite handsome aircraft with a solid and well-balanced appearance, but its poor flying characteristics contradicted the 'rule' which stated that 'if it looked right, it was right'. Both air-to-air shots of KV335 were taken on 20 April 1945. *Airbus Filton*

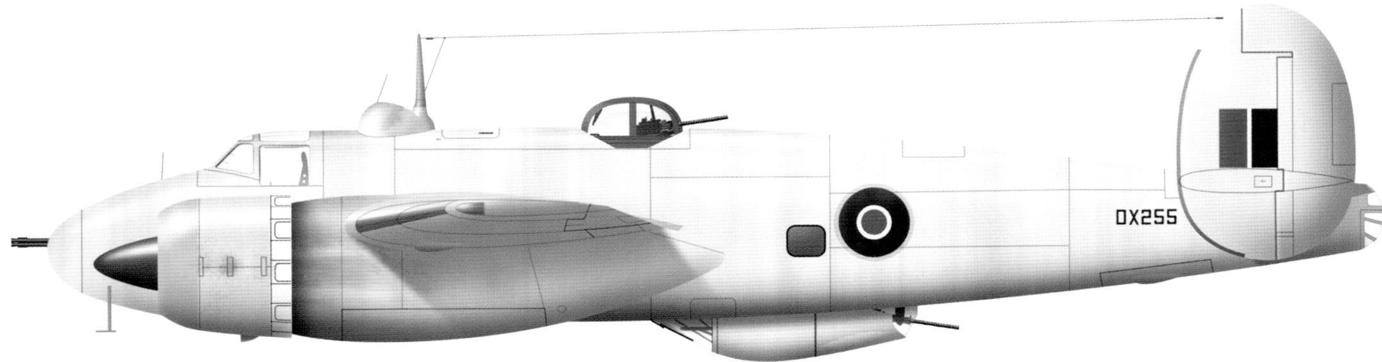

The second Buckingham prototype DX255 was the first to have armament fitted. *Tim Brown*

The Buckingham production order Acft/1915 for 400 aeroplanes covered serials in the run KV301 to KV893, but those actually built were KV301-KV346, KV358-KV372, KV402-KV450 and KV471-KV479, all of which were delivered between February 1944 and March 1946. In all 54 Buckinghams were delivered as B.Mk.I bombers with the rest as C.Mk.I transports, and some bombers were subsequently retrofitted. Not one joined a squadron and the vast majority experienced very short flying lives. Most were flown direct to store and then Struck Off Charge in 1947, although some were probably broken up even before then. A few were employed on test flying. The manufacturers used around a dozen, KV307, KV342 and KV360 found work with MAP's Centaurus Flight at Filton (where they undertook intensive flying for Centaurus development), at least ten were flown by A&AEE, another four by RAE, three by Rotol at Staverton on propeller development (including strain gauge tests on the propellers), one by Dunlop and some by a selection of experimental Flights and Trials Units. The Transport Command Development Unit had KV365, KV369 and KV404 to check out the courier version and in 1945 and 1946 flew these aircraft in the Mediterranean or Middle East theatres, while KV346 and KV471 flew with the Air Torpedo Development Unit at Gosport in 1945 and 1946. The last survivors appear to have been KV419 and KV479. KV419 was at Filton until at least the end of 1949 while KV479 went for scrap in June 1949 after being used by Dunlop for tyre development work. Here the objective was to improve the 'ride' for passengers when they were taxiing in civil airliners and the work involved an assessment of vibration when using high pressure tyres.

A total of 110 examples of a trainer version called the Type 166 Buckmaster was also produced which featured a new front fuselage with full dual control and side-by-side seating, although the rest of the structure was near identical to the Buckingham's. Prototypes TJ714 (flown on 27 October 1944) and TJ717 were converted from partially complete Buckinghams,

The Bristol Buckmaster T.Mk.I was a training version of the Buckingham. This view of RP185 in immaculate condition was taken after it had joined No 228 OCU in April 1949. *Crown Copyright – MoD*

The final member of the wartime 'Bristol twin' family (embracing the Blenheim, Bisley, Beaufort, Beaufighter, Buckingham and Buckmaster) was the Brigand torpedo bomber. The need to carry a torpedo died with the end of the war and the Brigand went on to operate as a general purpose bomber. *Crown Copyright – MoD*

Although the Buckingham failed to enter service, the very similar Bristol Type 166 Buckmaster did serve post war as a three-seat advanced trainer. This photo shows RP205 RCV-F on the ground at RAF Hullavington in about 1946 while serving with the Empire Central Flying School." *Peter R Arnold collection.*

and series machines used up sets of components made surplus by the reductions in Buckingham orders. These aircraft were used by Operational Conversion Units to train pilots to fly the Brigand and the last survivors were withdrawn in 1958. Finally, despite the ordering of a prototype (TK583), the Type 169 photo reconnaissance Buckingham was never completed.

In the end an aircraft planned in 1940 for production in 1943, but which suffered so many design and requirement changes that production was delayed until early 1944, could hardly have been expected to keep pace with the rapidly changing demands of air warfare. The many alterations gradually pushed up the Buckingham's weight and contributed to losses in flying quality, and when the aircraft was finally ready it was largely obsolescent in the tactical role. In the meantime the de Havilland Mosquito had become a great success and it was just not worth the trouble to make the Buckingham any better. Perhaps the farcical circumstances regarding manufacture of so many airframes that were sent direct to storage and scrap should have been avoided, but then the last year of war brought a lot of waste in the construction of several aircraft types, a good number having been made obsolete by the introduction of the jet fighter. The pace of progress meant that, despite being constructed in some numbers, the Bristol Buckingham was only allowed to leave a very small mark in aviation history.

Close-up of the Centaurus powerplant installation on the Bristol Buckingham. *Duncan Greenman, Bristol AirChive*

Structure

The Buckingham was designed and equipped as a four-seat bomber, the crew comprising pilot, navigator/bomb-aimer/under-gunner, wireless-operator and gunner. Each crew member had a separate station and armour plating was provided for them all. The mid-fuselage stressed skin wing was of the twin-spar type and had extruded upper and lower booms connected by web plates. Its ribbing was made from structures of sheet pressings and tubing. The inner planes had zero dihedral, the outer planes 2.5°, and metal-covered Frise type ailerons were incorporated together with split trailing-edge flaps; these were operated hydraulically. Spring tabs were fitted to the prototype in early May 1943. Power came from two Bristol Centaurus engines fitted to the inner main planes, each having a 14ft (4.27m) diameter Rotol constant-speed feathering propeller with four wooden blades, and the main undercarriage retracted backwards into the engine nacelles while the tailwheel retracted forwards into the fuselage.

The airframe was constructed almost entirely of metal with a semi-monocoque fuselage assembled from channel-section formers and bead-angled stringers manufactured in light alloy with Alclad skinning. The decision to use twin rudders was taken at the start of 1941 although it was acknowledged that a single fin was better for field of fire purposes. In 1945 KV322 only was fitted with an additional central dorsal fin for stability purposes but this proved to be of no value. The fixed surfaces of the tail unit were of stressed skin construction, the elevators were metal covered and the rudder control surfaces fabric covered. Four fixed machine-guns were mounted in the nose, four more in a fully rotating dorsal turret and a pair in a ventral turret. Both turrets were hydraulically operated and the latter was housed at the rear of a specially developed ventral 'bath' that was designed to give the navigator/bomb aimer the best possible downward view through a sloping optically flat aiming panel at the forward end. A variety of bomb loads could be carried in the internal bomb bay, but special doors were required when the 4,000lb (1,814kg) bomb was carried and these eventually become standard. The total capacity of the Buckingham's non-metallic self-sealing fuel tanks was 1,066 gallons (4,846 litres).

7 de Havilland DH.99/DH.101/DH.102 'Super Mosquito'

de Havilland DH.101

(For available DH.102 data - see text)

Type: Three-Seat High Speed Bomber

Powerplant: Two 2,180hp (1,626kW) Napier Sabre IV (NS.8SM) liquid-cooled inline engines

Span: 70ft 0in (21.34m),

Length: Unknown

Gross Wing Area: 710sq.ft (66.03m^2)

Flying Weight: Ministry assessment – 33,650lb (15,264kg)

Maximum Speed: 417mph (671km/h) at 26,000ft (7,925m) (Ministry assessment – 404mph (650km/h) at 25,000ft (7,620m))

Service Ceiling: Ministry assessment – 29,000ft (8,839m)

Armament: Bomber: 6 x short 500lb (227kg), 4 x short 1,000lb (454kg), 2 x 2000lb (907kg) or 2 x 1,900lb (862kg) bombs in bomb bay. 2 x 1,000lb (454kg) external; Fighter conversion: 4 x 20mm cannon, 4 x 40mm cannon

The fabulous de Havilland DH.98 Mosquito was an incredibly successful wartime combat aircraft and indeed was one of the world's first multi-role types to be built in fighter, bomber and reconnaissance forms. It will come as no surprise that there were several other proposed developments. Projects for which information is known include the DH.99, DH.101 and DH.102, and there was also an unnumbered version fitted with jet engines. The author has written about some of these before but in recent years a pair of drawings has appeared including a variant fitted with contra-rotating propellers which, although unidentified, may represent something like the DH.101. Information on a night bomber project is also reproduced in this chapter.

To set the scene, in May 1942 Specification B.11/41 was issued to cover the Hawker P.1005 medium bomber with twin Napier Sabre IV engines (which is described in Chapter Seventeen). However, in the autumn of 1941 de Havilland had suggested that a more powerful Mosquito could be built against the same draft requirement. This would also use two Sabres and was called the DH.99 – the project was quickly renumbered DH.101 and along with the later DH.102 it was also described as the Super Mosquito or 'hotted up Mossie'. The three-seat DH.101's predicted top speed was 417mph (671km/h) at 26,000ft (7,925m) (against the 430mph (692km/h) asked for in the draft B.11/41 document) and 4,000lb (1,814kg) of

This DH.102 model by Joe Cherrie is painted in standard prototype colours with yellow undersides. *Joe Cherrie*

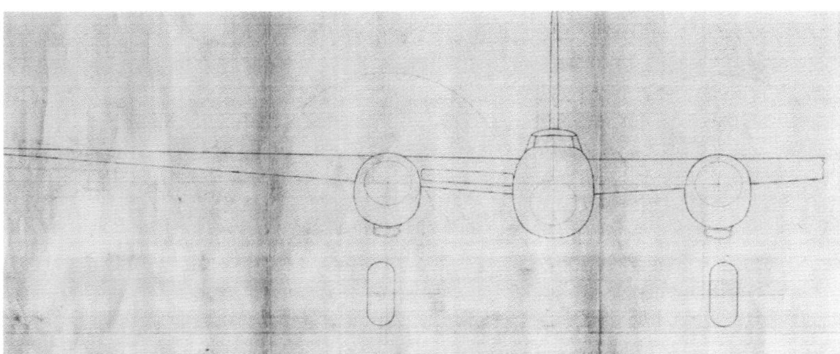

A drawing of de Havilland 'Aircraft B'. The contra-rotating propellers would help to avoid the heavy swing on take-off experienced by aircraft having blades rotating in the same direction. The propeller disc diameter was just about 13ft 10in (4.22m) and the wheels were offset to the nacelle centerline with a single vertical centerline drawn in next to it, which suggests that the DH.101 may have had an undercarriage arrangement not unlike the DH.103 Hornet fighter. *Bill Taylor*

bombs were to be carried internally with another 2,000lb (907kg) under the wings (the DH.101 could not carry the single 4,000lb (1,814kg) bomb). A range of 1,750 miles (2,816km) with a 4,000lb (1,814kg) load could be reached by carrying small external tanks – without these the range using just the 930 gallons (4,229 litres) of internal fuel was 1,450 miles (2,333km), but in this condition the 6,000lb (2,722kg) load was carried which reduced the maximum speed to 406mph (653km/h) and the ceiling to 27,300ft (8,321m). The 500lb (227kg) and 1,000lb (454kg) bombs were of the 'short', i.e. telescope fin, type. However, on 4 April 1942 de Havilland was notified that no Sabre power units would be available for this aircraft (insufficient Sabre production had been planned for the next two years) and the firm was advised to use Griffon 61s instead, but the expected lower performance from the Rolls-Royce engines meant that the DH.101 was quickly abandoned.

Since neither the Griffon inline nor the Bristol Centaurus radial was suited to the DH.101, de Havilland withdrew from the B.11/41 contest and replaced the DH.101 with an alternative slightly smaller aircraft which used the present Mosquito as its basis and was powered by the Rolls-Royce Merlin 61. This was to be a high-speed night and day bomber with a pressure cabin and three crew members and was called the DH.102. The company hoped it would be acceptable to MAP and the project was presented as a 'Mosquito Replacement' and labelled the Mosquito Series II and yet, with 5,000lb (2,268kg) of bombs aboard and either Merlin or Griffon powerplants, it was expected to be slightly slower than the Mosquito itself. Specification B.4/42 was allocated to cover the project and work began on the assembly of two prototypes which

Joe Cherrie's model of the DH.102 carries the serial MP478. *Joe Cherrie*

received the serials MP478 and MP481 under the order Contracts/Acft/1955. By October 1942 progress on these airframes was quite well advanced but little enthusiasm was felt for the DH.102, either by de Havilland or within the Air Staff. At the same time the firm was also working on the DH.100 (Vampire) jet fighter and DH.103 (Hornet) piston fighter, and the Air Staff eventually cancelled the DH.102 on 26 December 1942.

The newly discovered drawing of what is thought to be the DH.101, which is labelled 'Aircraft B', is undated but it seems almost certain that it was produced in about January 1942. This is because a drawing for 'Aircraft A' was discovered at the same time which shows the 'Jet Mosquito' and that is dated 25 January 1942, and it fits the time frame. The 'Jet Mosquito' was to be powered by two de Havilland Halford H.1 jet engines and a document dated June 1942 indicates that this would carry 2,000lb (907kg) of bombs and possess a top speed of 445mph (716km/h) at 40,000ft (12,192m). No project number was allocated to the jet aircraft. 'Aircraft B' had a Mosquito-style wing and fuselage with two Napier Sabre 20.S.I.M. engines and, most interestingly, contra-rotating propellers. Its span was 65ft 0in (19.81m) and the length (which includes the spinners) has been recalculated as 49ft 6in (15.09m) (not 47ft 6in (14.48m) as previously recorded) – most marks of Mosquito had a span of 54ft 2in (16.51m). The 65ft (19.81m) span does not match the official DH.101 figures, but one hopes that this is how the aircraft would have looked.

There is relatively little in the way of documentation to back up these drawings, but on 23 February 1942 de Havilland's C.C. Walker wrote: "We do fully realise the importance of producing a bomber with twin H.1 [jet] units. So far as our capacity to produce is concerned, if we were engaged on the fighter, the Sabre bomber and Mosquito development, we could do no more. There is, however, this further possibility. If the H.1 soon shows that it can do what is expected, we could do the H.1 bomber instead of the Sabre bomber. Much of the work we have done on the Sabre version would be of use in such a design, and two could be produced for the same production effort as one Sabre machine. The problem of getting a Sabre machine

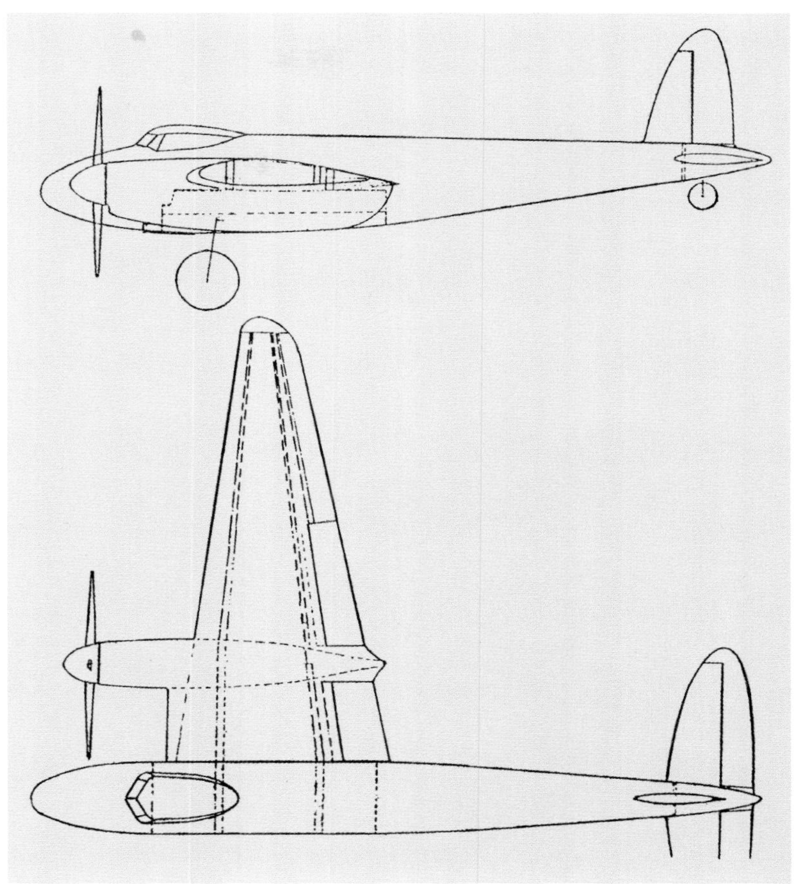

Drawing of the de Havilland DH.102 project. This proposed 'Super Mosquito' bomber would have had a crew of three.

Another view of the 'Super Mosquito' model, showing the four-bladed contra-rotating propellers. *Joe Cherrie*

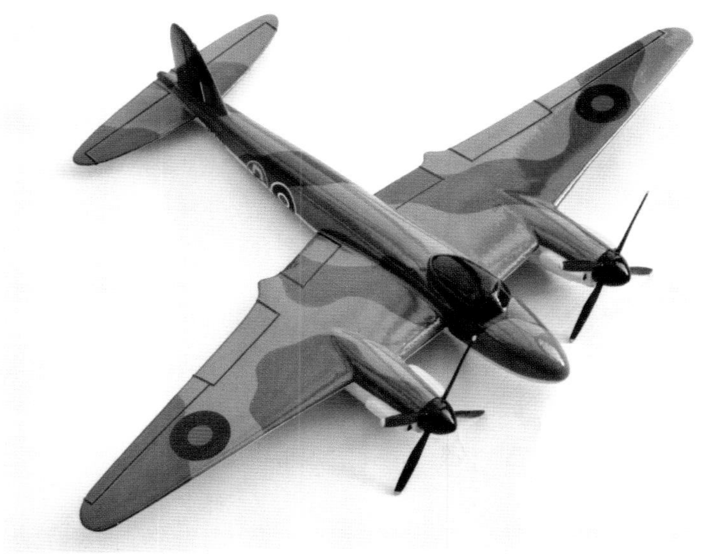

The de Havilland 'Aircraft A' Jet Mosquito was to be powered by two Halford H.1 jet engines. Its span was 56ft 6in (17.22m) and length 46ft 6in (14.17m). This model of the proposed Jet Mosquito was made by Joe Cherrie. *Joe Cherrie*

into production with its counter-rotating propellers, new installation and equipment problems with the skilled labour position as it is, is one which makes us look rather hungrily at the much simpler H.1 version. Substituting the H.1 bomber for the Sabre bomber is one of the possible alterations to be considered." The author has published this statement before in *British Secret Projects: Fighters & Bombers 1935-1950* but it contains the only known reference to contra-rotating propellers and links the two drawings together.

In April 1942 the Royal Aeronautical Society's Advisory Committee assessed the DH.101 and reported that the design was submitted as being: "...the best contribution to the national effort which could be made by the de Havilland Company". The principal reasons for this assumption included the following:

1. It used the same type of wood construction as the Mosquito and was designed by the same staff, and that would permit the saving of much time and experimental work.

2. The use of the Sabre engines would allow the high speed characteristics of the Mosquito to be retained but accompanied by an increase of dimensions, thereby permitting crew accommodation for accurate bombing, etc. and a useful bomb load.

3. The elimination of rear defence with extra crew stations etc. had a far-reaching effect on ease and date of production, the need for 'bottleneck' equipment etc., and performance.

The review was undertaken against the P.1005 and the Committee went on to recommend that Hawker's aircraft should be put into production, although by the time of its decision (on 26 April) de Havilland had in fact moved on to the DH.102.

From this author's point of view, the thought of a 'Mosquito II' in flight with Sabres and twin propellers is a fascinating. The Mosquito itself suffered from swing on take-off as a consequence of having two powerful Merlins with propellers rotating in the same direction. The author wondered if having two more powerful Sabres would exacerbate the problem but the late Flt Lt Norrie Grove DFM, who flew Mosquitoes, de Havilland Hornet fighters, Spitfires and many other aircraft, has explained that the size of the propellers and the engine revs were the problem, not the power of the engine. Swing is generated by the gyroscopic properties of the spinning blades and larger blades would make things worse. Contra-rotating propellers would of course solve the problem, as indeed would the introduction of handed engines where the single propellers on the two engines rotated in opposite directions. The latter were used by the de Havilland Hornet and did so much to make that fighter such a superb aeroplane. On handed engines the torque created by the two propellers was automatically cancelled out, while contra-rotating propellers did the same on each engine.

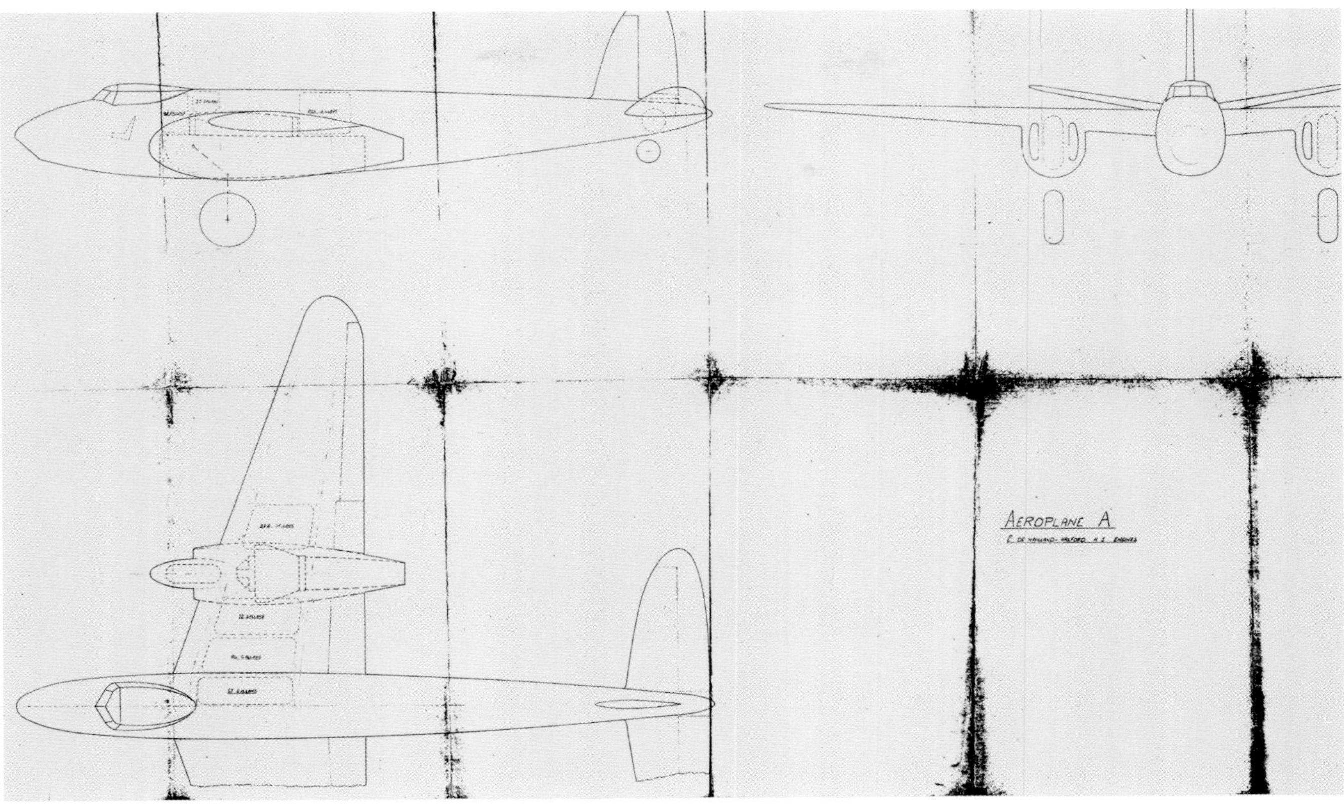

Fuel tanks directly behind the Jet Mosquito's cockpit would hold 67 gallons (305 litres). Tanks in each inner wing held 86 gallons (391 litres) and 72 gallons (327 litres) respectively, and one more outboard of the nacelles 52.5 gallons (239 litres), to give a total internal fuel load of 555 gallons (2,524 litres). *Bill Taylor*

It must be borne in mind that both Aircraft 'A' and 'B', which do not show official 'DH' designations, were most probably preliminary sketches. Nevertheless they are of great interest and do much to highlight the tremendous advances being made in piston engine and propeller technology at that time. The choice of the Sabre engine for the DH.101 would have provided some serious horsepower (well over 4,000hp (2,983kW) when added together). The fact that serials were allocated to the DH.102 qualifies the later project to appear in this book, and it has also provided the opportunity to present this new information as well.

de Havilland Night Bomber

During the research undertaken for this chapter a data table was found in the National Archives giving MAP estimates for a previously little known de Havilland night bomber. Presumably this would have been a scaled up Mosquito (but that is not certain) and it was a bigger aircraft than the DH.101. Span was given as 80ft (24.38m), gross wing area 825sq.ft (76.73m^2), operational weight 41,955lb (19,031kg) and fuel 1,150 gallons (5,229 litres). The powerplant was again two Napier Sabre NS.8.SM and the bomb load comprised twelve 500lb (227kg), six 1,000lb (454kg) plus two 500lb (227kg), four 1,900lb (862kg), or two 4,000lb (1,814kg). Maximum speed was given as 385mph (619km/h) at 25,000ft (7,620m), maximum range 2,150 miles (3,459km), and service ceiling 31,000ft (9,450m).

Structure

Both the DH.101 and DH.102 would almost certainly have been built along similar lines to the Mosquito.

The Mosquito was the world's first multi-role aircraft and this view, thought to be from 1942, presents one of the early night-fighter versions in the form of DD750, an all-black NF.Mk.II. *Phil Butler*

Although none of the Mosquito developments featured in this chapter were built, examples of the 'Mossie' itself continued in service for many years. This lovely de Havilland photo of PR.Mk XVI NS591 painted in photo reconnaissance blue was taken at Hatfield in 1946. *BAE SYSTEMS Heritage, Farnborough*

8 Fairey Spearfish and Strike Fighter

Fairey Spearfish

Type: Two-Seat Naval Dive Bomber and Torpedo Carrier
Powerplant: One 2,600hp (1,939kW) Bristol Centaurus air-cooled radial engine
Span: 60ft 3in (18.36m), Span Folded 19ft 6in (5.94m)
Length: 44ft 7in (13.59m)
Gross Wing Area: 530sq.ft (49.29m^2)
Maximum Weight with Torpedo: 22,021lb (9,989kg)
Rate of Climb: Time to 10,000ft (3,048m) 7.75 minutes
Maximum Speed: 292mph (479km/h) at 14,000ft (4,267m)
Service Ceiling: 25,000ft (7,620m)
Armament: 4 x 0.5in (12.7mm) machine-guns, two fixed in wings and two in turret; 1 x 2,000lb (907kg), 1,000lb (454kg) or 4 x 500lb (227kg) bombs, 1 x 18in (45.7cm) or 1x 22in (55.9cm) torpedo or 4 depth charges in bomb bay, 8 x rocket projectiles under wings

O.21/44

Type: Two-Seat Naval Strike Aircraft
Powerplant: Two 2,200hp (1,641kW) Rolls-Royce Merlin RM.14.SM air-cooled radial engines
Span: 60ft 0in (18.29m)
Length: 45ft 5in (13.84m)
Gross Wing Area: Not available
Maximum Weight: 23,700lb (10,750kg)
Rate of Climb: Not available
Maximum Speed: 360mph (579km/h) at 15,000ft (4,572m)
Service Ceiling: Not available
Armament: 4 x 0.5in (12.7mm) machine-guns, two fixed in wings and two in rear turret; bombs or torpedoes

Strike Fighter (at 13.11.45)

Type: Single-Seat Strike Fighter
Powerplant: Two 2,517hp (1,877kW) / 1,015lb (4.5kN) thrust AP-25 turboprops
Span: 51ft 0in (15.54m)
Length: 44ft 7in (13.59m)
Gross Wing Area: 390sq.ft (36.27m^2)
Maximum Weight: 23,100lb (10,478kg)
Rate of Climb: Time to 10,000ft (3,048m) 2.25 minutes
Maximum Speed: 494mph (795km/h) at 9,500ft (2,896m)
Service Ceiling: 38,500ft (11,735m)
Armament: 4 x 20mm cannon; 1 x torpedo, 2 x 1,000lb (454kg) or 500lb (227kg) bombs, depth charges or 6 x rocket projectiles

In April 1943 a new Specification for a two-seat naval dive-bomber and torpedo carrier, O.5/43, was issued against which designs were subsequently submitted by Cunliffe-Owen, Blackburn, Fairey and Folland. When proposals were requested by MAP in April Fairey submitted two main designs – a single engine aircraft with a powerful Bristol Centaurus engine and a rather ugly twin with two Rolls-Royce Merlins. Fairey emphasised most strongly its preference for the twin Merlin type on the score of performance and view

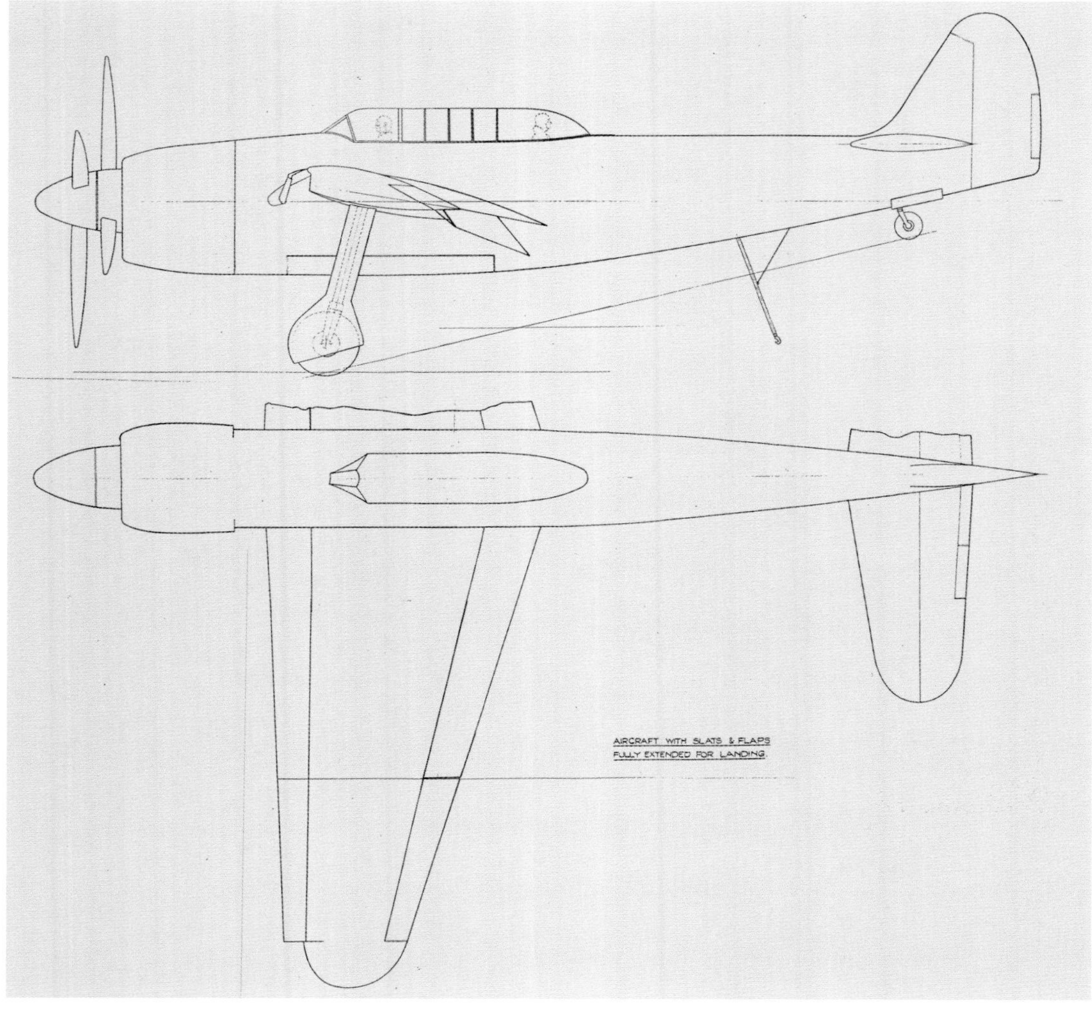
AIRCRAFT WITH SLATS & FLAPS
FULLY EXTENDED FOR LANDING.

Never previously published, this drawing shows Folland's proposal of 1 June 1943 to Specification O.5/43 which was called the Fo.119. It was rejected by the Ministry on 11 September 1943. The aircraft has contra-rotating propellers and the drawing shows the slats and flaps extended for landing. *Solent Sky Museum*

out, although in due course the conditions for the new aircraft in a dive were made more stringent which counted against the twin-engine design. In the end the Admiralty's decision to support the single Centaurus proposal was based on two main points:

(a). The Fleet Air Arm had no experience of twins or of aircraft of that size and weight on the deck.

(b). It was essential for the Pacific War campaign that a type reliable in engine and construction with normal means of handling should be available in production towards the end of 1945, or at the latest early 1946.

The single-engine design was selected by the Admiralty, but further developments with alternative engines were considered before an order was placed for three prototypes on 13 August 1943 to Contract Acft/SB.26862/C.20(b). Indeed, on the 23 August Fairey confirmed that a Bristol Centaurus 7 or 12.SM would be fitted in the first instance with the Rolls-Royce Exe 45 at a later date (the Exe was later dropped). In December O.5/43 was revised around Fairey's project and, although not listing a maximum speed, it did stress that best performance was required at heights between 5,000ft (1,524m) and 15,000ft (4,572m). A steady dive speed was not to exceed 300mph (483km/h) EAS and the crew would comprise the pilot plus an observer/telegraphist-air gunner. The design of the new torpedo bomber was led by Herbert Eugene Chapman who from 1943 was in charge of Fairey's project design team. As Fairey's chief designer Chapman proposed several ideas for full-span flaps and also a scheme for fitting two engines in tandem with a shaft drive for independent halves of co-axial propellers. He retired in 1957.

Opposite: Two further images of RA356, essentially an aerodynamic test airframe, taken in 1945. Note the prominent guides for the Fairey-Youngman area-increasing flaps. At certain angles the Spearfish was a not unattractive aeroplane.

Three walk-around views of the second Spearfish prototype RA360 taken in April 1947. Note the contours for the simulated dorsal turret fairing, the long undercarriage legs and the five-bladed propeller on the aircraft's Bristol Centaurus 57 engine. *Phil Butler*

The fourth prototype RN241, in effect a pre-production aircraft, pictured at the SBAC Show at Radlett on 13 September 1946. The rarely illustrated dorsal turret mock-up can be seen – initially the aircraft had flown without it. *Peter Green*

The prototypes were given the serials RA356, RA360 and RA363 and were to be built by Fairey's Hayes factory. The main design conference was held on 13 October 1943 and the type was subsequently named Spearfish. RA356 powered by a Centaurus 57 was the first to fly becoming airborne on 5 July 1945 at Heston piloted by Fairey chief test pilot Flt Lt Foster Hickman Dixon. This was rather later than planned, apparently in part due to development problems with the engine, but it was in time to allow RA356 to attend a special display and show of German and new British aircraft at Farnborough on 29 October. Work on RA360 and RA363 moved forward pretty slowly once the Spearfish production order had been cancelled and they did not fly until 11 April and 23 September 1947 respectively, their completion having been decided upon to permit them to be used for research work.

Fairey's Heaton Chapel facility at Stockport was given the task of building a fourth prototype, RN241 to Contract SB.27051 and first flown on 29 December 1945, and three more ordered to Contract SB.26862 (TJ175, TJ179 and TJ184). However, these last three were not flown - TJ175 was built but stayed on the ground while TJ179 and TJ184 were cancelled. A contract for 150 TD.Mk.1 production aircraft to be built at Heaton Chapel (and flown from Manchester's Ringway Airport) was subsequently cancelled and the Spearfish programme was abandoned. The first 50 were allocated serials TS915-TS935, TS963-TS990 and TT110 and the intention had been to fit Centaurus 58 units on the first ten production aeroplanes, a Centaurus 59 on the next 22 and Centaurus 60s to the rest. Production aircraft were also to have had even larger flaps with spoilers and small 'feeler' ailerons. Stockport-built RN241 was the airframe which came closest to the planned production standard in that it was fitted with a dummy underfuselage ASV Mk.XV radome and dummy gun turret. It was initially ordered as the prototype of a trainer version to a new specification T.21/43 and took part in the September 1946 SBAC Show at Radlett where pilot Peter Twiss demonstrated the advantage conferred by the ample Youngman area-increasing flaps, which could be set at four positions including housed retracted into the wing.

This photo of the then near brand new RA356 was taken at Heston on 17 September 1945. The aircraft had first flown from here on 5 July.

The Spearfish was one of the biggest single-engined aeroplanes ever flown, a fact acknowledged by Capt Eric Brown in his book *Wings of the Weird and Wonderful* (Hikoki, 2010) who flew prototypes RA356 and RA360. He found that the aircraft with its wide undercarriage was easy to taxi and on take-off there was only a mild tendency to swing to starboard. There was minimal change of trim when the flaps and undercarriage were raised but the top speed was disappointing and clearly not high enough. In cruising flight the controls were heavy and, before hydraulic powered ailerons had been fitted to RA360, the lateral control was so solid that the ailerons were difficult to move. Indeed, the aircraft at times exhibited such heavy controls that a pilot circling a carrier while waiting to land in bad weather would have to fly a very wide circuit, which most likely would mean that he could not see the carrier at certain times – not a good situation. The Spearfish had good longitudinal and directional stability but laterally it was unstable, and there was a near complete lack of warning for the stall either with everything up (98mph/158km/h) or everything down (76mph/122km/h). Since the approach speed was close to the stall speed this was an undesirable feature, but the landing performance itself was OK. On a baulked landing the application of full power gave a quite strong and rather sudden nose-up change of trim.

On 13 February 1947 RA360 was allotted to RAE Farnborough's Naval Aircraft Department where it was used to calibrate and proof test new arrester gear (although it did not arrive until 10 December 1947). After that the second prototype served with the Carrier Trials Unit at Ford until it was retired in mid-1952 and sold as scrap on 15 September. In the meantime RA356 was despatched from White Waltham to Luton on 4 November 1948 for a trial installation of the Napier Nomad engine (which in fact was never fitted), and later it was modified by Napier at Luton Airport for experiments with the firm's in-flight de-icing systems. Some experimental nozzles and a grid were placed to the rear of the cockpit and a water tank was mounted inside the fuselage, and the water-spray fittings allowed the aircraft to perform artificial ice-producing experiments. On 30 April 1952 RA356 was taken from Luton to RNAS Henstridge by road for ground instructional use, but then almost immediately it went to Yeovilton as scrap.

Having arrived at Defford on 9 February 1948, RA363 served with the Telecommunications Research Establishment (TRE) as a trials aeroplane for the ASV.XV (ASV.15) radar until it was damaged on 1 September 1949 when the undercarriage collapsed on landing. The aircraft was sold for scrap on 22 August 1950 after plans for repairs had been cancelled. Although completed, as stated TJ175 was not flown and it was eventually delivered to TRE at Defford by road as a source of spares. Earlier RN241 had had to force-land at Langley on 18 November 1946 after an engine failure, but later it was allotted to Fairey at White Waltham for engine cooling trials, and then on 1 September 1948 for trials of power-assisted flying controls. Authority was given for the aircraft to be Struck Off Charge on 24 July 1951. It is understood that other Spearfish fuselages may have been supplied to various training and research establishments.

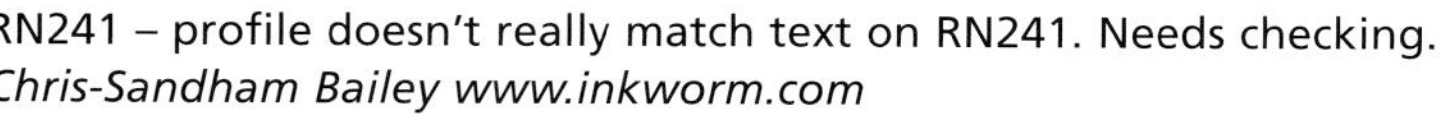
RN241 – profile doesn't really match text on RN241. Needs checking.
Chris-Sandham Bailey www.inkworm.com

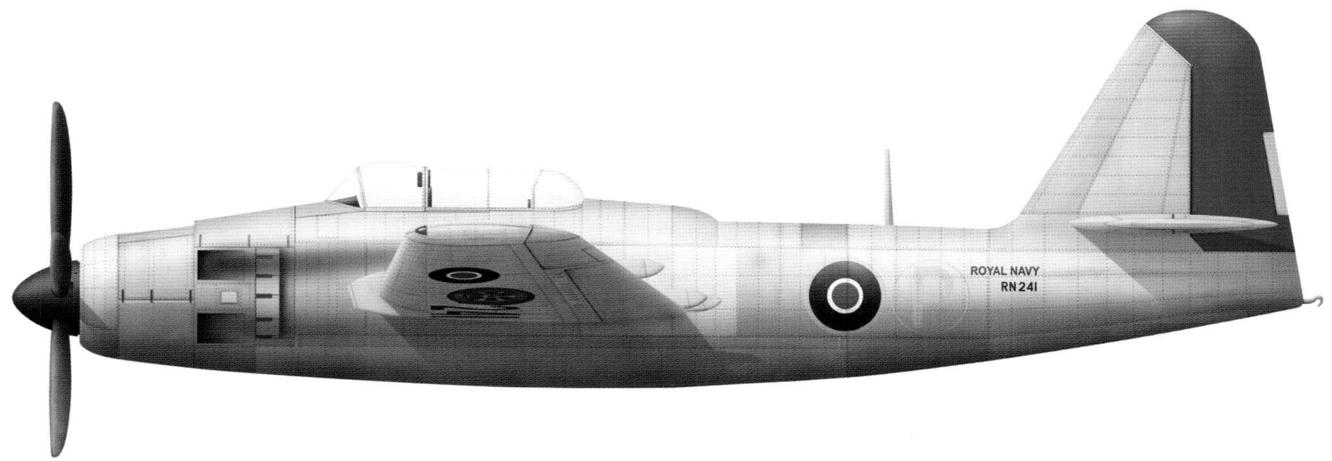

RA356 pictured at Luton after being modified by Napier in 1948 with equipment for creating artificial ice-accretion. Water was sprayed from the installation directly behind the cockpit onto the grid mounted above the fuselage level with the roundel.

Fairey Strike Aircraft and Strike Fighter

A higher performance development of the Spearfish with a twin coupled-Rolls-Royce Merlin powerplant was considered from mid-1944 onwards. Specification O.21/44 was written around this new naval strike aircraft and four prototypes were ordered to Acft/5173 with serials VD258, VD261, VD264 and VD269. The Merlins were to be mounted in tandem to drive co-axial three-bladed propellers and the pilot and observer were seated quite a distance apart – the pilot was in a cockpit placed above the forward Merlin while the observer came aft of the rear engine. The engines were fed by wing leading edge air intakes and the internal fuel capacity was 470 gallons (2,137 litres). Full design work commenced at the beginning of 1945 in the hands of Fairey's Stockport factory which, like the Spearfish, was to be the site where these aircraft were constructed. However, after the end of the war the O.21/44 project was cancelled following a review of future programmes.

The development of jet and propeller turbine engines (turboprops) began to gain momentum very quickly after the war and Fairey was asked to switch its effort to Specification N.16/45 for a strike aircraft powered by propeller turbine engines. (The development of turboprop engines to replace piston powerplants was one reason why the Spearfish was not taken into service - the arrival of these new power units would mean that any piston-powered aircraft would have at best a limited service career.) This new project became known as the Fairey Strike Fighter, it was to have a Rolls-Royce AP.25 twin-coupled turbine unit installed (later named Coupled Tweed) and was ordered in prototype form with three examples VP988, VR104 and VR123. However, the Strike Fighter programme was eventually dropped when Rolls-Royce abandoned its development of the AP.25, and after the aircraft itself had suffered from increasing weight. This work was now replaced by the design effort that led to prototypes and production of the Gannet anti-submarine aircraft which joined the Royal Navy in 1955, Fairey at last gaining production orders after so much development effort on this series of new naval aeroplanes. The Navy's strike fighter needs were eventually filled by the Westland Wyvern.

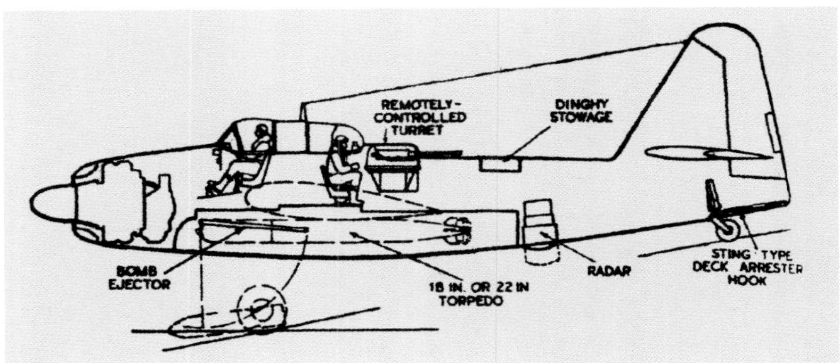

Side angle drawing showing the planned equipment layout for the Fairey Spearfish.

Below: Model of the Fairey Strike Fighter as first proposed in October 1944. *RAF Museum*

Spearfish Structure

The Spearfish's hydraulically-folding all-metal wing employed a two-spar structure with aluminium alloy sheet covering and was built in three main parts – a centre section integral with the fuselage and two outer sections. The short span ailerons were also made in metal with metal covering and retractable Fairey-Youngman all-metal flaps were fitted between the ailerons and fuselage in two sections per side. The fuselage was constructed in light alloy monocoque again in three sections – front fuselage to rear spar, rear fuselage to fin leading edge, and rear wedge – and it was formed from four light alloy extruded longerons with pressed sheet vertical frames covered by light alloy skin. The fin and tailplane were all metal except for the rudder which was fabric covered with a metal leading edge. The aircraft had a rather long main undercarriage which retracted outwards into the wings, a short tailwheel, two machine-guns were fitted in the wings outside the airscrew disc and two more in a remotely-controlled power-operated Frazer-Nash turret, although only a dummy turret was ever carried. There was a fuselage bomb bay to take the larger stores but rocket projectiles could also be loaded under the wings, and a Mk.XV ASV radar was to be carried in a retractable radome beneath the rear fuselage (again this was never fitted). In all 409 gallons (1,860 litres) of fuel could be carried in two 183 gallon (832 litre) tanks in the wing centre sections plus another single 43 gallon (196 litre) tank in the starboard centre section leading edge; an auxiliary 180 gallon (818 litre) tank could be fitted in the bomb bay to permit the aircraft to perform reconnaissance duties. On those aircraft that flew the Centaurus had a 14ft (4.27m) diameter Rotol five-blade constant-speed airscrew, but a reversible pitch airscrew was to be employed on later machines.

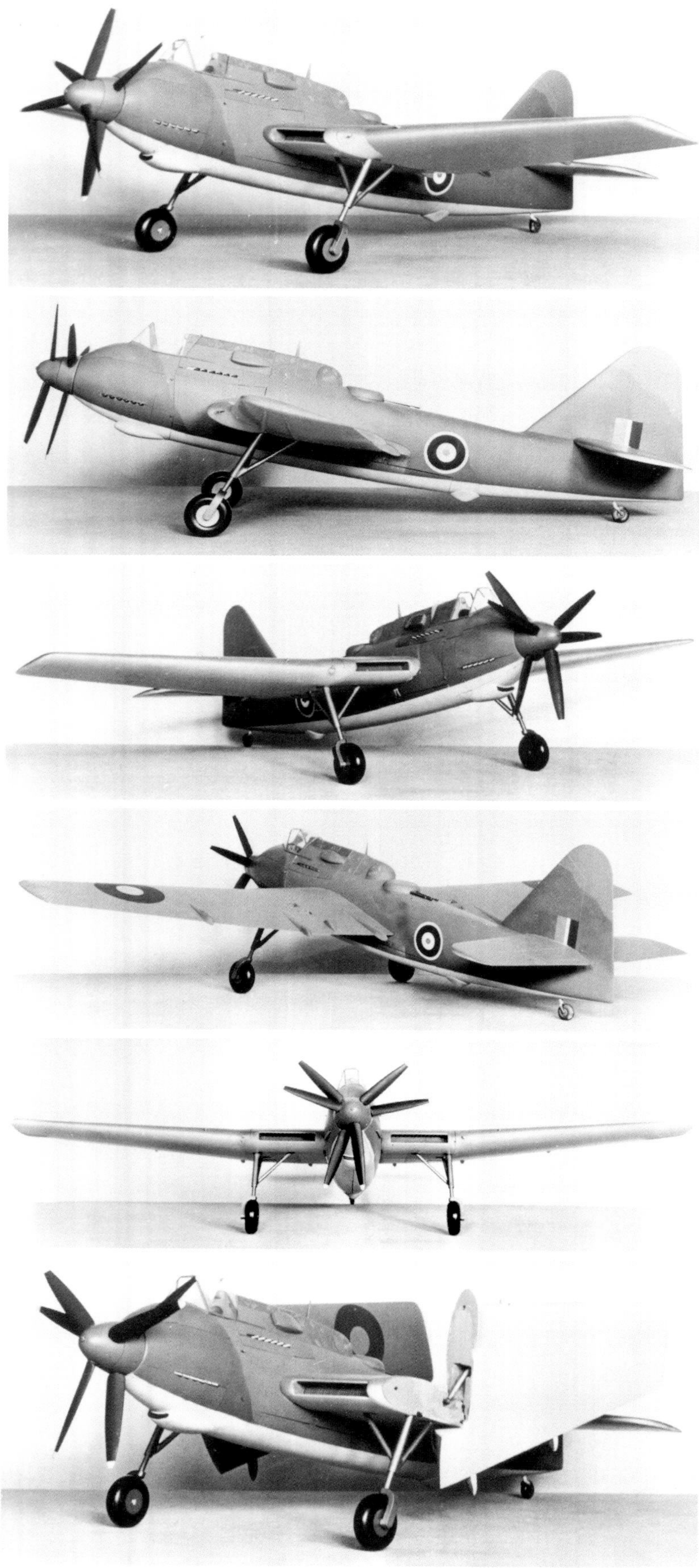

A series of 'walk-around' views of a model of the Fairey O.21/44 development of the Spearfish. Note the contra-rotating propellers and leading edge intakes. The photographs were dated 25 October 1944.

9 Folland Fo.108 and Fo.116

Folland Fo.108

Type: Engine Test Bed Aircraft
Powerplant: See text
Span: 58ft 0in (17.68m)
Length: 43ft 4in (13.21m)
Gross Wing Area: 588sq.ft (54.68m²)
Average Loaded Weight with Different Engines: 15,000lb (6,804kg)
Maximum Speed: 292mph (470km/h) at 15,000ft (4,572m)
Service Ceiling: No data available
Armament: None Carried

Most of the subjects covered in these chapters were prototypes or test aircraft for future fighter or bomber programmes – relatively few were produced to assess specific elements of aircraft aerodynamics or to try out new design features; in fact it was the modified versions of standard types collected together in Appendix 1 that were often used to fill the latter role. The Folland Fo.108, however, is almost unique in that it was designed purely as a test bed airframe for various types of piston engine. The traditional route for testing engines had been first to run them on ground rigs before trying them out in the air, in the great majority of cases using specially adapted production aircraft. However, during the late-1930s build up for war several British companies had new more powerful piston engines in the pipeline and to have a single basic airframe to test them seemed a sensible step forward. In due course the nine Fo.108 airframes completed and flown racked up quite a career record, but the fact that the type was nicknamed 'The Frightful' says much about its flying reputation.

In May 1938 the Air Staff issued Specification 43/37 for "The design and manufacture of single-engine type airframes for use in connection with the flight testing of aircraft engines of 1,500-2,200hp (1,120-1,640kW)". Had this document been issued after 1939 it would have received an 'E' prefix for 'Experimental', but prior to that date experimental specifications had no descriptive letter. The airframes were to be built in wood or composite construction for rapid manufacture and delivered without engines, and the front fuselage was to terminate in a way that would allow the attachment of different engines as complete units. In the first instance provision was to be made to install either the Bristol Centaurus or Napier Sabre but the aircraft's strength and stiffness was to be adequate to take any engine and airscrew installation. The wing construction was to be so arranged as to allow ducted radiators to be installed at a later date and, in the interest of simplicity and cheapness, a low structure weight was not a major consideration. The undercarriage was to be fixed. A crew of three would be carried (a pilot plus two observers to monitor the engine's performance) and the maximum speed had to be 300mph (483km/h) at 15,000ft (4,572m). Other designs submitted to 43/37 came from General Aircraft with its GAL.43 design (the GAL.43A version had the Centaurus, GAL.43B the Sabre), and Percival with its Type X with both Sabre and Centaurus engines (post-war the Type X was retrospectively renumbered P.26). Folland, however, was declared the winner.

P1775 seen in March 1942 with a Bristol Hercules VIII engine. Note that the undercarriage spats have been removed. *Phil Butler*

The idea was that the factories responsible for engine manufacture would fit the power units to be tested, but Folland was required to flight test the airframes before delivery. In addition, they of course had to be delivered to the engine companies in the first place and so Bristol Hercules engines were fitted to the Fo.108 airframes as 'slave' units to enable them to be flown and get to their destinations. In all 12 examples (P1774 through P1785) were ordered under Contract 953635/38 of October 1938 and there are still many gaps in their career histories, so the author is indebted to Phil Butler's article in *Aeromilitaria* (*Folland Fo.108* – Autumn 2006) for providing the most accurate information yet published. Some sources claim that P1778 flew with a Rolls-Royce Griffon, but his research confirms that this engine was never fitted; indeed no Rolls-Royce engine was ever installed in a Fo.108. However, the list of engines actually considered for testing was wide ranging, as a memo in the Rolls-Royce archive illustrates. This was written by Lt. Colonel Fell, Rolls-Royce's Chief Powerplant Engineer, who had attended a meeting with the Air Ministry on 13 March 1940 at which the delivery dates for Fo.108 aircraft were given, and the types of engines to be installed. These were as follows, but the plans were of course subsequently changed:

First aircraft: August 1940 –
Napier Sabre

Second aircraft: October 1940 –
Bristol Hercules VIII

Third aircraft: December 1940 –
Bristol Centaurus

Fourth aircraft: January 1941: –
Napier Sabre

Fifth aircraft: February 1941 –
Armstrong Siddeley Deerhound

Sixth aircraft: March 1941 –
Rolls-Royce Griffon

Seventh aircraft: April 1941 –
Rolls-Royce Vulture

Most of the assembly of the Fo.108s and their flight-testing was conducted at Staverton in Gloucestershire. The fuselages were constructed in Cheltenham at Folland's Experimental facility in Bath Road and the wings were made by a private company (Oddie, Bradbury and Cull based at Eastleigh Airport near Southampton) under a sub-contract. Folland's chief designer at Cheltenham on the Fo.108 (and the Fo.116 below) was Frank Radcliffe, the firm having dispersed some of its work from its main factory at Hamble to the Gloucestershire town following the outbreak of war. The production of these airframes appears to have been a slow process, in part because the demands brought by the war meant priority had to be given to more urgent programmes with labour being allocated elsewhere and in part because of the move to Cheltenham.

However, the first two Fo.108s P1774 and P.1775 were built and first flown from Eastleigh. P1774 fitted with a Sabre engine made its maiden flight in about February 1941 and by the end of that year it had joined Napier at Luton. During the Sabre trials programme it was tested with several examples of the engine and in 1942

P1775 again, this time photographed at Filton after a Bristol Centaurus IV had been installed. *Phil Butler*

experienced a forced landing. It is understood that the aircraft was written off after an accident on 14 September 1944 following the installation of a Centaurus engine. In fact details for the loss of P1774 and the date when it occurred are uncertain, but since the given date is the same as P1779 – which is confirmed – then 14 September may not be correct. In 1942 P1775 flew at Staverton with a Hercules VIII, and during 1943 it was at Farnborough flying with a Centaurus. This aircraft apparently crashed on 18 September 1944. P1776 completed its main trials with the Sabre at Luton in June 1943, but during ground running operations there on 1 March 1944 the aircraft was badly damaged by fire. The next example, P1777, was fitted with a Centaurus CE.13 (Vickers Warwick Mk.II bomber) engine but, after a short career, on 19 May 1942 it broke up in the air near Tewkesbury while performing a dive.

In appearance P1778 differed from the previous airframes in that it had wing air intakes and a streamlined Napier Sabre installation to test the Blackburn Firebrand fighter's powerplant (previous Sabre airframes had a chin intake). It operated out of Luton with the Sabre installed from 8 November 1942 onwards, having arrived there by 'slave' Hercules the previous July. In October 1945 it flew to de Havilland Engines at Hatfield to perform some propeller development trials (which were probably ground based), and the aircraft was sold in June 1947. P1779 was slated to receive examples of the Bristol Centaurus but this plan was abandoned. After receiving a Sabre I at Luton it crashed on 14 September 1944 after a very short flying life. The next aircraft, P1780, first flew (with a Hercules) from Staverton on 4 December 1942. By mid-January 1943 it was at Luton for Sabre trials, but by August 1943 was back at

Another Sabre test bed was P1778 which had this close-fitting cowling. Published sources have stated that this aircraft had a Rolls-Royce Griffon fitted, but this was not the case and no records of any Griffon installation have ever been uncovered. *Phil Butler*

Staverton. Its subsequent career is unknown. Next in the sequence to fly comes P1781, from Staverton on 15 May 1943. It was allocated to Bristol for Centaurus trials and in due course joined MAP's 'Centaurus Flight' at Filton, but was then written off when the engine failed after the aircraft had just taken off from Heston on 28 April 1944. Another Fo.108 to join the 'Centaurus Flight' was P1784 in June 1944, and this aircraft was struck off charge on 5 March 1945. The three other airframes, P1782/3/5, may never have been completed and were certainly never flown. P1782 had been delegated to test a Bristol Centaurus III engine plus a Rotol three-blade propeller as the powerplant for the Fo.116 below.

Approving the airworthiness of the Fo.108's airframe was a task given to two Gloster Aircraft test pilots, P.E.G. 'Jerry' Sayer and Michael Daunt, because Folland had no test pilot of its own available. It is thanks to these gentlemen's accounts that we have any idea of what the aircraft was like to fly, and indeed it was they who dubbed the aircraft 'The Frightful' since neither pilot enjoyed flying it at all. Daunt actually described it as "a bloody awful aeroplane" and it was he who was piloting P1777 when the wooden tailplane came off in a dive, followed by the disintegration of the propeller and reduction gear, during an attempt to determine the aircraft's maximum diving speed. Daunt survived but suffered considerable injuries. However, despite its poor flying qualities the Fo.108 did prove to be a good test bed for monitoring the performance of new engines, in part because the large size of the airframe provided plenty of space for test equipment to be installed and for the observers to work.

Folland Fo.116 Project

This later design from Folland was prepared against Specification E.28/40 which was issued in February 1941 cover a Fleet Air Arm Research Aircraft. The Fo.116 had a fairly similar configuration to the Fo.108 and was similar in size and had a fixed undercarriage, but its wing was placed higher on the fuselage. The objective was to perform a full scale investigation into the problems associated with the ever increasing weight of deck-landing aircraft and high lift devices were to be exploited to the full. In addition, the new type was to be capable of torpedo and dive-bombing operations and its all-up weight was not to exceed 20,000lb (9,072kg). A Napier Sabre engine was specified but in August 1941 this was replaced for the prototypes DX160 and DX165 by a 2,400hp (1,790kW) Bristol Centaurus III, these aircraft having been ordered in August 1941 under Contract Acft/741. A major feature of the Fo.116 was a variable incidence wing to allow the pilot to set the surface to any appropriate angle for take-off, landing or any flight condition, the fuselage staying at a normal angle. As such the wing could be positioned at angles between -1° and +14° and it was moved on wing spar pivots. There were also leading-edge slots and Fowler trailing-edge flaps to provide maximum lift. A twin-0.303in (7.7mm) defensive dorsal turret was mounted behind the pilot's cockpit.

A mock-up of the Fo.116 was built and the aircraft's span was to be 52ft 6in (16.00m), folded span 18ft 0in (5.49m), length 44ft 0in (13.41m), wing area 380sq.ft (35.34m^2) and top speed 263mph (423km/h) at 10,000ft (3,048m). The all-up-weight was estimated to

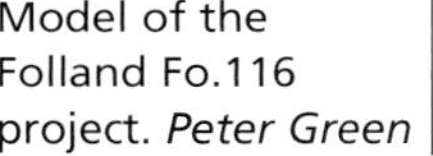

Model of the Folland Fo.116 project. *Peter Green*

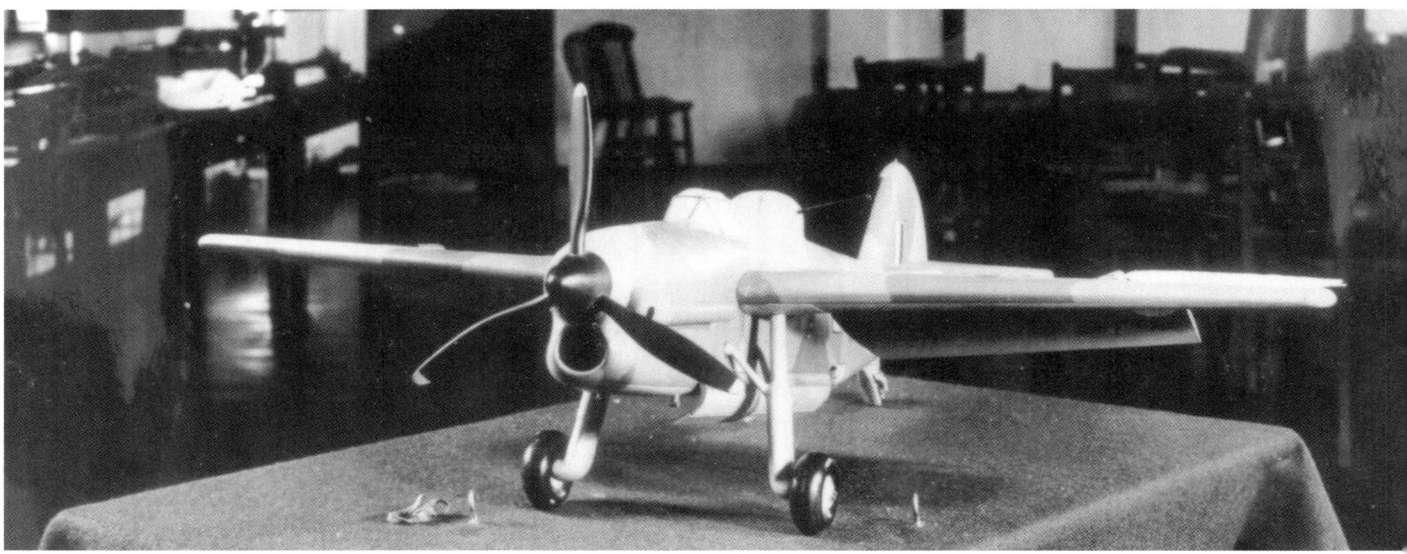

be 18,250lb (8,278kg) which, without the variable incidence wing in place, would have given the aircraft a minimum speed that was too high to achieve a carrier take-off or landing. Work on DX160 was underway during 1943 (some sources state that by then it was "half-built") and this airframe was to be fitted with basic flying equipment (instruments, radio and navigation) but no operational equipment. The latter was to be simulated by 'ballasting', although an aerodynamically accurate dummy turret was to be capable of being rotated in flight. By then, however, many of problems to be examined by the Fo.116 had been solved and the project was subsequently abandoned. The second aircraft DX165 was never started.

Folland Fo.108 P1776 seen with the covers off its Napier Sabre engine in a picture taken in January 1942.

Fo.108 Structure

To the rear of the bulkhead immediately behind the engine the Fo.108 was built as a standard airframe, but the characteristics and requirements of the various installed power units (inline/radial, water-cooled/air-cooled, etc.) meant that the forward appearances of individual examples were really quite different. The engines were installed complete with their cowlings and radiators. The Fo.108 was quite a big aircraft and fitting different engines presented problems of keeping the CofG the same on each machine; however, this was solved by having a sub-frame attached to the main engine bearer that could be made longer for lighter engines, thereby preserving the CofG. Although the one-piece wing was built in wood the fuselage was actually put together in semi-monocoque light alloy using frames and stringers. The wing itself was formed from box spars and girder-type ribs made in spruce and covered in plywood skins. Its leading-edge slats and mass-balanced trailing edge ailerons were also in wood with ply covering, but the split trailing-edge flaps were made in light alloy with light alloy sheet covering. Both fin and tailplane were cantilever structures built in wood but the rudder and elevators were formed with light alloy sheet ribs around a spar of steel tube; both had balance and trimming tabs. The aircraft had a large fixed undercarriage with spats over the wheels, although in due course these appear to have been removed from most airframes.

Below and overleaf: Original proposal drawing of the Folland Fo.108 with a Napier Sabre engine installed. *Solent Sky Museum*

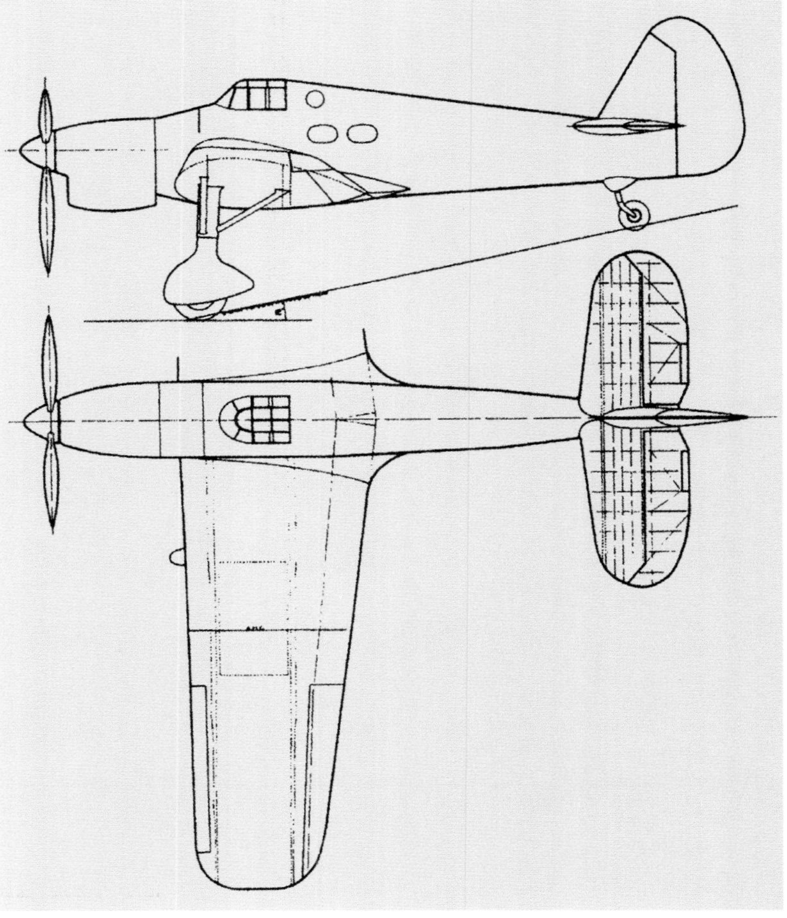

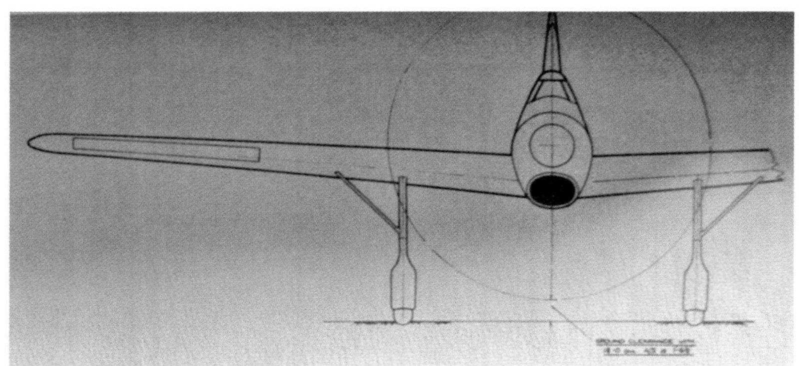

Bottom: The first Fo.108 P1774, without any serial number applied, is pictured with a Sabre II in place in August 1941.

Below: Original proposal drawing of the Folland Fo.108 with a Bristol Centaurus engine installed. *Solent Sky Museum*

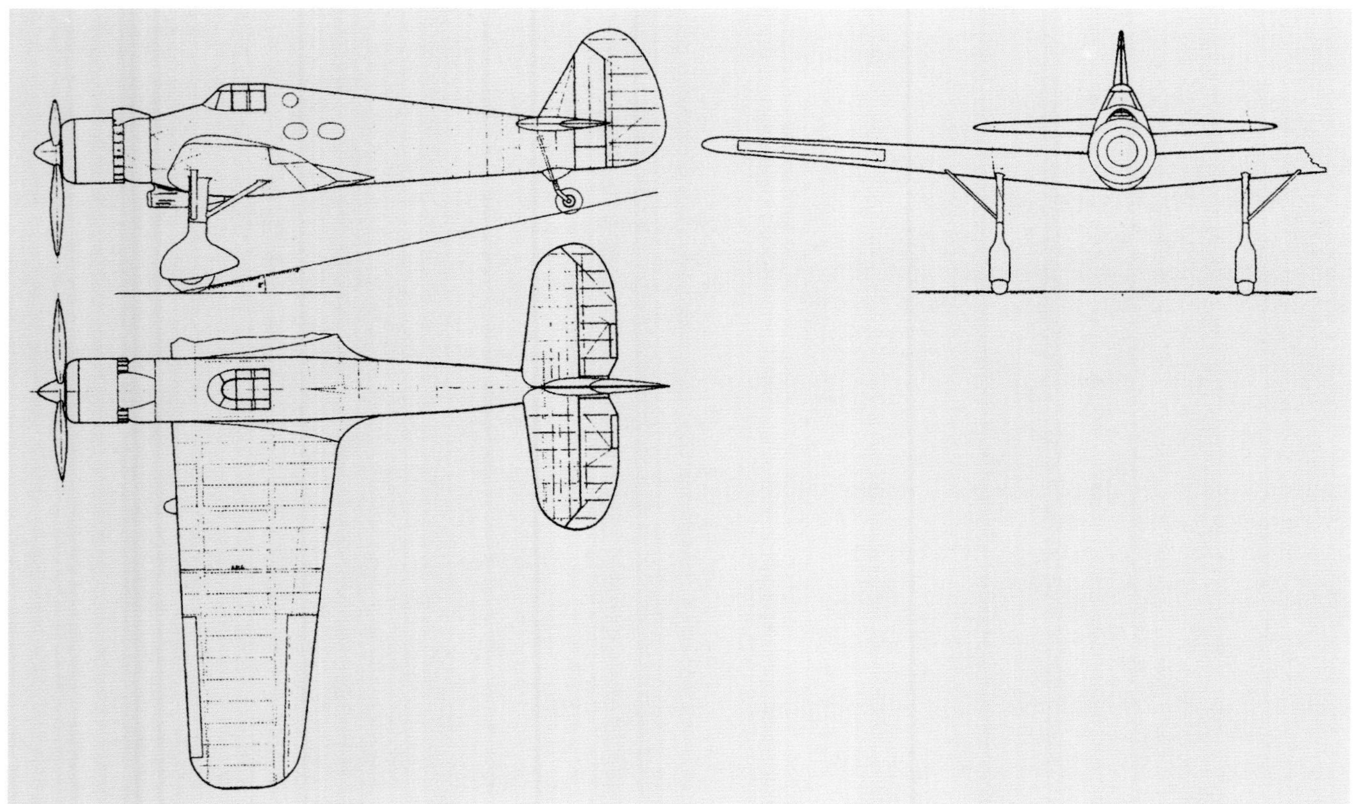

10 Folland Fo.117

Folland Fo.117

(Brochure Estimates – 2 September 1942)

Type: Single-Seat Single-Engine Fighter

Powerplant: One 2,500hp (1,864kW) Bristol Centaurus XII radial engine

Span: 36ft 0in (10.97m)

Length: 31ft 6in (9.60m)

Gross Wing Area: 224sq.ft (20.8m^2)

Maximum Weight: 9,749lb (4,422kg)

Maximum Speed: 468mph (753km/h) at 20,000ft (6,096m)

Rate of Climb: 4,950ft/min (1,510m/min) at sea level

Service Ceiling: 37,200ft (11,340m) – Absolute Ceiling 39,800ft (12,130m)

Armament: 4 x 20mm cannon

In the middle war years it was realised that current fighter types like the Hawker Typhoon were in many respects a bit too large to meet the current requirements for single-seat fighters. Consequently, in September 1942 Specification F.6/42 was issued for a smaller and lighter fighter, the document stating an armament of four 20mm cannon and a speed of 450mph (724km/h) at 20,000ft (6,096m), and this aircraft was to be superior in climb, speed and manoeuvrability to any fighter that might be developed out of Germany's superb Focke-Wulf Fw 190. Proposals were forthcoming from Airspeed, Boulton Paul, Folland, Hawker, Supermarine, Vickers and Westland and those from Folland and Hawker were favoured, the latter eventually being covered by a new Specification F.2/43 and flown as the Fury.

Folland Aircraft had been formed in 1937 at Hamble. The head of the company, Henry Philip Folland, was the former chief designer at Gloster Aircraft and the man responsible for the F.5/34 in the next chapter and several of Gloster's successful biplane fighters. His Fo.117 project generated some attention, particularly its contra-rotating airscrew which was then a new feature in fighter design. The Air Staff had assumed that the reason for having this smaller diameter propeller was to provide a smaller undercarriage and a more compact gun installation, but in fact Folland had used it to raise the wing in relation to the fuselage so that the exhaust and cooling air would be ejected above and below the wing roots, thereby reducing drag. The Fo.117 design was favoured by RAE Farnborough but there were doubts about the firm having the ability to develop and manufacture such an advanced aircraft quickly enough. By 13 November 1943 Folland's set up at Cheltenham and its ability to carry through the project had been thoroughly assessed and it was clear that the company could not do the job by itself, but Henry Folland was prepared to work with another firm. By 29 December several minor changes had been made to the design which had improved the Fo.117's performance figures and altered the all-up-weight to 9,170lb (4,160kg).

Someone else who supported the Fo.117 was Air Chief Marshal Sir Charles Portal, the Chief of the Air Staff (CAS), who felt the design had some particularly good qualities, especially in its potential manoeuvrability. Indeed the Folland and Hawker F.6/42 projects were discussed and compared very closely during January 1943. However, in March the Fo.117 was abandoned, in part because the country's design capacity was already overloaded and there were worries about squandering precious resources by giving a job like this to a company who would probably not have the aircraft ready in a sufficiently short period of time, Folland being relatively new and inexperienced in the job of fighter design. In addition, despite the Fo.117 offering a potentially better performance, Hawker's own project would be ready much earlier.

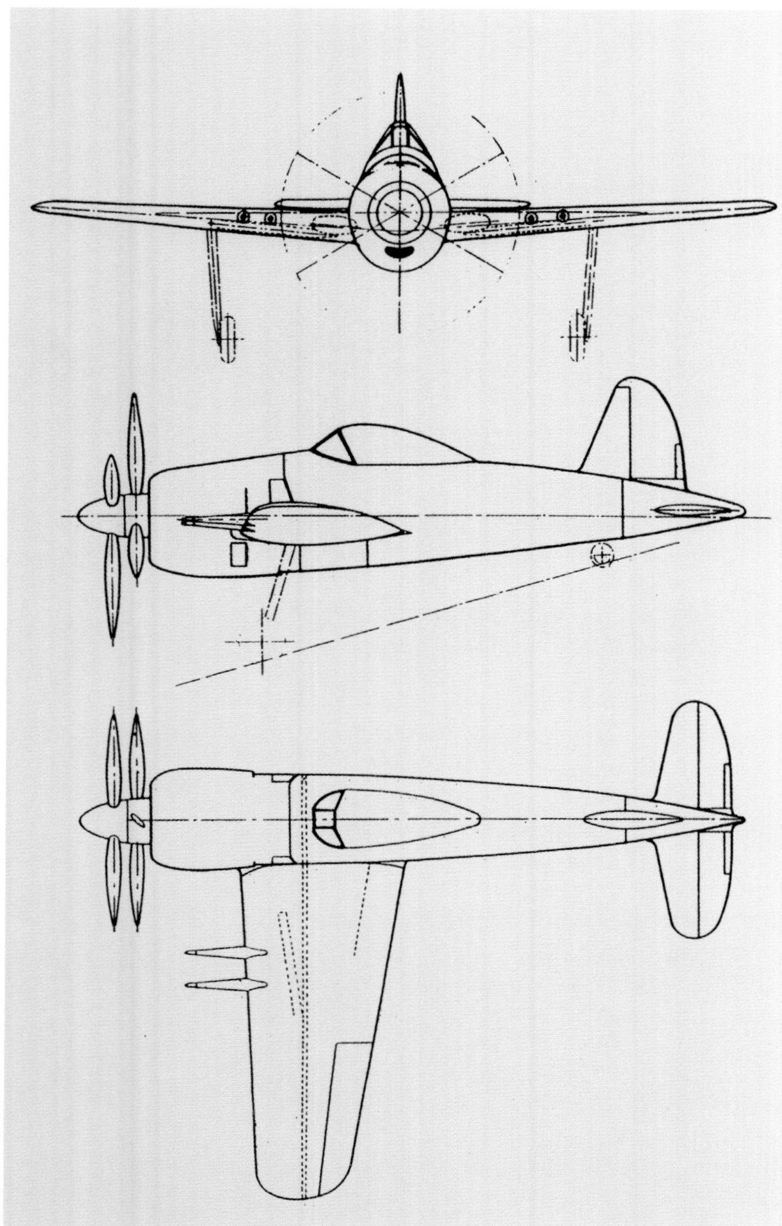

Manufacturer's drawing of the Folland F.6/42, which may be the Fo.117 or Fo.117A. It shows long-barrel 20mm guns and at the time of the initial proposal in early September 1942 a modified version of the 20mm had become available with a barrel some 18in (45.7cm) shorter, the use of which Folland recommended since it offered advantages to a single-seat fighter. *RAF Museum*

However, later in 1943 the project was revived as the Fo.117A, the revised design introducing a laminar flow wing while the 2,500hp (1,864kW) Centaurus XII still had a contra-rotating propeller. Plans were laid down for production aircraft to be produced by English Electric and six prototypes, RD104, RD107, RD108, RD113, RD115, and RD118, were actually ordered under contract SB26924 of 10 September to an updated Specification F.19/43. However, in the end they were never built and, at the time of writing, there are no further details available to describe these aeroplanes and compare them with the original Fo.117.

Structure

Folland's fighter would have employed conventional light alloy construction and it featured a one-piece wing, one-piece tailplane and one-piece main fuselage with detachable rear wedge (the latter had been found to be essential under service conditions). The wing consisted of a single main spar with skinning but there were auxiliary spars to transfer torque to the fuselage. There was a split landing flap of 25% chord hinged about the rear auxiliary spar, and for the ailerons a simple flap with minimum leakage through the hinge. On the fuselage the skin was supported by stringers and transverse frames and the tail used a two-spar structure with a smooth flush-riveted skin covering. The Bristol Centaurus XII with its two-speed supercharger had an 11ft 6in (3.51m) six-blade contra-rotating airscrew, and the four 20mm cannon were mounted in the wings outboard of the propeller disc. The cabin floor formed the top centre section covering of the wing and the lower portion of the fuselage in this region served as both fuselage and wing; the latter could be detached so that the main 100 gallon (455 litre) fuselage fuel tank could be removed. There was a second fuselage tank of 30 gallons (136 litres) behind the rear auxiliary spar and a 51 gallon (232 litre) auxiliary tank was also available. The wide-track main undercarriage retracted inwards into the inner wing.

The rival design to the Fo.117 was the Hawker Fury, and prototype LA610 is shown here in 1946 powered by a Napier Sabre VII engine. LA610 first flew with the Sabre in March 1946 – most Fury prototypes flew with the Centaurus, although LA610 had previously flown in 1944/45 with Rolls-Royce Griffon powerplants (see Appendix 1).

11 Gloster F.5/34

Gloster F.5/34

Type: Single-Seat Fighter

Powerplant: One 840hp (626kW) Bristol Mercury IX radial engine

Span: 38ft 2in (11.63m)

Length: 32ft 0.5in (9.76m)

Gross Wing Area: 230sq.ft (21.39m^2)

All-Up-Weight: 5,400lb (2,450kg)

Rate of Climb: Time to 15,000ft (4,572m) 7.8 minutes

Maximum Speed: 315mph (507km/h) at 16,000ft (4,875m)

Service Ceiling: 32,500ft (9,900m)

Armament: 8 x 0.303in (7.7mm) Browning machine-guns

An important step in the development of single-seat fighter aircraft during the mid-1930s and the start of the British build up for war with Germany was the issuing of Specification F.5/34 in November 1934. This document brought together for the first time several important elements that would be critical in a fighter's ability to deal with the high speeds and performance of new German bombers – namely a high rate of climb to put the fighter in a good position to make an attack, a heavy offensive armament to ensure a kill was made (six or eight Browning machine-guns with 300 rounds of ammunition for each gun), and other modern features including a retractable undercarriage, enclosed cockpit and oxygen supply. The main parameters for F.5/34 were a speed of 275mph (442km/h) at 15,000ft (4,572m) and a service ceiling of 33,000ft (10,060m). Although the privately-developed Hawker Hurricane and Supermarine Spitfire in the end offered a superior performance to the types produced to F.5/34, and resulted in no production orders being placed for any F.5/34 design, in their own way the prototypes that were built and flown against the specification did their bit to help move the art of fighter design forward out of the biplane age.

Of the four prototypes constructed from the F.5/34 design competition the Bristol Type 146 and Vickers Type 279 Venom were grounded before the outbreak of World War II, thereby disqualifying them from receiving full coverage here. The Gloster F.5/34 (it never received a name) and Martin-Baker M.B.2 (Chapter Nineteen), however, did continue flying after September 1939. The F.5/34 was the last complete fighter design undertaken by Henry Folland for Gloster and two examples were built, K5604 and K8089. They were constructed at Hucclecote, and Gloster historical accounts state that the priority given at the time to the company's production aeroplanes (the Gauntlet and Gladiator biplane fighters) slowed the F.5/34 programme down.

The first flight date of the first Gloster F.5/34 has been the subject of much research and debate over many years and is currently still unknown, but it appears to have taken place in either May or June 1937. Records do show that K5604 was flown on 21 June 1937 by an RAF pilot (Gloster test pilot Jerry Sayer had performed the first flight) and photos of the aircraft flying appeared in *Flight* for 1 July 1937 as part of the magazine's coverage of the RAF Display at Hendon on 26 June, which K5604 attended. The journal reported that this: "...eyeable machine of advanced design" performed such aerobatics that:

"...after a dive it must have zoomed for something like 4,000ft [1,220m]". It was also at the SBAC Show at Hatfield on 28/29 June and here the *Flight* report noted how the Gloster display was like a "duet". After Flt Lt Michel Daunt had completed his aerobatics in the Gladiator biplane, Jerry Sayer in the F.5/34: "...screamed across the sky, then climbed vertically and carried out the sort of aerobatic display which we still do not expect from low-wing monoplanes."

After these very public appearances the aircraft got down to its flight testing and in due course was flown to A&AEE (then still at Martlesham Heath) for official trials. It was still in A&AEE hands after the move to Boscombe Down was made in August and September 1939, and after war had broken out K5604 spent five months with the Performance Squadron at Boscombe serving primarily as a 'hack' aircraft until it was retired from flying. The only changes made to the airframe during its flying career were alterations to the propeller reduction gearing to get rid of some severe airframe vibration plus modifications to the main landing gear. Afterwards K5604 served for several years as a non-flying ground instruction airframe at No 3 School of Technical Training at Blackpool (as 2232M), before finding its way to Oldham to join No 325 ATC Squadron.

K8089 is thought to have made its maiden flight in November 1937, but again the true date is unknown. On 6 December it arrived at RAE Farnborough where it continued flying until 23 January 1940, spending time with the

The sole completed Bristol Type 146 prototype to F.5/34, K5119, first flew on 11 February 1938, but after completing its official trials at A&AEE the aircraft was damaged in a taxying accident at Filton on 28 May 1938 and deemed not worth repairing. It was scrapped and a second example K8088 was not finished. Two former employees at Bristol (Messrs Ronnie Ellison and Jock Campbell) once described the Type 146 as "a forlorn hope" because the project fell so far behind its Gloster and Vickers rivals, in part because the sleeve-valve Bristol Perseus radial engine originally earmarked for the aiframe was not ready in time.

The first prototype built and flown to F.5/34 was the small Vickers Type 279 Venom PVO-10, a company-finded aeroplane which first became airborne on 17 June 1936. At times during its career its flying was restricted by engine troubles and the airframe was scrapped in 1939. The Venom's span was 32ft 9in (9.98m), length 24ft 2in (7.36m), wing area 146sq.ft (13.58sq.m), all-up-weight 4,156lb (1,885kg) and top speed around 325mph (523km/h) at 15,000ft (4,572m). The powerplant was a 625hp (466kW) Bristol Aquila AE.3S radial, again the eight 0.303in (7.7mm) machine-guns were mounted in the wings and once more a metal structure was employed with stressed skin covering.

This picture of K5604 was taken at Hucclecote around the time of its first flight in 1937.

The Gloster F.5/34 again pictured near to or on the date of its maiden flight. *Phil Butler*

Wireless & Electrical Flight and the Engine Research Flight. It also took part in a set of trials against Spitfire Mk.I K9944 and a French Air Force Curtiss Hawk 75A-2, where K8089's rate of climb was found to be superior. After grounding the second F.5/34 followed the same path as the first and joined No. 3 SofTT at Blackpool (as 2231M) – both aircraft were apparently there by mid-March 1940 – and then some years later it was moved to Oldham. The two airframes were scrapped at Oldham in the later stages of the war.

One reason why the Gloster F.5/34 (and the Bristol 146 and Vickers Venom) failed to win any orders was that they began flying rather later than the clearly superior Hurricane and Spitfire, which were first airborne in November 1935 and March 1936 respectively. That meant that these private venture aeroplanes were well advanced in their flight testing before their inferior rivals were even flying. This was a piece of good fortune because the F.5/34 designs would clearly have been outclassed in the Battle of Britain. However, there was a proposal by Roy Fedden at Bristol Engines to re-engine the Gloster F.5/34 with a Taurus power unit, which although more powerful and heavier was actually smaller in diameter. It offered a potentially better performance and the extra weight forward was to have been balanced by a new fuel tank fitted to the rear of the cockpit, but it remained a drawing only.

Well known air-to-air view of the first Gloster F.5/34 K5604. The aircraft has no guns.

K5604 photographed in the New Types park at the RAF Display at Hendon in June 1937. The beautiful de Havilland DH.91 Albatross transport sits behind.

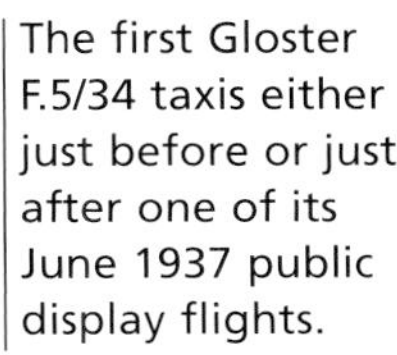

The first Gloster F.5/34 taxis either just before or just after one of its June 1937 public display flights.

The incomplete airframe of the second F.5/34 K8089 shows the wing ports for the four machine guns. *Phil Butler*

Structure

The Gloster F.5/34 had a light alloy monocoque fuselage with stiffeners and formers, and its one-piece cantilever wing had light alloy spars from tip to tip with steel and light alloy ribs and duralumin stressed-skin covering, split flaps and fabric-covered Frise ailerons. The cantilever tailplane and the fin were all-metal but the elevators and rudder used fabric covering. Although the main wheels retracted rearwards into the wings when folded away they still protruded clear of the wing lower surfaces. However, in this condition they were strong enough to take the aircraft's full weight and therefore reduce damage should a wheels-up landing have to be made (when retracted the tailwheel protruded in a similar manner); the designers acknowledged that this feature brought a small reduction to the maximum speed. The Mercury was fitted with a 10ft 6in (3.20m) diameter de Havilland three-blade controllable-pitch propeller and four machine guns were mounted in each wing outside the airscrew disc. Total fuel capacity was 68 gallons (309 litres).

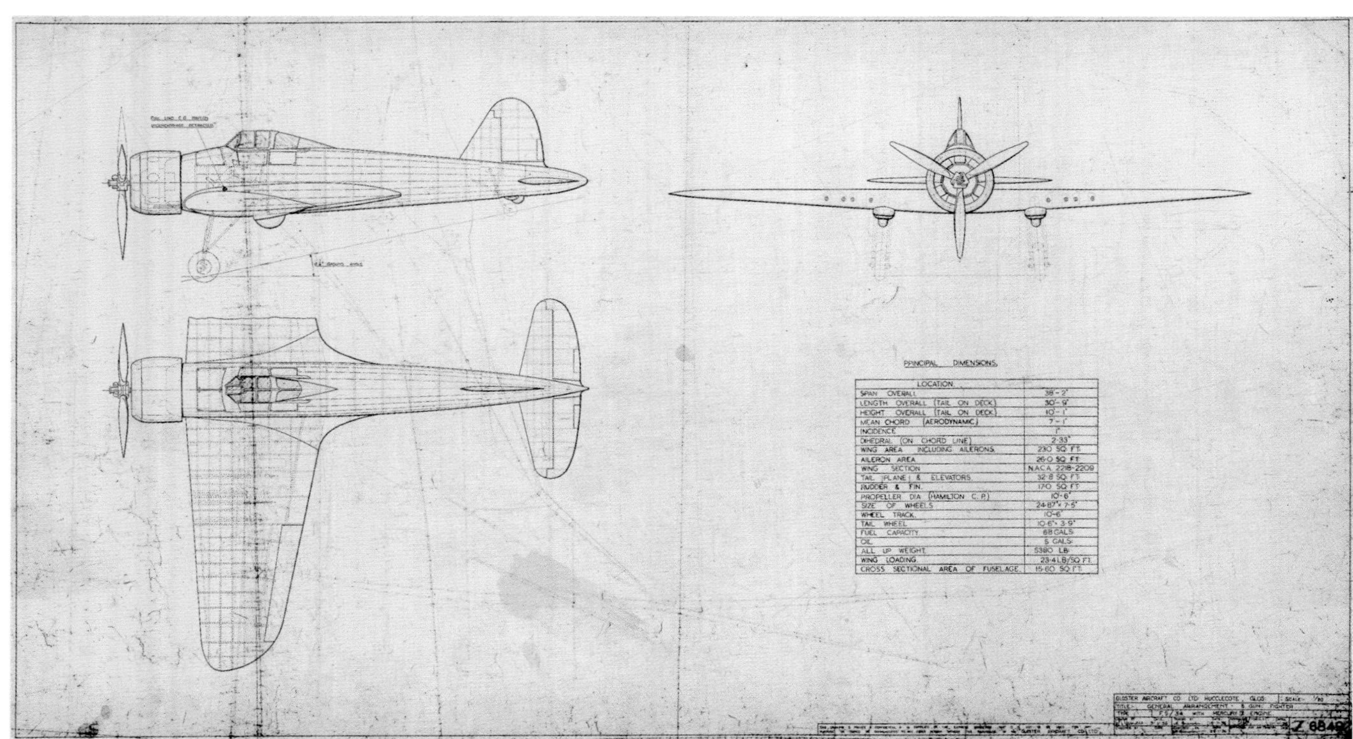

PRINCIPAL DIMENSIONS.

LOCATION	
SPAN OVERALL	38'-2"
LENGTH OVERALL (TAIL ON DECK)	30'-9"
HEIGHT OVERALL (TAIL ON DECK)	10'-1"
MEAN CHORD (AERODYNAMIC)	7'-1"
INCIDENCE	1°
DIHEDRAL (ON CHORD LINE)	2·33°
WING AREA INCLUDING AILERONS	230 SQ FT
AILERON AREA	26·0 SQ FT
WING SECTION	N.A.C.A. 2218-2209
TAIL PLANE & ELEVATORS	32·8 SQ FT
RUDDER & FIN	17·0 SQ FT
PROPELLER DIA (HAMILTON C.P.)	10'-6"
SIZE OF WHEELS	24·87" x 7·5"
WHEEL TRACK	10'-6"
TAIL WHEEL	10·6" x 3·9"
FUEL CAPACITY	68 GALS
OIL	5 GALS
ALL UP WEIGHT	5380 LB
WING LOADING	23·4 LB/SQ FT
CROSS SECTIONAL AREA OF FUSELAGE	15·60 SQ FT

Original manufacturer's drawing of the Gloster F.5/34 dated January 1936, i.e. produced well before the first machine had been built. Span at this stage was 38ft 2in (11.63m) and length (tail down) 30ft 9in (9.37m). *The late James Goulding via Jet Age Museum*

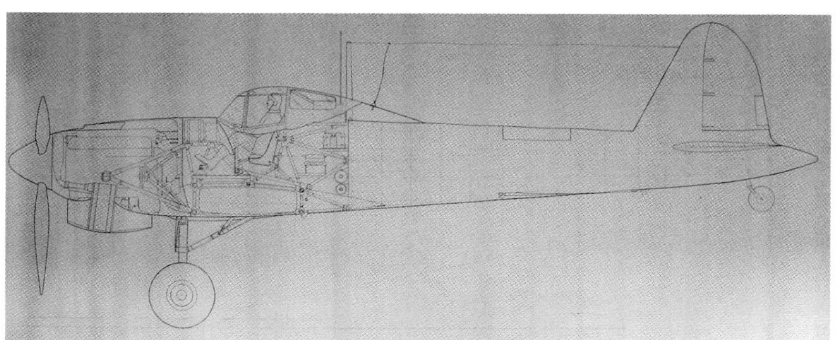

Original Gloster drawing from November 1939 which shows a proposed single-seat Griffon-powered Fleet Air Arm fighter clearly developed from the F.5/34. At the time the Navy had new requirements for single and two-seat fighters which led to the Blackburn Firebrand and Fairey Firefly respectively, and this design is almost certain a proposal against those specifications. *The late James Goulding via Jet Age Museum*

12 Gloster F.9/37

Gloster F.9/37

Type: Single-Seat Day and Night Fighter

Powerplant: Two 1,050hp (783kW) Bristol Taurus T-S(a) (TE.1) radial engines
*Two 900hp (671kW) Taurus T-S(a) III radial engines
**Two 885hp (660kW) 12-cylinder Rolls-Royce Peregrine inline engines

Span: 50ft 0.5in (15.25m)

Length: 37ft 0.5in (11.29m)

Gross Wing Area: 384sq.ft (35.71m²)

Tare Weight: 8,828lb (4,004kg), **9,222lb (4,183kg)

Maximum load: 11,653lb (5,245kg) = flying weight on trials, **12,108lb (5,492kg) - two guns only

Rate of Climb: 2,030ft/min (619m/min) at sea level

Maximum Speed: 360mph (579km/h) at 15,000ft (4,572m)
*332mph (534km/h) at 15,200ft (4,633m)
**330mph (531km/h) at 15,000ft (4,572m)

Service Ceiling: *30,000ft (9,144m), **28,700ft (8,748m)

Armament: 2 x fixed 20mm Hispano cannon in nose, 3 x fixed 20mm cannon in upper mid-fuselage (in L8002 only). Provision under centre wing for 2 x 20lb (9.1kg) bomb carriers

Apart from Britain's first jet aircraft (the E.28/39 covered by the next chapter) and the country's first jet fighter (the Meteor), for the author one of the most interesting types to emerge from the Gloster Aircraft Company based on the edge of the Cotswold Hills in middle England was this attractive twin-engine piston fighter. It originated from a proposal made in 1935 for a turret fighter and two prototypes were ordered to Contract 697972/37, which flew with different engines and were to be used as test aircraft for a proposed night-fighter development. Many published sources have indicated that Gloster called the aircraft the G.39. In fact this is completely untrue. The 'G' series of Gloster aircraft type designations was made up (it is understood) by an historian in the late 1940s to simplify his classification of the company's aircraft. Sadly, that 'system' has filtered through in publications to the present day but it was never used by Gloster at the time these aircraft were being developed because it did not exist.

The 1935 project for a Bristol Aquila-powered twin engine turret-armed fighter was made against Air Ministry Specification F.34/35, the aircraft sporting nose-mounted machine

Model of the Gloster F.34/35 project that preceded the F.9/37.

guns and a dorsal turret. In fact such was the interest generated by the Gloster F.34/35 that a prototype was ordered in February 1936 with the serial K8625. It was eventually cancelled but Gloster was able to continue its twin-engine fighter under a new specification, F.9/37. The chief designer on this work so far had been H.P. Folland who had joined Gloster in 1921, but in 1937 he moved to British Marine Aircraft at Hamble (later retitled Folland Aircraft). His successor was W.G. Carter who arrived with a strong track record. Carter had worked for Sopwith Aviation and in 1923 took over as chief designer for Hawker Aircraft, before leaving in 1925 to be replaced by Sydney Camm. Spells with Shorts, de Havilland and Avro followed before his appointment at Gloster in 1937 where, with his experience, he was well placed to refine Folland's design into the F.9/37.

Specification F.9/37 and Operational Requirement OR.49 were issued on 15 September 1937 and asked for a fighter that could achieve speeds of at least 300mph (483km/h) and which could reach an altitude of 15,000ft (4,572m) in a maximum of 6.6 minutes. The powerplant was to be a pair of Rolls-Royce Kestrel KV.26 or Bristol Taurus T-S(a) engines, the pilot in the nose cockpit would have two 20mm cannon as his forward-firing armament while the observer had a retractable turret with a battery of four 0.303in (7.7mm) machine-guns. However, in the late autumn of 1938, early in the development process, the amidships cockpit was dropped which turned the Gloster F.9/37 into a fixed-gun single seat fighter, and then in November came a proposal to fit a battery of three more 20mm in the position vacated by the turret in the upper fuselage behind the pilot. These would fire forward over the cockpit hooding, the fuselage being bulged to accommodate such formidable weaponry. The plan was accepted and the rear guns were eventually fitted into the second F.9/37. The second prototype also had the nose cannon installed but for its early test flights the first aircraft had the nose gun ports plated over, and most probably never carried any guns at all.

The two F.9/37s were given serials L7999 and L8002 and would prove to be the first and last piston-engined fighters designed for Gloster by George Carter. L7999 was powered by two Bristol Taurus 14-cylinder air-cooled radials while, instead of receiving the Kestrel powerplant, L8002 had a pair of Rolls-Royce Peregrine 12-cylinder liquid-cooled engines with chin radiators (the engine currently used by the production Westland Whirlwind fighter). Assembly of L7999 was started in the Gloster Experimental Department at Hucclecote in February 1938 and the first flight was made on 3 April 1939. Gloster's chief test pilot, Flt Lt P.E.G. 'Jerry' Sayer, was in the cockpit and the early test sorties performed by both Sayer and his test pilot colleague at Gloster, Michael Daunt, demonstrated performance and handling that showed great potential; in fact the F.9/37 achieved speeds in excess of 360mph (579km/h).

View of the brand new unpainted Gloster F.9/37 prototype L7999 powered by Bristol Taurus engines. Note that the propellers have spinners.

The type's preliminary trials moved forward with great speed and proved so successful that by 23 May it was possible to take L7999 on a cross-country flight to RAF Northolt for a special Air Ministry display staged specifically for a group of Members of Parliament. This exercise was to show the MPs how the money made available for the expansion of the RAF was being spent, and Hawker Hurricanes, Fairey Battles and other types were inspected. The F.9/37 made a brief and spectacular high-speed flypast before returning to Hucclecote, and apparently left quite an impression. However, it was to be five years before details of this 'hush-hush' aircraft were released officially and, consequently, the aeronautical press could only report on a "new aircraft with two engines that was probably a fighter".

Following further flight testing at Hucclecote, L7999 was despatched to A&AEE Martlesham Heath on 8 July 1939 for its official performance, handling and maintenance assessment. Sadly this was cut short after the aircraft was badly damaged in a belly landing at A&AEE on 27 July early in the course of its trials. By 3 August L7999 had been returned to Gloster at Hucclecote by road where it was rebuilt with different Taurus engines, T-S(a) IIIs replacing the original T-S(a)s, the essential difference being a de-rating of the supercharger to reduce the boost pressure from +5.25 down to 4.5lb/sq.in maximum. The aircraft was back at A&AEE (now at Boscombe Down) on 4 April 1940 but thanks to delays caused by long periods of unserviceability, the unreliability of the new engines and the allotment of L7999 for gunnery trials, only part of the original test programme was ever completed. However, this did include flights to examine its top speed, ceiling and climb performance, a brief handling assessment and a maintenance check.

Available pictures suggest that there was only ever one air-to-air photographic session with the F.9/37. Note that the spinners are now removed and the nose gun ports are plated over.

L7999 banks away from the camera to reveal the underfuselage colour scheme with the wing serials in opposite tones.

In fact Boscombe Down's report of 31 July 1940 was very praiseworthy. The cockpit layout was described as generally good with the view to the front and side excellent – the only criticism was the poor view to the rear. On take-off there was a slight tendency to swing to the right but this was easily overcome by use of the rudder, and the take-off itself was good but the F.9/37 took some time to reach a speed of 140mph (225km/h) which was the minimum speed for flight on one engine. If an engine failed before reaching 140mph there would be no alternative for the pilot but to throttle back the good engine and land straight ahead. Handling trials were conducted at a weight of 11,460lb (5,198kg) and all of the controls were found to be light, effective and well harmonised, their heaviness increasing slightly with speed. Flat turns were made at speeds up to 250mph (402km/h) and a slight vibration of the ailerons was experienced at speeds between 140 to 180mph (225 to 290km/h). A&AEE's pilots judged from the tests that were completed that the machine was stable in all conditions of flight and about all axes, with the exception of the climb with cooling gills fully open. Here the longitudinal stability was poor, but on one of the ceiling climbs the gills were half closed and the F.9/37 became stable again. For the approach and landing the flaps and undercarriage were found to go down quickly and the aeroplane became nose heavy. The best approach speed was found to be 90 to 95mph (145 to 153km/h) and the landing was straightforward and easy. If the engines were opened up to go around again after a bad approach the aircraft became tail heavy but could be held until re-trimmed. During A&AEE testing the best altitude achieved was 28,000ft (8,534m).

In general, the maintenance facilities were felt to be very good, and to conclude the aeroplane was described as "easy and pleasant to fly". The controls were not considered heavy for a twin-engined fighter and, from the brief handling tests completed, the stability appeared satisfactory. With the reduced power T-S(a) III Taurus a top speed of 332mph (534km/h) at the full throttle height of 15,200ft (4,633m) was recorded. Gerry Sayer's report for the manufacturers confirmed that the F.9/37's controls were: "...light, but positive, and the aircraft was entirely stable throughout the entire flight envelope".

The Rolls-Royce Peregrine made quite a difference to the F.9/37's appearance but without being detrimental to the type's good looks. The nose angles show clearly that the two cannon are fitted and protrude some way ahead of the skinning. The upward angle of the guns is discernable.

As noted, the second F.9/37, L8002, was fitted with Rolls-Royce Peregrine engines which provided even less power and further reduced the top speed to 330mph (531km/h), a situation not helped by the extra weight of the engines. These factors were also detrimental to the rate of climb but not to the aircraft's manoeuvrability and control – in fact both machines proved remarkably manoeuvrable and docile and could be rolled and looped in comfort, making them perhaps one of the most manoeuvrable twin-engined aircraft types flown to date. Gerry Sayer took L8002 into the air from its Hucclecote birthplace for the first time on 22 February 1940. Apart from the new engines and their nacelle shape, the only differences from L7999 were a modified undercarriage with longer doors and the Peregrines were 'handed' for improved take-off control.

Several versions and developments of the F.9/37 were considered for other requirements, including one prepared by Carter (together with an all-new twin-boom pusher design) to Specification F.18/37 (which led to the Hawker Typhoon). The 'F.9/37' proposal had a new nose and fuselage and twelve 0.303 (7.7mm) Browning machine-guns in the nose. In addition, the early plans to fit a turret in the F.9/37 were repeated in a design to F.11/37 which was eventually satisfied by the Boulton Paul P.92 (Chapter Four). There was also an F.11/37 bomber to be powered by Hercules HE.6.SM engines and, to help standardise and facilitate their production, both of these 1937 projects would have used the same centre wing, centre sections and engine installations as the F.9/37. Finally and most importantly a modified F.9/37 was offered as a two-seat night fighter to Specification F.18/40 of November 1940 and given the name Reaper.

Gloster found that the gross weight of the F.9/37 could be increased from 11,500lb (5,216kg) to as much as 14,500lb (6,577kg) for the F.18/40, which allowed the substitution of the Taurus installation by Rolls-Royce Merlin XXs in a move that would substantially improve the range, endurance and military load. In general, all of the requirements of F.18/40 were met by the proposal except that it carried four cannons rather than six. MAP considered the design a "particularly attractive idea" and on 13 October 1940 N.E. Rowe, DTD, wrote to tell Gloster that the project was to go-ahead. One of the F.9/37s was to be converted to carry fixed forward-firing 20mm guns, a Browning turret and an AI radar, and new build aircraft would follow. Indeed it was considered that having the F.9/37 already flying ought to give a lead of many months over any rival designs (which were submitted by several manufacturers).

But these plans proved to be very short lived. In mid-December 1940 it was calculated that a reasonable number of F.18/40s (or production F.9/37s) would not be in the air until the end of 1942, and so on 18 December the F.18/40 project was placed on a low priority. By now there were possibilities for a night-fighter Mosquito from de Havilland, while Gloster itself needed to concentrate on jet powered aircraft. Nevertheless, it was to be 1 May 1941 before a final decision was made not to proceed with the F.18/40 project. The Gloster Reaper carried four nose cannon beneath the cockpit, its estimated top speed was 390mph (628km/h) at 22,500ft (6,858m) and a partial mock-up was examined on 26 October 1940. For some flight tests L8002 was especially ballasted to represent having the F.18/40's second crewman on board.

Picture of the dorsal cannon fitting installed in the second F.9/37 L8002. *Jet Age Museum*

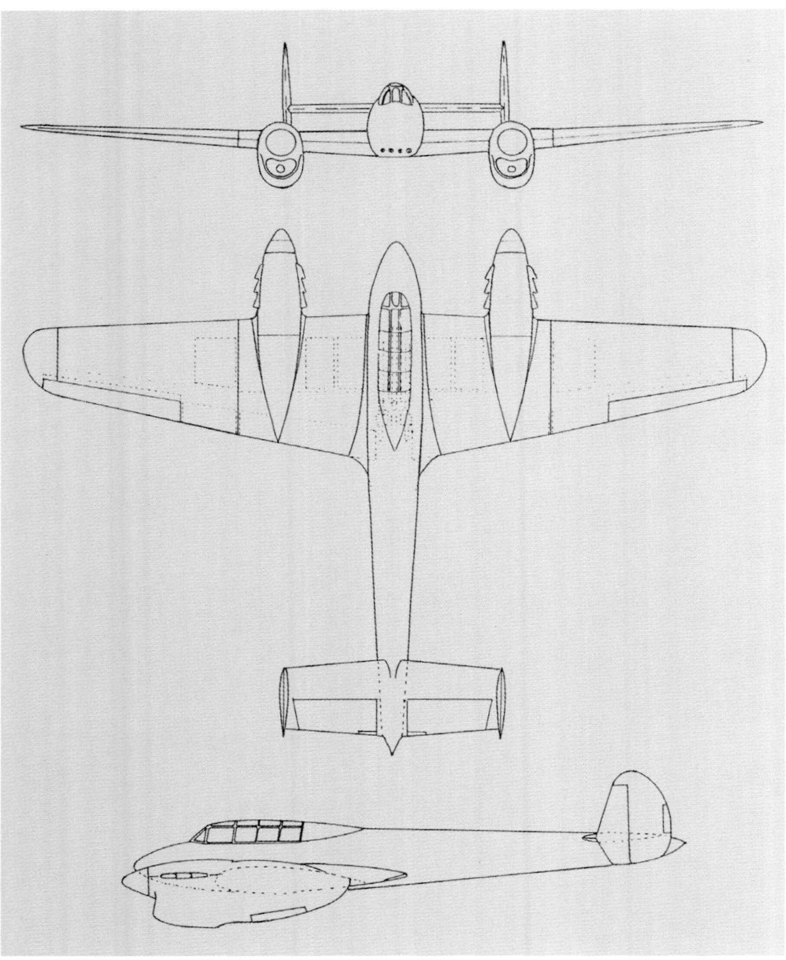

The two-seat Gloster F.18/40 Reaper project would have been another handsome aircraft as seen in this three-view drawing. The Reaper name was used by Gloster on several proposals and projects from the late 1930s to the early 1950s.

By late November 1940 L7999 had returned to the manufacturers where it was allocated for conversion to F.18/40 configuration. Some modification work appears to have been carried out but this was eventually stopped (apparently with some reluctance). In January 1941 Sayer wrote a report about the Frise ailerons made as a modification with a rather blunt nose. There was a large gap at the nose (around 1.25in (31.75mm)) plus a small gap at the upper shroud so that the aileron trailing edge was almost invariably above the hinge line with the shroud projecting outside the wing profile. Sayer said that at high speeds the aileron would stiffen up 'solid' and the trailing edge would droop by as much as 0.75in (19.05mm), almost certainly due to the projecting shroud. L7999 remained in Gloster hands until 2 April 1942 when Michael Daunt flew it to RAF Halton where it would serve as a ground instruction airframe. Although photographs of the aircraft appear to have been taken at Boscombe in February 1940, L8002 was not tested by A&AEE. The second aircraft was allotted to Gloster in February 1941 before being taken on the charge of RAF Cosford on 25 April 1942, again in a ground instruction role. A magazine reported in late 1948 that the "remains" of L8002 survived at Cosford until "recently" (presumably beyond the end of the war). The airframe was certainly at Cosford (reportedly in derelict condition) in March 1945.

Sadly the F.9/37 never acquired a production contract. The nine-month delay in repairing the first prototype after the July 1939 accident cannot have helped its prospects. In addition, although a long-range heavily-armed fighter like this (a type missing from the RAF's inventory) might have had some effect in the air war over France in May 1940 it would not have changed the outcome. On 28 November 1940 Air Marshal Joubert declared that Gloster's fighter would be out of date by the time it entered production. Indeed by 1942 when Gloster's fighter was expected to enter service, types such as the de Havilland Mosquito and the Bristol Beaufighter had taken the state of the art beyond that offered by the F.9/37. And of course by then the firm's work on jet aircraft had become far more important. Nevertheless, the F.9/37 was a handsome aircraft with numerous features of considerable interest, and at least for a period during 1940 it was most probably the most heavily armed fighter in the world.

Side view of a single-seat design that eventually matured into the F.18/40. This Single Seat Heavy Fighter project was also called Reaper on the drawing and it was 37ft 10in (11.53m) long. Armament was four 20mm cannon and eight Browning machine guns all mounted in the lower nose. The drawing is dated 27 April 1938. *Jet Age Museum*

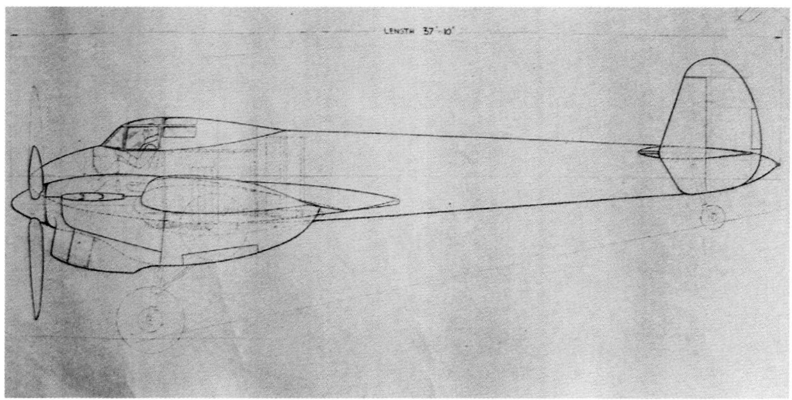

Images showing the partial mock-up of the F.18/40 Reaper, which comprised a forward fuselage, port wing centre section and port Merlin engine nacelle. Note the radar aerial in the nose. *Jet Age Museum*

Forward cockpit detail inside the F.18/40 mock-up. *Jet Age Museum*

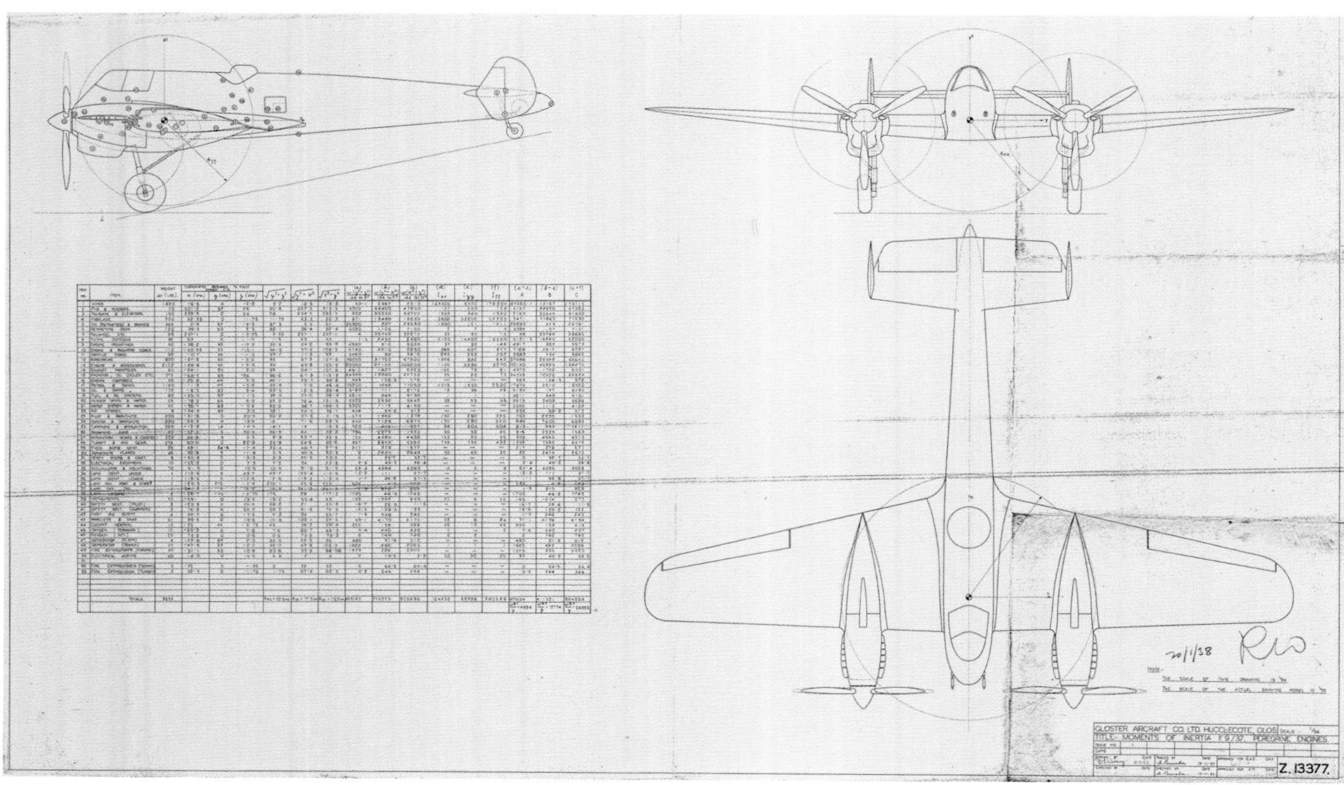

Drawing of the Peregrine-powered Gloster F.9/37.

Structure

The F.9/37's attractive layout was enhanced by the twin-rudder tail being retained from the earlier F.34/35 project. From the start Gloster planned for dispersed production by semi-skilled operators and so the aircraft's sub-assemblies, jigging and tooling were kept as simple as possible. The wing comprised a Dural tapered structure built up on two I-section parallel spars and there was also a Dural false spar to carry the inboard flaps. The centre plane used rolled skin while the two outer wing sections (which carried the ailerons and outboard flaps) were covered by stressed skin. The flaps and trimmers were covered in Dural sheet, the tailplane and fins in stressed skin, but the ailerons, elevators and horn-balanced rudders were all fabric covered. The maximum fuel capacity with the fuel housed in four wing tanks including two in the centre wing was 170 gallons (773 litres). Both aircraft were fitted with standard Rotol variable-pitch three-blade metal airscrews and spinners of 10ft 0in (3.05m) diameter.

The fuselage construction was stressed skin monocoque throughout on a rib skeleton of Dural section with some steel. The main ribs between the spars were made of Dural and steel tubing with sheet and strip for bulkheads, stringers and skins. A detachable nose allowed

Above and bottom opposite: When flown for the camera L7999 was camouflaged in 1939 day fighter colours – upperworks in Dark Earth and Green; engine cowling, fuselage and tail undersurfaces silver; wings black and white underneath. These in-flight photos are undated, but were taken during summer 1939 or summer 1940.

access to the instruments and gun camera and both the Avery or Dowty main undercarriage and tail wheel were retractable, the former folding rearwards into the engine nacelles with no twisting points. A pair of forward-firing 20mm Hispano cannon was installed beneath the pilot just forward of the rear spar and these were inclined at an angle of 12° to the horizontal line of flight. Three more would go behind the pilot again inclined at 12° from line of flight and firing over the pilot's hooding. Thanks to the aircraft's short nose the two forward 20mm barrels had to protrude out beyond the metal surface.

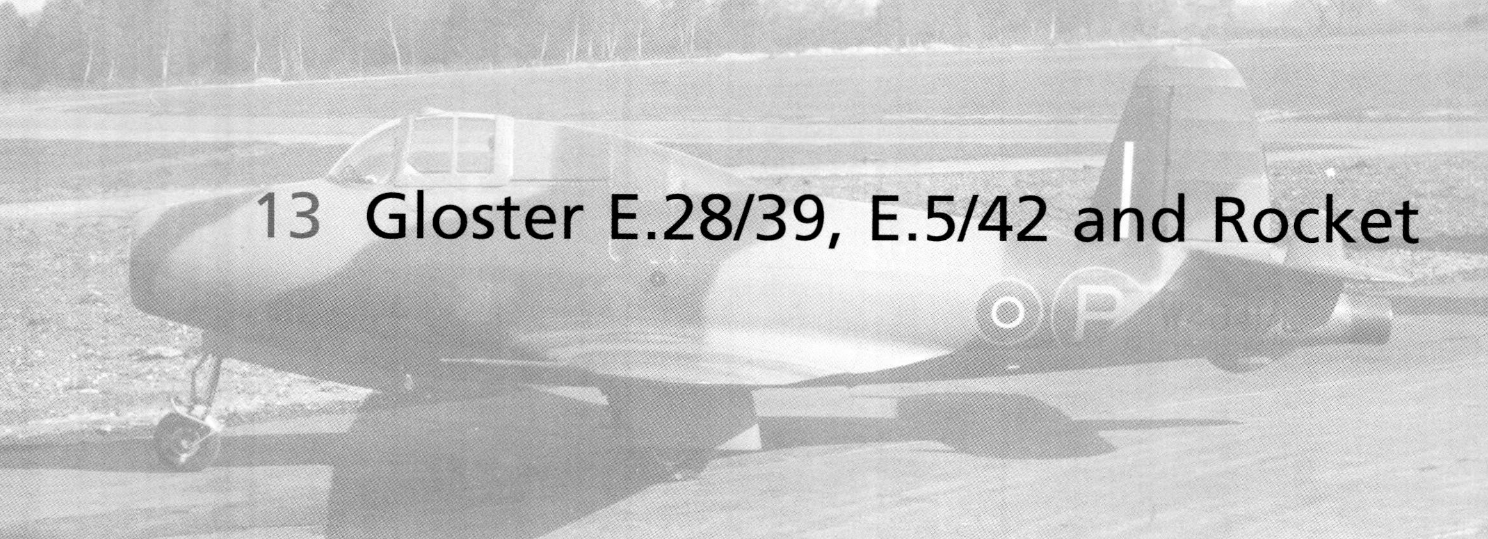

13 Gloster E.28/39, E.5/42 and Rocket

Gloster E.28/39

Type: Single-Seat Jet-Powered Research Aircraft

Powerplant: See text

Span: 29ft 0in (8.84m)

Length: 25ft 3.75in (7.71m)

Gross Wing Area: 146.5sq.ft (13.62m^2)

All-Up Weight: See text

Rate of Climb with W2B engine: Over 3,000ft/min (914m/min) at 1,000ft (305m)

Maximum Speed: See text

Service Ceiling: See text

Armament: None, although Specification E.28/39 listed four 0.303in (7.7mm) machine-guns

Some of the subjects in this book have had relatively little published material devoted to them, others have featured extensively in magazine articles, but the Gloster E.28/39 research aircraft, Britain's first jet aeroplane to fly, has quite rightly received probably more detailed coverage in many works than any other in the chapter listing. Hopefully, however, the reader will still find some new information in this modest history of the type.

The very early part of British jet aircraft history was dominated by the E.28/39 and the Gloster Meteor, the nation's first jet fighter. The twin-engine Meteor prototype first flew in March 1943 and the type became a huge success and stayed in production until well after the Second World War was over. What is not so well known, however, is that in 1943 Gloster proposed another twin engine jet fighter which, unlike the Meteor with its wing-mounted engine nacelles, had both power units housed inside the fuselage. The project was called the Rocket, and it followed a single-engined fighter design called the E.5/42 which was to have been built in prototype form. These are also discussed.

The design of the E.28/39 (the number is the Specification that covered the aircraft) was begun by George Carter and his team, working in close collaboration with Air Commodore Whittle (the designer of the jet engine), before the outbreak of war. On 30 August 1939 Contract SB.3229 was placed by the Air Ministry for two experimental aircraft and several designs were considered including one with armament in the nose and having (in order to clear the jet stream) a 'tadpole-like' rear fuselage supporting the tail. This was a mid-wing monoplane with the jet unit placed below the pilot but in the end it was decided to proceed with a very clean low wing monoplane layout. For security reasons the aircraft was also known by the code name 'Weaver'. A Mock-Up Conference was held on 22 April 1940 and during that year low speed wind tunnel tests on the design were performed by RAE's Aerodynamics Department.

Testing of the first aircraft, W4041/G ('G' signifying it required a day and night 'Guard'), began in the form of taxi trials at Hucclecote in April 1941. The engine was the Power Jets W1X which was not built for flight, although on 8 April during these tests the aircraft did leave the ground for a short period to a distance of about 200 yards (183km) and a height of about 6ft (1.85m). The first true maiden flight was made from Cranwell on 15 May 1941 by Gloster chief test pilot 'Jerry' Sayer. An 850lb (3.8kN) thrust Power Jets W1 engine was installed and it was found that the E.28/39 compared well with the best Spitfire of that time. Cranwell was chosen

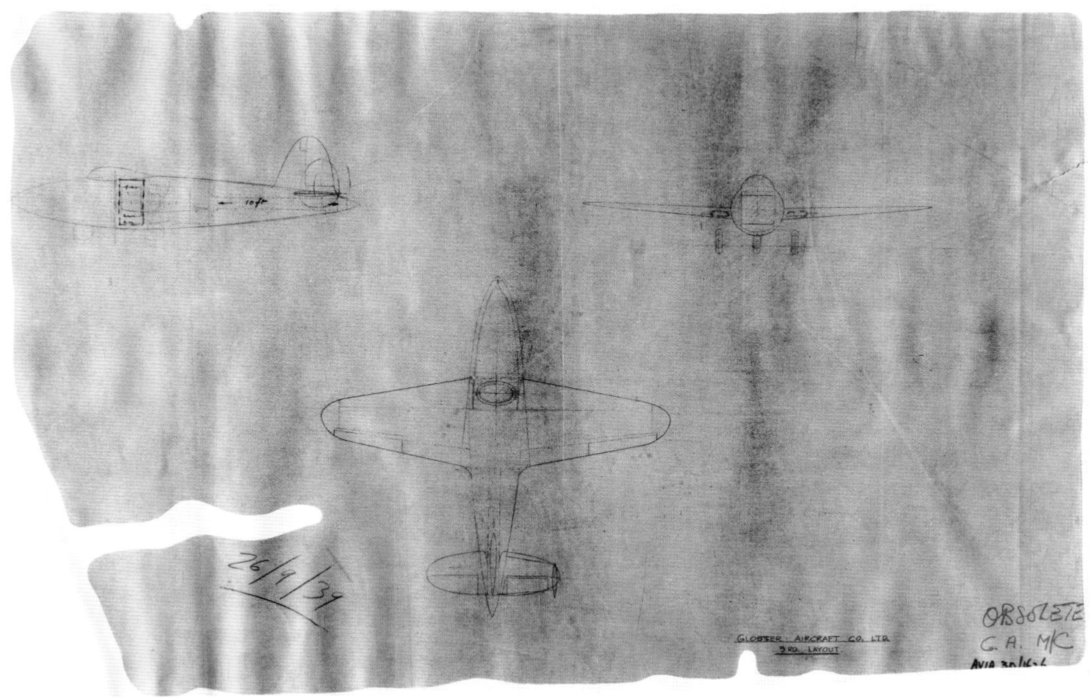

Drawing showing the E.28/39 'third layout' dated 29 September 1939. This comes quite close to the aircraft that was eventually built, but plenty of changes still had to be made. However, it does feature tip fins. *National Archives AVIA 30-1626*

Gloster E.28/39 drawing dated 18 July 1940. Here the length is given as 26ft 3.7in (8.02m).

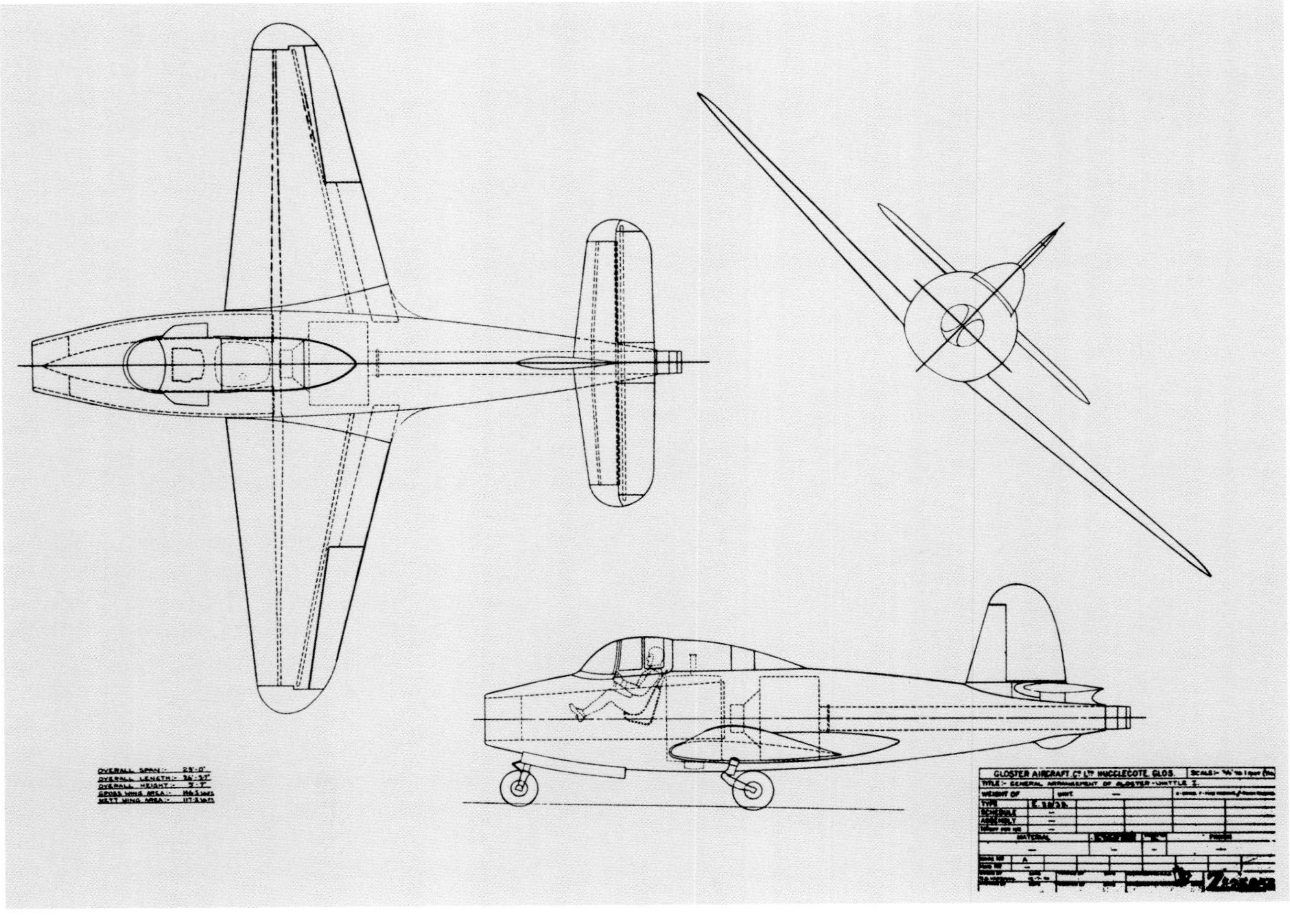

This view of Gloster E.28/39 prototype W4041 was taken at Brockworth immediately before taxying trials began in April 1941. The strip seen along the rear fuselage is thermal paint to record any effects of engine heat on the skins.

A similar view of W4041 taken later in its career at Farnborough with camouflage applied, tip fins in place and an extended nosewheel leg. The pilot is thought to be Sqn Ldr C.G.B. Charles McClure. *Rolls-Royce Heritage Trust*

Rare image of the second E.28/39 W4046 taken in June 1943, probably at Farnborough.

as the venue because of the need to reduce the risk present in early flights by having airfield conditions as ideal as possible (Boscombe for example was rejected because of its undulating runway surface). For security the aeroplane was housed in a hangar at the extreme west end of the airfield and admission to the hangar was by special pass only. Also for reasons of security subsequent tests were undertaken at a different airfield, Edgehill which was roughly half way between Gloster and Power Jets at Lutterworth. The next engine to be installed (in January 1942) was the 1,050lb (4.7kN) thrust (at 17,000rpm) Power Jets W1A and tests were carried out by both Gloster test pilot Michael Daunt and Air Ministry test pilot Wg Cdr H.J. Wilson. In December 1942 the flying programme was transferred to Farnborough where performance tests showed a maximum speed of 365mph (587km/h). It was found that the speed did not vary greatly with height but the problem of 'surging', where the engine appeared to backfire, was encountered for the first time.

Meanwhile, the second aeroplane W4046/G had been completed with a Rolls-Royce (Rover) W2B engine and first flown at Edgehill on 1 March 1943 (the engine delivered 1,350lb (6.0kN) static thrust at 16,350rpm). On 19 April W4046 was demonstrated to Prime Minister Winston Churchill at Hatfield and on 3 May it went to Farnborough for intensive flying. The all up weight was 3,950lb (1,792kg) and with this more powerful engine the performance was naturally better than that achieved by W4041 with the W1A. A speed of 435mph (700km/h) was recorded and a height of 23,500ft (7,163m) was reached in 12.5 minutes. It was found that the thrust given by the engine when landing was rather high, making the approach more difficult than in a propeller-driven aircraft. This also had the effect of making the speed of a 'glide' from altitude very high, although this was partly due to the lack of a propeller which would act as a brake in these circumstances while a clean propeller-less aeroplane picked up speed very rapidly. Most of these tests were carried out by Sqn Ldr D.B.S. Davie, Wg Cdr Wilson and Gp Capt A.H. Wheeler.

In June 1943 a 1,520lb (6.8kN) W2B engine (at 17,000rpm) was installed in W4046 and a speed of 466mph (750km/h) at 10,000ft (3,048m) was recorded with the engine slightly overspeeding. The aircraft's forward speed would normally increase slightly with altitude but in this case it was found necessary to throttle back at higher altitudes to avoid surging. W4046/G could reach 35,000ft (10,668m) in 26 minutes, aerobatics were performed (particularly by Sqn Ldr C.G.B. McClure) and the fuel tank was found to be sensitive to negative *g*, thereby preventing fuel from reaching the engine (it was found possible to restart the engine in the air). The aeroplane was also found to zigzag slightly at high speeds. W4046 was lost in a crash on 30 July 1943 after the aileron controls had jammed at 36,000ft (10,973m) but Sqn Ldr D.B.S. Davie was able to escape in what was probably the longest parachute descent recorded to date.

By this time W4041 had been test flown at Barford St. John with a 1,600lb (7.1kN) Power Jets W2/500. Its performance with this engine was much the same as W4046 with the more powerful W2B but a height of 41,600ft (12,680m) was reached without surging occurring. The pilots were Gloster's Michael Daunt and John Grierson and after the loss of W4046/G it was decided to modify the aileron controls – flying was resumed at Farnborough in March 1944 with a more powerful W2/500. A new tailplane was also fitted which featured endplate fins to cure the zigzagging experienced at high speeds. By this stage metal-covered control surfaces had also been introduced and the original NACA section wing had been replaced by a Gloster wing of special high speed design. It was found that the latest engine surged at 25,000ft (7,620m) and had to be modified accordingly in order to avoid this. Flying resumed again in April and on the 25th the aeroplane was taken to 43,000ft (13,105m) at which point it was still climbing, but since the cockpit was not pressurised it was impossible for the pilot to go any higher. Maximum speed was now 480mph (772km/h) and the all up weight through having additional equipment installed was around 4,200lb (1,905kg).

| *Below and overleaf:* Further views of W4041 taken during its flying career at Farnborough.

right: There are few known photographs of the second E.28/39 W4046. Here the aircraft is pictured (most likely) at Farnborough, the venue for most service views of Britain's first jet aircraft. *via Graham Pitchfork.*

W4041 photographed in colour at Farnborough on a showery day in 1944. *Barry Jones*

To close its flying career W4041 had a later design of engine fitted, the W2/700 developed directly from the W2/500, after which the aircraft was used to gather performance data. It was modified by the addition of a wing-mounted pitot comb and other special instruments to permit research on the effect of compressibility in high speed dives. Some very high Mach numbers were recorded by pilot Sqn Ldr B.H. Moloney (Mach 0.93 was achieved on 27 August 1944) and a considerable amount of valuable data was accumulated for high speeds and altitudes. W4041 made its final flight on 20 February 1945 and in 1946, after being used for several exhibitions, it was put on public display in the Science Museum in London. (Author's note: the engine thrust figures given here originate from an Air Ministry document and differ from other sources.)

Gloster Meteor prototype DG202/G. This particular aircraft first flew on 24 July 1943.

Gloster E.5/42 Project

The starting point for Gloster's series of jet aircraft designs using fuselage-mounted engines was of course the E.28/39. In January 1942 work began on a single-engine fighter development that Gloster named the 'Ace' and which, armed with four 20mm cannon in the lower nose, was expected to provide a maximum speed of 490mph (788km/h) at 30,000ft (9,144m). On 29 January 1943 a Contract (SB.26236) was awarded for three prototypes, NN648, NN651 and NN655, against Specification E.5/42, the document being raised specifically to cover the fighter. The aerodynamic characteristics of the E.28/39 were carried through into the new type which featured a similar layout but introduced a longer fuselage and a solid nose, wing root intakes and a T-tail. All three airframes were to be powered by a single 3,000lb (13.3kN) de Havilland H.1 jet and the design had a single main wing spar running through the fuselage. The E.5/42 was known as the Gloster-Halford fighter (Frank Halford was responsible for the de Havilland engine – earlier designs using Power Jets units were described as Gloster-Whittles) but a number of original documents call the aircraft the Gloster A.9, and others refer to the specification as F.5/42.

On 23 and 24 February 1943 a mock-up of the E.5/42 was inspected at Bentham and later in the year a model of the fighter was tested in the then brand new Farnborough high-speed wind tunnel. As work proceeded there was

In the latter part of its flying career W4041 had small finlets fitted to the outer part of each horizontal tailplane. However, in readiness for some public displays held in 1945 the aircraft was refurbished and the finlets were removed. *Jet Age Museum*

Below and overleaf: Model of the Gloster E.5/42. *Joe Cherrie*

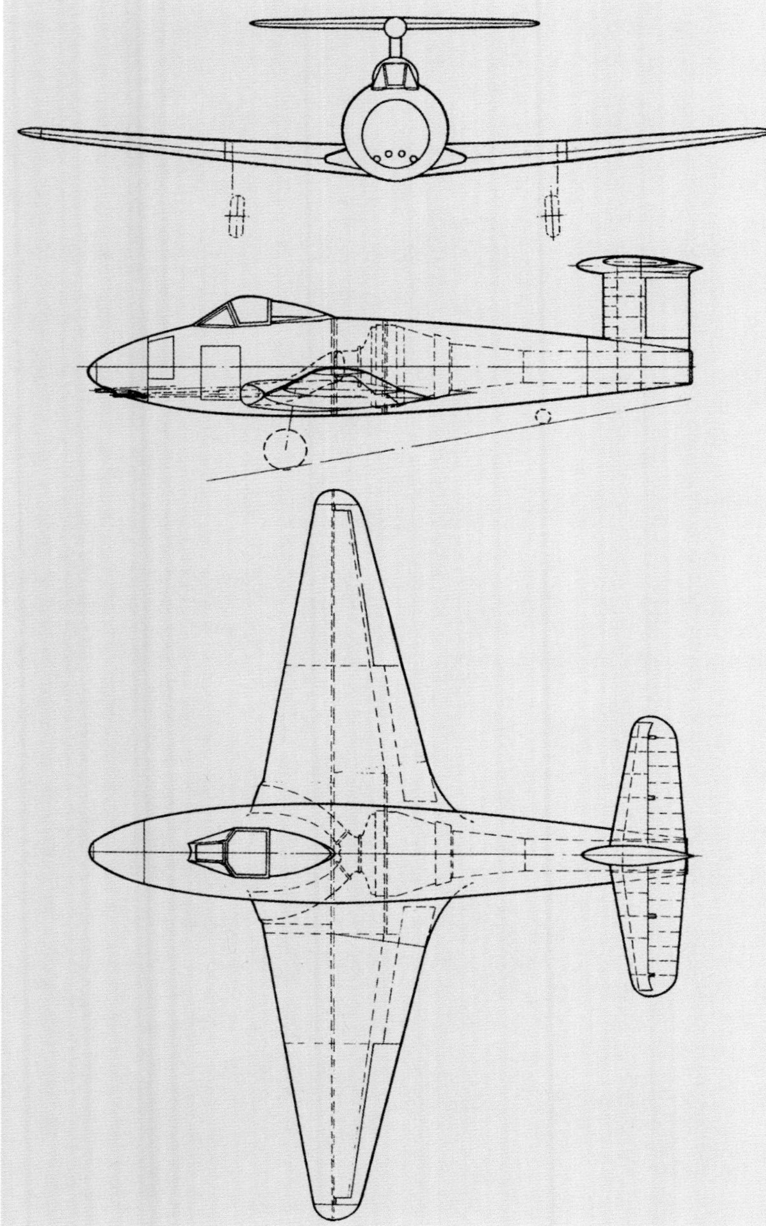

some debate as to the value of this single-engined type against the concurrent twin-engined Meteor and in the end the latter prevailed. However, it is understood that by November 1943 the manufacture of the first E.5/42 (a 'flying shell') had commenced in Gloster's experimental works at Bentham, but in due course the 'Ace' project was replaced by a new design called the E.1/44 which eventually reached flight test status (but not until 1948). In its final form the Gloster E.5/42 was to have had a span of 35ft (10.7m), all-up-weight of 8,300lb (3,765kg), estimated top speed 520mph (837km/h) at 30,000ft and an operational ceiling of 48,000ft (14,630m).

Gloster Rocket Project

A recently discovered original drawing showing the Gloster Rocket (numbered P.149) is dated 28 June 1943 and the design has twin jetpipes along the sides of the rear fuselage. It appears that a second version called the P.150 was drawn in July, which quite probably was the layout represented by a drawing originating from RAE Farnborough that shows a tail jetpipe. The date of the RAE drawing is unknown but it does seem likely that this would have been prepared later than the original from Gloster. The original brochure that accompanied the P.149, and which itself is undated, outlined an aircraft that was to be based on the E.5/42 but which introduced a twin side-by-side engine arrangement with two 2,200lb (9.8kN) thrust B.37 jet propulsion units in the fuselage (the B.37 eventually became the Rolls-Royce Derwent). These were placed in roughly the same position as the de Havilland engine in the E.5/42 and the fuselage had been made fatter in order to make room for the new powerplant. Later developments of the B.37 were expected to offer 2,500lb (11.1kN) of thrust and in 1943 such a high level of power was not yet available from any single power unit that would be suited to an aircraft of this type. An engine capable of giving 5,000lb (22.2kN) of thrust on its own would at this stage be too large and too heavy for a fighter.

The other changes shown by the Rocket against the E.5/42 centred on the fuselage behind the cockpit and the wing centre section – the front fuselage, outer wings, main undercarriage and tailplane would be the same

The Gloster E.5/42 fighter project from 1942. *Jet Age Museum*

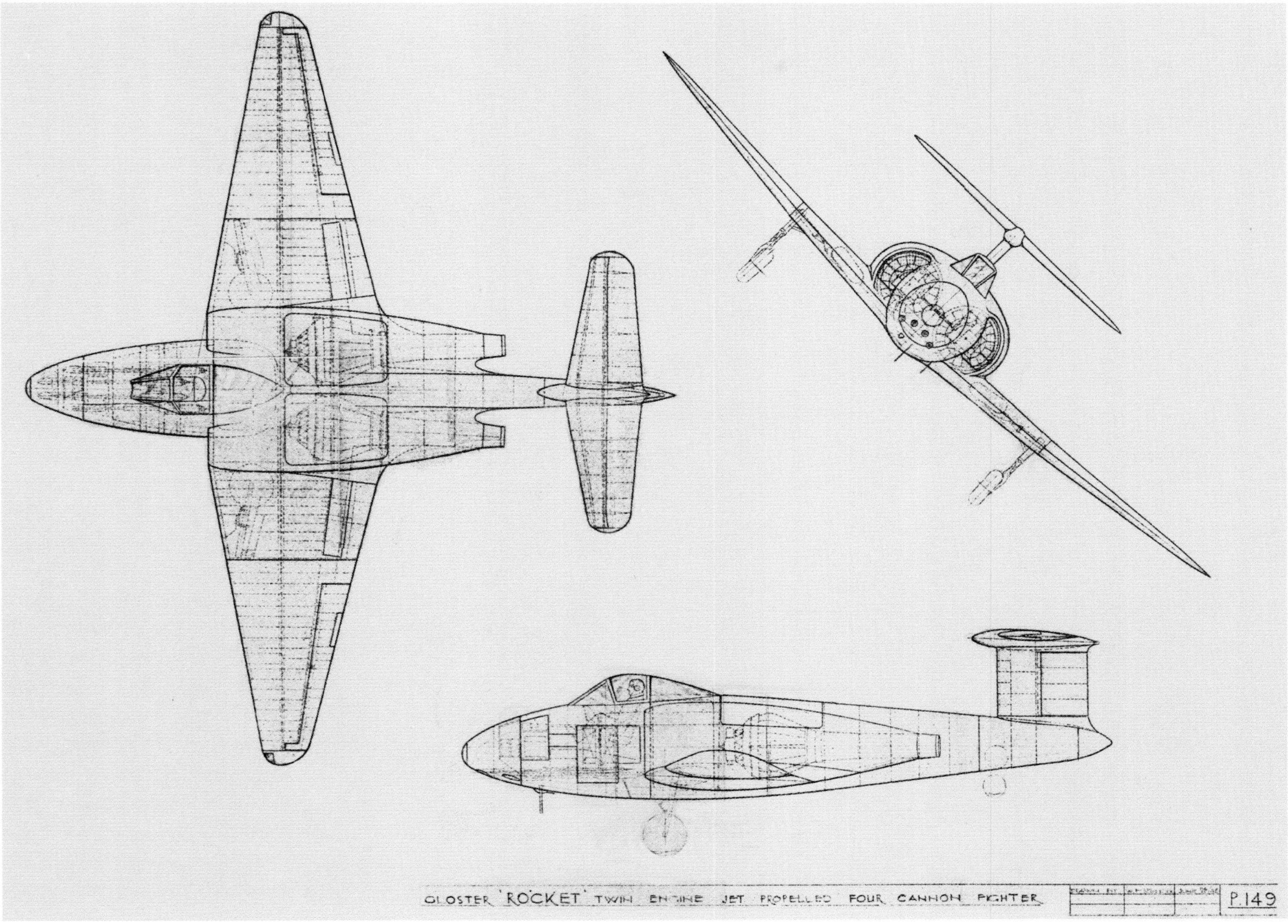

The twin-engine Gloster Rocket development of the E.5/42 as first proposed in mid-1943. The similarity to and changes from the single-engine aircraft make an interesting comparison. *Jet Age Museum*

except for some necessary strengthening. Both the E.5/42 and the Rocket were to be fitted with an RAE 'high-speed' wing section first developed for and used by the E.28/39. It is assumed that the Rocket would have employed a structure similar to the E.5/42 and that it would have been built in light (aluminium) alloy. Even for 1943 one might consider that the Rocket's appearance did not look particularly modern, but it had a neat nose and forward fuselage and a highly tapered wing with long ailerons along the outer portion of the trailing edge. On the P.149 drawing the B.37s were mounted just ahead of the wing root trailing edge and received air from side intakes placed alongside the cockpit; their jetpipes were faired quite beautifully onto the sides of the rear fuselage. The horizontal tailplane was also tapered and sat on the top of a straight non-tapered fin which had a large rudder. Four 20mm cannon were mounted in the lower nose and a tailwheel undercarriage was employed with Dunlop main and tail wheels.

Model of the Gloster Rocket with tailpipe made by Joe Cherrie. *Joe Cherrie*

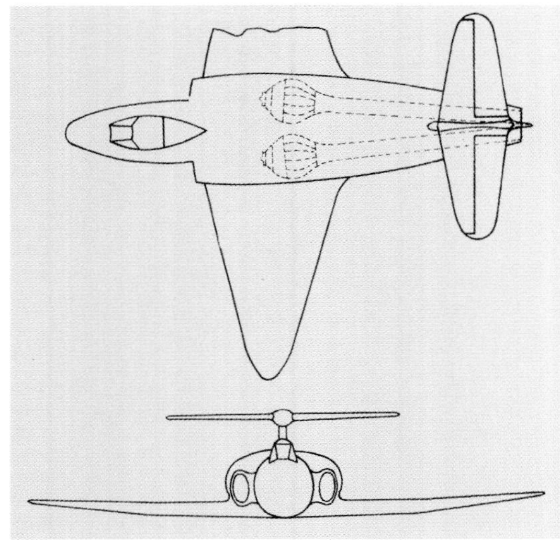

The rough RAE Farnborough drawing that shows the Gloster Rocket with a tailpipe. *National Archives AVIA 15-1933*

The Rocket had a span of 38ft 0in (11.58m), its length was 32ft 3in (9.83m), height over the hooding 9ft 3in (2.82m), and gross wing area 225sq.ft (20.9m^2). The fuel tank capacity was given as 250gals (1,138lit) and the gross weight was estimated to be 9,000lb (4,082kg), the latter including full fuel, four cannon and protection (armour) that was to be capable of handling 0.303in (7.7mm) gunfire at the front and 20mm fire from the rear. The aircraft's maximum speed at altitudes up to 10,000ft (3,048m) was estimated to be 545mph (877km/h), and between 10,000ft (3,048m) and 40,000ft (12,192m) 550mph (885km/h). Rate of climb was given as 7,650ft/min (2,332m/min) at sea level and the absolute ceiling 54,000ft (16,459m). If the aircraft cruised at 400mph (644km/h) the sea level range was 265 miles (426km). The introduction of 2,500lb (11.1kN) thrust B.37 engines would increase the top speed to 560mph (901km/h) at all heights, sea level rate of climb would rise to 9,150ft/min (2,789m/min) and the absolute ceiling to 55,000ft (16,764m).

The first Gloster E.1/44 prototype TX145 pictured at Moreton Valence in November 1947. This project replaced the E.5/42 and was also named 'Ace'. *Jet Age Museum*

RAE liked the Rocket design, the aerodynamics of which potentially appeared to be rather better than the E.5/42 and would produce less drag, but Frank Whittle considered that a better solution would be a super fighter fitted with a more suitable powerplant than the B.37. By 9 October 1943 the Rocket had been redesigned with a tricycle undercarriage, but the lack of documentation beyond the end of that year suggests that the project had by then been rejected and the work on it abandoned. The series of Gloster studies into fighters with fuselage engines eventually progressed to the flight test of the straight-wing E.1/44 Ace prototypes, the first of which flew on 9 March 1948. However, that was at a time when fighters with straight wings had become out of date and the trend was to produce fighters with swept wings that were capable of transonic and even supersonic speeds.

E.28/39 Structure

The E.28/39's structure was for the period completely conventional. The wings were of single-spar stressed-skin construction (with multiple ribs) which formed a D-shaped torsion box in conjunction with the leading edge. The Dowty main undercarriage retracted inwards aft of the main spar and, thanks to the very thin wing, the undercarriage doors and the wing upper surface had to be bulged slightly to accommodate the wheels; the nose wheel folded under the cockpit. A false rear spar supported the split flaps and the ailerons (the latter each had a spring-balance tab and an outboard mass-balance) and the control surfaces were manually operated by chain and cable controls. The tailplane and mass balanced elevators sat on a fairing above the end fuselage to the rear of the fin. The fuselage was also built of light alloy with stressed skins and the jet engine was mounted aft of the main wing spar, the jet pipe being led out through the monocoque rear fuselage to the extreme tail. Air for the engine entered through a nose intake passing to either side of the pilot through two ducts. In order to keep the rear fuselage cool a small amount of air was allowed to escape past the tail pipe through a small annular hole. A fuel tank of 81 gallons (368 litres) capacity was situated immediately behind the pilot and the cockpit was fitted with a number of experimental instruments, the standard blind-flying panel not being installed because of the lack of space.

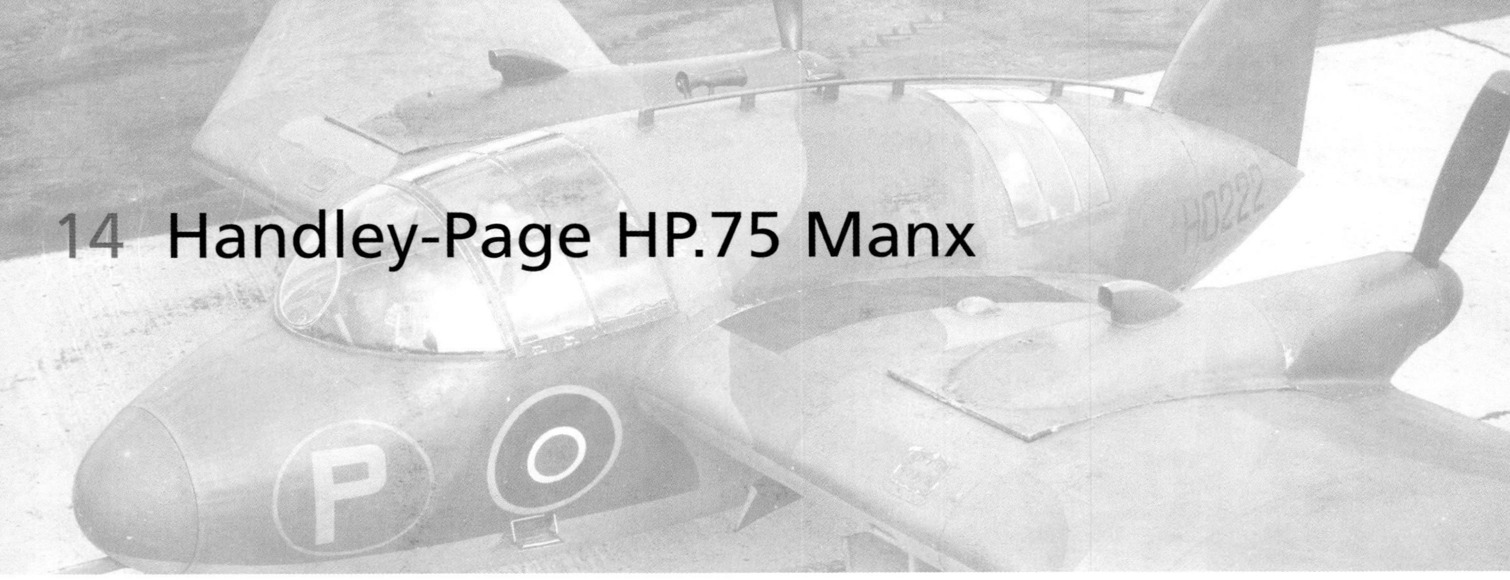

14 Handley-Page HP.75 Manx

Handley-Page HP.75 Manx

Type: Twin-Engine Two-Seat Tailless Research Aircraft

Powerplant: Two 140hp (104kW) de Havilland Gipsy Major II air-cooled inline engines

Span: 39ft 10in (12.14m)

Length: 18ft 3in (5.56m)

Gross Wing Area: 245sq.ft (22.79m²)

All-Up Weight: 4,131lb (1,874kg).

Rate of Climb: 555ft/min (169m/min) at 1,000ft (305m)

Maximum True Air Speed: 146.5mph (235.7km/h)

Ceiling: 10,470ft (3,190m)

Armament: None

Tailless aircraft have been built at almost every stage during the history of flight. A report written in early September 1943 by the Royal Aircraft Establishment's Tailless Aircraft Advisory Committee noted that they had flown reasonably well but had not in general held their own with other types (the Committee was formed in July 1943 to assess and provide information on tailless and tail-first aircraft). The reason was simple – the reduction of drag was not sufficient to outweigh the disadvantages introduced by the difficulties of trim, control and stability. Overall, there were two main arguments in favour of tailless aircraft. Their drag was low and in military types the field of fire to the rear was excellent. The saving in drag over conventional types was very little for small aircraft because of the relatively large body, but the saving increased as aircraft size increased. Also, the tailless type would lend itself to the fitting of gas turbine engines and thus enable full advantage to be taken of laminar flow wings.

Various methods of overcoming the difficulties associated with tailless types had been proposed, but as far as Great Britain was concerned there had been little forward progress since 1934 when development of the Westland Hill Pterodactyl had been abandoned. In fact since then only two small tailless aircraft had actually flown, a twin-engined Handley Page aircraft nicknamed the 'Manx' and a Muntz-Baynes glider. The Muntz-Baynes was better known as the Slingsby-Baynes Bat since Slingsby Sailplanes had built it. Mr L.E. Baynes was the chief designer at Alan Muntz Ltd and this was a one-third-scale' prototype for a larger Muntz design. A tail-first powered aircraft had also been built and flown by Phillips and Powis (which is the subject of Chapter Twenty-Three) but considerably more progress has been made in America, mainly by Northrop who had designed a tailless aircraft weighing 150,000lb (68,040kg) and which would become the XB-35 bomber prototype.

A project for a flying wing/tailless research aircraft was put together by Handley Page's designer Gustav Lachmann in 1936. It was nicknamed 'Manx' by the firm from at least the start of taxi trials, but the aircraft was not designated HP.75 within the company's project listing until 1945; the name was also made official at around the time it was shown to the press in September 1945. A theory to support the creation of the Manx was put forward in 1939. This was a concept for a large flying wing aircraft that would accompany the bomber stream (flying in daylight) at its rear to provide a defensive rearguard. Bombers were usually

General view of the Handley Page Manx taken late in its career.

Pictures taken in September 1942 at Radlett when the Manx was ready for taxi trials.

attacked from astern and several of these large flying wing aircraft would be present. The aircraft needed a short fuselage to permit two large gun turrets to be fitted (their short length was important from a CofG point of view) and these would contain Hispano cannon. No information has been found detailing the design of these large aircraft, which in essence were heavy defence fighters.

The Manx project was undertaken by a separate research department set up by Handley Page and Lachmann at Edgeware and in 1938 the task of building the scale model test airframe was passed to Dart Aircraft, a company based in Dunstable in Bedfordshire which had been responsible for the manufacture of a small number of ultra-light aeroplanes. However, Dart Aircraft had troubles producing the new type (primarily of a financial nature) and Handley Page had to get involved to sort things out and get the work completed. The finished airframe did not arrive at Radlett until just after the outbreak of war and the demands within the company for its Halifax bomber meant progress continued to be slow. Taxi trials were started on 29 February 1940 and high speed taxi trials followed on 5 March, but the aircraft did not respond well and at this time it was considered useless to try and make further attempts to get it to leave the ground. Pilot J.H. Cordes (who only ever taxied the Manx) reported that he felt "something might collapse" at any moment. That brought things to a stop for a long time, and then in March 1941 an inspection revealed a serious deterioration of the wing structure and another year's delay followed as the upper and lower wings had to be renewed.

After repairs and modifications (including the fitting of a central fin) were complete the aircraft was given a 'B' condition mark H-0222 (on the airframe it was written H0222). Taxi trials recommenced on 12 September 1942 but there were further difficulties. On one of the runs the aircraft bounced and soon after landing its nosewheel broke which left some damage to the fuselage. Repairs and a stronger undercarriage were required which brought another long holdup and taxying did not resume until 14 May 1943. After a main tyre failure new twin mainwheels were fitted and a maiden flight of ten minutes was finally achived on 25 June 1943 with Handley Page's chief test pilot Flt Lt James R. Talbot in the cockpit. The second and third flights were performed in August and October, but Flight 4 was not made until 29 June 1944 when a new

The Manx's initial engine installation. *Handley Page Association*

The rear-facing jettisonable hinged tailcone to the observer's position is shown in a photo made in October 1944. *Handley Page Association*

retractable main undercarriage and a fairing to cover the nosewheel and fork had been installed, which worked satisfactorily. An observer (E.A. Wright) was taken aloft for the first time the next day and these flights marked the start of by far the most intensive period of flying undertaken with the aircraft, with 14 flights in all completed by 5 December.

Test pilot Sqn Ldr Robert Kronfeld flew the Manx from Radlett on 4 and 10 November 1944 at a take-off weight (with the observer aboard) of 4,103lb (1,861kg). He observed that the aircraft flew starboard wing low and the recorded rates of climb were 555ft/min (169m/min) at 1,000ft (305m), 495ft/min (151m/min) at 2,000ft (610m) and 415ft/min (126m/min) at 3,000ft (915m). On an earlier flight he had recorded a cruise speed with the undercarriage up of 125mph (201km/h) at 1,700ft (518m), and with it fully down 108mph (174km/h) at 1,400ft (427m). Kronfeld was an Austrian Jew who after the rise of Nazism had become a British subject. He was a glider specialist, having been a pre-war champion and a sailplane designer (on 20 June 1931 he became the first man to fly a glider across the English Channel and then glide back on the same day).

On 6 December 1944 Kronfeld compiled a report summarising his flying in the Manx. He was originally called upon to give an opinion about the aircraft's lack of performance, which he initially put down to the fact that it had turned out to be more than 1,000lb (454kg) heavier than the estimated design weight. However, Godfrey Lee (who had been put in charge of Handley Page's Research Department once Lachmann, as a German citizen, had been interned for the duration of the war) had stated that the performance even at the present weight of 4,100lb (1,860kg) should be better than the approximately 130mph (209km/h) ASI obtained, but in fact position error measurements suggested that the corrected EAS would be 145mph (233km/h), which Kronfeld felt was not bad for an aircraft of this size fitted with two Gipsy Majors. However, there were possibly other factors behind the problem, concerning elevon angles, slots in the endplates and rudders (which were intended to minimise the shielding effect of the endplate on the elevons), aerodynamic losses through interference of engine cowlings, wing and fuselage, and the efficiency of the airscrew (the diameter of the airscrews was limited by ground clearance). Kronfeld suggested that fitting some fixed-pitch wooden airscrews (possibly four-bladers) might give a better performance and allow the airscrews to be further away from the trailing edge.

One problem brought about by the poor performance was the aircraft's low ceiling at this stage, which was insufficient to allow stalling and spinning tests to be carried out in reasonable safety. Indeed, the aircraft had all of the characteristics of a very underpowered one and, therefore, an engine failure during take-off and climb could easily be disastrous, and single-engine flight seemed out of the question at any time. More powerful engines were most desirable. From the longitudinal stability and manoeuvrability standpoint some pilots had experienced troubles with oscillation, but

Rare images of the Manx flying, possibly taken in June 1945. Note the retracted undercarriage. *Handley Page Association*

Kronfeld felt that the characteristics of a tailless aircraft were different to a normal type and their worries were generally unfounded. Whilst the HP.75's ailerons and rudder were comparable to normal aeroplane controls, there was something unusual in the reaction fore and aft which might easily be alarming to pilots inexperienced in such aircraft. This was their reaction to the unusually high speed at which tailless aircraft would obey elevator movements, the accelerations felt as a consequence and the feeling that the oscillations could become difficult to control if the stick was not held very steady.

What was required were measures to decrease the longitudinal manoeuvrability. A radical step already suggested was the fitting of a rider plane, which undoubtedly would reduce manoeuvrability and make the aircraft less sensitive to the CofG position, but in fact Kronfeld was rather against the rider plane. His main objection was that it would inevitably end up in a "front tail aircraft" (which as the drawing shows would have happened) and this would involve many complications in calculation and design and might easily be the cause of further unforeseen troubles. His experience in flying three other types of small tail first aeroplane had left him unfavourably impressed with their handling and their restricted view from the pilot's seat. Other possibilities would be to increase the sweepback, or reduce the size of the elevons (a move which he suggested should be tried) or to gear down the elevator control leaving the ailerons as they were, or to introduce some form of mechanical or hydraulic damping gear inserted in the control circuit of the elevator control.

Kronfeld closed by saying that: "Provided the damping of the quick period oscillation can be improved and more powerful engines fitted, the H-0222 should, because of its general good handling characteristics, make a good scale model of a large future transport or military type. The handling, apart from the shortcomings dealt with, is quite pleasant and normal in normal conditions of flight, glide and moderate turns. (Steeper turns and stalls have not been tried.) Compared with other tailless types, this aircraft is, to my mind as a prototype, a success in several ways and well worth while developing." He added that from all of the tailless types he had flown H-0222 was the only one which had a really satisfactory

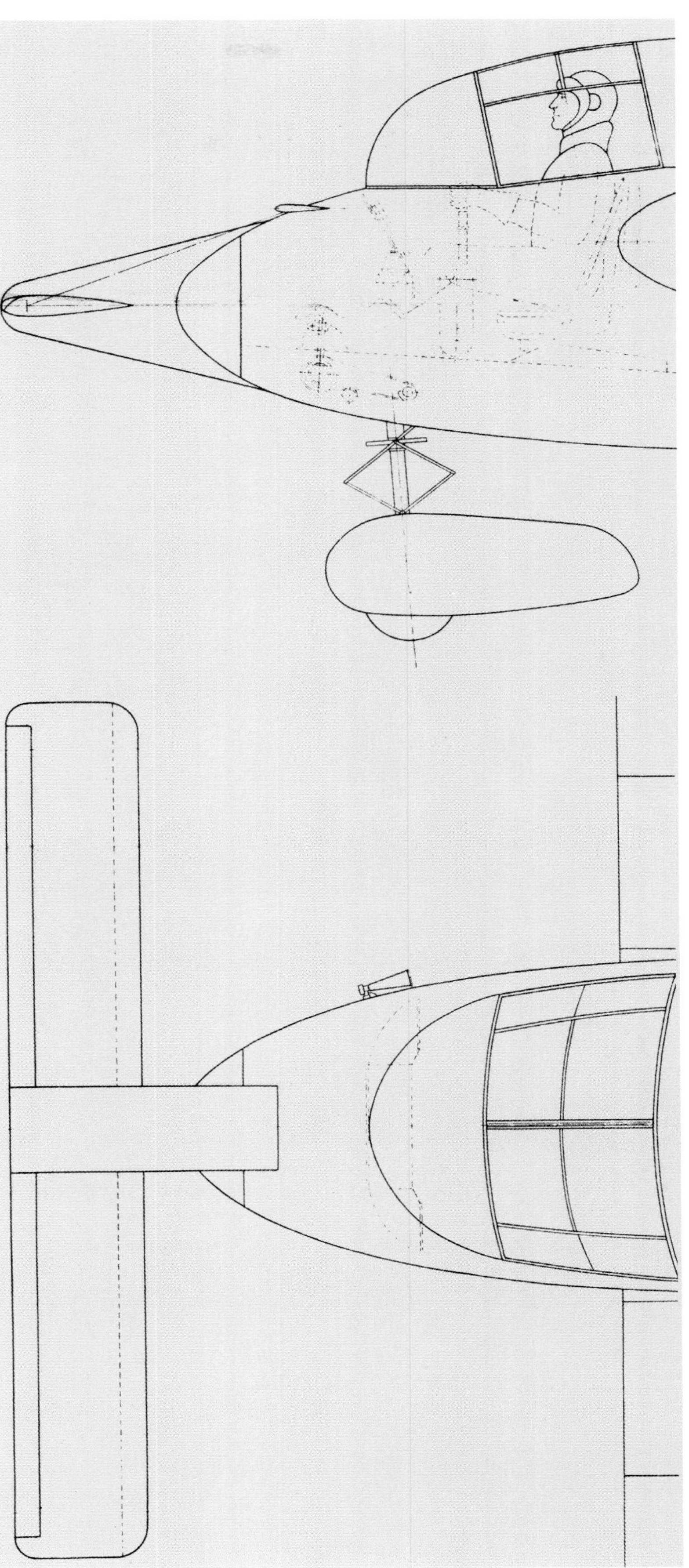

Manufacturer's drawing of the rider plane which was to be fitted to the Manx, but in the end the installation was never carried out.
Handley Page Association

The Manx pictured in October 1945 after the engine installation and spinners had been modified. Note the twin main wheels. A Handley Page Halifax A.Mk.IX is parked behind. *Handley Page Association/Phil Butler*

undercarriage. Apart from the fact that the springing of the main wheels was on the hard side, the present arrangement seemed very satisfactory from a handling point of view. Take-off and landing were easy and the behaviour in side wind take-offs and landings was better than with most orthodox aircraft of a similar weight and performance. He hoped that Handley Page, having gone a long way towards the solution of the problem of tailless aircraft, should make every effort to eliminate the existing faults of this type through an intense modification and test programme.

In September 1945 the HP.75 Manx was demonstrated to the press for the first time, photographs appearing in *Flight* for 11 October. The work of building the rider plane was sub-contracted to Percival Aircraft because they had skilled woodworking staff available when Handley Page did not, and the new surface was delivered in June 1945 but never taken into the air. Talbot had continued the flying programme during 1945 but, after he and 'Ginger' Wright were killed in the crash of the prototype Hermes airliner, Kronfeld took the Manx aloft for its final two flights (numbers 30 and 31) on 2 and 3 April 1946. On these sorties he was accompanied by observers Noel Brailsford and J. Steele and the pilot generally observed that: "...the machine seemed to be a considerably improved aircraft when compared with my impression when I last flew it", which had been before some modifications had been made. Defects were now found within the wooden airframe which in May saw it grounded. Vibration was one problem that helped bring an end to the programme because it caused fatigue in the bearings (although Kronfeld

A near contemporary of the HP.75, but later in timescale, was the General Aircraft GAL.56 glider. During 1943 a number of tailless projects were put forward by British aircraft firms but it was evident that there was not sufficient basic information to enable any designer to go ahead with confidence on a large aircraft of this type. Therefore MAP decided that experiments should be put in hand to obtain this information. Since the most serious problems were those of trim and control it was felt that tests in flight were most important and the first large piece of new research was based on two types of flying wing, one V-shaped and the other U-shaped, which were fitted to four identical glider fuselages designed and built by General Aircraft. These either had a U-shape wing or different V-shape wings with various angles of sweepback and they were built strictly to MAP requirements. Most of the flying programme took place after the war had ended, but the first GAL.56 glider (TS507) made its maiden flight on 17 January 1945. These aircraft proved very difficult to fly and TS507 killed its pilot (Sqn Ldr Kronfeld) in a crash on 12 February 1948.

described the level of vibration as "reasonable" during his last flights on the aircraft), and many glued joints in the wooden airframe had by now deteriorated. Throughout its career the Manx always experienced problems with engine cooling and with vibration through having two-blade propellers behind the wing. The aircraft was subsequently stored at Park Street, and then burnt in 1952.

Long before then it had been realised that un-escorted bombers could not survive in daylight and the large scale aircraft had been taken no further. The author is left with a feeling that it was rather a shame that the Manx was not tested more since its configuration may have supplied valuable data for the tailless aircraft proposals and projects that were produced after the war. Kronfeld must have felt the same but later Godfrey Lee did go on to create another new wing form in the crescent wing used by the Victor V-Bomber. However, by the time that aircraft flew Kronfeld had tragically died flying a tailless General Aircraft glider.

Structure

The HP.75 Manx was a small swept-winged tailless research aircraft built in wood and driven by two pusher propellers. It featured a short stocky fuselage, which had a small

The aircraft's de Havilland Gipsy Major II engine installation. *Handley Page Association*

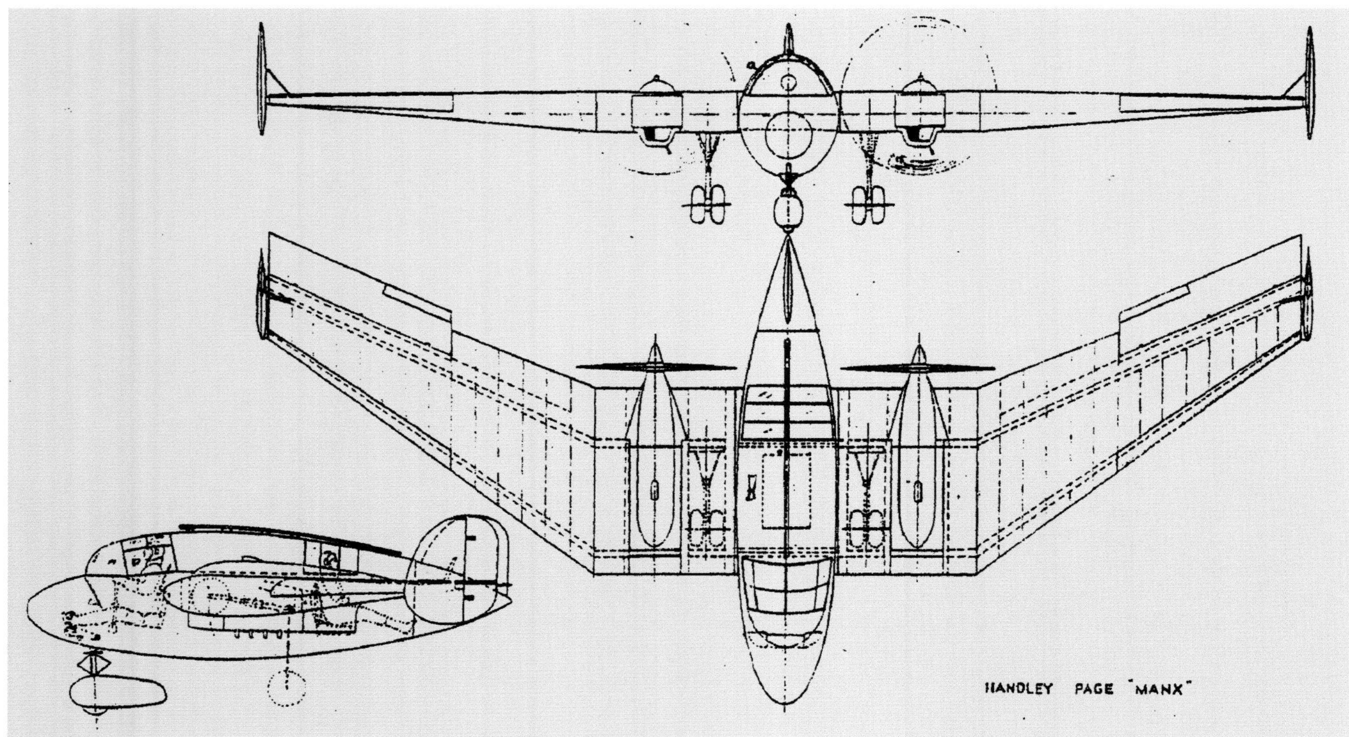

Original manufacturer's drawing of the HP.75 Manx. *Handley Page Association*

central fin to supplement its wingtip fins and rudders, and seating for a pilot forward and an observer towards the rear both with glazed canopies. To leave in an emergency the observer could jettison the tail cone. The engines were housed in the centre fuselage between the crew and these drove by means of flexible drive shafts pusher two-blade propellers of 6ft 2in (1.88m) diameter mounted in the straight wing centre section.

The swept and tapered outer wings had wingtip rudders and also on the outer wings were leading edge slots and trailing edge elevons, while control was conventional using ailerons. No flaps were fitted to this aircraft but, as noted above, there were plans to fit a forward rider plane which would trim out any moment changes caused by the large-chord flaps after they had been installed. At the start of its career the aircraft had pogo stick legs to its Dunlop tricycle undercarriage and suffered shimmy on the nose leg. The main wheels were later replaced while the rear engine nacelles were extended with spinners. In flight the mainwheels could be retracted but the nose leg remained extended and consequently was given a streamlined fairing over the wheel. A 15 gallon (68 litre) fuel load would give a flight time of one hour.

Another September 1942 photo showing the aircraft's extended-chord elevons, unfaired nose wheel and single main wheel. *Handley Page Association*

15 Hawker Hotspur

Hawker Hotspur

Type: Two-Seat Interceptor Turret Fighter

Powerplant: One 1,025hp (764kW) Rolls-Royce Merlin II liquid-cooled inline engine

Span: 40ft 6in (12.34m)

Length: 32ft 10.5in (10.02m)

Gross Wing Area: 261.6sq.ft (24.33m^2)

All-Up weight: 7,650lb (3,470kg) fully armed; 6,580lb (2,985kg) maximum flown by RAE

Rate of Climb: Time to 15,000ft (4,572m) approximately 10.5 minutes

Maximum Speed: 316mph (508km/h) at 15,000ft (4,572m)

Ceiling: Approximately 28,000ft (8,534m)

Armament: 4 x 0.303in (7.7mm) Browning machine-guns in turret, provision for 1 synchronised Vickers machine-gun on port side of fuselage

Hawker Aircraft is most remembered in the mid-1930s for its development of the superb Hurricane single-seat fighter which did so much to win the Battle of Britain. What often gets forgotten, however, is that two other monoplane combat aircraft were produced by the company at the same time – the Henley light bomber which was actually used as a target tug, and the Hotspur two-seat fighter of which the prototype K8309 was the only example to be constructed. As such these aircraft allowed the company to break away from its long tradition of producing biplane types.

The Hotspur's design began as a tender made in August 1935 to specification F.9/35, against which the Boulton Paul Defiant was also ordered. F.9/35 required a new two-seat type to replace the Hawker Demon and the enclosed turret would enable a gunner to operate his guns at speeds of 300mph (483km/h) or more (i.e. the gunner was completely sheltered from the wind), something not possible in the past with open cockpit fighters. The prototype Defiant K8310 first flew on 11 August 1937 and was followed by a long production run. By comparison the Hotspur rather fell behind – prototype drawings for the aircraft with metal wings were produced during 1936 and 1937 and these were completed in 1938. The Hotspur's construction began in the Kingston Experimental Shops in 1937, K8309 having been ordered against contract 453461/35 of December 1935, but a second machine (serial K8261 to the same contract) was cancelled and plans for the production of the type by Avro under Specification 17/36 were abandoned in 1937.

The Hotspur was essentially a modified version of the Henley, although from most angles it did look quite different. The fighter's fuselage was slimmer (which reduced the span) and the rear fuselage was lower which gave a 'straighter' shape compared to the Henley's rather curvier body; the fin was also larger. A January 1938 report from Gp Capt Robert Saundby, making use of wind tunnel data, noted that: "There is really nothing to choose between the Defiant and the Hotspur in performance". But he added that: "Whereas Boulton Paul have been most enthusiastic about their design, Hawkers have shown less interest and the flying trials of their first prototype are not likely to take place before the end of May." In fact K8309 was first flown on 14 June 1938 from Brooklands in the hands of Hawker test pilot Flt Lt Philip G. Lucas, but since the decision to abandon production had

This photo of prototype Hotspur K8309 in its original form with a dummy turret fitted is one of a series taken at Brooklands in July 1938.

been taken by this time there was no attempt to upgrade the prototype to full military standard; the wooden turret and ballast was the closest the aircraft ever came to carrying weaponry. In 1939 the wooden turret mock-up was removed and replaced at first by a faired covering and then by a new extended rear cockpit to cover the observer. The aircraft had originally been given a natural metal/silver dope finish but it was now painted with camouflaged upper surfaces and yellow undersides.

Three different pilots subsequently flew K8309 at Farnborough as part of a set of handling trials and they found that a tendency to swing to the left on take-off persisted until a speed of about 130mph (209km/h) had been achieved. Acceleration in the air was slow and a lot of right rudder was required when the speed dropped to 120mph (193km/h). The elevator trimming tab was not very effective at low speeds either and the surface was sluggish at low speeds, but at 240mph (386km/h) the elevator was reasonably light and effective. However, the ailerons were described as very light and effective at all speeds and effective down to the stall, while the rudder was effective but very heavy which meant that the harmony of the controls was spoilt. The stall

Despite flying until February 1942, it appears that few or no air-to-air photos of the Hotspur were ever made.

The Boulton Paul Defiant, in fact the prototype K8310. Unlike the Hotspur, the Defiant was produced in large numbers, but was never regarded as a great success.

with flaps up occurred at 74mph (119km/h) and with flaps down at 61mph (98km/h), in both cases without warning outside of the attitude of the aircraft itself.

Once the appraisal of the Hotspur's flying characteristics had been completed, the aircraft was employed by RAE on trials to examine new flap and dive brake configurations, the work continuing for over two years from 1939 until February 1942. On 12 February 1942 K8309 had to make a forced landing on Yately Common in Hampshire when pilot Flt Lt W.D.B.S. Davie was performing some gliding tests for a variable-drag flap. After it had been throttled back for the aircraft to perform a prolonged glide the Merlin engine would not restart and Davie had no option but to 'land'. Fortunately he was unhurt and there no was fire. Despite the engine and airframe being considered as repairable, the effort that this would entail could not be justified and so the Hotspur's quiet career came to a close. That the type was not put into production was in part due to the limited capacity available for quantity production of additional new designs – the much more important Hurricane had Hawker itself fully occupied while Gloster Aircraft, a sister company within Hawker Siddeley, had been given production of the Henley. However, the relative lack of success of the Defiant as a fighter compared to the Hurricane, and concept of the turret fighter as a whole which wartime experience showed was flawed, suggests that taking the Hotspur no further was probably a wise move.

This image from August 1941 shows K8309 after the turret had been faired over and the aircraft had been camouflaged and fitted with long canopy. *Phil Butler*

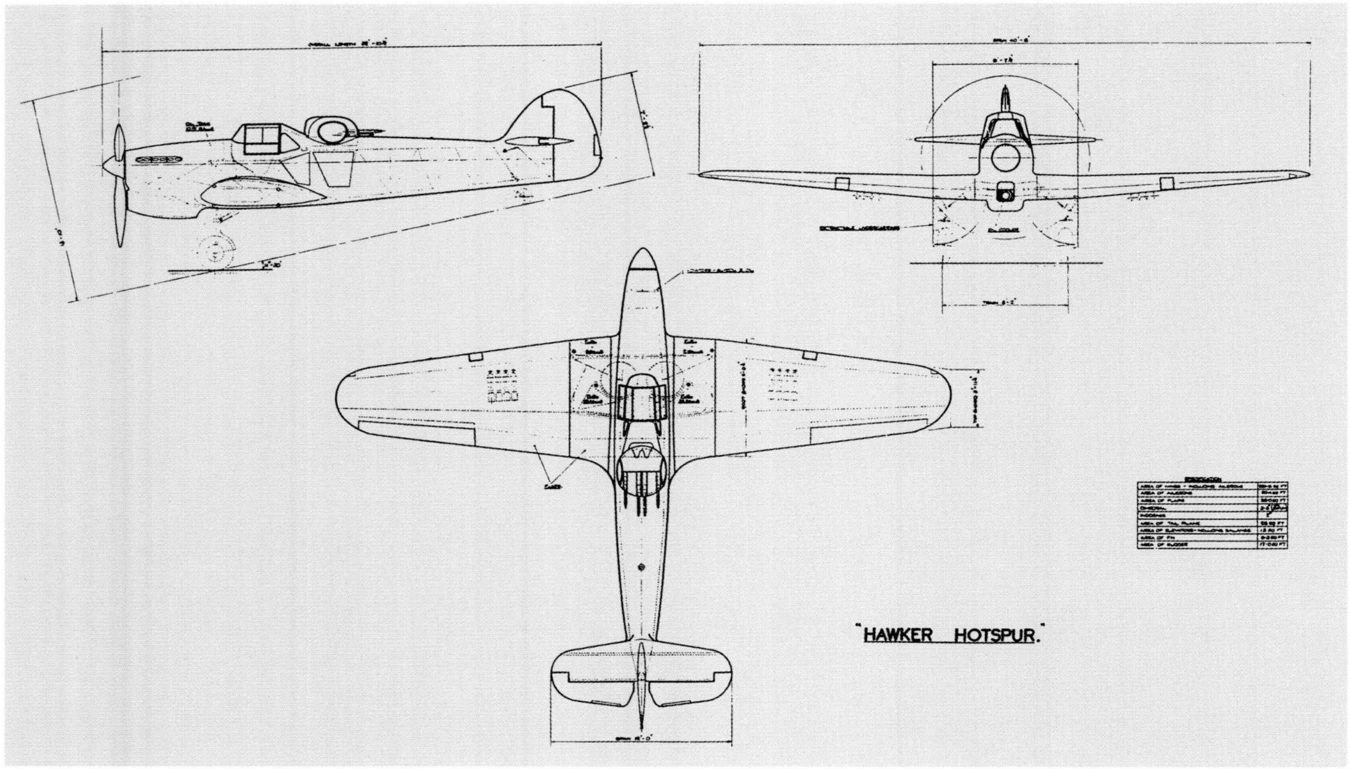

Hawker drawing showing how the Hotspur would have looked with its fully armed four-gun turret in position.

Structure

The Hotspur's fuselage structure was similar to the company's Hurricane single-seat fighter, and the outer wings were interchangeable with the Hurricane and the Henley light bomber to help with the standardisation of spare parts and ease of quantity production (but without the Hurricane's wing guns of course). Construction was generally all-metal using tubular frames, the wings had stressed skin but the rear fuselage and control surfaces were fabric-covered. Split trailing edge flaps were fitted together with a Hurricane-type inward retracting undercarriage, and the tail unit and airscrew were also similar to the Henley and Hurricane. The Merlin II used a glycol radiator mounted in a similar manner to the Henley and the engine was fitted with a de Havilland three-blade two-position propeller. The machine guns were to be housed in a power-driven fully enclosed Nash & Thompson turret in the rear cockpit, the pilot's cockpit sloping down to the turret. A plan to install a Vickers machine gun in the wing appears to have been an idea from Hawker since it was not required by the covering specification. The rudder was horn-balanced and the elevators were mass-balanced with an inset horn balance and trimming tabs. After the removal of the turret the cockpit was extended to cover the observer's seat.

Manufacturer's drawing showing how the Hotspur prototype appeared after its turret had been removed.

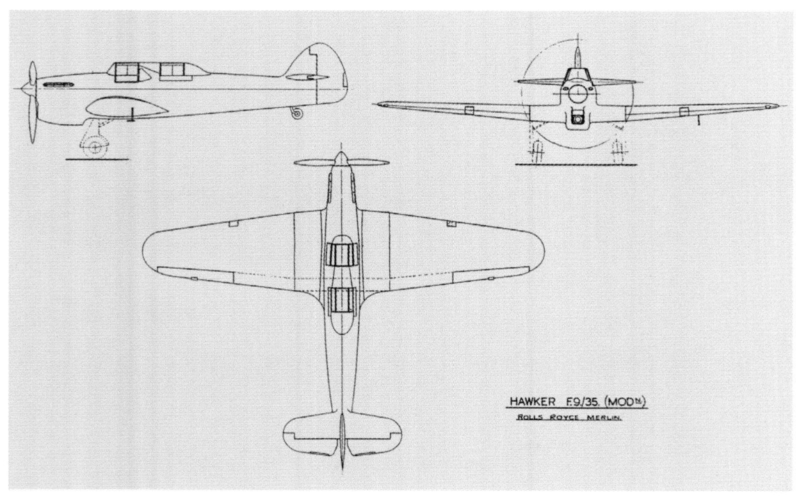

16 Hawker Tornado

Hawker Tornado

Type: Single-Seat Fighter

Powerplant: One Rolls-Royce Vulture liquid-cooled X-type engine

Span: 42ft 0in (12.80m)

Length: 32ft 6.5in (9.92m)

Gross Wing Area: 283sq.ft (26.32m^2)

All-Up-Weight: Vulture production aircraft 10,600lb (4,808kg)

Armament: 12 x 0.303in (7.7mm) machine-guns

Performance: A variety of figures are given for the Tornado both by primary sources, or published sources which refer to original documents. Therefore, it seems best to list a selection:

P5219 with a 1,760hp (1,312kW) Rolls-Royce Vulture II had a maximum speed of 396.5mph (638km/h) at 20,800ft (6,340m), and time to reach 20,000ft (6,096m) was 6.6 minutes.

Estimated figures with a 1,790hp (1,335kW) Vulture III installed indicated 413mph (665km/h) at 22,000ft (6,706m) and a ceiling of 34,000ft (10,363m).

R7936 with a 1,980hp (1,476kW) Vulture V: 402mph (647km/h) at 21,800ft (6,645m) and 6.9 minutes to reach 20,000ft (6,096m). The maximum altitude recorded while flying from Langley was 29,600ft (9,022m).

The 2,120hp (1,581kW) Bristol Centaurus IV fitted in HG641 (which produced an over-powered aeroplane) gave a reported performance of 393mph (632km/h) at 18,000ft (5,486m) and a ceiling of 32,500ft (9,906m). However, data dated 18 December 1941 taken from official tests with the Centaurus CE.4.SM at 10,600lb (4,808kg) weight gave a top speed of 430mph (692km/h) at 24,000ft (7,315m) and a service ceiling of 34,500ft (10,516m). Ten minutes were required to reach 20,000ft (6,096m).

The Hawker Tornado should perhaps have appeared in the Appendix, since it is essentially a Hawker Typhoon with a different engine and the Typhoon was built in large numbers. However, the engine arrangement featured different cooling systems, and then one prototype was used to test an altogether different engine – and it is an interesting story. The Typhoon became one of the first British cannon-armed fighters, and Specification F.18/37 of 9 March 1938 which led to it requested a top speed of not less than 400mph (644km/h) at 15,000ft (4,572m), a ceiling of not less than 35,000ft (10,668m) and maximum weight of 12,000lb (5,443kg). The key for the new type was a new power unit – the Napier Sabre or Rolls-Royce Vulture, two engines which offered great increases in power over earlier types. Hawker's proposals won the subsequent design competition and orders were placed in December 1938 to Contract B.815124/38 for two prototypes each of what for a period were called the 'R' and 'N' fighters (Rolls-Royce Vulture and Napier Sabre respectively). However, at the time the two engines were in the experimental stage and nobody foresaw that both would have troubled development programmes, which in the case of the Vulture proved fatal and thereby brought an end to the Tornado. Indeed, one wonders if

Pictures of the first Hawker Tornado prototype P5219 in its original form with the ventral radiator. At this time the aircraft had an incorrect camouflage scheme on its undersides and the Temperate Land Scheme for fighter types had also been applied on the upper surfaces, albeit incorrectly.

the Vulture was ever likely to have had a successful career since an Air Staff memo from as early as 4 January 1939 noted that: "...the Vulture is ahead of the Sabre, but the Sabre does promise advantages in horsepower, a better shape and therefore a better engine, and therefore a better aeroplane".

Design work on the 'N' Sabre aircraft actually began on 5 April 1937 and the first drawings were submitted to the Ministry in July, around a year before the F.18/37 design competition. The layout drawings for the 'R' Vulture fighter were commenced in October and wind tunnel models of both 'N' and 'R' fighters went to RAE for testing in mid-April 1938. On 30 August 1938 Hawker was informed of its success in winning the competition and the Mock-Up Conference for both types was held at Kingston on 16 December. The two were to have interchangeable centre fuselages, rear monocoque, tail units and wings but with alternative engine mountings to suit the Vulture and Sabre respectively. An armament of twelve Browning machine-guns was initially specified by F.18/37 as an alternative to the cannon-armed fighter which became the Westland Whirlwind, but subsequently this was replaced on most Typhoons by four 20mm cannon. However, some sources indicate that the thick wing used on these fighters was designed to take cannon from the start. The names Tornado and Typhoon were given to the 'R' and 'N' fighters in August and on 6 September 1939 respectively, but delays with the Sabre meant that it was the Tornado prototype P5219 that flew first.

P5219 with a Vulture II engine was transported from its birthplace in the Experimental Shop at Kingston to Langley on 31 July 1939 and made its first engine run on 18 September (the guns were not fitted). Taxi trials began on 1 October and the first flight was made on 6 October from Langley with Hawker test pilot

This colour scheme was rectified at a later date together with the addition of the normal large yellow 'P' on the fuselage sides.

P5219 is seen in its second form with the radiator mounted underneath the engine.

Flt Lt Philip G. Lucas in the cockpit. However, thanks to buffeting caused by having the radiator bath located amidships beneath the mainplane, the preliminary handling trials proved unsuccessful and the radiator had to be moved further forward. Vibration was experienced due to the onset of compressibility in the region of the ventral radiator when speeds were approaching 400mph (644km/h), and was shown by both flight and wind tunnel tests, so it was decided to move the radiator to directly underneath the nose (the Typhoon had a chin radiator from the start). The first flight with the new position was made on 6 December 1939 and it was found that problems with engine cooling had also now been eased by the modification, but the aircraft's directional stability was unsatisfactory. During the summer of 1940 the rudder area on P5219 was increased to improve the directional problem, prior to which a maximum speed of 384mph (618km/h) had been recorded in March 1940 but with some control instability. This latter modification was also made to the Typhoon prototype and the first flight of P5219 with a larger fin was made by Lucas on 16 May 1940 (which also proved that a straight line take-off was now possible).

Tailwheel doors were added soon afterwards to further improve the airflow underneath the aircraft. Shortly afterwards P5219 went to the Rolls-Royce airfield at Hucknall for more trials work on the airframe, and it returned to Langley in July after being fitted with a Rotol C/S Schwarz three-bladed 13.2ft (4.02m) diameter airscrew. It was also now fitted out to receive its twelve Browning machine-guns. On 27 March 1941 P5219 made a first flight with a Vulture V, but in July all flying on Vulture V engines had to be suspended owing to fractures being found in connecting-rod bolts. On 23 June 1943 the aircraft joined de Havilland for trials duties, and indeed throughout its life P5219 was employed on test work until it was Struck Off Charge and "destroyed" at Hawkers during August 1943.

Lucas took the second Tornado P5224 on its maiden flight on 5 December 1940, the trip having been delayed by the programme's loss of priority described shortly. The second aircraft had the radiator in the forward position, a production Vulture II installed and additional window panels to improve the view to the rear. P5212, the first Typhoon, went to Langley on 21 January 1940, its Sabre engine was run for

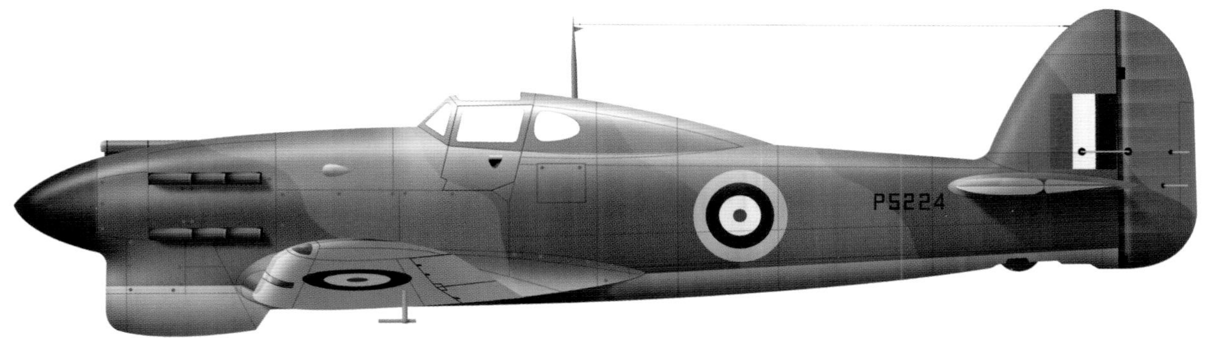

Tornado P5224 had the chin radiator from the outset and extra window panels behind the cockpit. *Tim Brown*

Rear view of the second Hawker Typhoon prototype P5216.

the first time on 1 February, and it first flew with a de Havilland 14.0ft (4.27m) Hydromatic airscrew in place on 24 February 1940. The second prototype Typhoon P5216 armed with four cannon (P5212 had twelve machine guns) first flew on 3 May 1941. However, for a period there were more Tornados available than Typhoons on test flying and much of the general aerodynamic work performed by the Vulture aircraft was also vital to the Sabre aircraft's programme. Another pilot to fly P5219 was Flt Lt Dick Reyell, while Flying Officer Gordon Seth-Smith flew P5224 and R7936 (below) – both of these pilots spent time on attachment to Hawker.

P5224 went to A&AEE at Boscombe Down for a brief period in October 1941 having been fitted with a Vulture V (during April it was decided to fit Vulture V engines in all Tornados from the start of production). At a take-off weight of 10,690lb (4,849kg) its handling was described as indistinguishable from the Typhoon, the stall in the clean condition came at 82mph (132km/h) and with the flaps and undercarriage down at 61mph (98km/h). A&AEE's report noted that had an extra pound of engine boost been

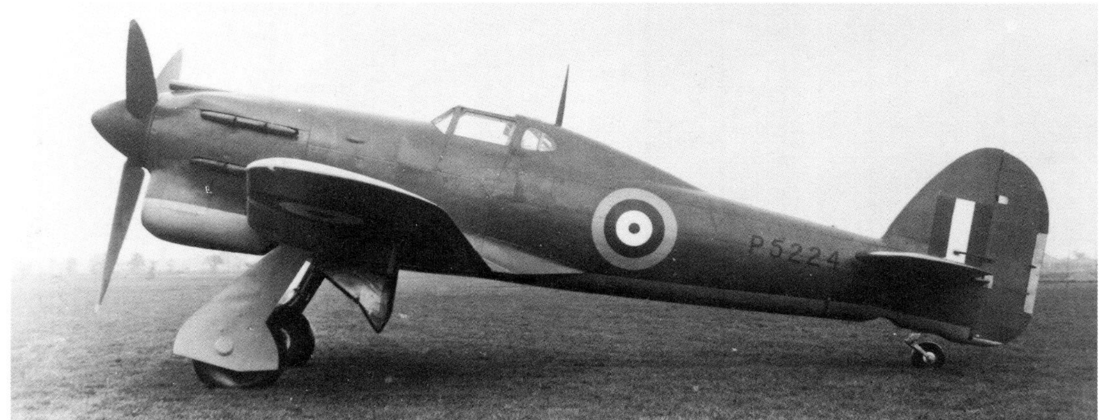

A comparison in shapes (1). Side angle views of the second Typhoon P5216 and the second Tornado P5224. The Tornado now has the larger rudder. Note the extra row of exhaust stubs required for the Vulture.

available then this aircraft could have reached a top speed on the level of over 400mph (644km/h). Following its visit to Boscombe, in December 1941 P5224 moved on to Farnborough for further trials and it stayed there on RAE charge until April 1943 when it went into store at No. 20 MU at Aston Down. In all it made 46 flights from Farnborough which were mainly concerned with diving trials and "rear-view mirror drag". P5224 was finally cut up at the Salvage Centre at No 50 MU at Oxford, having been moved there on 20 September 1944.

On 10 July 1939 a production order was placed for 1,000 aircraft from Hawker – 500 with the Vulture engine and 500 with the Sabre. The first batch of Tornados was to be constructed at Kingston, but on 23 October 1940 the Tornado programme was transferred to Avro since that company had experience with the Vulture and its problems (the engine also powered Avro's Manchester bomber). Such high expectations for long production runs for the Tornado were based on the fact that the engine was expected to be available more freely than the Sabre. Some Tornados were to have cannon, but all cannon-armed Tornados were subsequently cancelled on 17 February 1941 when the decision was taken to give the limited number of these weapons currently available all to Typhoons. In March 1940 the decision had been made to manufacture the four-cannon wings at Gloster and twelve-machine-gun wings at Kingston, but at Whitsun 1940 the priority given to the combined Tornado/Typhoon programme was removed due to the critical situation of the war, and to enable Hurricane output to be accelerated. This move held up the ordering of materials and arranging of sub-contracting and on 12 June Hawker chief Sydney Camm wrote to the DTD (N.E. Rowe) expressing the opinion that the Tornado and Typhoon should not have been stopped. He added that they should proceed immediately, and after long discussions with the Ministry in July the programme was reinstated.

The cannon fighter in service. Hawker Typhoon Mk.IA EK183 is seen on the strength of No 56 Squadron.

A comparison in shapes (2). Nose angle views of the only production Tornado R7936 and a production Typhoon with its four 20mm cannon armament.

right: Avro-built Tornado R7936 with contra-rotating propeller fitted, photographed at Staverton, Rotol's test aerodrome.

Below: Close up of R7936's contra-prop installation. This de Havilland photo is dated 2 February 1943.

Contract 121248/39 covered Avro's Tornado production but only R7936 to R7938 were to be produced before this was cancelled. Avro fitted a Vulture V into the first production Tornado, but the Vulture suffered from persistent connecting-rod fractures and its career record in the Manchester proved to be appalling. Finally, on 15 October 1941 the engine's development was halted in a move which put also paid to any production plans for the Tornado, and Rolls-Royce was allowed to concentrate on its better and much more reliable Merlin and Griffon engines. In fact on 28 August Camm had suggested that the Tornado should be dropped because he considered that no aeroplane designed around the Vulture V could compete in performance with an aeroplane designed around the Rolls-Royce Merlin 60. All work on the Tornado development and production programme was stopped on 15 October. However, R7936 had first flown at Avro's Woodford airfield on 29 August 1941. It was similar in appearance to P5224 but lacked the rear window panels and two days later it was at Langley where it was flown by Philip Lucas. During the autumn it was also flown by some service pilots who, apart from the view to the rear, liked the aircraft a lot in terms of its performance and handling.

The second and third production machines R7937 (at Woodford) and R7938 (despatched to Rolls-Royce to assist with Vulture development) were never brought to flying standard. But for some time R7936 found employment as an engine and airscrew test bed, going first to Rolls-Royce on 8 March 1942 to have the Vulture modified to drive a contra-rotating propeller. In late 1941 the first completed contra-rotating propeller was delivered from Rotol to Rolls-Royce at Derby and it was tested on a Vulture in February 1942. On 21 September R7936 joined Rotol at Staverton for tests with six-blade contra-props and on 21 December it went to de Havilland Engines at Hatfield in the same role. It moved to Hawker's airfield at Langley on 25 March 1943 but was back at Hatfield on 21 January 1944. Hawker's wartime notes state that the contra-prop was found to have a marked destabilising effect on the aircraft. R7936 was finally delivered to No. 43 Group (Maintenance Command) to be scrapped in April 1944.

A preliminary scheme for a long-range Tornado was forwarded to the Ministry by Hawker on 5 March 1940. Then during June 1940 Hawker began work on the design of a Wright Duplex Cyclone engine installation for the Tornado and the drawings were completed on 4 July. An engine was delivered to Hawker during October and in January 1941 a letter was received from the Ministry stating that this American engine was to be installed in a Tornado prototype and in production. However, on 9 July 1941 MAP suspended all work on the Wright Duplex Cyclone installation without any hardware having been flown.

The installation of a Bristol Centaurus engine in the Tornado was first discussed in January 1940. On 24 April Camm told Rowe of a move to make a trial installation which would necessitate the building of an additional prototype airframe, although it was 20 September before the firm received confirmation to go ahead. By mid-December a new centre fuselage was being built for this airframe while the rear fuselage had been taken from the production line and an existing set of Tornado wings were to be fitted. In November a Centaurus mock-up installation was applied to P5224 before that prototype received its Vulture, and Contract SB.21392/C.23(a) was issued to cover the new aircraft. The completed prototype was taken to Langley on 22 September 1941. However, owing to the dropping of the Tornado in October the Ministry renamed the aircraft the 'Centaurus-Typhoon', but this was not agreed to by Hawker since the fuselage was still very similar to the Tornado and it would not be possible to make a similar installation in a Typhoon fuselage. Unlike the Sabre, the Vulture installation could not be mounted over the front wing-spar connecting structure. In fact the adoption of the Centaurus in place of the Vulture had not been a simple procedure – the engine mounting and centre fuselage had to be completely rebuilt.

The first flight of HG641 was made by Philip Lucas on 23 October 1941 with a Centaurus IV CE.4.SM and a three-blade Rotol constant-speed propeller in position. The project was really part of the background work that would lead to the Centaurus-powered Hawker Tempest II fighter and HG641 had no guns. Thanks to vibration, however, the early flights were unsatisfactory and it was thought that the problem came from disturbed airflow caused by having the exhaust pipe in close proximity to the cooler fairing and wing undersurface. Modifications were thus made to the exhaust collector ring, and the single exhaust pipe (on the port side) was re-set to an angle of 20° above the thrust line, but the changes brought no improvement. Therefore, HG641 was

Walk-around views of the last Hawker Tornado, the Bristol Centaurus test bed HG641, taken at Langley in October 1941 in its original form. Note the three-bladed propeller and the exhaust pipe beneath the cowling.

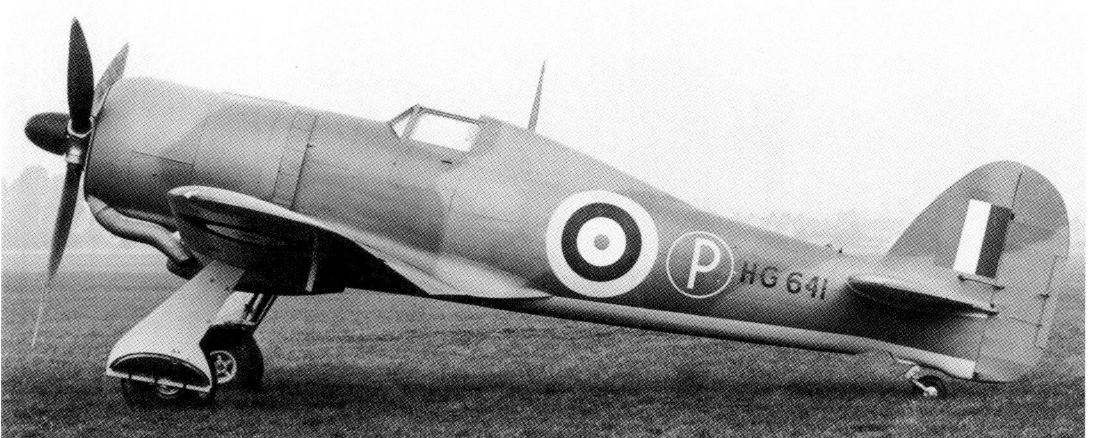

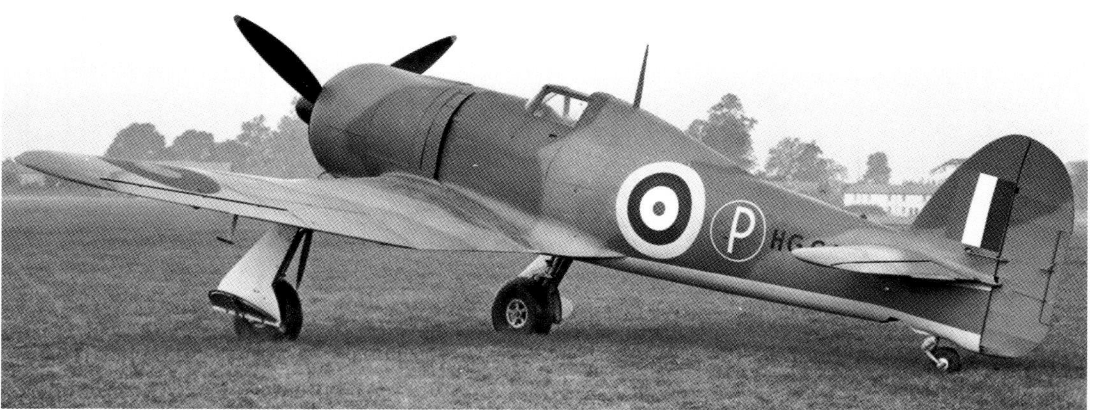

refitted at Kingston with a redesigned engine cowling and exit areas for the cooling gills. In addition an enlarge spinner now fully enclosed the propeller hub. The refitted airframe, which also had a new engine with a two-speed supercharger, was returned to Langley in the middle of November but the first flight proved to be very short after fumes and smoke found their way into the cockpit. Oil had collected in the under panel and was heated by the exhaust pipe immediately beneath, so deflector plates had to be fitted to the exhaust pipe to cure the new problem. HG641 passed into the hands of Bristol Engines at Filton on 3 February 1943 (by which time it had a four-blade Rotol propeller) where it was used in the Centaurus development programme. In August 1944 this last Tornado was delivered to 43 Group (Maintenance Command) for scrapping.

The production serials allocated to Tornados were R7936-R7975, R7992-R8036, R8049-R8091, R8104-R8150 and R8172-R8197, 201 aircraft in all to be built by Avro at Chadderton. Further orders followed for

HG641 was later fitted with a four-bladed propeller and a much-modified cooling arrangement with a deeper lower section ahead of and blended into the wing. The line of six gun ports in the wing identifies the use of a Typhoon Mk.1A airframe. This picture, again taken at Langley, was made in November 1942.

another 200 Tornados under Contract B.97616/40 (X1056-X1090, X1103-X1117, X1166-X1195, X1220-X1264, X1297-X1326 and X1343-X1387 all to be built by Cunliffe Owen at Eastleigh), and 360 more to Contract Acft/944 (EG708-EG747, EG763-EG801, EG819-EG845, EG860-EG897, EG915-EG959, EG974-EG994, EH107-EH156, EH171-EH211, EH228-EH261 and EH280-EH304 for manufacture by Avro's Yeadon factory at Leeds).

With the problems surrounding the Vulture engine the Tornado was never likely to reach service, although it is understood that relatively little engine trouble was experienced by the Tornado. It was the Manchester bomber that suffered repeated Vulture engine failures, usually in climbing flights with heavy loads (prototype P5219 did, however, experience a failure in the air on 31 July 1940 and was damaged during the subsequent forced landing). Despite the Typhoon suffering development problems as well, the Tornado's sister aircraft entered service in September 1941 and eventually over 3,300 examples were built, the type recording a hugely impressive service career after reliability problems with the Napier Sabre had been cured. Alongside the Hurricane and Typhoon, and the Tempest and Sea Fury that followed, the Tornado gets rather forgotten in the list of Hawker piston-engine monoplane fighters, but it was a valuable design and the few airframes that did fly contributed a lot of important trials and research work in a wide field of experiment.

Structure

The Hawker Tornado had two-spar all-metal wings that were interchangeable with the Typhoon. They utilised stressed skin construction, there was no centre section and each wing was attached to the fuselage by four lugs – two per spar. The forward half of the fuselage had a composite structure with a braced tubular framework in steel and light alloy while the rear portion aft of the cockpit was monocoque with light alloy frames of stringers and formers; the structure was covered by metal skins. The rear end of the rear fuselage was built separately and had an integral fin and the tail unit was covered in stressed-skin. Only the rudder was fabric covered. Again the rear fuselage was interchangeable with the Typhoon, but to accommodate the Vulture engine the Tornado front fuselage had to be extended forward by 12in (30.48cm) while the wings were located approximately 3in (7.62cm) lower on the fuselage sides. The twelve machine-guns were to be mounted six per wing outside the propeller disc and the aircraft used a Hawker Hurricane-type undercarriage. There is no evidence to indicate that any Tornado actually carried its guns but in some cases provision appears to have been made to fit them. For the Centaurus engine the airframe was unchanged from when a Vulture was in position.

17 Hawker P.1005

Hawker P.1005

(Brochure figures unless stated)

Type: Three-Seat High Speed Bomber

Powerplant: Two 2,180hp (1,626kW) Napier Sabre IV (NS.8SM) liquid-cooled inline engines (alternative two Bristol Centaurus radials)

Span: 70ft 0in (21.34m)

Length: 54ft 0in (16.46m)

(Fighter: Length approx 51ft 0in [15.54m])

Gross Wing Area: 677sq.ft (62.96m^2)

Flying Weight: 34,000lb (15,422kg)

(Ministry assessment – 33,710lb [15,291kg])

Rate of Climb: 10.5 minutes to 20,000ft (6,096m)

Maximum Speed: 415mph (668km/h) at 24,000 ft (7,315m)

(Ministry assessment – 400mph [644km/h] at 25,000ft [7,620m])

(With Centaurus 390mph [628km/h])

(With high altitude version of Sabre – 430mph [692km/h] at 36,500ft [11,125m])

Service Ceiling: 34,000ft (10,363m)

(Ministry assessment – 28,500ft [8,687m])

Armament:

Bomber: 4 x short 1,000lb (454kg), 2 x 2000lb (907kg), 2 x 1,900lb (862kg) or 1 x 4000lb (1,814kg) bomb. Some documents indicate 2 x 0.303in (7.7mm) machine-guns in nose

Fighter: 6 x 20mm cannon

Both: 4 x 0.303in (7.7mm) machine-guns in optional turret

For the Hawker Aircraft Company the period 1935 to 1966 embraced the start of the monoplane age with the Hurricane through to the death of its chief designer Sir Sydney Camm. With the exception of the Henley day bomber of 1937, all of the company's designs from those years which reached hardware were either fighters or at least were devoted to the development of fighter type aircraft. Even the jet-powered P.1127 and Kestrel experimental V/STOL prototypes of the 1960s were prepared to some extent with the advance of fighter technology in mind. Of course many of the firm's production aircraft were duly adapted for fighter-bomber/ground attack/strike duties (dependent on the role title at the time), but the Henley was the only Hawker bomber design from this period to reach production (the modest numbers built were actually used as target tugs). Even more curious perhaps, Hawker's penchant for fighters ensured that no twin-engine proposal from Kingston during those 30 plus years ever reached construction. However, had events during the 1941-42 period gone differently then neither of these 'records' would have been established.

In late 1940 Hawker schemed a project for a high speed light bomber called the P.1005 which (ultimately) was to be fitted with two Napier Sabre IV engines (at the time the Sabre was a promising new engine in which the Ministry was showing great interest). The project was started because it was felt most strongly that the RAF needed a new type of aircraft which could be developed either as a high speed bomber or a high speed long range fighter, particularly with a heavy offensive armament for the night fighter role. The value of high speed was that it decreased the time the aircraft spent over enemy territory, thereby increasing the safety of its crew and making

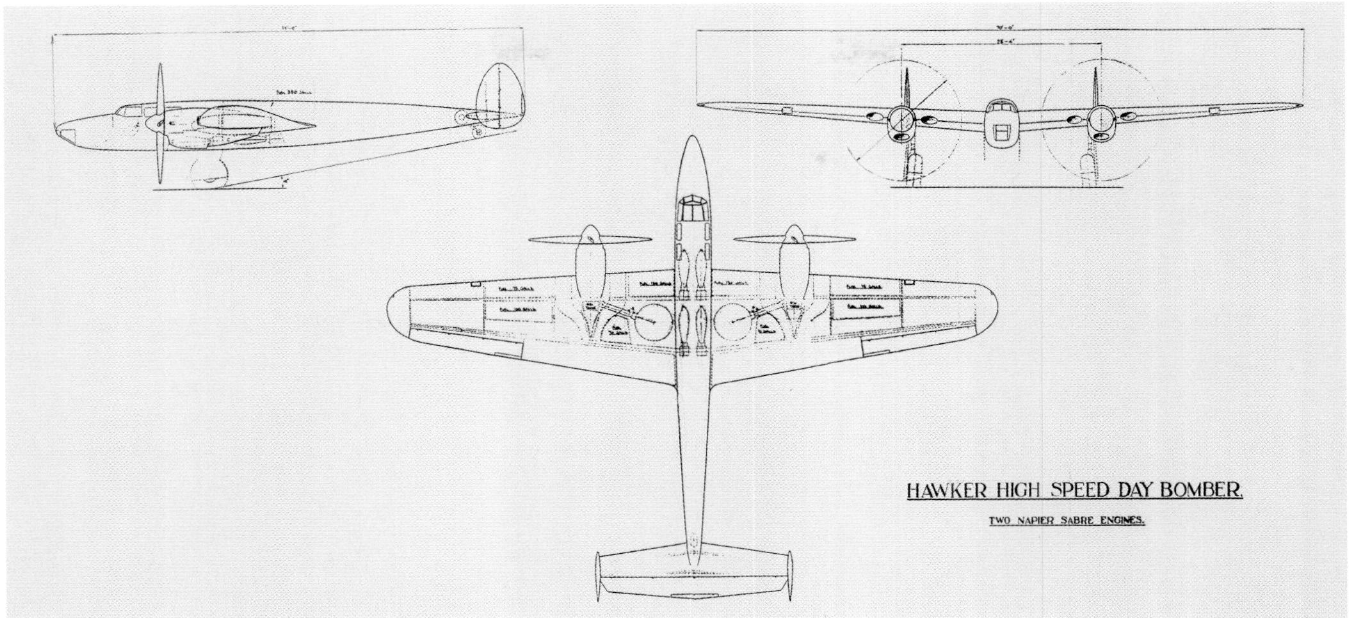

The original general arrangement drawing for the Hawker P.1005 high-speed day bomber.

daylight raiding deep into enemy territory possible. The speed and range combination would also permit operations to be carried out during the short summer nights when the slower heavy bombers could not operate. In addition, the production and maintenance advantages gained by using the same basic airframe for two types could be immense.

The design would be satisfactory, however, only if its speed exceeded 400mph (644km/h) and Hawker felt that the experience gained with its Typhoon single-engined fighter could be used in developing this aeroplane. The P.1005 design showed no defensive armament but provision was in place for a circular 41in (104cm) diameter retractable power-operated turret in the dorsal position which, if required, would contain four 0.303in (7.7mm) machine-guns with 1,000 rounds per gun. The turret and its guns were designed to retract into the fuselage, leaving just a small protrusion (shown on the fighter version drawing) to disturb the streamlining; the turret would of course require a fourth crew number in the form of a gunner.

The P.1005 brochure was submitted to the Ministry of Aircraft Production in December 1940. An appraisal completed on 4 February 1941 by Capt R.N. Liptrot from the Research and Development (Aircraft) department indicated that the P.1005 showed some merit over the new high speed unarmed de Havilland Mosquito because it offered: "...more normal equipment and a higher bomb load and did not attempt to rely solely on its speed and evasive power for safety". Soon there was talk of production orders but one problem was that in its use of the Sabre engine the P.1005 would draw heavily on the supply required for the Typhoon. However, the P.1005 was considered to be the best proposal so far for a light bomber designed around two Sabre engines and an outline specification B.11/41 was eventually written around the aircraft in December 1941. B.11/41 was approved in May 1942 along with its Operational Requirement OR.110 and the maximum speed requirement was given as 415mph (668km/h) (reduced from 430mph (692km/h) in the draft document) and ceiling (100ft/min/30m/min climb) 33,000ft (10,058m) (instead of 35,000ft (10,668m)). The Bristol Centaurus was listed as an alternative power unit to the Sabres and the reserve torsional stiffness in the wing was not to be less than that already obtained on the Hurricane and Typhoon; the aircraft's tail plane and rear fuselage were also to have the same reserve factors as those aircraft. By now the bomb load had been pushed up to 4,000lb (1,814kg).

In January 1942 Liptrot assessed a revised version of the P.1005 submitted by Hawker, the main alteration being a reduction of wing area by 12% but with the span unchanged. The smaller wing reduced the fuel tankage to 950 gallons (4,320 litres) and Liptrot commented that the higher taper ratio resulted in bad lift distribution with consequent loss in overall lift. A top speed of 409mph (658km/h) at 25,000ft (7,620m) was predicted but the changes would, he declared, reduce the range by 70 miles (113km) and the ceiling by 1,000 to 1,500ft (305 to 457m). Camm's calculations for carrying a 4,000lb (1,814kg) bomb load showed an

increase in wing loading from 46 to 49lb/sq.ft (20.8 to 22.1kg/sq.m) and there was a modest increase in cruising speed, a 2,000ft (610m) loss in ceiling and 40 mile (64km) reduction in range. Overall, Liptrot considered the revised wing to be quite unacceptable and that it introduced some real risks.

In general there was a lot of indecision in regard to ordering the P.1005 and how it would fit into the production organisation. One element was the growing potential and capability of the de Havilland Mosquito, but there were also competing designs from Bristol (the Buckingham – Chapter Six) and the Sabre-engined DH.101 Mosquito development from de Havilland (Chapter Seven). Indeed, some in the Air Staff felt that the P.1005 did not offer a sufficient advance to warrant large scale production, although by November 1941 there were provisional plans to order 1,000 'Camm bombers' (as the type was often called in official documents – it was also referred to as the 'Hawker Sabre bomber'). In general the Air Staff considered the fighter version to be entirely secondary to the main bomber role.

Two P.1005 prototypes were ordered and serials HV266 and HV270 were allotted to them in December 1941 (or possibly in late November) under Contracts/Acft/1712. A partial mock-up was built by Hawker and the Mock-Up Conference was held on 27 February 1942. However, in mid-March, at an Aircraft Supply Council Meeting, it was agreed that Buckingham production should be set at 25 a month and no production orders should be placed either for the Hawker Sabre bomber or a DH.101 fitted with Griffon engines. In Hawker's case the company's single-engine fighter production was not to be prejudiced by working on the bomber. Then on 11 April the Royal Aeronautical Society's Advisory Committee was asked to assess the Buckingham, DH.101 and P.1005 and to suggest the most suitable type for quantity production during the 1943-45 period, thereby eliminating any duplication. The prospects for both DH.101 and P.1005 were embarrassed by the fact that the latest version of the Sabre engine would not be available in time for either, and this was why the Centaurus was considered as an alternative for the P.1005

The partial full-size mock-up built by Hawker was officially assessed in late February 1942.

and the Rolls-Royce Griffon for the DH.101 (see Chapter Seven). It was soon established that the present edition of Griffon power output and weight made it unsuitable for either aircraft.

The Committee indicated that the P.1005 should be selected since the Buckingham really fell into a different category and had already been ordered, and also by this time de Havilland had moved on to the Merlin-powered DH.102 project. But in coming to these conclusions the Committee added that if the Minister was really going to consider a high-speed long-range patrol fighter as well then none of the types offered gave what was required, namely a certain 440mph (708km/h) speed with a range of over 2,000 miles (3,218km). In fact no solution was available for this requirement except by the employment of buried engines in the fuselage with a shaft drive.

On 10 June 1942 the Deputy Controller of Research and Development gave verbal instructions that the order for the P.1005 was to be cancelled. No production capacity was expected to be available before the end of 1944 at least and so the company was recommended to cease work on the two prototypes. Hopeless production prospects through a shortage of capacity were the main problem, not any shortcomings in the design, but the growing potential of the Mosquito had also inhibited the progress of the Hawker bomber (it appears that very little progress had been made in building the prototypes). In due course, during the middle war years considerable development and service problems were experienced with the Napier Sabre engine which, had the P.1005 been continued, would undoubtedly have affected the bomber's progress into service. Consequently, it is hard to predict if the P.1005 would ever have progressed beyond the prototype stage given the fact that Hawker's Typhoon and Tempest fighters were regarded with great value by the Ministry – the P.1005 was unlikely to have found preference over either.

Two other companies undertook some work against Specification B.11/41. The first was Armstrong Whitworth but its design study was unofficial with no project number allocated to it. That usually meant just a small proportion of the design team would have

The de Havilland Mosquito eventually proved to be a success in many roles, including those envisaged for the P.1005. This picture shows DZ313, a B.Mk.IV.

Model of the P.1005. *Joe Cherrie*

been involved – once full project status was reached rather more of the company workforce would have been put onto the project, but no submission to the Ministry appears to have been made. The other company was Miles Aircraft (Philips and Powis) who offered its M.39 project (Chapter Twenty-Three), one of the famous Libellula designs produced by the firm. Further proposed versions of the P.1005 were the P.1011 with Power Jets gas turbine engines, the P.1013 with remotely controlled guns and the P.1015, which was the variant with Centaurus power units. Later in 1944 came the P.1033 with Rolls-Royce Eagle piston engines while the P.1034 had two of the new B.41 jets from Rolls (which was later named the Nene). One further twin piston-engined design from Hawkers which never saw the light of day, and for which no drawing is currently known to exist, was the P.1037 twin-boom Rolls-Royce Griffon-engined fighter project which, according to the master Hawker project list file, was studied during September 1944. This design has always intrigued the author because Sydney Camm's products at Hawker were usually most attractive with beautiful lines, and he wonders how this might have shown through on a twin boom fighter.

The high-speed fighter version of the P.1005 with a different nose and six 20mm cannon (two only visible from side on). The small dorsal fitting indicates the position of the wireless operator's station or the alternative gun turret.

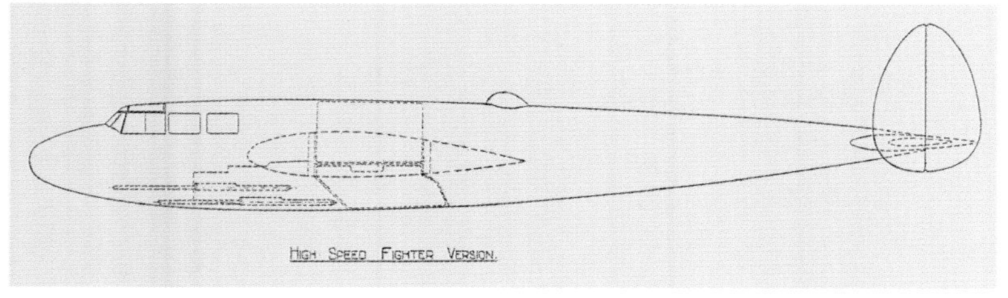

Structure

The P.1005 was a mid-wing monoplane with 3.5° of dihedral on the main wing, a comparatively narrow fuselage and twin fins and rudders. It employed conventional all-metal construction using light aluminium alloy throughout, flaps and ailerons were fitted to the wing trailing edge and, thanks to the choice of twin fins and rudders, the aircraft had a full length elevator. Each engine was fitted with a 14.0ft (4.3m) diameter four-bladed propeller, the original fuel capacity was 1,100 gallons (5,000 litres) and there was to be a crew of three comprising a pilot, navigator and wireless operator. The sideways-retracting main undercarriage hinged just inside the engine mountings and folded into the thick centre-wing section. The maximum bomb load in the internal weapon bay was originally 2,000lb (907kg), but eventually this was capable of holding combinations up of bombs of up to 4,000lb (1,814kg) in total.

The high-speed fighter version of the P.1005 was originally just a simple conversion with two forward firing 20mm cannon added to the retractable turret's machine guns. Later, however, there was a more substantially modified aircraft with a new nose and six 20mm cannon with 250 rounds each, all mounted beneath the cockpit. The turret was still optional (it was common to both types) but there was now an alternative wireless operator's station, while the fuselage fuel tanks were designed to permit a through passageway from the cockpit. There was also provision for additional removable fuel tanks.

Other Twin-Engine Bombers

Information has been traced for two other twin-engine bomber designs, one of which was ordered as a prototype while the other is previously unpublished, but insufficient material is available to make the first into a full chapter. Consequently they have been grouped with the P.1005.

Blackburn B.28

The B.28 was a private venture high speed light bomber proposed by Blackburn in 1939. It was to be powered by two Rolls-Royce Griffons and had a span of 54ft 9in (16.69m) and length with its tail down of 39ft 0in (11.89m). The project was covered by Specification B.3/40 and the B.28 was expected to achieve at least 400mph (644km/h) at 18,000ft (5,486m). Its warload was two 500lb (227kg) or four 250lb (113kg) bombs and for defence there was a four-gun turret. A partial full-size mock-up was built and a single prototype, X8500, was ordered in 1940 to Contract B.81965/40. The Instruction to Proceed for the contract was made on 6 June 1940, but in due course the programme was cancelled.

The full size mock-up of the Blackburn B.28. *BAE Systems Brough Heritage*

Folland Bomber

A model of a high speed light bomber design from the war years is held by the Solent Sky Museum at Southampton. It shows a Folland design but no information is known about the project. It may be the Fo 113/Fo 114. Its turret has two-machine guns.

Model of the Folland twin-engined bomber.
Phil Butler

18 Hillson Bi-Mono and 'Slip-Wing' Projects

Hillson Bi-Mono and 'Slip-Wing' Projects

Type: Single-Seat Research Aircraft
Powerplant: One 200hp (149kW) de Havilland Gipsy VI air-cooled inline engine
Span: 20ft 0in (6.10m)
Length: 19ft 6in (5.94m)
Gross Wing Area: As biplane 132sq.ft (12.28m^2); as monoplane 66sq.ft (6.14sq.m)
Loaded Weight: As biplane 1,940lb (880kg); as monoplane 1,850lb (839kg)
Rate of Climb: Not available
Maximum Speed: Not available
Ceiling: Not available
Armament: None

As aircraft grew ever heavier during the 1930s there were numerous experiments and theories for reducing weight on take-off, or the problems created by high weight. In-flight refuelling was one important system to be developed during this period, but another solution could be to increase the aircraft's wing area specifically through the addition of a second upper wing, which would then be discarded after take-off – a 'slip-wing'! Such a feature might also permit aircraft to operate away from large, vulnerable airfields. In the 1920s and 1930s several designers and companies offered ideas along these lines, but it was the onset of war that got things moving. However, the push came not through one of the major aircraft firms but instead from a little-known company.

In 1940 F. Hills and Son of Trafford Park in Manchester proposed a light and cheap fighter that could operate from grass surfaces and roads by means of a 'slip-wing'. Hills and Son were actually a woodworking firm but in the aivation field, where they built light aircraft, they traded as Hillson. The fighter proposal was made by W.R. Chown, Hillson's managing director, and his designer Norman Sykes, and despite receiving no official support the company began work on a private venture aircraft to test out their theory. This was called the Bi-Mono and the team effort was led by assistant chief designer Ernest Lewis; the aircraft never received a military serial or civil registration. In the early stages (at least) the Bi-Mono's 'slip-wing' had a much larger span than its main wing, but this may have been rejected prior to the start of flight testing (there are no pictures of the aircraft flying with the larger wing). In due course a 'slip-wing' of the same span was fitted and this smaller alternative gave a much neater and more compact appearance. There were reservations about the safety of discarding a wing in flight but, with help from RAE representatives, several ground runs and various tests and modifications eventually saw the little aircraft cleared for flight. RAE also performed all of the required wind tunnel testing and wing stiffness experiements. Such was the speed put into the project that it took just seventy-two days from the start of design work to the completion of the Bi-Mono and its readiness to fly. The engine was a de Havilland Gipsy Six.

The maiden flight took place at Barton in early 1941 and both biplane and monoplane configurations were tested, but without the wing being slipped. On 16 July 1941 the Bi-Mono took-off from Squires Gate airfield at Blackpool in the hands of Hillson test pilot P.H.

Photograph of the Hillson Bi-Mono taken in November 1941 without the 'slip-wing' in position. The relatively large pilot's cabin shows just how small this attractive little aeroplane was. *Phil Butler*

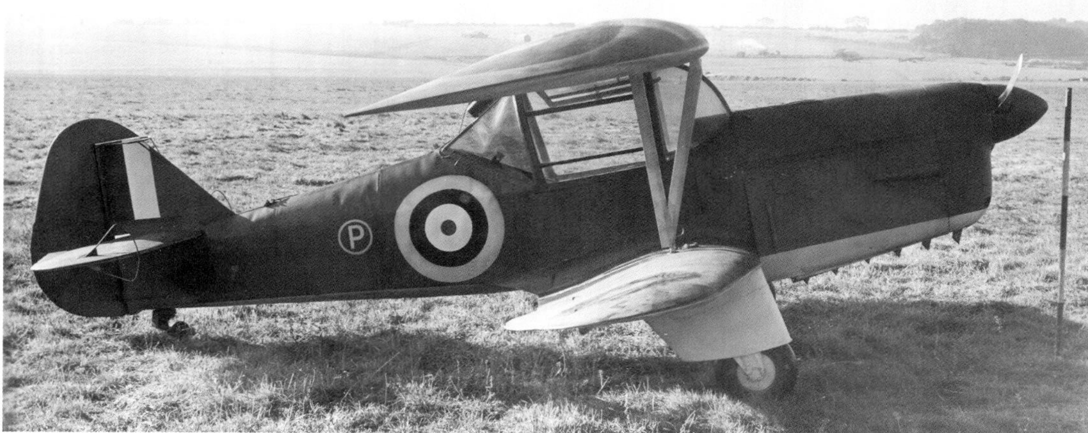

Similar view of the Bi-Mono but with one of its additional wings now in place. Both views were taken at Boscombe Down. *Phil Butler*

Richmond, while Chown, his designer and RAE staff followed in a Lockheed Hudson to observe. At an altitude of 4,500ft (1,370m), and flying over the sea at about 5 miles (8km) to the west of Blackpool to avoid hitting anyone or anything on the ground, the upper wing was jettisoned safely and satisfactorily. There proved to be no problems in controlling the aircraft during and after the alteration to the aircraft's configuration, there was no change in trim and the only real result was a gentle and controlled loss of a few hundred feet in height. In the middle of October 1941 the Bi-Mono arrived at A&AEE Boscombe Down to undergo an official evaluation. No reports appear to survive but Tim Mason's book *The Secret Years* notes that: "...the maximum level speed as a biplane was less than the stalling speed of the monoplane", which meant that releasing the 'slip-wing' brought an immediate stall. Landing in the monoplane condition was also stated to be like "a high-speed kangaroo". The 'slip-wing', which weighed 90lb (41kg), was detached by mechanical means.

Another designer to put a lot of effort into the design of 'slip-wing' aircraft of various kinds was Noel Pemberton-Billing. Indeed, Hillson in due course gained the contract to build the prototype of his PB.37 'slip-wing' dive-bomber project, which in fact was an altogether more complex aircraft than the Bi-Mono. The 'lower' component comprised a pusher monoplane powered by a 290hp (216kW) engine while the manned 'slip-wing' upper component was a tractor monoplane with a 40hp (30kW) piston engine. The manufacture of this aircraft began early in 1940 but was halted in the July when its construction was well advanced (some sources indicate that it was fairly close to being finished). The PB.37 was never flown. Since it could not be reused Pemberton-Billing referred to the discarded wing as the 'scrap-wing'.

The 'slip-wing' research was taken further when Hillson flew its FH.40 Mk.I, a Hawker Hurricane fighter adapted to carry and jettison a 'slip-wing'. Hurricane Mk.I L1884 (which by the time of its adoption for the task had received the Royal Canadian Air Force serial RCAF321) was fitted with a plywood-covered two-spar wooden upper wing of similar outline to the fighter's standard wing. The new surface and its fittings weighed 693lb (314kg) and had an area of

The Hillson FH.40 – a Hurricane converted to receive a 'slip-wing'. As L1884 this aircraft had been shipped to Canada in 1939 as one of a batch sent for RCAF service before Canadian production got underway. There it was numbered '321' and after returning to the UK it was employed in this new role. Note the 'N'-shaped struts and how high the upper wing sits on the aircraft.

328sq.ft (30.50sq.m), and N-shaped struts were used to attach it to the lower wing with supplementary diagonal struts joining the fuselage sides. The only other change made to the basic airframe was a 10% increase in elevator area to provide extra control. After numerous problems and delays the aircraft was first flown as a biplane from Sealand near Chester on 26 May 1943. However, controversy and argument saw the Hurricane flying programme abandoned in mid-February 1944, without the wing ever having been slipped in flight.

Ken Ellis in his article on the 'slip-wing' (*Back to the Biplane* in *Air Enthusiast 107*) notes that in today's terminology the additional surface would be described as: "...a lift augmentation device". For a small company like F. Hills and Son to begin such a project like the 'slip-wing', and to take it so far, was a quite extraordinary achievement in the face of wartime conditions and priorities at the Ministry, but the effort eventually faded away as more practical and modern aircraft were developed. The possible need for a 'slip-wing' fighter disappeared and it is a fact that the cost and labour required to produce what in effect were 'scrap' wings would have been difficult to justify during wartime. Published sources have never mentioned the fate of the Bi-Mono and few details of its individual flights or its performance figures appear to be available.

No serial number can be seen in this view of the 'slip-wing' Hurricane flying as a biplane. The upper wing was never jettisoned in flight.

Structure

The Bi-Mono had a fuselage built in steel-tube with fabric covering and wooden wings. To ensure sufficient stiffness the 'slip-wing' was attached to the lower wing by means of an interplane strut and there was also an attachment on the top of the cockpit canopy. As stated, two upper wings were designed with different wingspans, the shorter version having the same span as the lower fixed wing while the larger form appeared to have around 40% more span. There was a fixed tailwheel undercarriage and to begin with a fixed-pitch two-blade wooden propeller. However, when the Bi-Mono began its official trials a de Havilland constant-speed two-blade metal propeller had been fitted. Fuel was housed in the lower wing leading edges.

19 Martin-Baker M.B.2

Martin-Baker M.B.2

Type: Single-Seat Fighter

Powerplant: One 1,020hp (761kW) Napier-Halford Dagger III air-cooled engine

Span: 34ft 6in (10.52m)

Length: original configuration 34ft 2in (10.41m), final configuration 34ft 9in (10.59m)

Gross Wing Area: 212sq.ft (19.72m^2)

Take-Off Weight: 5,400lb (2,449kg)

Rate of Climb: 2,200ft/min (671m/min)

Maximum Speed: 305mph (491km/h) at 9,250ft (2,819m)

Service Ceiling: 29,000ft (8,839m)

Armament: 8 x 0.303in (7.7mm) Browning machine-guns

Martin-Baker Aircraft's first design to fly was the M.B.1 light aeroplane which employed a new method of construction that subsequently found its way into the company's fighter prototypes. The company's first fighter was called the M.B.2, and this aircraft qualifies for the book because it was still in existence when war broke out in September 1939 and survived for some time afterwards.

Design of the M.B.2 got going in 1935 and the construction of the single prototype began in March 1936. With such a simple structure it was thought that putting this aircraft into production would be a cheap and quick process. The project was a private venture but it was designed against Specification F.5/34 which had been issued to industry in November 1934. This document requested a speed of 275mph (442km/h) at 15,000ft (4,572m) and a service ceiling of 33,000ft (10,058m). The M.B.2 was first flown by Capt Valentine Baker, a partner in the company and its test pilot, on 3 August 1938, the flight being made from Harwell because the firm's airfield at Denham was too small to test a powerful fighter aircraft. On 5 November the machine was flown to A&AEE at Martlesham Heath for official trials.

A&AEE's maintenance appraisal of December 1938 declared that the accessibility of the fixed undercarriage wheels and oleo legs compared unfavourably with the retractable chassis used on other fighters. The flight test report, dated 1 February 1939, stated that on take off the aircraft developed a strong tendency to swing to starboard once the tail was up, and full left rudder was barely efficient to check the swing which continued after the aeroplane was airborne and only gradually diminished as the speed increased. In the air the behaviour of the controls was influenced considerably by the fighter's lack of stability. The elevator was the most effective of the three controls and was light and effective both at low speeds in the glide and at high speeds, and the response was quick. It became slightly heavier with increase in speed and it was too sensitive on the glide. The ailerons were light but not sufficiently effective at low speeds, and became heavy as the speed was increased. The rudder was insufficiently effective to provide adequate control to overcome the tendency to swing to starboard at low speeds engine on. This tendency gradually diminished as the speed increased, but slight application of rudder at cruising speeds and above produced a rapid swing of the nose quite disproportionate to the amount of rudder applied. The report stressed that a larger and more effective rudder was required.

The M.B.2 photographed after the first form of vertical fin had been fitted. The designation 'M-B-I' painted on the side of the rear fuselage was carried during early test flights. *Martin-Baker*

Directionally, the M.B.2 was unstable for small angles of yaw, the instability increasing with speed. The result of this instability was that quite small movements of the rudder produced a quick initial yaw and the effect on the pilot, who tended to be thrown to one side or other of the cockpit, was not pleasant. In conclusion the M.B.2 was considered not pleasant to fly and required great concentration to fly accurately in turns and in level flight.

On 24 May 1939 the M.B.2 made its first flight, from Northolt, with a larger fin and rudder and in June it was bought by the Air Ministry and given the serial P9594. Between 12 June and 1 July further official trials were performed where it was found that on take off the tendency to swing to the right still persisted but could now be overcome by use of a little left rudder. The rudder control was now reasonably light and at cruising and full out level speeds the rudder was moderately light and effective, but it became slightly heavier with increases in speed (in a dive). The other controls were of course unaltered and were now out of harmony, the ailerons being heavy by comparison and very ineffective at low speeds. Overall the modification to the rudder had made the control considerably more effective and it now compared favourably with the rudders on aircraft of similar type.

P9594 spent a period of time at the Air Fighting Development Unit (AFDU) at RAF Northolt before returning to Martin-Baker late in 1939. It is understood that the type's only public perfromance came at a flying display held at Heston on 26 May 1939 when Baker

The M.B.2 (with M-B-1 marks) is cleared for another flight. *Martin-Baker*

This picture of the M.B.2 was taken after the larger fin had been fitted and the aeroplane had been given the military serial P9594. The fixed undercarriage was selected by the designers for simplicity and the port side also contained the oil cooler. *Martin-Baker*

The crash post fitted to the M.B.2 to protect the pilot in the event of a nose-over landing is shown here in the extended position.

demonstrated it with some style and flair. *Flight* magazine reported that he took the machine up to 10,000ft (3,048m) and put it into what appeared to be a vertical dive with engine off; also particularly impressive was the tightness of the M.B.2's turns. It appears unlikely that the M.B.2 was flown very much (if at all) after the outbreak of war, and in March 1942 the fighter was still at its birthplace. It is presumed that the airframe was eventually scrapped. Overall the M.B.2 offered no major advantages over the far superior Hurricane and Spitfire and its fixed undercarriage was a very out-of-date feature. The fighter's Dagger engine made a noise like a sewing machine.

Rare view showing the M.B.2 in flight.

The M.B.2 zooms over a cameraman at very low level.

Structure

The M.B.2 used a simple basic structure of steel tubing and bolted joints. It had a straight tapered wing and as originally built there was no fin. Instead the rudder was mounted on the fuselage end and it was hoped that the aircraft's flat-sided fuselage would provide enough directional stability, but during early flight tests Baker found that he could not get the aircraft to go where he wanted. Consequently, a small vertical surface was soon added above the end of the fuselage (which was in place when the aircraft began its official trials) and this was later enlarged. The wing had a triangular spar (a single spar built up of steel tubular members) and was fabric covered aft of the spar (as was the rear

Views showing the forward fuselage of the M.B.2 and its Napier Dagger installation. These were taken after the aircraft had been bought by the Air Ministry in mid-1939.

fuselage), but the forward fuselage and wing were covered by easily removable metal skin panels. The tail had a cantilever steel tubular structure and both the rudder and elevators were also built in steel tube. All control surfaces were fabric covered and the eight machine-guns were mounted within the wings. A crash post that extended automatically was fitted so that in the event of a nose-over landing the risk of injury to the pilot (and any damage to the aircraft) was reduced; this was kept in the raised postion for take-offs and landings.

The fixed undercarriage was enclosed in two trouser-type fairings and the fighter's Napier Dagger engine had a fixed-pitch two-blade propeller. A total of 83 gallons (377 litres) of fuel were carried in two fuselage tanks. Although named M.B.2 the airframe was at one stage marked M-B-1 in lieu of its civil registration G-AEZD, something that for many years has created plenty of confusion over identities.

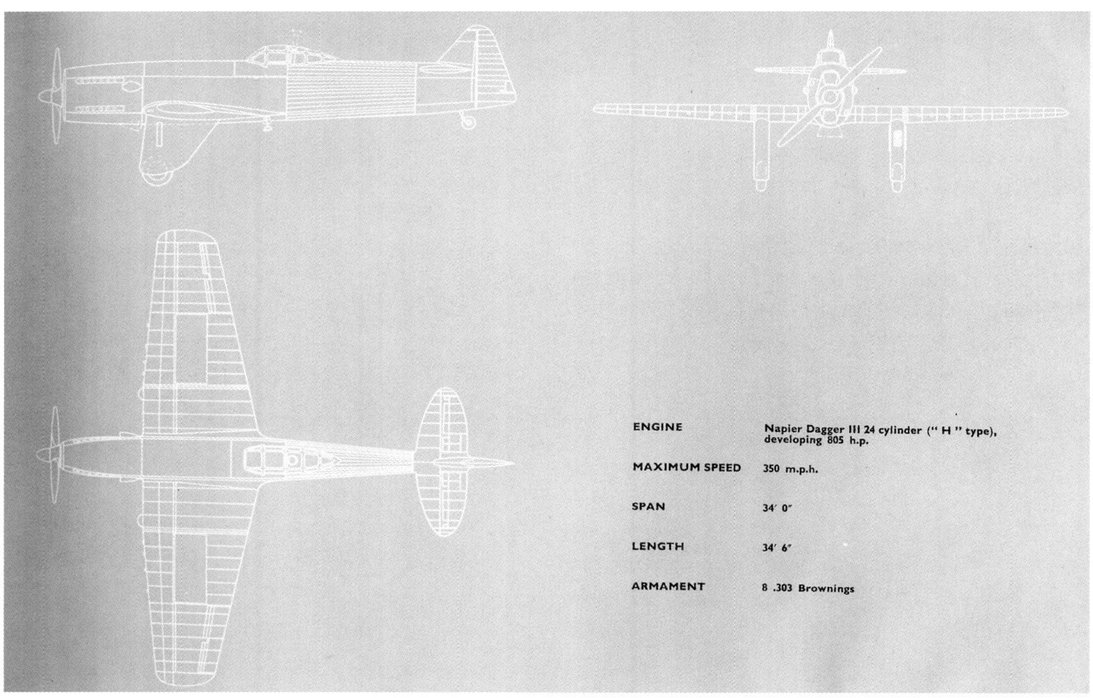

ENGINE
Napier Dagger III 24 cylinder (" H " type), developing 805 h.p.
MAXIMUM SPEED
350 m.p.h.
SPAN
34' 0"
LENGTH
34' 6"
ARMAMENT
8 .303 Brownings

Manufacturer's drawing of the Martin-Baker M.B.2. *Chris Gibson*

20 Martin-Baker M.B.3

Martin-Baker M.B.3

Type: Single-Seat Fighter

Powerplant: One 2,020hp (1,506kW) Napier Sabre II liquid-cooled inline engine

Span: 36ft 0in (10.97m)

Length: 35ft 4in (10.77m)

Gross Wing Area: 262.5sq.ft (24.41m^2)

Take-Off Weight: Unknown but c12,000lb (5,443kg)

Maximum Speed: 430mph (692km/h) at 20,000ft (6,096m)

Service Ceiling: (expected) 35,000ft (10,668m).

Armament: 6 x 20mm Hispano cannon

The M.B.2 was followed by the M.B.3, three examples of which were ordered against Specification F.18/39 of May 1939 and Contract 1165/39; however, the order was not finally issued until 11 August 1940. F.18/39 was raised especially to cover the M.B.3 project and was issued to Martin-Baker on 4 May 1939. It detailed an all-up weight of 12,000lb (5,443kg), a top speed at 15,000ft (4,572m) of not less than 400mph (644km/h) and, again, structural strength, simplicity and accessibility were the order of the day. Initially the specified engine was the Rolls-Royce Griffon, although F.18/39 stated that a Rolls-Royce Merlin RM.2.SM was to be installed in the first instance (because at that stage the Griffon itself had not yet flown). In fact three Merlins were ordered by Martin-Baker from Rolls-Royce Hucknall in May 1939, three Griffons were ordered two months later, and by May 1940 three Merlin X engines had been delivered to Martin-Baker. However, despite company head James Martin's preference for a Rolls-Royce powerplant the M.B.3 was eventually fitted with a Napier Sabre II, but just why that happened when Rolls-Royce engines were available has so far proved impossible to find out.

Work on the M.B.3 was started during the financial year 1938/39 and the three prototypes were given the serials R2492, R2496 and R2500; the order also included another complete set of mainplanes fitted with twelve 0.303in (7.7mm) Browning machine-guns. However, although developing and building the M.B.3s was of course Martin-Baker's primary objective, the effort was slowed down by the company's growing order book. By mid-1941 the firm had dealt with requests from Fighter Command and others to undertake such work as a manual jettisonable hood for the Spitfire and a twelve-gun nose for the Douglas D.B.7 Havoc. These side issues brought mixed blessings – a reputation for dealing with 'urgent' jobs brought in the cash to enable Martin-Baker to finance its fighter prototypes, but these orders constantly retarded their manufacture and thereby increased their cost substantially. As a result the team was for a time forced to concentrate on completing only the first M.B.3 prototype.

Another point was that Martin-Baker was not a member of the Society of British Aircraft Constructors (the SBAC), a situation which the firm felt made its efforts to sell the fighter more difficult. In fact the M.B.3 was not highly regarded by everyone in the Air Ministry. The Chief of the Air Staff, Air Chief Marshal Charles Portal, wrote on 15 December 1940 (admittedly well before first flight) that the aircraft was: "...no advance on the [Hawker] Tornado (Chapter Sixteen) and Typhoon and was unlikely to be ready until much later" and he did not

Side view of R2492, seen here with the cockpit canopy and side door open. Note the yellow 'P' prototype marking alongside the cockpit. The tailwheel was retractable. *Del Holyland, Martin-Baker*

think that there was: "...much object in proceeding further with it unless there was any marked production advantage over either of the others". Scientist Henry Tizard, also in 1940 in a review of new forthcoming combat aircraft, stated: "My first impression was to suggest that this should be cut out but the airframes can be made by firms such as the Hercules Cycle Co. who have had no previous experience of high grade aircraft work. This might be important."

An RAE report from April 1941 predicted that the M.B.3 when powered by a 1,850hp (1,380kW) Napier Sabre NS.1.SM engine would have a top speed of 402mph (647km/h), and with a 2,040hp (1,521kW) NS.4.SM in place this would rise to 418mph (673km/h). The respective altitudes for these speeds were 19,000ft (5,791m) and 20,000ft (6,096m) and the engine powers would be supplemented by another 130hp (97kW) and 140hp (104kW) respectively due to the effects of the exhaust. At a weight of 12,000lb (5,443kg) the estimated service ceilings with these engines were 30,700ft (9,367m) and 32,800ft (9,998m), and absolute ceilings 31,500ft (9,601m) and 33,600ft (10,241m). This information is recorded here because, with the early loss of the sole M.B.3 prototype to fly, relatively little in the way of detailed performance data was collected for the type.

The first prototype, R2492, fitted with a Napier Sabre II, made its maiden flight on 3 August 1942 from Wing in Buckinghamshire, but the first two flights both had to be terminated after one circuit of the airfield due to engine overheating, and the aircraft was grounded for a period while efforts were made to improve the radiator cooling. Baker reported that in the air the aeroplane had excellent flight characteristics, it was easy to fly and was highly manoeuvrable, and it handled perfectly with good directional stability. However, on 12 September at the start of its tenth flight the M.B.3's engine seized soon

R2492 was the only MB.3 to be completed. Its flying career lasted just ten flights. *Tim Brown*

after taking off from Wing and with the aircraft at a height of no more than 100ft (30m). A crank on one of the Sabre's sleeve valves had failed and Baker attempted to land in a field, but he was forced to turn to port to avoid a farmhouse, his wing clipped the ground, the aircraft cartwheeled and it burst into flames. Tragically, Capt Baker was killed.

Since the M.B.3 never reached A&AEE there is also little available information giving details of its flying qualities, although a letter from James Martin in the Rolls-Royce archives states that the top speed: "...appeared to be 430mph (692km/h) at 20,000ft (6,096m)" and 'Bake' had flown it with "hands and feet off". After the crash there was no point in building another airframe to the same design since the time this would take would ensure that the M.B.3 was left behind by new developments (it is understood that construction of the second M.B.3 R2496 had started). The loss of the M.B.3 was a big setback to the company, but for James Martin the loss of his great friend and business partner Val Baker was a huge blow. It sowed the seeds in his mind for what would become a passionate interest in aircrew safety, which of course culminated in his work on ejection seats that the company continues to this day. It was also a pity that there was never an opportunity to assess the destructive power of six 20mm guns.

Structure

The experience gained in manufacturing the M.B.1 and M.B.2 was carried over to the M.B.3 but, whilst retaining the essential characteristics of the earlier designs with a fuselage primary structure built in steel

Below and overleaf: Official Ministry views showing the Martin-Baker M.B.3 from front, side and rear angles. They were all taken at the same time in August 1942. Note the wide track undercarriage.

Doctored image showing the M.B.3 R2492 with a bubble canopy, a feature which was never introduced to the aircraft. Had there been time to fit this canopy it would have made the M.B.3 a handsome aeroplane. *Chris Gibson*

tubing, the new aircraft introduced many new features. Metal stressed-skin panels with flush riveting replaced all of the fabric covering and the straight tapered wing was formed as a torsion-box around a laminated steel spar. This gave a remarkably strong and stiff structure in which there was no perceptible flexing. The M.B.3 had six wing-mounted 20mm cannon placed outboard of the undercarriage which made it at the time of its development the most heavily armed fighter in the world. The Napier Sabre 24-cylinder H-type engine was cooled by radiators placed underneath the wings with the coolant radiator on the starboard side and the oil-cooler under the port wing, and it was fitted with a three-blade

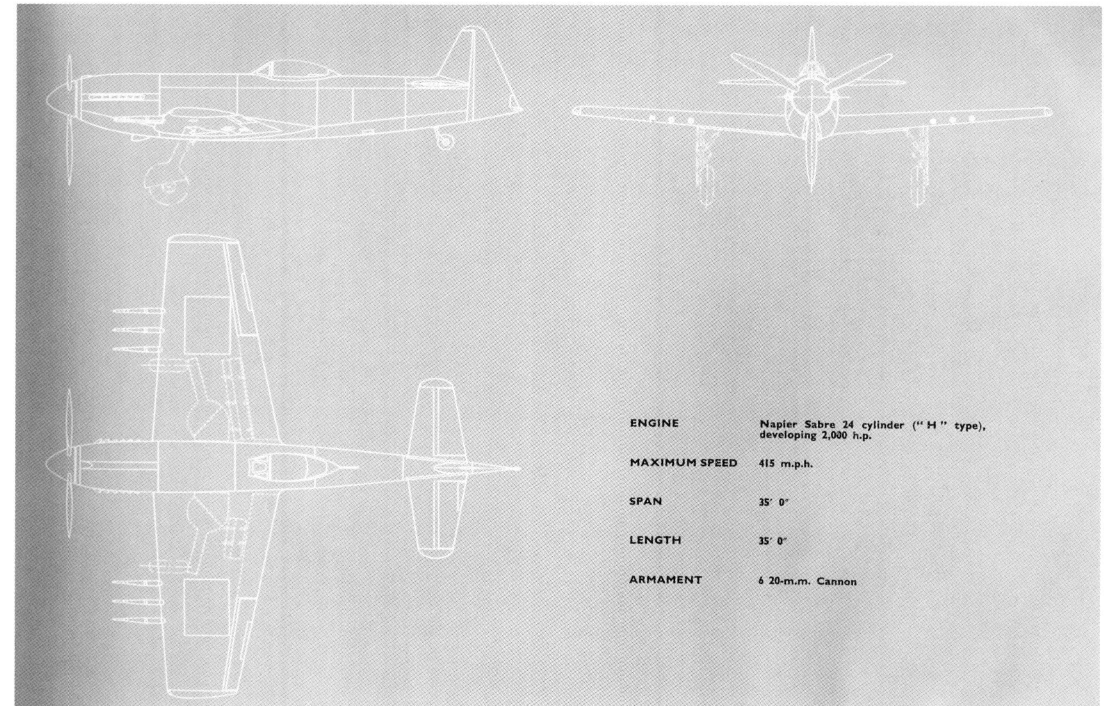

ENGINE
Napier Sabre 24 cylinder (" H " type), developing 2,000 h.p.
MAXIMUM SPEED
415 m.p.h.
SPAN
35' 0"
LENGTH
35' 0"
ARMAMENT
6 20-m.m. Cannon

Manufacturer's drawing of the Martin-Baker M.B.3 with a bubble canopy. *Chris Gibson*

variable-pitch airscrew. James Martin's own design for a simple pneumatically controlled undercarriage was employed, which had a wide track and folded inwards into the inner wing, and the wing flaps were also pneumatically operated but they could only be positioned fully up or fully down. The fin was pointed (or tapered), a feature common to all Martin-Baker fighters, and it must be pointed out that photographs which show the M.B.3 with a bubble canopy and no dorsal spine have been 'retouched'. The aircraft never appeared in that form but apparently it was a planned modification.

M.B.4 Fighter Project

Work on the follow-on M.B.4 and M.B.5 projects (Chapter Twenty-One) began during the 1939/40 financial year. James Martin had always wanted to use a Griffon engine on his fighters but the Bristol Centaurus was also considered as an alternative, and preliminary drawings were made for an M.B.4 with this engine. However, once the Griffon was finally available to Martin-Baker all other alternatives were dropped. A drawing of the M.B.4 found in the National Archives which originated from RAE Farnborough shows an aircraft with a supercharged Rolls-Royce 37-litre V/12 Griffon (the engine first specified in F.18/39) rated at 1,440hp (1,074kW) at 15,000ft (4,572m) and fitted with a 12ft 0in (3.66m) diameter three-blade variable pitch propeller. The wings, rear fuselage and fin appear to be near identical to the M.B.3, but the M.B.4 in this form was abandoned. The drawing is not dated.

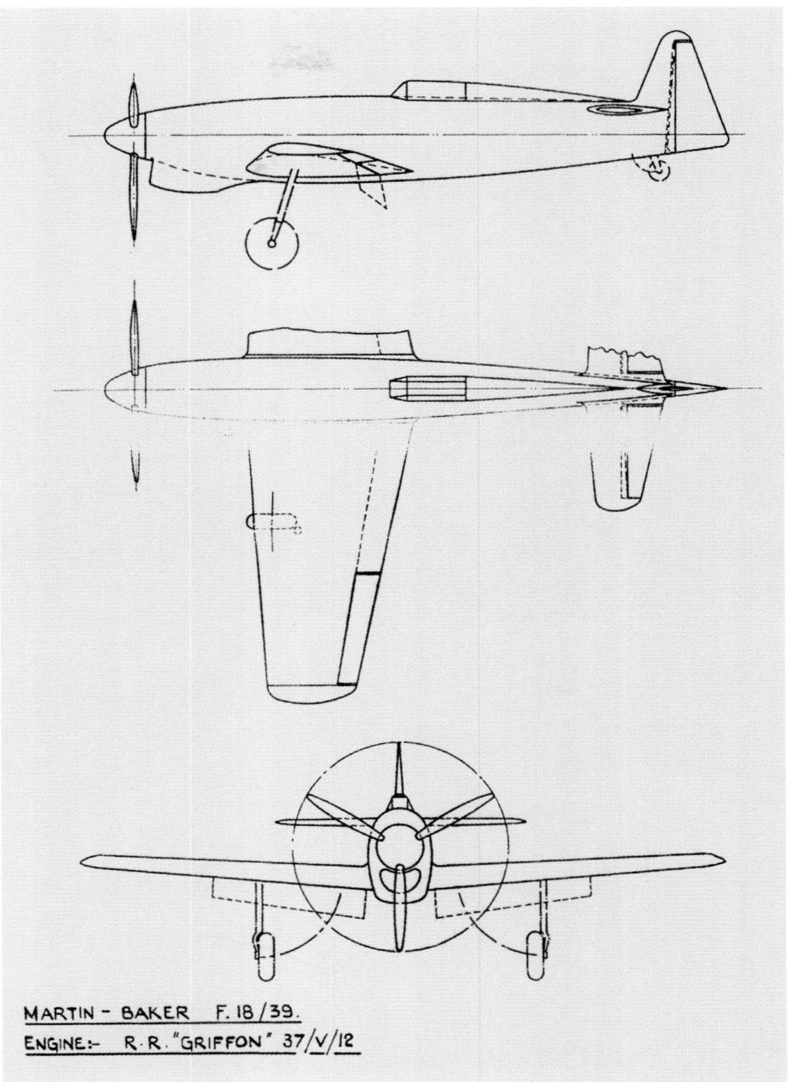

Drawing showing the Martin-Baker F.18/39 M.B.4 project powered by a Rolls-Royce Griffon engine. *National Archives AVIA 14/64/27*

21 Martin-Baker M.B.5

Martin-Baker M.B.5

Type: Single-Seat Fighter

Powerplant: One Rolls-Royce Griffon 83 liquid-cooled inline engine rated at 2,340hp (1,745kW) in MS gear, 2,120hp (1,581kW) at 12,250ft (3,734m) in FS gear

Span: 35ft 0in (10.67m)

Length: (with final tail unit) 37ft 9in (11.51m)

Gross Wing Area: 262sq.ft (24.37m^2)

Maximum Weight: 12,090lb (5,484kg)

Rate of Climb: 3,800ft/min (1,158m/min)

Maximum Speed: 395mph (636km/h) at sea level, 460mph (740km/h) at 20,000ft (6,096m)

Service Ceiling: 40,000ft (12,192m).

Armament: 4 x 20mm Hispano cannon

The Martin-Baker M.B.5 was the most glamorous and impressive of the three Martin-Baker fighters to be built, and indeed was one of the most spectacular of all of the prototype aeroplanes produced in Britain during the Second World War. It was highly rated by pretty well all of the pilots who flew it, it was a spectacular aerobatic display aircraft and made a very good gun platform, but the end of the war and other factors ensured that the type would progress no further than a single prototype. The M.B.5 was a sleek low-wing aeroplane and articles written in *Flight* magazine in 1945 and 1947 actually called it the M-B V – in those days of course individual marks of British Service aircraft were also designated using Roman numerals. The airframe used the serial R2496 which indicates that it was the second M.B.3 modified or rebuilt. Indeed, in many respects Martin-Baker designs were 'Meccano kits' and for the M.B.5 it is understood that the pilot's cockpit was just moved to a different pair of frames within the fuselage. Construction of the prototype was completed at Denham by the spring of 1944 but plans for a second M.B.5, which presumably would have become R2500, were cancelled on 14 May 1943. In fact, apparently as early as October 1944, James Martin was informed by the Ministry that his M.B.5 would not enter production because service entry would take too long.

In February 1944 the company was running a night-and-day shift to get the M.B.5 completed. Capt Bryan Greensted, the chief test pilot of Rotol who had been heavily involved with the development of variable pitch airscrews, took R2496 on its maiden flight from Harwell on 23 May. It was decided to make the first flight from Harwell because this field provided a much larger runway than Wing where the M.B.3 had flown. As a result, R2496 had to be moved by road from Denham, a task which provided a great opportunity to demonstrate the quality of Martin-Baker's design and construction and the ease of accessibility provided in the airframe. During the morning of 23 May the aircraft was dismantled at Denham and loaded onto a 'Queen Mary' trailer, it was then towed to Harwell, another period of time was required to unload and reassemble it, and then during the afternoon the fighter was handed over to the test pilot in an airworthy condition. Such swift progress would not have been possible with other fighter types. However, Greensted found on this first flight that the M.B.5 was directionally unstable and would not fly straight. Consequntly, R2496 was

The Martin-Baker M.B.5 R2496 seen as-built with the original fin and rudder. Note the metal cable holding the rear fuselage to the ground. *Del Holyland, Martin-Baker*

This ground view of R2496 in its original form shows the aircraft's sleek lines over the forward fuselage and propellers. Note the wide-track undercarriage.

grounded while the rear fuselage was modified to provide better longitudinal stability (later on a larger fin and rudder were fitted).

When *Flight* first reported on the M.B.5 in November 1945 it was unable to quote performance figures, but could confirm that the aircraft's climb with +25lb of boost was "startling". This account came from R2496's first public appearance, an RAE Farnborough 'At Home' exhibition and flying display held on 29 October which was the first post-war event of its kind. The M.B.5 was the only aircraft

An official photo of R2496 taken in January 1945. The Ministry still called the aircraft the 'F.18/39', not M.B.5, although the specification no longer applied. Note the lowered undercarriage doors.

Port side view of R2496 showing further forward detail of the aircraft. *Chris Gibson*

present to have contra-rotating propellers and one critical observer described its general appearance as: "...a cross between a [P-51] Mustang and a V2 rocket". At the end of its display R2496 lost its sliding canopy when the pilot opened it during the approach, fortunately without damaging the tailplane. Soon afterwards the engine failed spectacularly while Greensted was demonstrating the M.B.5 to Prime Minister Churchill and senior RAF Fighter Command officers at Farnborough, including the Chief of Staff. After performing combat climbs and aerobatics the engine suffered a broken piston which filled the cockpit with fumes and forced Greensted to jettison the hood while flying at some 400mph (644km/h); he managed to make a safe wheels-down dead-stick landing on the runway.

On 1 March 1946 the M.B.5 went to A&AEE at Boscombe for a brief maintenance and engineering appraisal and the resulting report was glowing in its praise. It declared that the M.B.5's general layout was excellent and infinitely better, from the engineering and maintenance aspect, than any other similar type of aircraft. R2496 went to A&AEE again on 15 April and flight trials were completed on 21 May, and on 17 April AVM John Boothman flew it while on a visit to Boscombe. After his single flight he was able to report that it was: "...quite an outstanding aircraft in so far as control and stability are concerned. I have seldom flown an

R2496 prepares to take-off from Farnborough in 1945. *Phil Butler*

aircraft which combines the positive stability of the American fighter with the extreme manoeuvrability usually associated with ours." Boothman added that the top speed was about the same as the Hawker Tempest and Spitfire Mk.XXII, but thought that its climb was somewhat down on both of these aircraft. His only adverse criticism was: "...that it does not accelerate well even in a dive and undoubtedly its thick [wing] section would bring on compressibility effects at a fairly low speed".

The M.B.5's next duty was to take part in a Ministry of Supply exhibition of British aircraft and equipment at RAE Farnborough which was held from 27 to 30 June (this was not the annual SBAC Show). The demonstration of the aircraft by Sqn Ldr Jan Zurakowski at this event has long been remembered as a truly outstanding and breathtaking performance by all who saw it. Zurakowski, at the time serving with 'A' Squadron at Boscombe and one of the finest aerobatic and test pilots ever, flew R2496 from Boscombe and back every day and apparently rated the M.B.5 as the best he had ever flown. Apart from high speed aerobatics, his display included an extraordinary demonstration of slow flying control with a series of stalled 'falling leaf' manoeuvres.

On 24 July 1946 A&AEE issued a flight test report on the M.B.5, although since the type would not be entering production an extensive trial was thought unnecessary. The aircraft was flown throughout at a take-off weight of 11,145lb (5,055kg) which included full fuel and radio but without the guns, ammunition and any armour plate. The pilot's view out and the

The M.B.5 seen at the event held at Farnborough in June 1946. *Phil Butler*

The MB.5 R2496 with its original rudder, which was replaced in the search for better lateral stability. *Tim Brown*

wide undercarriage made taxying easy and, using neutral rudder trim and slight nose down elevator trim, the take-off was straightforward with no tendency to swing; the aircraft became airborne at 75mph (121km/h) ASI after a fairly short run. The M.B.5 had split trailing edge flaps which could only be selected either up or down, so a take-off would be made without flap and there was little change of trim on retracting the undercarriage. With flaps and undercarriage up, slight warning in the form of mild buffeting was given just before the stall which occurred at about 83mph (134km/h) with a mild wing drop. All controls remained light and effective down to the stall. With the flaps and undercarriage down again there was little warning of the stall at 65mph (105km/h), but the rate of sink near the stall appeared high. Most figures indicated that the aircraft was longitudinally stable, and easily trimmed to fly hands and feet off at 10,000ft (3,048m) and at 25,000ft (7,620m) altitude. Its manoeuvre characteristics were good and the

R2496 taxis out, in the process presenting the cameraman with the opportunity to record rear fuselage and empennage detail. The aircraft has the original fin, and note the open radiator shutter door lowered from the rear of the cooling duct. *Del Holyland, Martin-Baker*

The M.B.5 is seen taxying with flaps lowered. They had no intermediate position and were not used for take-offs.

M.B.5 showed no tendency to tighten in turns. The lateral and directional characteristics were also satisfactory and the aircraft was steady in dives to the maximum permitted speed – no compressibility effects were experienced up to the limiting Mach number of 0.75 quoted by Martin-Baker. By 1946 standards the rate of roll appeared to be low, but none of the normal aerobatic manoeuvres presented any difficulties.

The controls were well harmonised throughout the speed range, although some pilots complained of a lack of feel and response. The report noted that this lack of feel was doubtless due to the spring tabs fitted to all three controls. At low speeds the ailerons were light and comparatively ineffective and lacking in self-centring qualities. However, the aircraft's powers of manoeuvre were good but a tendency towards rudder overbalance was reported at high powers and low speed. A normal approach could conveniently be made at 100mph (161km/h) ASI and the deceleration on throttling back was rapid. Landing was easy and there was little change of attitude from the approach to touch-down. Overall the report concluded that, in general, the M.B.5 was easy and pleasant to fly and was highly rated by all who flew it in regard to its flying qualities. It was felt that its combination of steady flight behaviour, good control and excellent pilot view should make the M.B.5 a very good gun platform. However, against present standards the aircraft's

Well known view of the fighter before the serial R2496 had been applied to the rear fuselage. *Del Holyland, Martin-Baker*

Poor quality but a relatively rare flying shot of the M.B.5. *Del Holyland, Martin-Baker*

performance was described as disappointing and it was felt that it was underpowered. This opinion was based on the result of poor acceleration and a low rate of climb. However the maximum level speed performance could not be checked because of insufficient engine cooling which restricted the power available. That criticism of the performance surprised this author since so many reports relating to the M.B.5 have praised its speed so highly, quoting a maximum of 460mph (740km/h) at 20,000ft (6,096m) which was exceeded in the UK most probably only by the Napier Sabre-powered Hawker Fury prototype, by the Supermarine Spiteful (Chapter Thirty-Two) and by the twin-engined de Havilland Hornet prototypes.

It is known that R2496 was at RAE by 15 August 1946 having flown to Farnborough direct from Chalgrove. However, the RAE Flight Log gives no details of further flights with the M.B.5 until November 1947. Wg Cdr Maurice A. Smith flew the aircraft at about that time and the account of his trip from Chalgrove airfield was published in the 18 December issue of *Flight*. (Chalgrove had been leased to Martin-Baker to allow the firm to conduct some early ejection seat trials.) Smith was immediately impressed by the size and "brutal appearance" of the aircraft and its powerplant, and such was the power of the Griffon that it was necessary to anchor the aircraft for the engine run up – a steel cable was employed which ran: "...from one of the main wheels through a pulley attached to a lug in the ground beneath the tail, then up to the rear end of the fuselage". After release the only unpleasant feature Smith noticed on the ground was "the most distracting stroboscopic effect of the contra-props when taxying into the sun", but this effect was not so apparent in the air when the blades were turning faster. The visible cross-over point for the two sets of blades was at 12 o'clock.

Even when taxying only a small movement of the throttle gave a substantial response and Smith described the take-off as delightful – "...the surge of torque-free power was magnificent to experience". By this stage the

R2496 prepares to take-off from Farnborough in 1945. *Phil Butler*

Griffon had been given a 'peace-time' rating of +18lb boost and Smith used only +12lb to get off, so the thought of using the original +25lb of boost was quite intimidating (the engine had been derated because of a shortage of 130 octane fuel.) After leaving the ground, speed built up rapidly and it was clear that the airscrew (on which the blades could not be feathered) had a great bearing on the fighter's performance characteristics. The lack of torque on take-off was one example, but what Smith described as: "...an immediate and unusually powerful response to rpm or power changes over a wide speed range" was another. The engine was virtually vibration free and the volume of noise experienced inside the cockpit was described as "low". When Smith approached a stall in a climbing attitude he could almost "feel the blades digging into the air, as if it were literally hanging on the prop".

At 8,000ft (2,438m) he cruised "very sweetly" at around 315mph (507km/h) (it hadn't taken long to reach that altitude) and he found that both the ailerons and elevators were light without being over light. He thought that the control right around the roll was "exceptional", and a loop at about 360mph (579km/h) with only a slight increase in power "went according to the book". When he returned to the Chalgrove circuit in readiness to land Smith reached 465mph (748km/h) ASI, at which point the aircraft "felt as smooth and solid as one could wish", and the control in a wide vertical turn made at this speed was just as excellent. Slowing down to land Smith found that the airscrew's retarding effect from throttling right back was like "pulling on a hand brake". In all the important aspects of equipment and control the M.B.5 had set a very high standard.

R2496 was at de Havilland Hatfield from 15 November to 31 December 1947 for propeller trials, and in 1948 the aircraft went back to RAE Farnborough. On 5 May it was flown to Wattisham to join the Air Ministry Servicing Development Unit to permit a maintenance schedule to be prepared for the type. What happened to the aircraft after that isn't known,

Right top to bottom:

The aircraft seen parked outside its hangar. *Phil Butler*

R2496 runs up its Griffon engine. *Phil Butler*

The M.B.5 taxis out for another flight. *Phil Butler*

R2496 performs a flypast for the cameraman. *Phil Butler*

and in fact the biggest mystery surrounding the M.B.5 relates to its final fate, which is still very obscure. The aircraft did not receive a Ground Instruction Airframe number and it was the case that aircraft joining the Servicing Development Unit were usually returned to flight condition very quickly. Its remains were at RAF Bircham Newton in the early 1950s, in use either as a 'target' or for fire-fighting training. Many historians and enthusiasts are frustrated because the end of the M.B.5's story is still unknown.

Numerous observers have credited the M.B.5 as being perhaps the best piston-powered fighter of its day, and indeed one of the finest ever built, and had jet-powered fighter aircraft not made such rapid progress it seems quite possible that Martin-Baker's last fighter would have entered production. Although James Martin did produce drawings for other piston and jet fighter projects, soon afterwards his company switched to the lucrative business of ejection seats which keeps it going to this day.

Official assessors praised the M.B.5 cockpit (seen here during the aircraft's construction) very highly. *Del Holyland, Martin-Baker*

Structure

The M.B.5 fuselage was built with steel tubing and was covered with light, detachable metal panels. The engine was a two-stage two-speed supercharged Rolls-Royce Griffon 83 and by 1946 the propeller was a 'double three' de Havilland contra-rotating unit (prior to this the aircraft had used a Rotol propeller). The Griffon was cooled by air from a laminar flow duct placed beneath the fuselage aft of the cockpit in an arrangement that looked quite similar to marks of the North American P-51 Mustang powered by the Rolls-Royce Merlin. This radiator

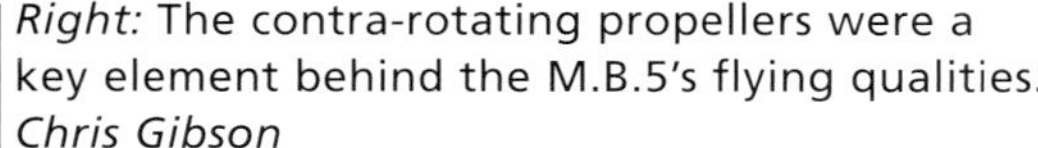

Right: The contra-rotating propellers were a key element behind the M.B.5's flying qualities. *Chris Gibson*

Above: Here the M.B.5 has the enlarged tailplane that was fitted to counter the aircraft's directional instability.

Left: Undercarriage leg detail. *Phil Butler*

Below: Close up of the radiator. *Phil Butler*

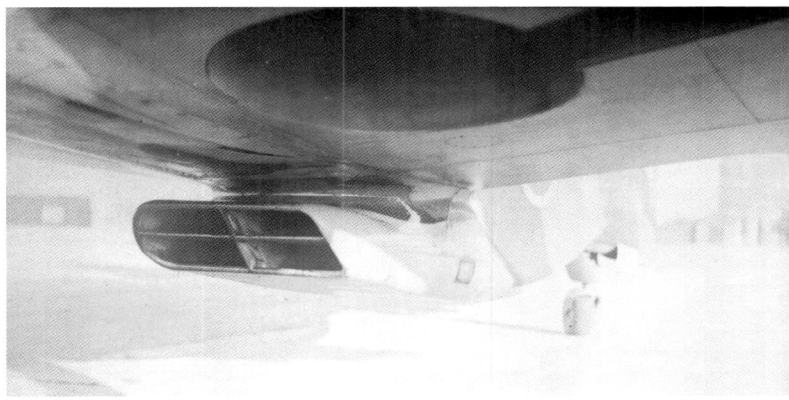

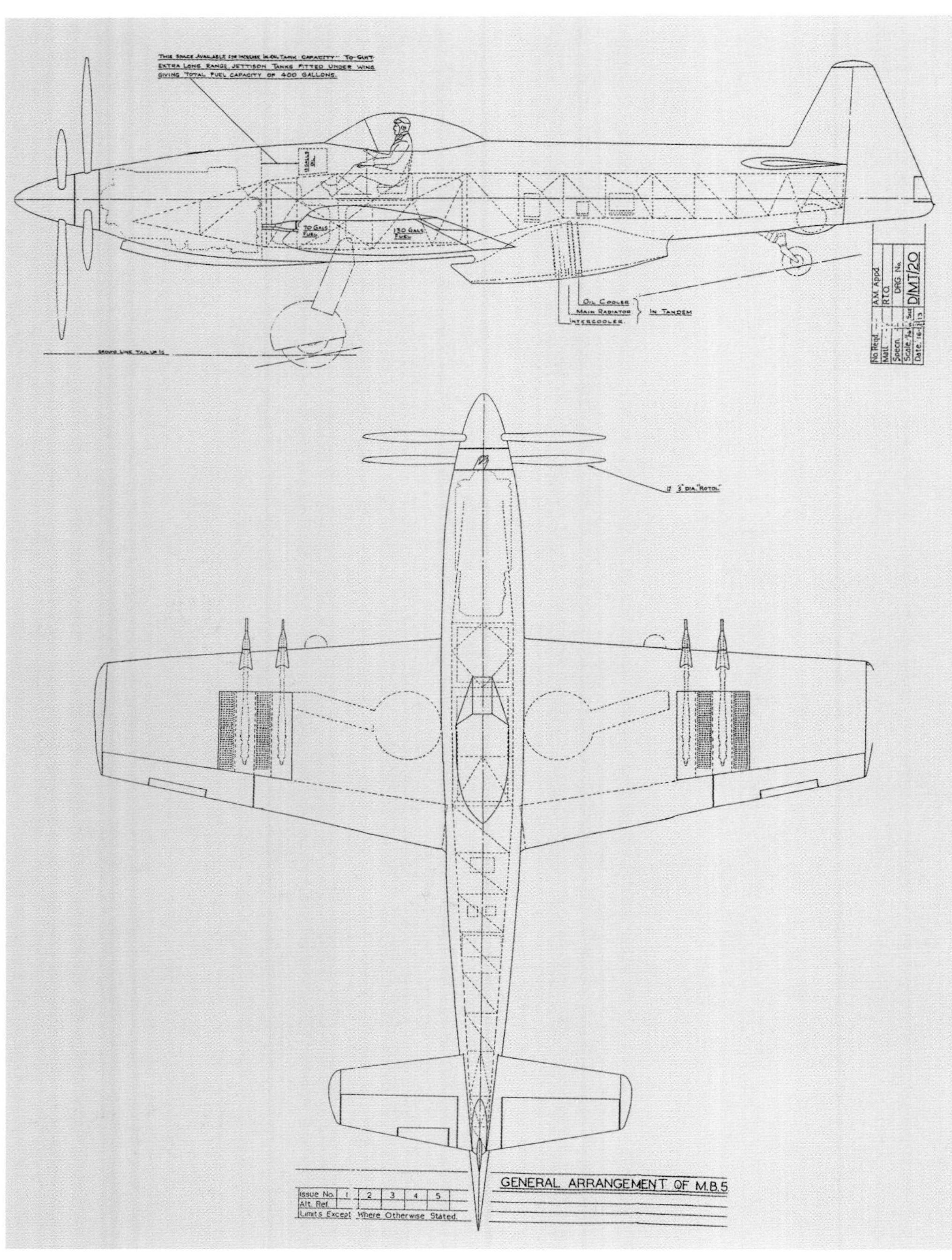

Original Martin-Baker drawing of the M.B.5 which is dated 16 December 1943.

position left the fuselage nose very clean and slim and the long spinner over the hubs of the airscrews carried the lines almost to a point. The duct had three radiators placed one behind the other – first the intercooler, then the main cooler and at the back the oil cooler. This unusual arrangement offered the advantage that, when warming up, the heat from the main radiator prevented coring of the oil, and full oil pressure was obtained within a few minutes of starting up. The Griffon unit was basically identical with that fitted in the Supermarine Spitfire Mks.14 and 21 except that those aircraft had five-blade single airscrews. The lack of contra-rotating propellers on most Griffon-engined Spitfires created substantial problems of swing on take-off, but because they gave no swing the M.B.5's contra-props permitted a greater level of take-off power to be used and they improved the aircraft's performance at altitude.

Great efforts were made to ensure that the M.B.5's cockpit was well laid out with all pilot's controls easily and readily to hand, and a neat one-piece transparent sliding 'teardrop' canopy was fitted. The wing, which was little different from the M.B.3 and M.B.4, had a single spar which with the leading edge formed a strong torsion-box and the flying controls were operated by torsion bars that provided light operation – it is certain that the wings from the incomplete second M.B.3 prototype found their way onto the M.B.5. Fuel was housed in a pair of fuselage tanks – a 70 gallon (318 litre) tank was placed in front of the cockpit and a larger 130 gallon (591 litre) tank came behind the pilot. All three flying controls were fitted with spring tabs, trimming was provided on both the rudder and elevators and the aircraft had pneumatically-operated split flaps on the wing trailing edge. Four 20mm cannon were to be mounted in the wings and the wide-track tail-wheel undercarriage had inwards-retracting wheels. Again the angular fin and rudder marked the design as a Martin-Baker product.

22 Miles M.20

Miles M.20 (DR616)

Type: Single-Seat Fighter

Powerplant: One 1,300hp (969kW) Rolls-Royce Merlin XX liquid-cooled inline engine

Span: 34ft 5in (10.49m)

Length: 30ft 9in (9.37m)

Gross Wing Area: 234sq.ft (21.76m^2)

Loaded Weight: 8,000lb (3,629kg)

Rate of Climb: 2,300ft/min (701m/min) at sea level

Maximum Speed: 333mph (536km/h) at full throttle height of 20,400ft (6,218m)

Absolute Ceiling: Estimated 33,700ft (10,272m); Estimated Service Ceiling 32,800ft (9,998m)

Armament: 8 x 0.303in (7.7mm) Browning machine-guns

The Miles M.20 'utility' fighter of 1940 was the result of an effort to address the urgent need for new fighters as part of the background to the Battle of Britain. The work was undertaken by Phillips & Powis Aircraft Ltd, which in 1943 became known as Miles Aircraft Ltd, but the name of designer Frederick George Miles (the company's technical director) was attached to several designs produced in the years prior to this change and the M.20 was one of them (some Ministry documents just called it the 'Miles fighter').

Previously, in 1938 Miles had produced a design for a wooden, cheap to produce, single-seat fighter which made use of components from Miles' Master trainer aircraft. It also featured the Master's gull wing and was to be powered by an 880hp (656kW) Rolls-Royce Peregrine I engine. The project was called the M.20 and a mock-up was officially inspected at Woodley on 27 January 1939 by the Secretary of State for Air, Sir Kingsley Wood, but it did not proceed. Then in June 1940 the company undertook some preliminary work on a new version (later known as the M.20/2, with the 1938 design becoming known as the M.20/1), but only to a stage which enabled approximate weights and performance to be predicted and to enable discussions with MAP to begin. A meeting between Miles design staff and the Air Minister took place on 13 July 1940 and he agreed to support the project provided the firm kept its promise to complete the aircraft's construction inside three months of this date. Contract B140247/40 was placed for one prototype and in view of the urgency it was crucial that all non-essential services were deleted to reduce weight and the manufacture of parts and to ease maintenance.

In order to assist a rapid design and construction process the following lines were adopted:

(a). Wooden construction throughout, which would mean employing wood-working labour that was available immediately.

(b). Non-retracting undercarriage and tailwheel.

(c). Deletion of all hydraulics (standard items of hydraulic equipment were in short supply).

(d). Use of an existing powerplant. In fact the fuselage was designed to fair in with a standard Bristol Beaufighter Mk.II's Merlin XX engine powerplant.

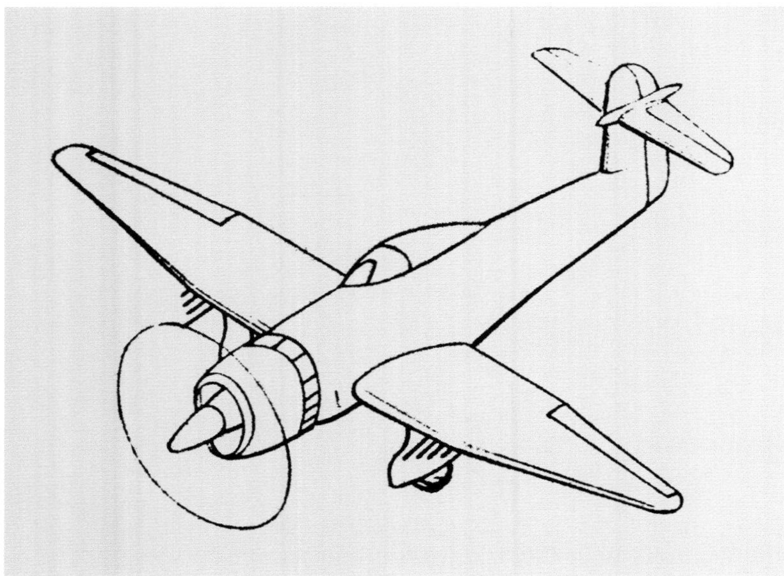

This sketch shows a Westland project which was designed in November 1939 as a simple easy- to- produce interceptor fighter along the same lines as the Miles M.20. It would have had a span of 41ft (12.50m), wing area 240sq.ft (22.32m2) and all-up weight 7,200lb (3,266kg). Powerplant was one 1,400hp (1,044kW) Bristol Hercules engine, four guns appear to be installed in each wing, the undercarriage was fixed and the tailplane and empennage were similar to the company's Whirlwind twin-piston fighter. The estimated maximum speed was 336mph (541km/h) at 15,000ft (4,572m). *Westland Archive*

(e). Standard parts. These were to be used wherever possible and included a Miles Master control box and flying controls, Hurricane gun mounting fittings, and the standard Beaufighter engine installation complete with a slightly modified cowling.

The fighter was covered by Specification F.19/40 and despite these austerity requirements it was expected to have a maximum speed of not less than 350mph (563km/h) at 21,000ft (6,400m) and a service ceiling of 32,000ft (9,755m). One Rolls-Royce Merlin XX would power the aircraft and the armament was eight Browning machine-guns. The specification was dated 29 August 1940.

In the end Miles had the aircraft flying well inside the stipulated three months. The firm realised, however, that in attempting to get an equivalent performance to current fighter aircraft, with the handicap of a thicker wing (21% thickness/chord ratio made necessary by the wooden construction) and the fixed undercarriage, it had a difficult problem. This was overcome by reducing drag, the surface drag for example being aided by the fact that the thick ply skin made an excellent surface which, combined with a suitable paint finish, could hardly be bettered by any other form of construction. Special fastening to ensure tight fittings and reduce leakage drag also proved vital (Miles used a design of its own), while the fuselage lines were laid out to avoid any double curvature, thus rendering the skinning process a simple matter.

The construction team was led by Walter Capley and the prototype with 'B' mark U9 (and later serial AX834) first flew on 15 September 1940, just over nine weeks after the start of design work. For the occasion it was piloted by Miles' chief test pilot Flt Lt Tommy Rose and from the 21st of that month a programme of test flying was commenced

Two photographs showing the Miles M.20/2 in its earliest form with 'B' mark U9. It later became AX834.

which proved that the aircraft had a good performance, although a high wing loading meant a longer take-off and landing run than the Hurricane and Spitfire. Flying continued until 6 February 1941 when AX384's brakes, which had frozen in the free position due to a prolonged period flying at altitude, failed to stop pilot Hugh Kennedy from sliding into the gravel pit at the end of the runway. He was unhurt, but the trials were brought to an abrupt end and AX384 was eventually scrapped, appearing on the dump in 1948. Although having flown well, the type had failed to ignite any real enthusiasm. Government scientist Henry Tizard reviewed the M.20 in an official Ministry report and noted that: "...it has flown but is in difficulties through spinning trouble. I have not yet been able to discover any real argument in its favour. The only argument put forward which carries any weight with me is that it has an extremely good view, better than that of the Hurricane." In fact the aircraft had shown a marked reluctance to recover from a spin, but this problem was solved very early on. It was caused by the tailplane blanketing the rudder, and the simple cure was to move the tailplane further aft and square off the end of the fuselage in the side view.

Another official report written by Sir Archibald Sinclair, the Secretary of State for Air, on 30 December 1940 confirmed that the M.20's performance was not good enough for day use and the armament was inadequate for day or night use. However, a fighter was needed for catapulting from ships for convoy defence and the M.20 might be suitable as a relatively cheap expendable type. The forecast performance was more than adequate to deal with the Focke-Wulf Fw 200 Condor long-range bomber which was currently a threat to Allied convoys and shipping and the M.20 also had a good range. It was recommended therefore that, subject to the agreement of the Admiralty, the development of the M.20 prototype might continue in the limited role of a shipborne expendable fighter, but no production order would be placed until it was known if the aircraft could be catapulted from the light naval type of catapult. Sinclair added that small wheels projecting slightly below the fuselage as a replacement for the normal undercarriage would make landings in the sea safer. (Another memo from 30 December actually states that an order for twelve Miles M.20s had already been placed for development purposes, but this was incorrect).

Consequently, by early April a second prototype, the M.20/4 was flying. This machine had been produced as a private venture to counter to the threat posed to naval convoys by the Condor, but it would be unable to land back on board ship and so would have to ditch in the sea (this role was eventually filled by the Hurricat version of the Hurricane flown from Catapult Aircraft Merchantmen). This second prototype showed subtle differences from the first – for example the spinner was more pointed and the undercarriage fairings were thinner. Specification N.1/41 of 3 July 1941 was subsequently issued for the new naval role – an arrestor hook was to be added and the top

A view taken after the M.20's upper surfaces had been camouflaged and the lower surfaces painted in trainer yellow. The serial AX834 has now been applied.

speed was a more modest 300mph (483km/h) at sea level with service ceiling 20,000ft (6,096m). There were few other changes and with 'B' mark U-0228 the new machine was covered by the same Contract B140247/40. Some reports have indicated that parts of the first aircraft found their way into the second, and the proximity of the M.20/2 crash and M.20/4 first flight dates suggest that could easily be the case, but there is nothing in the surviving company records to confirm it.

Flight handling trials were underway by 8 April in the hands of Miles Aircraft's assistant test pilot Flt Lt Hugh Kennedy and later that month U-0228 went to A&AEE Boscombe Down to undergo a brief assessment. The flying was limited by engine troubles but the tests that were completed were made at a start weight of 7,560lb (3,429kg). There was a strong tendency to swing to the left on take-off but this was overcome by the use of full (and immediate) opposite rudder, although if the swing was allowed to develop it could not be checked. When the flaps were used they took a considerable time to come up and there was very little sink, and no noticeable change of trim. The M.20 appeared to be stable around all axes and at all speeds but in flight all of the controls were heavy and the ailerons were over-balanced, the latter being most noticeable in dives in bumpy air and at low speeds. The aeroplane was dived to 450mph (724km/h) ASI and the acceleration (with a fixed undercarriage) was described as remarkable, while the absence of wind noise around the bubble hood made this high speed "feel quite pleasent". The overbalance of the ailerons was most noticeable but associated only with small movements – for large movements they became moderately heavy. In a dive the aircraft behaved normally and recovery was straightforward. The stall with the flaps up was 90mph (145km/h) ASI and with them down 73mph (117km/h) ASI. Problems were highlighted with the airframe construction and layout but the pilot's view from the bubble-shaped canopy was considered to be excellent, although the fixed undercarriage introduced a real element of danger in the event of a forced landing in the sea.

This aircraft made a second visit to Boscombe later in the summer to assess its suitability as a naval fighter; this was after the military serial DR616 had been allotted. Gun firing trials were made on 24 July over Sidmouth Bay and it is understood the the particular Merlin XX fitted in DR616 was a rogue, which for no clear reason spluttered at

The M.20/4 was DR616 seen here. Note the slimmer undercarriage leg fairings and the ports in the wings for the machine guns, and that there are fuselage catapult points underneath the cockpit. There appears to be few if any images of an M.20 in flight and none at all showing this second aeroplane with its serial DR616. It apparently defied all attempts to be photographed with the number in view!

times and made banging noises. The report, dated 18 September 1941, stated that flights were again made at 7,560lb (3,429kg) weight, which represented full ammunition for the guns but only 110 gallons (500 litres) of fuel, and the estimated service ceiling was 32,800ft (9,998m), although the highest altitude achieved was 32,000ft (9,754m). The coolant radiator's performance fell within the requirements for temperate summer conditions but not tropical summer conditions.

In mid-September 1941 DR616 went to Farnborough but was back with its manufacturer by the last day of the year, it was delivered to 24 Squadron on 21 February 1942 but on 19 March it was returned to the makers and placed in store in a hangar on the Davis Farm site. Struck off charge on 22 May 1943, DR616 was broken up in the Repair & Service Department in November of that year. In the end the M.20 was not ordered into production because of the RAF's success in the Battle of Britain and the adoption of the Hurricat to fill the short-term requirements of convoy defence. The need for such an aircraft passed by, but this fighter remains a remarkable effort and achievement by its manufacturer.

Structure

The M.20 was a quite small aircraft and its two-spar wing was built in wood except for the tips and root fairings. The ribs were placed very close together to prevent the plywood skin from wrinkling under load, but to reduce weight all spar joints were deleted, the spars being continuous from tip to tip. A strong metal casting was attached to the front spar on which the main undercarriage tube was bolted. Pneumatically-operated split flaps and Frise-type ailerons with differential travel were fitted and there were four guns per side. The fuselage was semi-monocoque formed of longerons and formers and covered by plywood or fabric. The cabin was for its time an unusual design in so far as the pilot's head and shoulders projected above the top fuselage lines. It had a bullet-proof windscreen and Perspex rear cover which afforded a greatly improved view over contemporary types, particularly to the rear. Internal fuel totalled 148 gallons (679 litres) with all of it housed in the wings (additional long range fuel could be carried in underfuselage drop tanks), and the engine had a two-speed, single-stage supercharger and drove a Rotol three-blade constant-speed propeller.

23 Miles M.35, M.39 and M.39B Libellula

Miles M.35

Type: Single-Seat Tandem-Wing Research Aircraft

Powerplant: One 130hp (97kW) de Havilland Gipsy Major air-cooled inline engine

Span: Front wing 20ft 0in (6.10m); rear wing 20ft 6in (6.25m)

Length: 20ft 4in (6.20m)

Gross Wing Area: Front wing 45.0sq.ft (4.185m^2); rear wing 87sq.ft (8.09 m^2)

Maximum Weight: 2,000lb (907kg)

Maximum Speed: Unknown

Service Ceiling: Unknown

Armament: None

Miles M.39B

Type: Single-Seat Tandem Wing Research Aircraft

Powerplant: Two 130hp (97kW) de Havilland Gipsy Major IC air-cooled inline engine

Span: Front wing 25ft 0in (7.62m), rear wing 37ft 6in (11.43m);

Length: 22ft 4in (6.81m)

Gross Wing Area: Front wing 61.7sq.ft (5.74m^2), rear wing 187sq.ft (17.39m^2)

Maximum Weight: 3,200lb (1,452kg)

Rate of Climb: 1,100ft/min (335m/min) at 4,500ft (1,372m)

Maximum Speed: (RAE figure mid-1944) 166mph (267km/h) at sea level (this was less than that measured by Miles, and by the time of its second RAE visit the speed had dropped to 164mph (264km/h) at sea level, possibly through airframe deterioration)

Service Ceiling: Unknown

Armament: None

Miles M.39 Project

Type: Three-Seat High-Altitude Bomber

Powerplant: Two Rolls-Royce Merlin 61 piston engines or three Power Jets W.2/500 gas turbines

Span: Front wing 37ft 6in (11.43m); rear wing 55ft 9in (16.99m)

Length: 35ft 10in (10.92m)

Gross Wing Area: Front wing 139sq.ft (12.93m^2);rear wing 417sq.ft (38.78m^2)

Maximum Weight: 26,750lb (12,134kg)

Cruise Speed: Merlin engines 360mph (579km/h)

Service Ceiling: Unknown

Armament: 2 x 20mm cannon and 6,000lb (2,722kg) bombs. Maximum range with this load and Merlin powerplant 2,900 miles (4,666km)

In 1941 George Miles of Phillips & Powis (Miles) became aware of the accident rates associated with deck landing on a carrier, due largely to the poor forward view on the approach of various service aircraft. Another weakness was the waste of time taken in folding and unfolding the wings, so he decided to investigate the possibilities of using unorthodox layouts to eliminate these shortcomings. It eventually became clear that a tandem wing arrangement might improve the view and eliminate wing folding. Miles' tandem wing 'monoplane' concept would have a leading plane that would carry a substantial proportion of the total weight, and the centre of gravity (CofG) would lie somewhere amidships between the two wings.

The name 'Libellula' (a generic name for a certain species of the dragonfly family) was chosen for this and all subsequent tandem wing arrangements. The two wings were connected by a short fuselage and the CofG would always lie forward of the leading edge of the rear wing and aft of the trailing edge of the forward wing. The forward wing's loading would also always be greater than for the rear wing, usually between the ratios 2.5:1 and 1.25:1. The very large range of CofG movement possible with the Libellula was to be partly due to the tandem wing and partly to its use in conjunction with Miles' patent retractable auxiliary aerofoil flaps-cum-elevator arrangement to be fitted on the forward wing (eventually only in the M.39B below). This not only provided a very large range of lift coefficient for the front wing but also a means of varying the available wing area without variation in lift coefficient. In this way the wing area could be varied at will to correspond with the optimum value for any given condition of loading. It could also provide a means of varying the area of elevator available for longitudinal control, and in this way it could be varied at will to correspond with any given speed of flight. This was accomplished by having a small portion of the trailing edge of the outboard portion of the wing hinged to form a slotted flap, which in the Libellula was used to effect longitudinal control by operation, in effect, as an elevator.

The first Libellula type was the M.35, and this aircraft was completed in just six weeks from the start of its design, with the maximum number of people engaged in working on it never more than twelve. It was planned as a 'rough' flying mock-up to investigate the Libellula's aerodynamic possibilities in general, but more specifically for the ship-borne long range fighter project as submitted to MAP in 1941. However, due to the lack of a suitable engine, and the firm's decision not to use a shaft drive in order to accelerate the aeroplane's completion, it was necessary for the M.35 to carry a very heavy load of ballast to obtain the design CofG position. Consequently, when flight tests showed that the aircraft was unstable longitudinally it was found impracticable on such a small machine to carry the CofG sufficiently far forward to cure this effect. The duration of the individual flight tests was also restricted by inadequate cooling, which the firm had expected with this rather crude installation (which was all that could be done in the short time and with the restricted labour that was available).

Much valuable information was gained with the M.35, however, which was given B mark U-0235. Taxying trials were undertaken by its designer George H. Miles on 1 May 1942 at Woodley but it is understood that the aircraft showed no inclination to leave the ground and it possibly did not fly that day. Nevertheless, in due course it was able to fulfil its objective in showing that the tandem wing was feasible and controllable. A point which in particular had previously been in doubt, and which according to a Miles document was satisfactorily cleared up by the M.35, was the possibility of obtaining adequate directional and lateral stability and control on an aircraft of this nature. As a result the firm was encouraged to go ahead with a 5/8th scale flying model which became the M.39B.

A paper written by George Miles in April 1944 outlined some of the theories behind the tandem wing concept, and how it offered certain advantages not shared by orthodox or other unorthodox types. For some time nearly all of the improvements in the performance of conventional (orthodox) aeroplanes had come primarily from increased power, new means of propulsion (jets), increased wing loading and attention to detail design. One limitation on the orthodox form was that it was now much too sensitive to small changes in the position of the CofG. Along with tailless layouts like the Manx (Chapter Fourteen), a possible direction for a new aerodynamic configuration could be a tailfirst design, although there would be difficulties – for example tailfirst would still be sensitive to CofG movements (but a larger range of CofG would be possible). There were numerous other potential advantages, including:

Manufacturer's artist's impression of the Libellula naval fighter project. Note the guns in the lower nose.

U0235 (it should have been written U-0235) seen in June 1942 after receiving an additional tailwheel. *Peter Green*

View of the M.35 U0235, Miles' first Libellula design to fly. *Peter Amos*

1. Both leading and main plane would contribute to the aircraft's total lift, thereby eliminating the parasitic drag associated with a conventional tailplane.

2. Maintaining trim at low speeds would be easier. The nose-down pitching of a conventional wing-tailplane associated with its centre-of-pressure movement due to increasing incidence called for maximum negative lift from the tail unit just at the point when the greatest overall lift was required, a situation aggravated substantially by high-lift flaps. On the tandem the lift of the two planes was additive, so backward movement of the centre-of-pressure called for an increase in lift on the leading surface to maintain trim.

3. Because of the division of lift between the two wings, as on a biplane, a reduction in span might be possible which would benefit the structure weight.

4. Losing the rear tail and concentrating the powerplant near the CofG could reduce the aircraft's length considerably, again cutting the structure weight and enhancing the manoeuvrability. Indeed, these final points would mean the elimination of the weight and drag of tailplane and elevators which contributed nothing to the overall lift, and the elimination of the weight and drag of the long fuselage required to provide the necessary leverage for orthodox tailplanes and elevators.

M.39 Designs

The naval fighter project was not taken up, but a Libellula design called the M.39 was also prepared against the requirements of Specification B.11/41 for a medium bomber capable of high speeds and altitudes (the document actually covered the Hawker P.1005 in Chapter 17). It was the lack of official interest in the naval fighter that prompted

George Miles to look at a design which corresponded very roughly with B.11/41, and it was for this that the 5/8th scale flying mock-up was planned. Proposals for the M.39B were completed in June 1942 and the aeroplane first flew on 22 July 1943 with George Miles again the pilot; it was given 'B' mark U-0244. It is understood that MAP became pretty annoyed when it learnt that both the M.35 and the M.39B had been built in secret as private ventures, without the Ministry's knowledge. It must be emphasised that the M.35 and M.39B differed enormously. As stated, so far this had all been a private venture effort but on 16 September 1943 MAP agreed to award a development contract which included the purchase of the M.39B (it was given the serial SR392 but was this was not allotted until 12 February 1944).

A letter written by George Miles to Colonel H.G. Bunker of the USAAF (US Army Air Forces) on 7 October 1943 reviewing the programme so far declared that at this time only the first of a series of front wings had been tried on the M.39B, which had a comparatively simple form of flap. Miles was still planning to try out some alternative front wings later on which would embody more effective high lift devices and which were to be similar in design to those proposed for the full-scale M.39. The level of measured drag on the M.39B was very promising because, although it was a very clean aircraft, it had been impossible to keep the engine nacelles down to the correct size for an exact scale model, and in addition neither the cabin nor windscreen were as clean as they would be on the full size machine. The take-off compared well with an orthodox aeroplane of similar power and the climb was definitely better than Miles had expected. Stability with the controls fixed was satisfactory. The M.39B was given a third central fin which was intended to serve as an additional safeguard and flight tests were carried out both with and without it fitted . The letter noted that the impression the design team had gained was that the aeroplane's handling characteristics were improved with the additional fin area, although George Miles thought that the centre fin was much larger than was really necessary.

When the firm's preliminary tests had been completed George Miles' plan was to dismantle the machine to make certain structural alterations to the rear, which flight tests had indicated were advisable. This was not unexpected since major design alterations had been made halfway through the M.39B's construction due to the non-availability of the original type of engines specified and these had resulted in a rather flexible rear wing (trouble with this source had been anticipated). Small alterations were also to be made to the ailerons and rear flaps since on the first flights these were shown to be somewhat overbalanced. Although this snag was easily cured by the addition of trailing edge strips, Miles proposed to move the hinge points forward slightly. (Note: At the start it was also planned to have an observer in a cabin just ahead of the rear wing and there were two small windows for him in the upper fuselage. However, no observer was ever

The M.39B marked as U-0244 before it received its official serial SR392 in early 1944. *Tim Brown*

The sole M.39B U-0244 photographed in August 1944. The aircraft is in the configuration in which most of its flight test programme was conducted.

U-0244 seen in flight with George Miles in the cockpit.

carried and when the rear fuselage was re-skinned to improve the fuselage torsional stiffness these windows were deleted).

Miles' October 1943 letter was sent to AAF Materiel Command at Dayton, Ohio to see if the USAAF would be interested in the concept. This was before the M.39B had been stall tested. Bunker's covering letter to AMC noted that MAP was: "...only mildly interested in this venture, which is strictly on a speculative basis". MAP's Controller of Research and Development (CRD – Air Marshall J.E. Serby) had requested AMC's opinion as to whether it would be worthwhile to invest in a full development programme with Miles. The Design Unit of the AMC Aircraft Laboratory made a brief study of the data and the reply made by John H. Ober raised the following points:

1. The only aircraft under development in the US against which the M.39B could be compared was the Curtis XP-55 fighter. This had first flown in July 1943 and crashed on 15 November 1943 due to its inability to recover from an inverted stall.

2. It was thought that the M.39B would possess the same undesirable stall characteristics as the XP-55, namely, settling at a trim angle of approximately 90°.

3. Although it could not definitely be predicted that the M.39B would exhibit this uncontrollable settling trim condition following a stall, it was strongly recommended that stalls and stall recovery be demonstrated before any serious consideration be given to the designs.

4. There was no known aerodynamic advantage to the Miles arrangement. It was believed that the canard type aircraft owed its recurrence to the general misconception of the direction of tail loads. With conventional aircraft the CofG was generally aft of the aerodynamic centre. If low-moment wing sections were employed with a conventional arrangement an up tail load was required to balance the aircraft at low speeds contrary to the general conception that the tail load acted downwards. The only advantages to be gained from such an arrangement were in equipment layout, and a smaller overall span (for a given weight and wing loading).

Clearly, Air Material Command was not particularly impressed with the Libellula concept and it remained to be seen if flight testing would show problems with stalling.

U-0244 was first received at RAE Farnborough on 17 January 1944, but after three flights a more reliable undercarriage retraction system had to be fitted. After Miles staff had completed the work the M.39B (now SR392) was returned to RAE on 24 April, but three accidents brought further and considerable delays. Firstly, the aircraft was slightly damaged when it came into contact with a crane, then a pilot forgot to lower the undercarriage before making a landing which damaged the propeller tips and the fuselage and nacelle undersurfaces, and finally having been parked tail to wind it was blown over backwards by an aircraft running up in front of it which resulted in damage to the central fin and aft end of the fuselage. Other mishaps had occurred at Woodley during initial taxi trials when the nosegear attachment failed, and during maintenance in the experimental flight shed when the aircraft fell back onto its rear fuselage and was damaged.

Farnborough's August 1944 report noted how brief flight tests had shown that the handling characteristics were normal for an aircraft of this power and wing loading and did not differ from those of conventional aircraft.

This relatively poor quality image of the M.39B shows how the pilot's view below was limited somewhat by the forward wing.

Another air-to-air of the M.39B, this time taken during official trials with serial SR392.

This air-to-air image of SR392 shows how unorthodox for its time, and yet most attractive, the Libellula configuration was. *Peter Amos*

The CofG was about 40% of the distance between the quarter-chord points of the two wings forward of the quarter-chord point of the rear wing. Therefore, in normal flight the front wing was taking about 40% of the aircraft's weight. The take-off was very easy (the nose wheel making it simple to correct any tendency to swing) but the effect of having the front flap was that the aircraft needed to be pulled off the ground very firmly. At 80mph (129km/h), however, the M.39B would fly itself off. However, with the then present amount of lift on the front wing, for landing it was not possible to use more than about 10° of flap on the rear wing, so to permit the aircraft's capabilities to be explored more fully would require further development work to provide adequate high lift. The front flap was not powerful enough to balance the moment produced by lowering full rear flap, and in flight it was recommended to lower the front flap before the rear flap. It was also important to select the correct combination of flap settings in order to maintain trim in flight.

The aileron control was described as being rather sluggish at speeds below 85mph (137km/h) (which did not help landing in gusty weather) and with the central fin in place the directional control was [only?] adequate. Longitudinal control was satisfactory and good turns were possible on rudder alone or ailerons only, but a sudden application of aileron created yaw and the nose would rise. On cutting one engine the aircraft would immediately bank in the direction of the dead engine, there was a rapid decrease in speed and the nose would then drop, the aircraft entering a steep spiral if no corrective action was taken. Single engine flight was unpleasant because of the low speed (80mph (129km/h) or a little more at 3,000ft (914m)) and a large rudder load was required, but height could be maintained and no aileron was required. No stall trials were to be conducted until tail parachutes had been fitted.

The M.39B completed a second spell at Farnborough between August 1944 and February 1945 and this time the stall was examined. Few external changes had been made to the aircraft, although a new nose contained a venturi pitot for reading low air speeds and two anti-spin parachutes had been packed into the main wing (one aft of each engine and at a total weight penalty of just 5lb (2.27kg) [should this be 50lb?]). At the stall the nose dropped and recovery was straightforward, but it was not always easy to recognise since the manoeuvre was gentle and entailed a loss of no more than 100ft (30m). There was no difficulty in controlling the aircraft when the front wing had stalled if the stick was eased forward or the front wing flap was raised. The stall was assessed in two CofG positions and the minimum recorded stalling speed was 59mph (95km/h). AAF Materiel Command's predictions had been proved incorrect!

When these trials were completion the aircraft went back to Miles to have the 'high-lift' front wing finally fitted. On the inboard section of the M.39B's front wing Miles

Model of the Miles M.39B matched with a false sky to give an impression of this delightful aeroplane in flight.

retractable auxiliary aerofoil flaps were installed in such a way that as they were extended they followed a path parallel to the chord line, thus progressively increasing the wing area. Their extension could be stopped at any desired point so that the optimum wing area corresponding to the prevailing conditions of loading would be provided. In addition these flaps were interconnected with the flaps on the rear plane so that, as soon as extension of the forward flaps was commenced, the rear flaps started to lower. In this way trim was maintained at all times to correspond with any position of loading. For flying at low speeds such as take-off or landing the forward flaps were fully extended, and when the maximum coefficient of lift was required, such as at touch down, this was obtained by fully depressing them by the normal full rearward movement of the control column.

This rebuild was designed to improve the flaps-down elevator power – the outboard flaps became the elevators (retaining their slotted form) while as stated the inboard wing was rebuilt to incorporate the retractable external-aerofoil flaps. In a letter to *Aeroplane Monthly* in July 1991 former Miles engineer Graham K. Gates noted that the flap mechanism included: "...a very simple method of progressively coupling the flaps to the elevator motion – when the flaps were retracted they were not influenced by elevator movements at all, but when extended they went up-and-down with the elevators". As such they were retractable external-aerofoil elevators and the aircraft was now used to explore a much larger range of CofG (apparently 16in/40.6cm, compared to 1.6in/4.06cm at RAE). This required modifications to be made to the main landing gear drag stays to permit the wheels to be

On the completion of its official testing the M.39B was painted yellow and given the post-war B mark U4. It is seen here piloted by Hugh Kendall. The venturi pitot is well shown.

Artist's impression of the full size Miles M.39 bomber project.

moved further aft. The aircraft was painted yellow, it now had Class B marking U4 and flight tests confirmed that the new forward wing gave a higher coefficient of lift, which made the take-off run shorter and cut the landing speed by around 6%. In the cockpit for most of these sorties was Hugh M. Kendall, Miles' assistant test pilot.

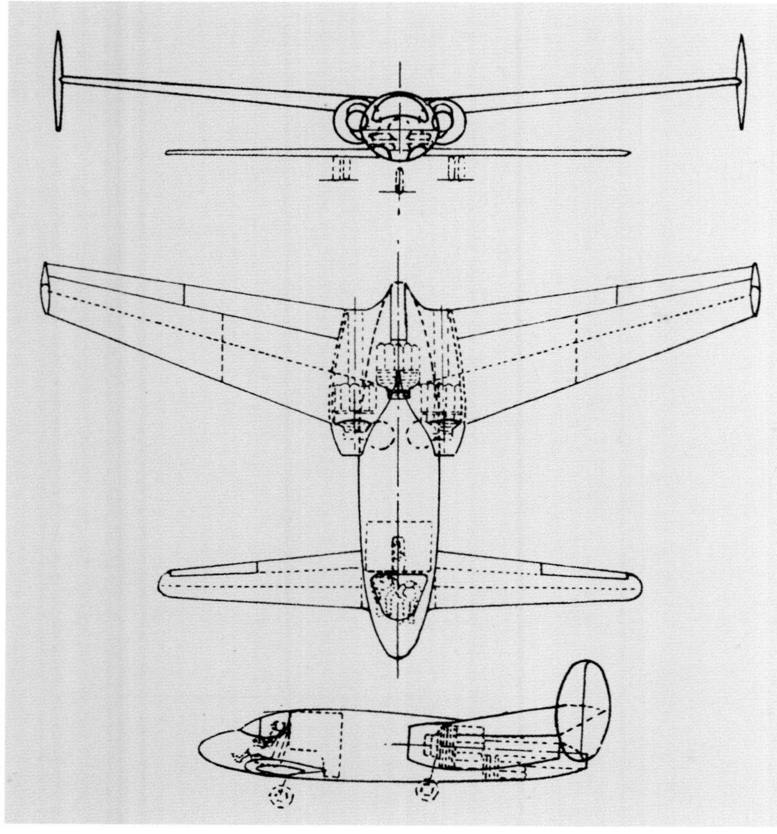
Drawing of Miles' 1944 M.63 project for a jet-powered Libellula. Three jet engines are mounted in the rear fuselage.

An M.39 prototype was ordered in November 1943 to Contract Acft/3461 and given the serial number RR910 but it was never built. Furnished with additional flight data from the M.39B, in May 1944 George Miles projected a tri-jet version of the Libellula design called the M.63 which was submitted to the Postmaster-General as a potential high-speed mailplane, but despite receiving enthusiasm for the idea the full-scale aeroplane remained stillborn. That was a pity since a jet-powered Libellula flying at the late 1940s SBAC Shows at Radlett and Farnborough would have been a thrilling spectacle. The M.39B was finally scrapped in 1948 after none of Miles' numerous full-size Libellula proposals had been accepted. Overall, the Libellulas were a truly fascinating family of aeroplanes.

Structure

The M.35 had a standard Miles all-wood structure with ply and skin covering. The forward tapered surface with a straight leading edge was constructed as a mono-spar wing while the rear surface with its straight centre section but swept outer portions had a conventional two-spar frame. Tip fins and rudders were fixed to the rear wing and both horizontal surfaces were equipped with flaps. There was a fixed tricycle undercarriage and the aircraft had a single pusher engine with a fixed-pitch two-blade propeller of 5ft 6in (1.68m) diameter, its size being limited by the small ground clearance available at the rear of the aircraft.

The M.39B was built on similar lines with a single-spar forward and twin-spar rear wing and a wood structure. However, all of the rear wing was now swept (21° 48' at the leading edge), the span of the forward 'tail' was rather less than the main wing, the undercarriage could be retracted and the twin-blade wooden airscrew had a diameter of 6ft 6in (1.98m). As built the aircraft's rear wing was fitted with plain flaps inboard and ailerons outboard and the front surface had slotted elevators inboard and slotted flaps outboard. The flaps on either wing could be lowered independently but lowering the flaps on the front wing caused the elevators to droop, giving added lift. End plate fins and rudders were attached to the rear wing and a central fin was mounted on the fuselage. No trimmers were provided on any control. At a later stage a different type of auxiliary front tail and flaps was fitted in order to give high lift. Also, the engine cooling was revised, the air originally exhausting through the rear nacelles but later more conventionally at the bottom of the firewalls, fairings being added to the back of the nacelles.

The full-scale M.39 bomber was to have had a purely metal structure and its three crew members were to be sited in a pressurised cockpit with the bomb bay placed amidships. Again a tricycle undercarriage was to be employed and two 20mm cannon were housed in the forward wing roots. The M.39 would have been powered by two Rolls-Royce Merlin engines but it was proposed to install three Power Jets W.2/500 units later. These would have given a speed of 500mph (805km/h) at 36,000ft (10,973m). The Libellula configuration made the substitution of jets for pistons a pretty straightforward process.

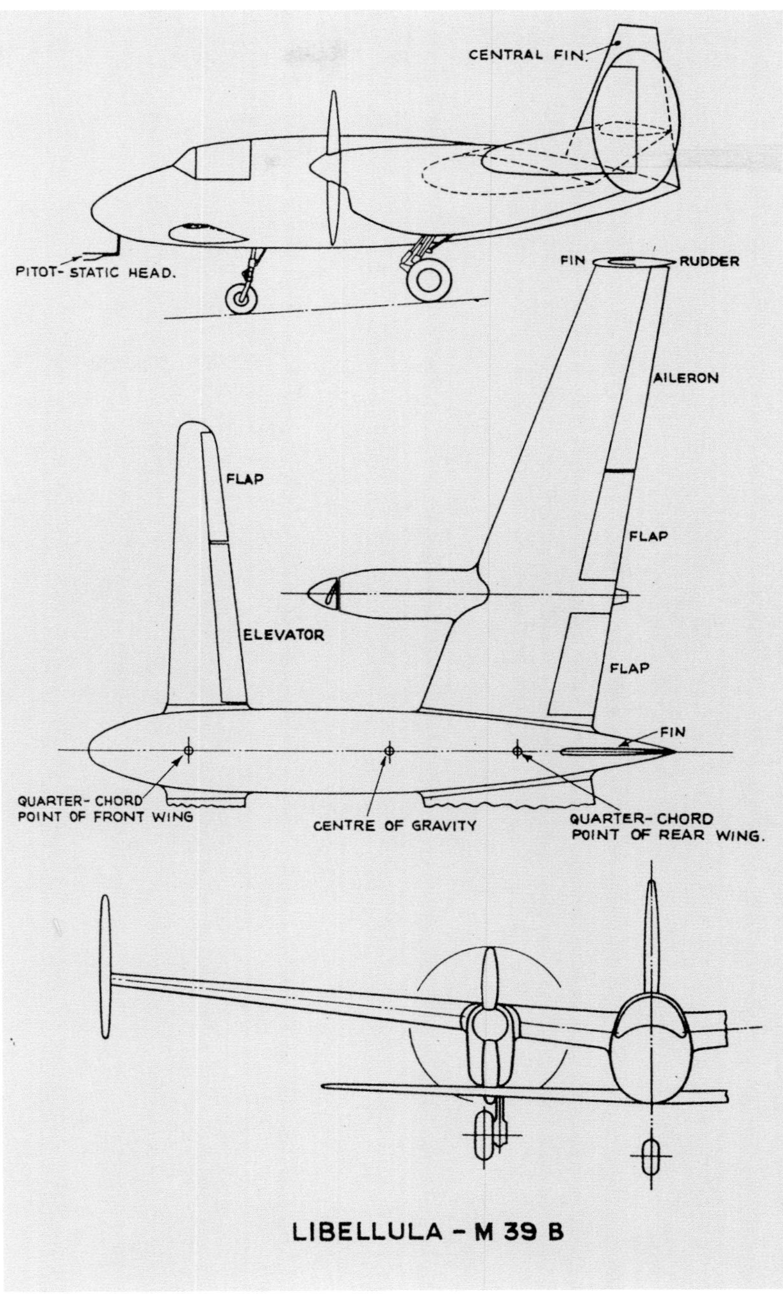

RAE drawing of the Miles M.39B. *National Archives*

24 Napier-Heston Racer

Napier-Heston Racer

Type: Single-Seat Racing Aircraft

Powerplant: One 2,450hp (1,827kW) Napier Sabre liquid-cooled inline engine

Span: 32ft 0.5in (9.77m)

Length: 24ft 7in (7.50m)

Gross Wing Area: 167.6sq.ft (15.59m^2)

Maximum Weight: 7,200lb (3,266kg)

Rate of Climb: Never established

Maximum Speed: Estimated 480mph (772km/h)

Ceiling: Never established

Armament: None

The Napier-Heston Racer was not specifically designed with any military purpose in mind. It was just part of an attempt to break the World Speed Record. On 26 April 1939 the record was claimed for Germany by Fritz Wendel with a figure of 469mph (755km/h) achieved in a Messerschmitt Me 209. With the potential power offered by the new Napier Sabre engine, it was felt that the record could be brought back to Britain for the first time since the days of the Schneider Trophy racing seaplanes of the early 1930s. Consequently an order was placed with Heston Aircraft Ltd for two aeroplanes designed specifically for the task, with Lord Nuffield bearing the cost. (When *Flight* first publicised the Racer in April 1943 it called it the Nuffield-Napier-Heston Racer, and other accounts have used Heston Type 5 Racer or Heston High Speed Aircraft). The detail design was undertaken by the Heston team led by George Cornwall, although Arthur Hagg (at the time working for Napier and a specialist in low drag engine ducting) laid down the general outline. Heston was actually a manufacturer of light aeroplanes but a specialist in wood construction, and wood was ideal for this aircraft since it was light but very strong for its weight, using steam and molds it could be shaped into complex curves, was immune from the fatigue cracking problems experienced in metals, and would provde a very smooth surface without 'waves' (since it exhibits many of the properties of today's advanced plastic materials, wood has been described as 'God's own composite'). Before the war Hagg had worked for de Havilland for many years, and from 1943 he became chief designer and technical director at Airspeed.

The Racer was produced at the instigation of Napier Engines and design work commenced in December 1938, with parts manufacture beginning soon afterwards. At the time the Sabre was top secret and untested (the Racer was one of the first aircraft to use it) and the project was originally proposed to the Air Ministry as an engine testbed. But it was not officially sanctioned as a racing aeroplane which is why it had to proceed as a private venture and why Lord Nuffield had to underwrite the whole project. It was decided that, apart from an unorthodox cooling system, there should be no features that would not be found in a normal aeroplane. Parts for the two planned airframes were made together to ensure in the case of an accident that a 'second string' was available, and wood was also chosen as the build material because it was quicker to work with when only two machines were to be produced. Those sub-contractors involved with the project all supplied their parts free of charge.

The wing had thin-section aerofoils designed specifically for high speeds (thickness/chord ratio at the roots was 16.2%,

The Napier-Heston Racer only achieved one (inadvertent) flight, which ended in a crash-landing. *Tim Brown*

at the tips 9%), a multi-ducted underfuselage air intake and a low profile Perspex canopy that would spoil the airflow as little as possible but provide sufficient view. Saunders-Roe helped with the manufacture of the wings with its own 'Compregnated' wood – multiple laminations bonded with impregnated resin under high pressure. Unusually, the maximum ordinate of the wing was located at 40% of the chord, which was further back than normal to prevent the onset of shock stall (the separation of the boundary layer behind the shock wave) to speeds higher than were to be flown. Since the 3km (1.86 mile) speed record course had to be followed at an altitude of less than 100ft (30m) above sea level, delicate and accurate handling of the aircraft would be vital at such low levels and high speeds. Consequently, when near the neutral postion the control surfaces were geared to give very small movements from relatively large movements with the stick and rudder pedals. However, the gearing was increased close to the maximum control angles to permit the full range of travel to be used.

The novel cooling system was designed to avoid the drag-producing 'whiskers' of an underslung radiator. In brief it used ducted cooling and there was a special Gallay radiator located in the bottom of the rear portion of the fuselage. The speed of the air entering the radiator duct was reduced gradually by increasing the area of the duct, to the point by

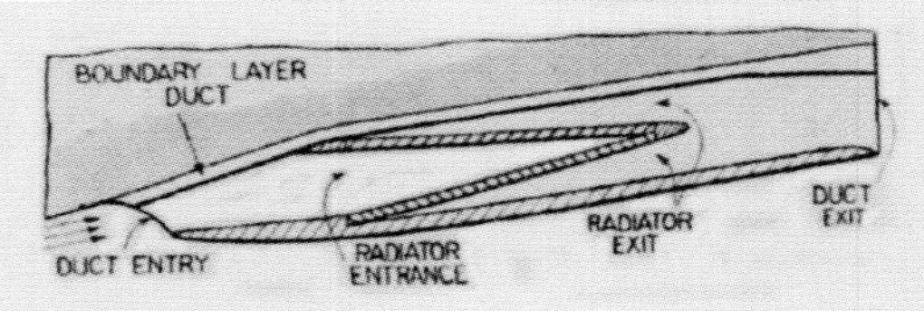

The principal behind the ducted Gallay radiator is shown with this manufacturer's sketch.

Similar picture of the Racer but taken in different light, which enhances more of the aircraft's contours.

Broadside view of the Napier-Heston Racer with the tail end raised on a trellis or frame. Note the droop rear fuselage which contained the radiator duct.

the time it reached the radiator where it was travelling at about one third of the flight speed. It was then led to the two Gallay radiator surfaces which were set in a vee arrangement. These were of such large surface area that the air was flowing through them at approximately 30mph (48km/h), before passing out through the open end of the rear fuselage.

When war began in September 1939 the first machine was nearly complete and the second was around 60% finished. Since these were not military aircraft they were given the civilian registrations G-AFOK and G-AFOL, but the war halted work on the second machine. However, G-AFOK was taken to completion and had its first ground run on 6 December 1939, but a series of wing and airscrew vibration tests prevented any taxi trials from being made until 12 March 1940. Then, because the aircraft was loaded to 43lb/sq.ft (210kg/m^2), a startling figure for the time, the team had to wait for suitable weather conditions to make the first flight. It is quite remarkable that the work of completing and preparing the aircraft continued right through the first nine months of the war!

Opposite bottom and left: Two views of the Racer taken at Heston, without the cockpit canopy in place which was the condition of the aircraft for its one and only flight. The Dowty 'levered suspension' undercarriage is well shown. *Phil Butler*

Taxying tests revealed that problems such as excessive swing or any tendency to ground loop were not present, and the torque reaction proved to be far less than had been expected. G-AFOK made its first and only flight on 12 June 1940 from Heston Aerodrome piloted by Sqn Ldr G.L.G. Richmond, Heston's chief test pilot. It actually left the ground prematurely during a high speed run in take-off configuration after a hefty bump had pushed the airframe into the air. The canopy was not in place and the undercarriage was extended throughout. Unfortunately, thanks to engine overheating the flight had to be terminated after just five to six minutes. Richmond also experienced inadequate elevator control (it is understood that he was also scalded by steam from a broken radiator fitting) and he had no option but to make a quick forced landing. The aircraft was inadvertently stalled when possibly as high as 30ft (9m) above the airfield and hit the ground so heavily that the undercarriage was pushed through the wings. The tail was also broken off and the Racer was damaged beyond repair. Richmond was badly burnt but survived.

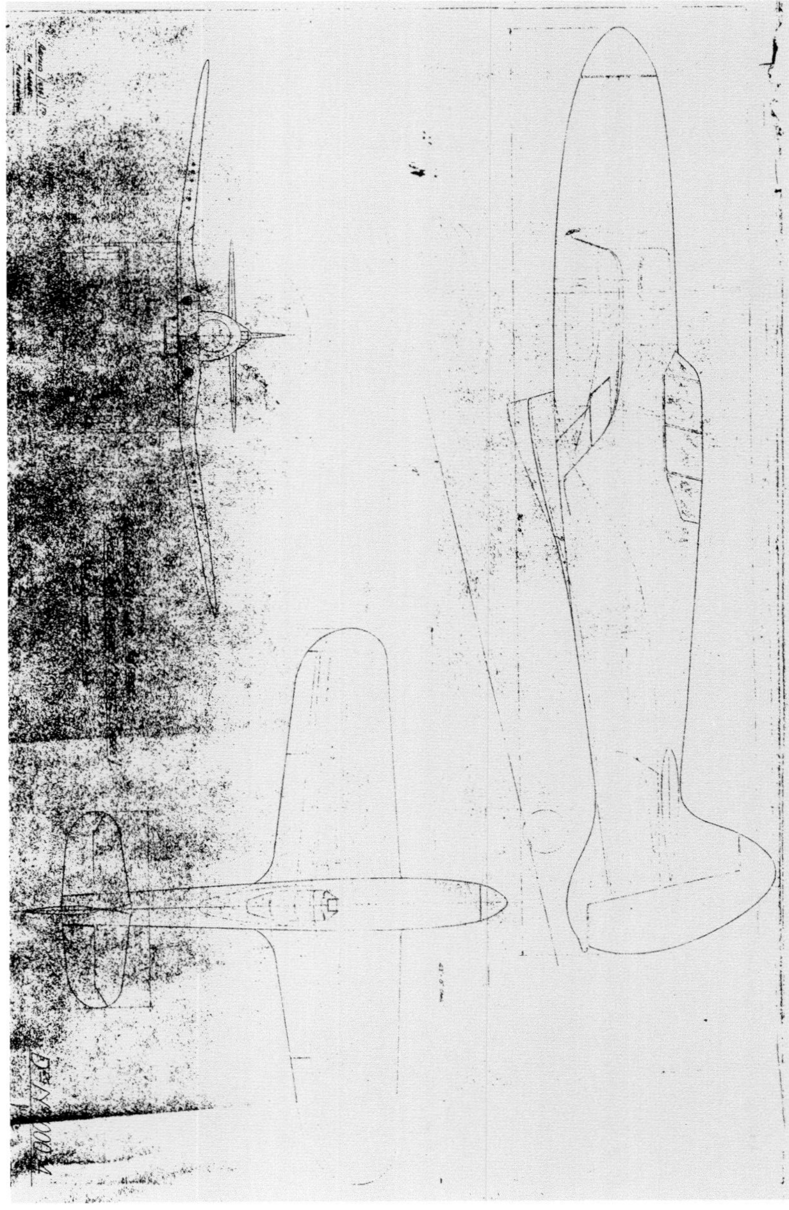

Little is known about this sleek 'Napier Sabre' fighter design from Airspeed, not even a date. But its similarity to the Racer is most marked, and the fact that Arthur Hagg spent some of the war with Airspeed may mean that this was his handiwork. However, at the time of writing this can only be conjecture. A bigger aircraft than the Racer, the fighter's wing is less tapered and its fuselage is slimmer. Span is 43ft 0in (13.11m) and length 36ft 0in (10.97m), each inner wing houses a 60 gallon (273 litre) fuel tank and 12 machine-guns are housed in the wings, six per side. A version with a fixed undercarriage was also drawn.

It is open to debate as to what might have happened to the Racer had it flown successfully. Would it have brought the speed record back to Britain? We will never know. But when the war was over it was a jet aircraft (the Gloster Meteor) which regained the World Speed Record and the day of piston types like the Racer was gone. Wendel's record in the Messerschmitt, however, did last until August 1969 as the highest speed achieved by a piston aircraft. Nevertheless, had it broken the record or not the Racer would most probably have supplied a good deal of important data for Britain's new high peformance aircraft.

Manufacturer's drawing of the Napier-Heston Racer.

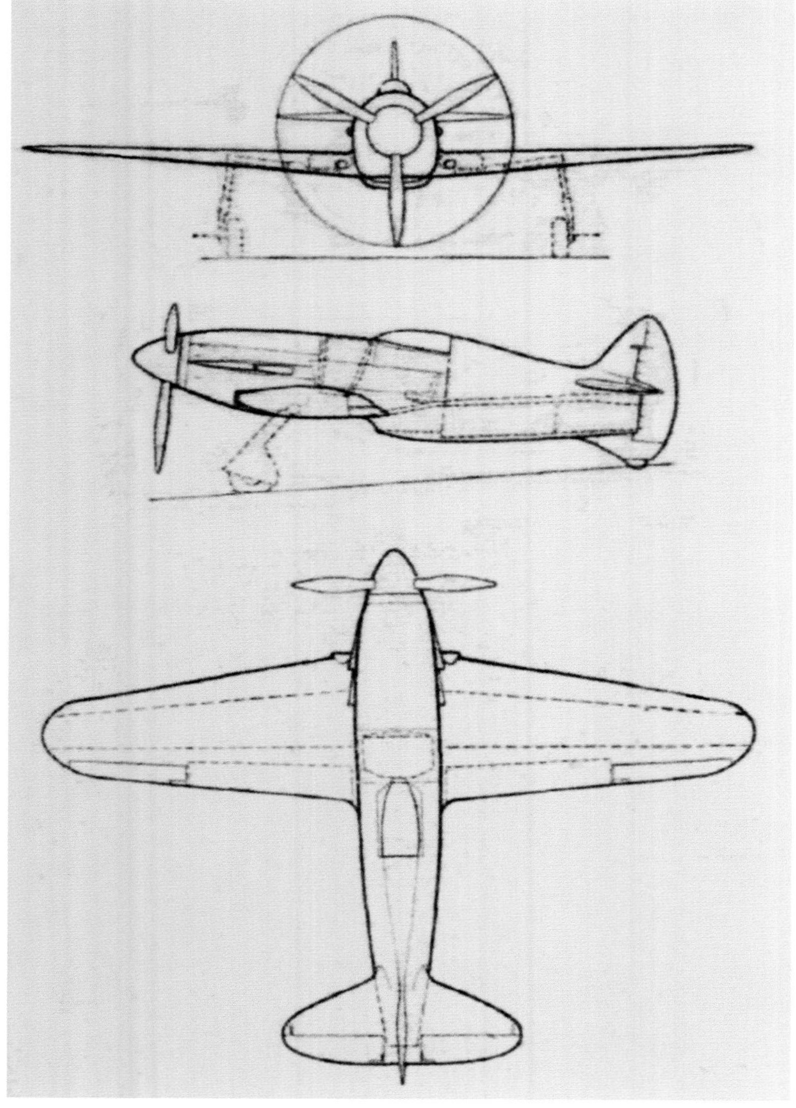

Structure

The small, compact and very clean Racer was built in wood with some metal fittings. The objective was to produce the smallest practical aeroplane for the task and the resulting machine was beautifully streamlined with a 'superfine' finish. It is understood that twenty coats of hand-rubbed lacquer contributed to the smooth surface finish and at critical points such as the wing leading edge it was polished and treated until no scratches deeper than 0.0005in (0.013mm) were present. The wings had box-type spars with birch ply skinning (the leading edge was pre-formed in a mould) and the control surfaces were all made in metal with fabric covering and were all mass balanced with trimming tabs. It had been expected that the Frise-type ailerons would would require careful setting of the tabs, but it was found that the wings damped out the torque reaction. The gap between aileron and wing on the upper surface was completely sealed. Birch ply was also used for the fuselage with spruce frames and stringers. The propeller on G-AFOK was a de Havilland three-blade constant-speed unit, but G-AFOL was to have received a de Havilland Hydromatic airscrew. Fuel was housed in a tank just forward of the pilot's instrument panel and its capacity of 73 gallons (332 litres) gave an endurance of 18 minutes. The undercarriage track was very wide and the engine weighed around 2,900lb (1,315kg), which at around 40% of the total weight was a very high figure.

25 Saunders-Roe A.37 'Shrimp'

Saunders-Roe A.37 'Shrimp'

Type: Two-Seat Four-Engine Research Flying boat

Powerplant: Four 90hp (67kW) Pobjoy Niagara III air-cooled radial engines

Span: 50ft 0in (15.24m), Length: original form 42ft 3.25in (12.88m), later possibly 42ft 8.75in (13.02m)

Gross Wing Area: 340sq.ft (31.62m^2)

Maximum Weight: 6,250lb (2,835kg)

Maximum Speed: Original form 149mph (240km/h) at sea level

Rate of Climb: Original form 635ft/min (194m/min) at sea level

Service Ceiling: Unknown. Highest altitude achieved during first MAEE trial 8,000ft (2,438m)

Armament: None fitted

In 1939 the Air Staff began to look at finding a replacement for the Short Sunderland patrol flying boat and raised Specification R.5/39 to define the project. Several companies submitted designs, one of whom was Saunders-Roe (Saro) who went further than the others in their effort when the firm decided to build a near half-scale flying model to assess the main proposal's aerodynamics and hydrodynamics – it was felt that producing the full size machine on its own was just too big a step to take. The scale aircraft was called the A.37 and nicknamed 'Shrimp', although in fact for a model it was relatively large. R.5/39 was abandoned in October 1939 and in 1940 a new requirement took its place under R.14/40 (which gave birth to the Short Shetland in Chapter Twenty-Seven). Nevertheless, Saro continued its scale model studies as a private venture.

Several subjects in this book were built as scale model aeroplanes, either for a specific type or to test new aerodynamic features for possible new types. By the end of the 1930s the art of aircraft design had reached a point where a new aeroplane could no longer be built for a just a few hundred pounds – the task was much bigger with new and expensive materials and techniques, and it was also very difficult to make major changes to an airframe once it had gone into production. No longer was designing 'by eye' or 'by guess' enough, careful analysis of shapes in the wind tunnel and the most elaborate calculations were the order of the day, but even then they did not guarantee a satisfactory result or provide all of the information required in the early stages of a new design. This was particularly so when a design departed considerably from previous layouts and practice, something more was needed and by 1940 several aircraft manufacturers had gone to the trouble of building actual scaled-down models of an important new type which they had proposed. In this way any doubtful features could be examined thoroughly and modifications made with nothing like the expense required to alter a full-size machine after it had gone into production. However, to be truly comparable with the larger aircraft the flying model had to be a replica in every way, which for the airframe was not really a problem. Strictly speaking it was the engines (and airscrews) that needed to be exact scale models and this was not always possible because it depended on what power units might be available. The choice of engine for the A.37 however, the Pobjoy Niagara, came

Early manufacturer's photo of the A.37 in its original metal finish parked on the slipway at Saro's Columbine Works at East Cowes in about September 1939. Note that the airscrews have not yet been fitted. In many photos the A.37 appears larger than it actually was. *Phil Butler*

from the fact that unusually it was very close to being an accurate scale model of a modern radial engine, the Bristol Hercules to be used by the S.38, Saro's R.5/39 proposal. This set the A.37's size at a scale of 1:2.2 against the S.38.

The A.37 was constructed in just seven months and its design was undertaken by Henry Knowler, who for nearly 30 years was the chief designer at Saro where he worked on many flying boats including the SR.A/1 jet fighter and huge Princess civilian airliner from the second half of the 1940s. The A.37 with civil registration G-AFZS was flown for the first time from its East Cowes birthplace in early October 1939 piloted by Flt Lt Leslie S. Ash, Saro's test pilot. During the first days of March 1940 the machine was shown to the press where it left a very favourable impression, *Flight* reporting that it was "not only fast and very manoeuvrable in the air but showed good sea qualities, clean running and absence of porpoising". Saro reported that the handling was easy and positive and that the A.37 had a very low alighting speed.

By mid-January 1941 G-AFZS was flying from Saro's facility at Beaumaris on Anglesey, and within weeks it had passed into the hands of the Marine Aircraft Experimental Establishment (MAEE) at Helensburgh on the River Clyde in Scotland. Both of these new facilities had been set up out of range of enemy air raids but Beaumaris was not a 'factory' making complete aircraft. Its primary purpose was to receive Lend-Lease flying boats (primarily Consolidated Catalinas) and install British equipment before they entered RAF service. The A.37's first official trials (at a weight of 5,700lb (2,586kg)) were finished in early March 1941 and brought high praise both for its flying and its water qualities. The take-off was described as "easy" with only a slight tendency to swing to starboard. Taxi behaviour was "very good", the hull was clean and "very seaworthy" for its size, the turning circle when taxying was small and the A.37 was easy to land if held at a small angle, but landing tail-down would make the aircraft leave the water again. The elevators were light

Saro A.37 Shrimp G-AFZS pictured flying just above the water probably early in 1940.

The aircraft in the foreground here is a production Saro Lerwick patrol flying boat (with its serial painted out by the censor). The picture was issued in April 1940 and its official caption describes the A.37, seen passing over its larger stablemate, as one of the world's smallest flying boats.

and effective, the ailerons slightly heavier, and the rudder was heavy and less effective, but overall the controls were reasonably well harmonised and the differences were quite small. One undesirable feature was that there was a tendency for the wing to drop if it was stalled without using flaps – the stall occurred at 62mph (100km/h) flaps up, 52mph (84km/h) flaps fully down. In addition the A.37 was used for a separate general trial that examined the use of flaps on flying boats for take-off, finding their best settings, etc, coupled with variations in certain conditions and different propellers.

The R.14/40 Shetland resulted in a joint programme between Shorts and Saro and eventually it was decided to use the A.37 to test elements of the new design in scale form, and particularly to help confirm the shape of the hull's planing bottom. From 22 April 1942 the aircraft was tested again by MAEE, and then on 13 November it went back to Beaumaris. After some modifications had been made (possibly at Cowes) the A.37 was test flown again by Saro on 29 July 1943 and on into August. In June 1944 it was taken under MAP control with the serial TK580 (Contract Acft/1371/C.20[b]) and trials made at MAEE

Another 1940 image of the A.37 with its hastily applied camouflage and RAF roundels coupled with a civilian registration. *Phil Butler*

through much of that year assessed scale versions of the Shetland's floats and elevators plus its single fin and rudder. The Shetland tail was tested in spring 1944 and was considered longitudinally stable over the permissible CofG range. However, the A.37 did not possess the Shetland's wing section so it was not possible to make really close comparison trials. The full results were given in reports dated 7 July and 12 October 1944 and under certain conditions problems were encountered with the elevator control, which was a worry since the A.37's tail was itself an exact replica of the Shetland's with the engine nacelles in the same relative position to provide the same slipstream effects.

The water stability trials also provided interesting results and the A.37 was tested at two standard weights, 5,700lb (2,586kg) and 6,250lb (2,835kg) which equated to 120,000lb (54,432kg) and 130,000lb (58,968kg) on the Shetland. Some problems were experienced with the floats, the starboard side appearing to provide less buoyancy than the port, but by July it was clear that increasing the float settings improved the planing characteristics and cut down spray. However, holding the stick forward of central on take-off and landing was dangerous since there was a tendency to swing to starboard and vicious porpoising. Moving the CofG forward made for violent porpoising during the later stages of the take-off run with the aircraft at times thrown out of the water. There were problems on landing as well, and the higher weight saw water being thrown into the propellers up to the hump (the point of maximum water resistance). The report indicated that the Shetland's stability limits should be satisfactory at the lower weight of 120,000lb (54,432kg) during take-offs and landings. With elevator control, however, the trim would be rather low with normal and forward CofG positions and porpoising would occur over the hump at take-off, and the problem would be wider at the 130,000lb (58,986kg) weight. It was found that the change from the original A.37 to the Shetland type tail gave little or no effect on the stability limits, but the Shetland tail gave a higher attitude over the hump and was more effective at take-off. (Note: this MAEE report called the aircraft the S.37).

On 7 July 1945 the A.37 was back at MAEE again (it passed between Beaumaris and Helensburgh on several occasions), but just a month later the unit was to return to its pre-war home at Felixstowe. The aircraft duly followed to the new venue and was subsequently tested with a further revised Shetland bottom (a new 1:1.5 fairing was added over the step) but this form proved unsatisfactory in that it created a lot of skipping both during the take-off and landing. Forced ventilation of the afterbody was also tried but gave little or no improvement. The A.37 was sold for scrap on 17 February 1949. It represented a fine effort by Saunders-Roe and was an aircraft that was pretty near viceless and a most effective test and research machine.

Structure

The Shrimp had a tapered cantilever wing of plywood and wood frames covered in plywood skin and fabric. It had Handley Page slotted flaps and tubular steel was used for the engine mountings. The single-step hull, however, was all-metal and skinned with Alclad, the floats were also skinned in Alclad and the latter were originally designed to represent the S.38, but here they were fixed, whereas on the full size aeroplane they were intended to retract. Twin fins and rudders (with no tabs) were fitted which, with the horizontal tail, were also assembled in wood with fabric on the moving surfaces. A single fin and rudder was fitted later on. The aircraft had no water rudder but used drogues to manoeuvre on the surface, the Niagara engines had 6ft 3in (1.905m) diameter twin-blade airscrews and the internal tanks held 50 gallons (227 litres) of fuel. Two crew, the pilot and a technical observer seated in tandem, were carried. When first rolled out the Shrimp had a natural metal finish, but by March 1940 it had been camouflaged.

26 Short S.31

Short S.31

Type: Two-Seat Four-Engine Research Aircraft

Powerplant: Four 90hp (67kW) Pobjoy Niagara III air-cooled radial engines; later four 115hp (86kW) Niagara IV

Span: 49ft 7in (15.11m)

Length: 43ft 7in (13.29m)

Gross Wing Area: 325sq.ft (30.225m^2)

Maximum Weight: 5,700lb (2,586kg)

Maximum Speed: 184mph (296km/h)

Rate of Climb: Unknown

Service Ceiling: Unknown.

Armament: None

Another firm to use a scale model aircraft to assess the design of a much larger aeroplane was Short Brothers with its private venture S.31, an exact half-scale prototype model of the firm's S.29 Stirling bomber. It was also known by its B condition mark M4 which, when it was first flown, was painted on the aircraft's fin. The S.31 was to be powered by four small Pobjoy Niagara engines and MAP's Director of Technical Development declared in a memorandum that it would be: "...of great value in proving the flying qualities and controls of the [bomber] aeroplane to a much greater extent than wind tunnel experimental work" (the classic benefit of having a flying model).

The firm originally thought that the model would fly in May or June 1938, about six months in advance of the bomber itself, but it was not, however, ready for taxi trials until September 1938. Nevertheless, the S.31 was constructed quite quickly at Rochester, taxi trials began on 14 September and it made its maiden flight from there on 19 September. The pilot was John Lankester Parker, Shorts' chief test pilot, he was accompanied by Hugh Gordon and the sortie was made in great secrecy. Overall the aircraft and its handling was considered satisfactory but it did suffer from a long take-off run, a point raised by A&AEE pilots at Martlesham Heath after they had seen the aircraft later that month. The solution was to increase the angle of the wing at take off, but this would mean changes to the design of the Stirling's wing-fuselage junction when the bomb-suspension structure in this part of the airframe was set and ready for production (it also meant that the S.31 would fly at a nose-down attitude while cruising). So instead, chief designer Arthur Gouge lengthened the main undercarriage struts to raise the nose on take-off, which added 3° to the ground angle. This resulted in a long main undercarriage for the bomber.

The S.31 returned to the air with its modified undercarriage on 22 November 1938 and soon afterwards more powerful Niagara IV engines were installed, Parker flying the S.31 successfully enough with these on 10 January 1939 although they could be temperamental. Immediately afterwards horn-balanced elevators were fitted to improve the longitudinal control but later a larger tailplane with normal elevators was introduced as a more satisfactory solution. However, this was not before the aircraft was demonstrated to the King and Queen by Harold Piper during a visit to Rochester on 14 March (the larger tail was first flown on 16 March). The aerodynamic data collected by the S.31 brought some benefits and modifications to the full-size Stirling, including an increase to the area of the flaps, while pilots Sqn Ldr E.J. Moreton, Harold

Poor quality image of the S.31 showing the scale model test aeroplane in flight in 1939 with its original colour scheme. *Peter Green*

Piper and Geoffrey Tyson used the S.31 as preparation to fly the Stirling, although the model was actually as manoeuvrable as a fighter. RAF fighter pilots were often bemused when they 'intercepted' the S.31 to find that this big four-engine machine was not much larger than their own aircraft.

In early 1940 the complete aircraft was set up in the 24ft (7.3m) wind tunnel at RAE Farnborough to test the airflow and drag caused by fitting a twin-cannon ventral turret and a Boulton Paul dorsal turret to the Stirling. After a rebuild it was flown again on 13 March 1942 by Lankester Parker (without the turrets) and the aircraft completed its 110th flight on 10 August. The Stirling made its first flight on 14 May 1939 and was used extensively during the war, intially as a bomber but latterly as a glider tug and civil transport. Once again a scale model had proved to be a useful research tool for a full-size aircraft.

The Short S.31 was scrapped after a take off accident which took place at the RAF airfield at Stradishall in Suffolk on 12 February 1944. There are also reports that the engines were 'time-expired' by late 1943, which may have been behind a decision not to repair the aircraft since, apparently, it was not too badly damaged. Pobjoy engines were very good designs, but at the time of the crash the company was in abeyance after Douglas Pobjoy had been directed to work for (and at) Rotol's works at Down Hatherley 'for the duration'. So the production of his company's engines and their spares, and overhaul, were at that stage and thereafter a problem.

Structure

The S.31 was built in wood and had an airframe which was near identical to the Stirling's with dummy turrets, bomb doors and landing gear. Its semi-monocoque fuselage and the two-spar wing with spruce booms and plywood webs were covered in plywood skins. The pilot and observer were seated in tandem with the pilot having all-round vision that was pretty good, but the observer crouched behind him had only a small circular window on each side to look out. There were four fuel tanks placed between the wing spars inboard of each engine nacelle, which themselves had two-blade wooden propellers. At the start the aircraft was painted aluminium but once war had broken out it was repainted in camouflage.

This image shows the S.31 after it had been repainted in 'prototype' colours following the outbreak of war. Note the dummy turret 'shape' of the nose. *Peter Green*

27 Short S.35 Shetland

Short S.35 Shetland

Type: Eleven-Seat Four-Engine Flying boat

Powerplant: Four 2,525hp (1,603kW) Bristol Centaurus VII air-cooled radial engines

Span: 150ft 4in (45.82m), Length: Mk.I 110ft 9in (33.76m)

Gross Wing Area: 2,636sq.ft (245.1m^2)

Maximum Weight: Mk.I 125,000lb (56,700kg), Mk.II 130,000lb (58,968kg)

Maximum Speed: Mk.I at 120,000lb (54,432kg) = 268mph (431km/h) at 2,000ft (610m)

Rate of Climb: Mk.I at 125,000lb = 900ft/min (274m/min) at sea level

Service Ceiling: Mk.I 17,000ft (5,182m)

Armament: See text for guns. Maximum 12 x 2,000lb (907kg) bombs

The superseding of the R.5/39 flying boat specification by R.14/40 in 1940 (Chapter Twenty-Five) resulted in both Saunders-Roe and Short Brothers submitting new designs. Eventually, the two competitors were told to submit a combined proposal and the result was the project which became the Shetland. Although primarily a Short design the two firms agreed to co-operate on its construction and Saro had the responsibility for the design and manufacture of the wing and the engine installation and some of the hull's hydrodynamic shape (which was assisted by the work undertaken with the Shrimp scale model in Chapter Twenty-Five). Shorts then produced the hull and tail unit and undertook final assembly. The wings were delivered from Saro by land.

R.14/40 dated 1 November 1940 asked for a four-engine flying boat capable of operating in any part of the world, and an aircraft of around 100,000lb (45,360kg) was visualised. The primary role was reconnaissance but it was to be capable of resisting attack by fighters and its speed was to be approximately equal to that of ship-borne fighters. An Issue II of the Specification was raised on 11 March 1943 to include a maximum continuous speed of 180 knots (207mph/334km/h) at 5,000ft (1,524m) while carrying 4,000lb (1,814kg) of bombs; the powerplant was four Bristol Centaurus engines and the aircraft would have a crew of eleven. Prototypes DX166 and DX171 were ordered to Contract Acft/761/C.20(b), and later Contract Acft/1361/C.20(b) was placed for ten more Shetlands with serials DZ765 to DZ774. This second order was placed at roughly the same time as the one for the prototypes but it had been cancelled by the time DX171 had switched to a civilian role. These machines would have been built at the Short Brothers' Windermere factory, although the prototypes were built at Rochester.

DX166 made its maiden flight on 14 December 1944 from the River Medway piloted by John Lankester Parker and Geoffrey Tyson, having been launched at Rochester on 24 October. Extensive flight testing by the manufacturer showed that it performed well both in the air and in the water and there were no major incidents during the initial test programme. An MAEE team also made three brief handling flights with the first prototype at Rochester and their report (dated 19 June 1945) noted that on the water the stability was good and the spray characteristics were normal. The take-off and landing were normal except that on landing, just after the hump, a

Compared to types like the Short Sunderland and Saro Princess flying boats, the Shetland tends to be rather ignored. It was, however, a majestic aircraft and a magnificent sight in the air. This picture of DX166 was taken in the summer of 1945 after the original camouflage paint had been stripped off. *Phil Butler*

wing would drop which made the float tend to dig into the water. In the air the rudder (with a Synchrome assister) and elevator controls were satisfactory over the whole speed range but the ailerons were excessively heavy, partly owing to friction. Overall the aircraft was described as generally pleasant to fly with the ailerons the only serious defect noticed.

The aircraft went to MAEE at Felixstowe on 17 October 1945 for official type trials and the report (14 February 1946) noted that the harmonisation of the controls was not good since the now power-assisted ailerons were very light and the elevators slightly heavy. Longitudinal stability in level flight was marginal but the asymmetric power behaviour was good and the critical speed at take-off low. In the water the manoeuvrability was very good (in spite of the non-reversible propellers) and the turning circle was at least as small as that of a Sunderland Mk.III or V. In addition the extremely light and positive throttle controls and the rapidity with which the engines responded gave confidence in narrow waterways. However, the water clearance of the propellers at 120,000lb (54,432kg) weight was not great and when taxying in a 15 knot (17mph/28km/h) wind, fine spray was taken through the downwind propellers when the engine speed exceeded 1,200 rpm.

The Shorts' seaplane works at Rochester is visible in the background of the three-quarter angle view of the first Shetland prototype. *Phil Butler*

On take-off at lower weights the swing to starboard near the hump could be corrected but at 120,000lb (54,432kg) a slight and momentary throttling of the port outer engine was necessary. When taking off at 125,000lb (56,700kg) weight the aircraft appeared rather dirty in rough water but the propellers did not suffer from spray. Landings were generally made at an ASI of 117mph (188km/h) to 121mph (195km/h) since at slower landing speeds the aircraft was liable to skip gently on touchdown. The Shetland's limiting speed (in a dive) at 97,000lb (44,000kg) weight was 301mph (484km/h) ASI, which equated to 287mph (462km/h) EAS, and at 120,000lb (54,432kg) it fell to 263mph (423km/h) ASI and 250mph (402km/h) EAS; special care was needed not to exceed the maximum permissible speed at heavy loads which was only a little higher than the maximum level speed. The aircraft stalled at 101mph (163km/h) ASI with engine off and flaps at 25° or 35° down and some warning of its approach occurred at 106mph (171km/h) through a gentle buffet of the whole airframe. At the stall a wing dropped fairly sharply and the ailerons would snatch.

The first Shetland prototype DX166 sitting on the River Medway at Rochester in May 1945. The aircraft is in 'grey' maritime camouflage. *Phil Butler*

This view shows DX166 flying early in its career still in camouflage. Note the 'glasshouse' canopy and the dummy nose and tail turrets.

Below: Two spectacular photographs of DX166 skimming over the water at high speed, possibly during a take-off and then a landing. It is understood that the shots were taken on 15 February 1945. *Phil Butler*

The type trials were interrupted by a visit to the show held at RAE Farnborough on 29 October 1945, the Shetland being: "...brought quietly over the field by a Felixstowe pilot to provide a dignified finale" to the day's flying. The trials were then curtailed by the complete loss of the first prototype on 28 January 1946 when DX166 was accidentally burnt out at its moorings at MAEE Felixstowe. The fire began at 06.30 hours and developed so swiftly that the fire boat was unable to help. The aircraft was burnt down to water level and then broke into two and the cause was eventually traced to a problem in the port Auxiliary Generating Plant. The fore and aft sections of the hull were retrieved but the salvage of other parts was abandoned because they could not be found in the deep mud on the bottom. The remains that were retrieved were seen on the Woodbridge scrap dump in early June. It did not really matter – the end of the war had already brought an end to the Shetland's military future and in truth the need for a new reconnaissance type like this had been fading since 1943.

Back in mid-1943, however, the RAF had begun looking at converting the Shetland into a transport aircraft and indeed there was a great deal of discussion over the idea. The necessary structural changes would not be too radical and the aircraft could carry a 10,000lb (4,536kg) to 15,000lb (6,804kg) load, while the small production numbers that would be required would still fit within production plans. From this point the Shetland was looked upon almost entirely as a civil aircraft. The early success of DX166's flight trials prompted further discussions in regard to orders, but then on 9 April 1945 it was officially declared that the RAF no longer required the Shetland. A plan to purchase six examples for RAF Transport Command was considered in July 1945 but at a meeting held on the 13th of that month it was decided that the Air Staff could not commit to taking this step. These machines would be far too expensive and could possibly absorb a whole year's funding for new transport aircraft.

Nevertheless DX171 was subsequently converted into a civil prototype S.40 Shetland II with civil registration G-AGVD, but the work took some time to complete (the new version meant DX166 became the Shetland I). The second aircraft was about 60% complete when the war against Japan came to an end but it was not launched until 15 September 1947. It first flew on 17 September and was then ferried to Belfast from its Rochester birthplace to receive its furnishings. A drawing from 1943 shows seating on two decks for 53 day passengers, but in the end G-AGVD was fitted out with space for forty day passengers or twenty-four sleepers, a galley, cocktail bar, toilets and washrooms. Cruising at 184mph (296km/h) and with a payload of 7,620lb (3,456kg) the aircraft would have a range of 4,650 miles (7,482km) – the distance from London to Bombay. However, by 1947 the British Overseas Airways Corporation (BOAC) was no longer interested in the Shetland II either, although there were thoughts towards a version fitted with Napier Nomad compound engines for operations over trans-ocean routes. In fact G-AGVD was considered as a Nomad test-bed and in September 1946 Short Brothers had proposed a design called the S.A.8 that was based loosely on the Shetland and had four Nomads as its powerplant, but this all came to nothing. In mid-September 1949 G-AGVD was allotted to Short Brothers & Harland in Belfast to go into store, and the aircraft was broken up at Queens Island at Belfast/Sydenham in 1951.

After the end of the war a lot of thought was given to the future of the flying boat and it was concluded that in certain areas and

A rare image of DX166 taxying, in this case on very calm water. From this angle the slab-sided Shetland in this colour scheme reminds one a little of a large battleship or aircraft carrier. *Phil Butler*

The civilianised Shetland Mk.II prototype DX171, but now with civil registration G-AGVD. It is pictured on the Medway on 22 September 1947. *Phil Butler*

circumstances a boat would still have advantages over a landplane. Consequently, plans were made and requirements raised towards acquiring a new type of military flying boat, but there was no likelihood of the Shetland filling the need since Air Commodore J.N. Boothman had declared that the type was very old-fashioned and out of date. However, in 1948 thoughts did turn once again to ordering the type against a new Specification R.2/48. In June 1949, however, a modified Shetland, which had been only one of the proposals tendered against R.2/48, was rejected as being too heavy and lacking sufficient range. The winning design came from Saro but work on that project was itself stopped in 1952, heralding the end of the flying boat as a maritime patrol aircraft in RAF service (although the Sunderland soldiered on with the RAF until 1959).

In the air a pilot could apparently throw the Shetland around the sky almost like a fighter, and yet when the war ended in 1945 it was the largest British aircraft flying. An article in *Flight* magazine reported: "…one cannot fully appreciate what a wingspan of 150ft [45.7m] actually is until seeing it in the shop. Then, standing at one end and seeing the other tip 50 yards away in comparison with people, one realises what this span really means". The height from the bottom of the keel to the tip of the fin was over 40ft (12m). The Shetland was indeed an immensely impressive machine and it deserves more attention.

Lovely angle showing G-AGVD about to settle on the water after another flight. *Phil Butler*

This lovely Charles Brown colour photograph of Shetland prototype DZ166 was taken over the British countryside on 31 May 1945. *RAF Museum*

Structure

Despite its substantial size, the Shetland was built as a mostly conventional aeroplane in a simple and straightforward manner best suited for ease of production. Aerodynamically, it was clean with few excrescences that would produce parasitic drag. The planing bottom was of V-form throughout with gently sweeping chines and a raking step. The hull skin plating was carried on stringers and frames and had an immensely strong keel structure based around an extruded section. It was the wing which used the most unconventional construction in the airframe since it was designed on the main spar torsion box principle used in gliders. Three spars were used but the front two including the main spar were both employed as sides of the torsion box, the box being covered in heavy gauge upper and lower skin plating. The rest of the wing had a lighter structure with chordal ribs stiffened with strips of metal. Frise-type fabric-covered ailerons were fitted, each with a trim and servo tab, together with metal-covered Handley Page slotted type flaps. The wingtip floats were fixed.

The defensive armament planned for the Shetland I comprised four forward-firing 0.5in (12.7mm) machine-guns in a nose turret and four more in a tail turret, two in a mid-upper turret, and one on each side of the hull; later two 20mm Hispano cannon were to have been installed in the mid-upper turret. However, DX166 was never fully equipped for military duties and had dummy nose and tail turrets but with no military equipment. The Shetland II used similar engines to the military Mk.I and on G-AGVD each of these drove 15ft 9in (4.80m) diameter four-blade de Havilland Hydromatic constant speed fully-feathering metal propellers; those fitted to the inboard engines were also reversing to help facilitate the Mk.II's handling on the water. Fuel was carried only in the wings – ten tanks on each side. DX166 had Hydromatic fully-feathering propellers of 15ft (4.57m) diameter.

The first and only Shetland I, DX166 had successful flight trials but fell victim to a fire at its moorings in October 1945. *Tim Brown*

28 Short S.36 and other Four-Engine Bombers

Short S.36 (Original July 1941 Estimates)

Type: Heavy Bomber

Powerplant: Four 2,000+hp (1,491+kW) Bristol Centaurus CE.3.SM air-cooled radial engines

Span: 135ft 9in (41.38m), Length: 101ft 0in (30.78m)

Gross Wing Area: 2,145sq.ft (199.5m^2)

Maximum Weight: 103,100lb (46,766kg)

Maximum Speed: 311mph (500km/h) at 20,000ft (6,096m)

Rate of Climb: Not given

Service Ceiling: 29,300ft (8,931m)

Armament: 10 x 0.5in (12.7mm) and 2 x 0.303in (7.7mm) machine-guns; maximum 23,500lb (10,660kg) bombs

The principal landplane programme at Short Brothers during the war was the Stirling four-engine heavy bomber first flown in May 1939, but battle experience would soon reveal that the aircraft was inferior in many respects to the slightly later Avro Lancaster and Handley-Page Halifax. Pretty quickly Shorts looked to improving the Stirling and the result was the S.36, often known as the 'Super Stirling' but which at the start of the studies in June/July 1941 was called the 'Stirling III'. It was not considered to be an all new design (at least by the Ministry) and was described as having a "general similarity" to the earlier aircraft. Specification B.8/41 was allotted to the project on 19 November 1941.

The Stirling's Bristol Hercules engines were to be replaced by four of the same manufacturer's Centaurus radials driving 15ft 3in (4.65m) diameter four-blade propellers. This change offered a gain in take-off power over the Stirling of about 50% while the aircraft's maximum weight also went up by 50%. Compared to the original aircraft the fuselage was longer, the straight tapered wings were modified and increased in span, and the empennage had been altered, but most of all the bomb carrying arrangements were far superior with a single centre bay now in place. This could take various loads including a single 8,000lb (3,629kg) bomb but there were also six more wing cells that could each hold a 1,000lb (454kg) bomb. However, a large proportion of what was described as the "bits and pieces" used in the Stirling's fuselage was retained. The defensive armament was two 0.5in (12.7mm) machine-guns in the nose, another four of these weapons both in mid-upper and tail turrets and there was an under turret with two 0.303in (7.7mm) machine-guns. The undercarriage had twin-wheel main units. In many respects the S.36 mirrored the work done on the Shetland (Chapter 27) and it would have employed the same sheet-web form of construction.

After his assessment MAP's Capt R.N. Liptrot concluded that the project was: "...well conceived and a logical next stage in the development of the heavy bomber". Its take-off and flight performance would be similar to the Stirling, although the S.36 could carry a much higher warload over a greater range, but he estimated that the maximum weight would be 105,000lb (47,628kg) and the top speed 295mph (475km/h) at 20,000ft (6,096m). For a distance of 1,000 miles (1,609km) the S.36 could take 23,500lb (10,660kg) of bombs against the Stirling's 14,000lb (6,350kg), and over the longer distance of 2,300 miles (3,701km) a load of

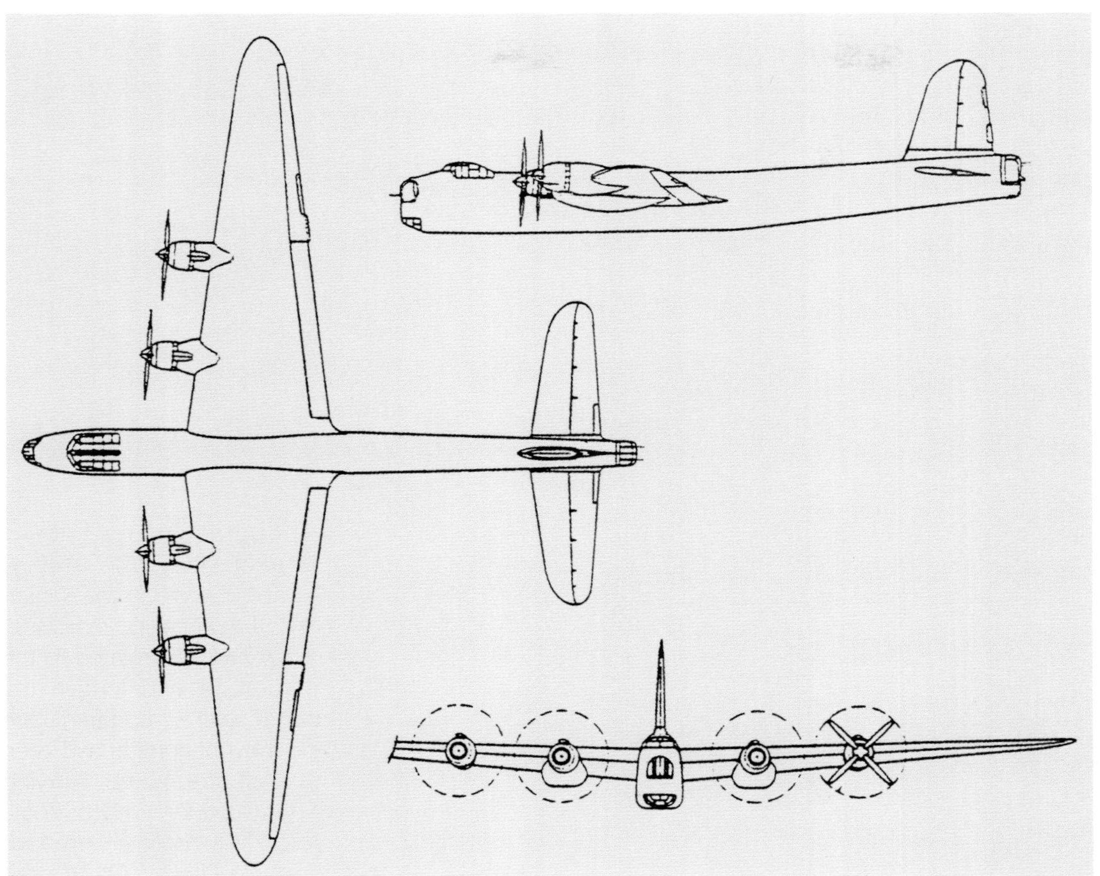

Three-view drawing of the Short S.36 'Super Stirling' dated 15 July 1941. Some of the gun turrets are not shown.

An example of the Short Stirling, the RAF's first four-engined heavy bomber of World War II.

10,000lb (4,536kg) against 4,500lb (2,041kg). Some people inside the Ministry were uncomfortable about proceeding with this new bomber but discussions between Arthur Gouge and Mr McPhie of Short Brothers and DTD and CRD from the Ministry, held on 9 January 1942, brought a decision to order two prototypes, the first without certain operational equipment but the second complete. These were subsequently given the serials JR540 and JR543 and a first flight was expected to take place in the autumn of 1943. A production order for 150 bombers was also discussed but the prototype order was cancelled by the minister on 29 May 1942, four months after it had been placed.

The Commander-in-Chief of Bomber Command, Air Marshal Arthur Harris, (Air Chief Marshal from March 1943) had in fact written on 11 May 1942 that the S.36 would "...eradicate the weakness of the present Stirling and with much bigger span wings it should be a better aircraft". But he added that its potential did not justify the problems that would be created in making a change in production from the original Stirling. Whether Harris had any influence on the decision is unknown, but just a couple of weeks later the manufacturers were told to stop working on

the project. Another important factor was that the Air Ministry was aware that by the time the S.36 entered service the inevitable increases in weight that accompany any new aircraft would have partially offset the gain in performance and bomb load that the S.36 offered over the Stirling. On 5 August Shorts decided to abandon the bomber altogether but it would carry on with work examining the addition of a split flap to its Gouge flap to minimise drag for landing, the results of which so far had shown great promise. The firm had already completed some work on this feature, in the process employing the S.31 half-scale Stirling (Chapter Twenty-Six).

S.36 Structure

See text.

Handley Page Heavy Bombers

During 1943 Handley Page made a serious effort to improve the capabilities of its Halifax four-engine heavy bomber, the studies culminating in the HP.65 'Super Halifax' project proposed in June. This was not ordered and by October the effort had moved on to a simpler redesign of the basic Halifax called the HP.66. This was ordered against Specification B.27/43 and it was proposed to call the type the Hastings B.Mk.1, while a further version with turbo-blower exhausts would be the HP.69 Hastings Mk.II. Three prototype development aircraft, SR650, SR654 and SR657 (as two Hastings Mk.Is and one Mk.II), were ordered in February 1944 while a fourth (SX553) was added in early April, all under Contract Acft/3401. The HP.69 was dropped later in April 1944, while the end of the war in 1945 brought an end to any requirement for the Hastings bomber. No drawings of the HP.66 are known to exist.

Handley Page High Altitude Bomber

What has been found recently is a drawing and sketch for a Handley Page high altitude bomber project from 1 December 1941. This was not given an 'HP' project number but it had some interesting features and relatively little in common with the concurrent Halifax. Most particularly the four-engined (Rolls-Royce Merlin 60s) were placed sideways in pairs buried in the wing roots and drove contra-rotating propellers. The roots themselves were consequently very thick and deep because behind the powerplants also came the stowage space for the main wheels of the tricycle undercarriage, another item of aircraft design which at the time was quite new. The

Two Bristol Hercules-powered Handley Page Halifax bombers fly in formation. The complete aircraft shown, LL599, was a Mk.III.

bomber had a large central body, relatively small twin fins, a nose turret, and also dorsal and ventral turrets set well towards the rear of the aircraft. The elevators and rudders appeared to be fabric covered but the rest of the airframe had metal skinning. This bomber would have had a span of 100ft (30.48m) and a length of 74ft 5in (22.70m). The source of the drawing is unknown but the High Altitude Bomber was designed by Godfrey Lee.

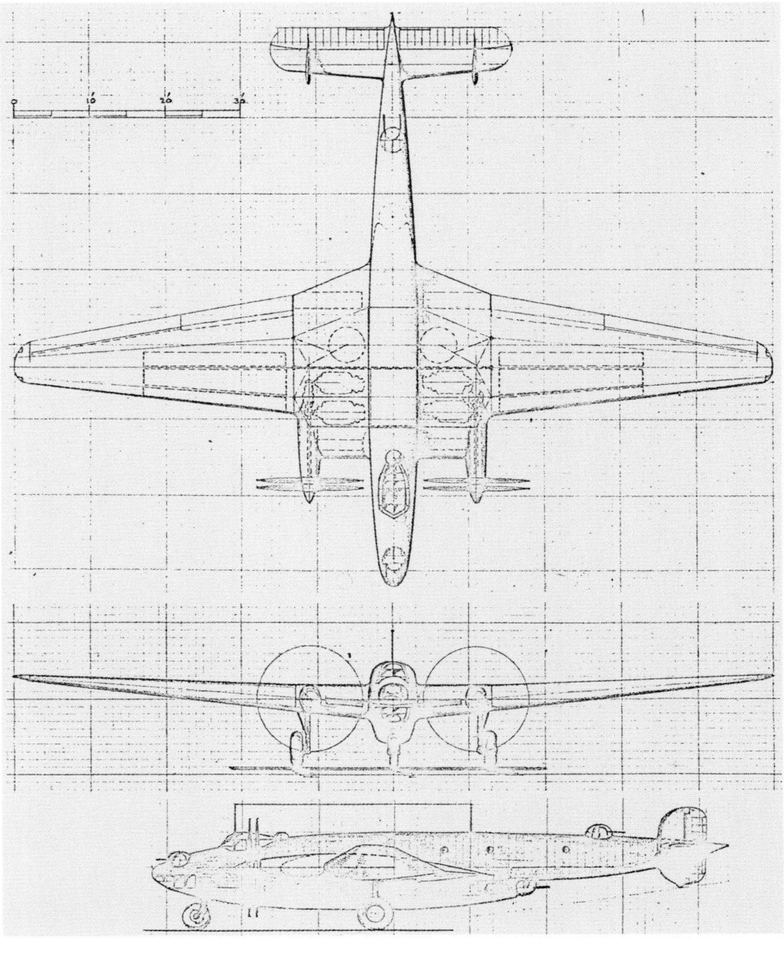

Above: The Handley Page High Altitude Bomber proposal of early December 1941. *The late Jim Oughton*

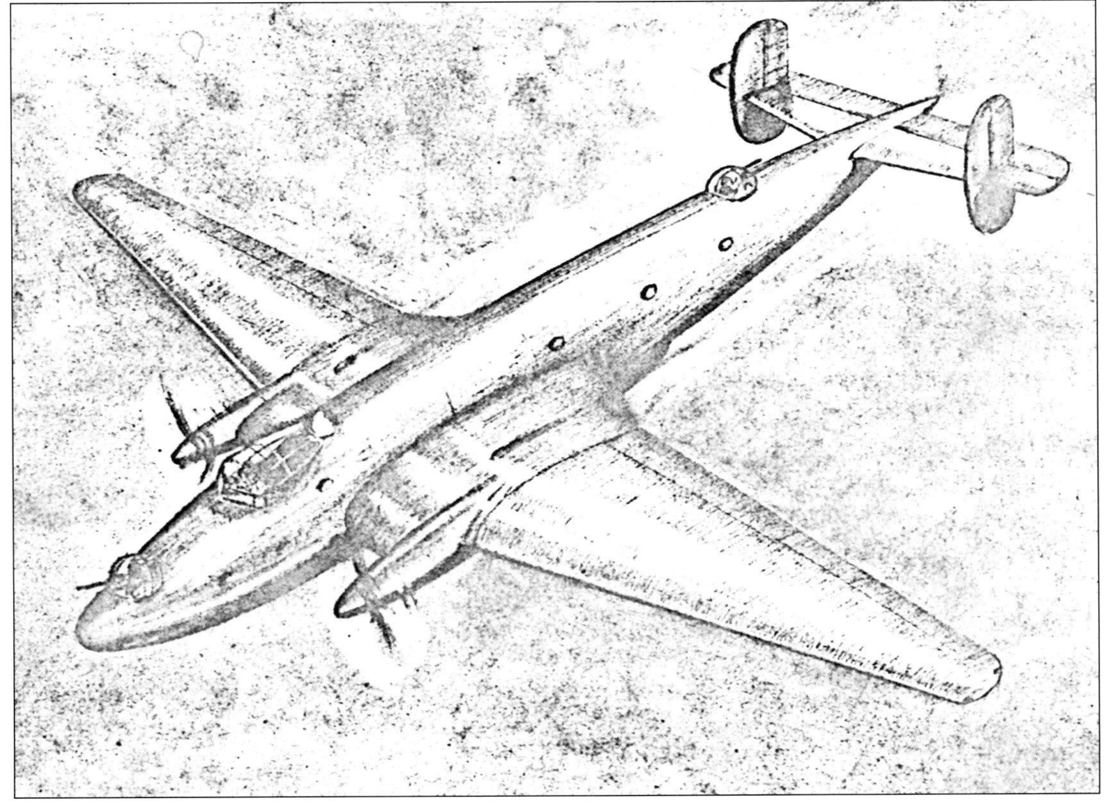

Manufacturer's artwork for the Handley Page High Altitude Bomber. *The late Jim Oughton*

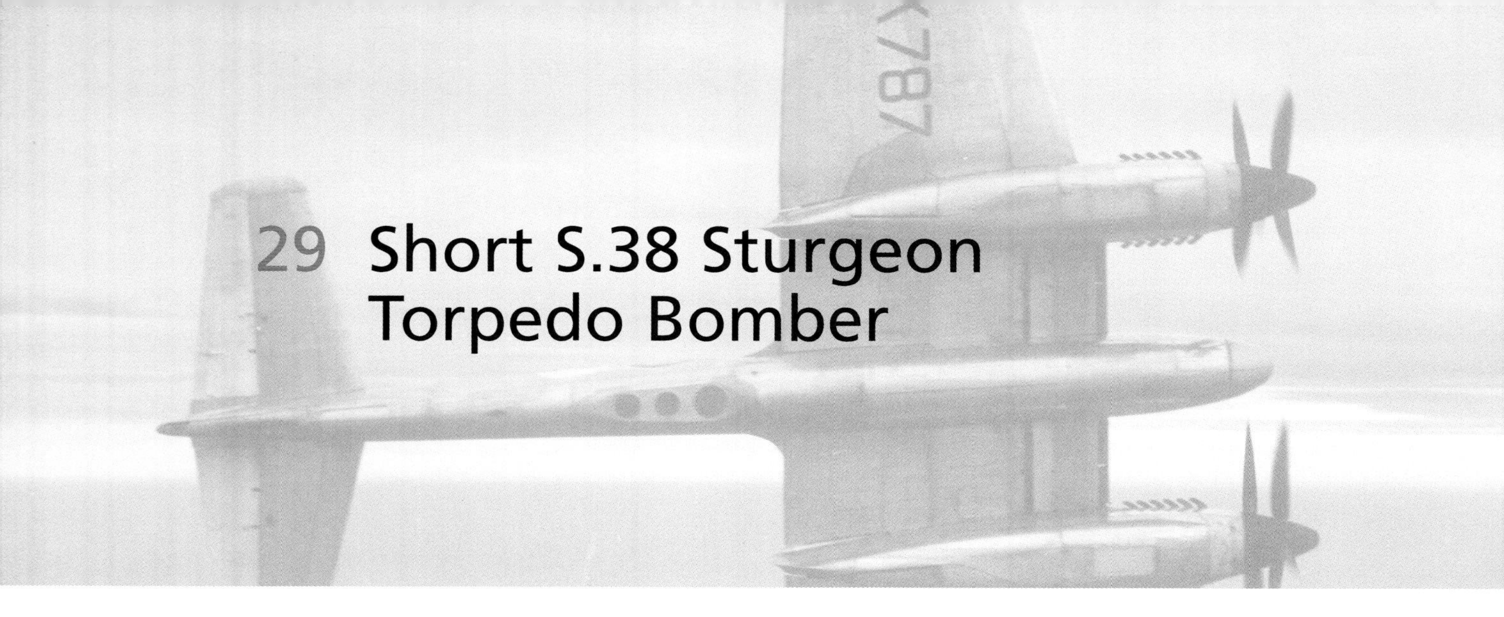

29 Short S.38 Sturgeon Torpedo Bomber

Short S.38 Sturgeon

Type: Three-Seat Naval Reconnaissance Bomber

Powerplant: Two 2,080hp (1,551kW) Rolls-Royce Merlin 140 liquid-cooled inline engines

Span: 59ft 11in (18.26m)

Length: 44ft (13.4m) (some sources give 45ft 6in (13.87m))

Gross Wing Area: 560.4sq.ft (52.1m^2)

Maximum Weight: 21,700lb (9,843kg)

Maximum Speed: 370mph (595km/h)

Rate of Climb: 4,180ft/min (1,275m/min) at 2,000ft (610m)

Service Ceiling: 35,700ft (10,880m)

Armament: 2 x 0.5in (12.7mm) machine-guns; 16 x rocket projectiles, 1,000lb (454kg) of bombs or depth charges

In 1943 several companies submitted projects to Specification S.6/43 which called for a naval torpedo bomber and reconnaissance aircraft. This was eventually split into separate requirements for a torpedo bomber (satisfied by the Fairey Spearfish in Chapter 8) and a reconnaissance type. Of the two designs submitted by Short Brothers (the other had a single Bristol Centaurus power unit), the firm's twin Merlin S.6/43 layout proved to be the most attractive for the reconnaissance role and Specification S.11/43 was produced for it. The document was issued to the firm on 12 February 1944 and stated a maximum weight of 24,000lb (10,886kg), a maximum length of 45ft (13.7m), span with wings spread 60ft (18.3m) and folded 20ft (6.1m), and maximum stowed height 17ft (5.2m), dimensions which would permit the aircraft to be operated aboard the Navy's carriers. No specific speed figure was given, just that the aircraft must have the highest possible top speed with the best performance at heights between sea level and 15,000ft (4,572m). Two Rolls-Royce Merlin RM.14.SM engines were specified (provision for rocket assisted take-off gear – RATOG – was also stated) and two machine-guns were to be carried, together with bombs or depth charges in a secondary bombing role. The design was called the S.38 (and later S.A.1 in the SBAC's universal post-war number scheme) and in due course it was christened Sturgeon.

Three prototypes of the Sturgeon Mk.I were ordered under Contract SB.27016/C.20(a) of 19 October 1943 and given the serials RK787, RK791 and RK794. They were to be built at Rochester but the construction process experienced some delays. Producing a twin-engined aircraft – a type new to the Navy – brought with it a lot of problems and breaking of new ground for the design team under C.P.T. Lipscombe and works team led by D.E. Wiseman. In fact the war had long ended when RK787 finally flew from Rochester on 7 June 1946 in the hands of company test pilot Geoffrey Tyson. Exactly a year before RK787 had been in the very early stages of assembly and it is understood that September 1945 had previously been the planned first flight date. The first prototype had no guns and the ports were faired over. Early flight testing with RK787 at an all-up-weight of 20,000lb (9,072kg) and using 100/150 grade fuel gave a maximum true level airspeed of 401mph (645km/h) at 18,850ft (5,745m) and a ceiling of about 38,000ft (11,582m). Five minutes were needed to reach 12,000ft (3,658m) and 27.4 minutes to get to 36,000ft

The first Sturgeon reconnaissance bomber prototype RK787 makes a high speed pass, it is thought during the 1947 SBAC Show at Radlett. *Shorts*

RK787 runs up its engines at Belfast. Note the Sunderland flying boats parked behind.

Spectacular view of the first Sturgeon reconnaissance bomber prototype RK787 banking away from the camera aircraft. Note the underfuselage camera ports, probably the reason why this particular image was taken.

(10,973m). This data was taken from manufacturer's graphs published in *The Aeroplane* of 18 October 1946 – more recent published sources have quoted lower top speeds.

Just twenty days after its first flight RK787 was put on exhibition at Farnborough, and again at Radlett for the SBAC Show in early September 1946. It does not appear to have performed any display flying at the Farnborough event but *Flight* magazine described the machine as "exceptionally compact". Following its first RAE tests RK787 moved to A&AEE Boscombe Down on 8 May 1947 for further trials and deck landings, and in early September it attended the next SBAC Show at Radlett where it was flown by Sqn Ldr John S. Booth. The report here noted that the Sturgeon was one of several relatively large aircraft to be rolled during their displays. However, on 10 October the aircraft crash-landed aboard the carrier HMS *Illustrious* after failing to catch an arrestor wire. The hook experienced a damping failure which made it miss all of the wires, a wingtip then clipped the carrier's island and RK787 nosed over. The wreckage was delivered to RNAS Ford for assessment before being returned to Rochester and struck off charge on 9 April 1948 to be held as a spares source for the second prototype. The remains of the airframe were still at Rochester in the early 1950s.

In the mid-1940s a key difficulty with landing any twin-engine piston aircraft onto an aircraft carrier deck was the lack of asymmetric control with one engine out that was required during the high power/low speed approach. The conventional de Havilland Mosquito (propellers rotating in the same direction which gave the additional problem of swing on take-off) could not realistically be deck landed on one engine, while the same firm's Sea Hornet fighter used handed propellers which removed of the swing problem but not the worry of asymmetry. Since the Sturgeon had shorter contra-rotating propeller blades there was optimism that the bomber would not experience this asymmetric weakness. Test pilot Capt. Eric Brown evaluated RK787 at RAE Farnborough in April 1947 but found that lateral control with one engine was: "...too heavy and spongy to bring the speed down to acceptable limits for such an operation". Indeed, this problem was never really solved until twin jet-powered aircraft became available with their engines placed closer to the centreline.

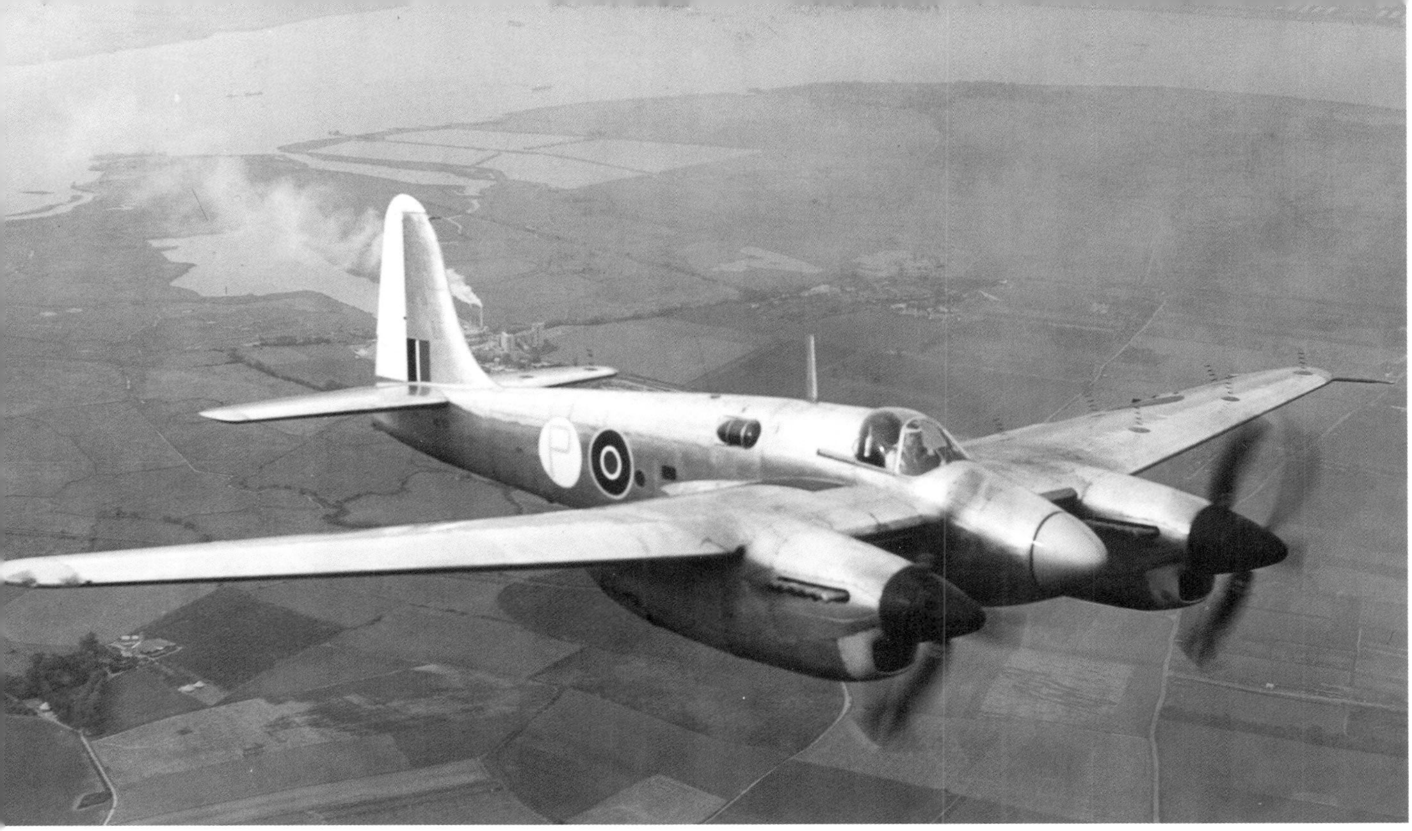

The original Sturgeon had graceful lines as shown in this picture, which also reveals the close spacing of its Merlin engines.

The Sturgeon was also a pretty fast aircraft and its speed at low level is evident here as RK787 is about to scream over the cameraman's head. Looks like it was a good day for drying the washing!

Charles Brown's colour views of Sturgeon prototype RK791 landing aboard HMS Implacable on 16 June 1948 are probably the only such images to have been made of this aircraft. *RAF Museum*

There appear to be very few photos of the second Sturgeon prototype RK791. This sad view, taken in 1954 and without its wings, shows the machine on the dump at Yeovilton.

Brown, however, was impressed with the Sturgeon's normal deck-landing performance, its very short landing roll and much of its flight characteristics in general. The stall characteristics, so important to a carrier aeroplane, were satisfactory with adequate pre-stall warning and no nasty wing drop on the clean stall at 92mph (148km/h); the all-down stall at 86mph (140km/h) was difficult to produce. Control response was good and the machine seemed well suited for its intended role. The aircraft undertook its arresting proofing trials at the same time and these proved to be near faultless, primarily thanks to the airframe's substantial strength. (A fuller account of Eric Brown's experience with the Sturgeon is given in his *Wings of the Weird & Wonderful*, another Hikoki title.)

The assembly of RK791 had also begun at Rochester but, thanks to delay and also that Short Brothers was in the process of moving, the airframe was eventually completed in Belfast and made its first flight from Sydenham on 18 May 1948. The pilot was John Booth who had become a test pilot in 1944 and who eventually flew for both Shorts and Saunders-Roe. On 16 June RK791 achieved a maiden landing aboard HMS *Implacable* and three months later it was employed on deck trials of the powered wing folding, joining No. 778 Squadron at Lee-on-Solent on 16 June and visiting HMS *Illustrious* two days later. On 26 October the second Sturgeon joined SDE Flight at RAE Farnborough for deck trials and undercarriage strain gauge work. Catapult trials took place on 27-29 April 1949 from the catapult installed at RAE, RATOG trials followed at RAE in August, but the aircraft was loaned to Shorts for several days to permit it to take part in the National Air Races at Elmdon (from 30 July to 1 August). On 13 December RK791 taxied over an airfield manhole cover which then collapsed causing damage to the starboard propeller, undercarriage and wing tip, and this ended its flying career and also the flight test programme for the Sturgeon bomber. Six months later RK791 was declared surplus to CS(A) requirements and allotted to Yeovilton for ground instruction use, leaving Farnborough on 23 June. In 1953/54 the fuselage was visible on the dump at Yeovilton, while RK791's wings are known to have been in store at Rochester in November 1954.

The S.38 Sturgeon had been designed essentially for operations in the Pacific as part of the preparations for the final drive against Japan, but when that conflict came to a close the Navy was left with a new bomber and nowhere to operate it. As a result the reconnaissance bomber did not go into production, but the Sturgeon airframe was adopted as target-tug aircraft. The third prototype RK794 was not completed as a bomber but became the first TT.Mk.2 tug prototype and very substantial alterations were made to the airframe including a longer nose. With new serial VR363 it first flew on 1 September 1948 and was followed by a second prototype (VR371) and a production batch of twenty-three aeroplanes (TS475 to TS497), which served the Royal Navy in the role through most of the 1950s. It is understood that the Sturgeon tug was very noisy on take-off, and the original bomber prototypes must have been the same.

Structure

The metal structured Sturgeon had a two-spar cantilever wing with heavy-gauge light alloy booms and plate webs. It was made in three pieces – a constant-chord centre section through the fuselage and two tapered outer planes. Frise-type ailerons with spring tabs and Zap area-increasing split flaps were fitted, the ailerons were fabric covered, and the outer wings could fold rearwards about the rear spar leaving the leading edge facing downwards. An all-metal monocoque fuselage was built in four pieces using stressed light alloy skins riveted to a longeron and stringer skeleton. Tail and fin were made integral with the rear fuselage structure but the rudder and elevators were metal and fabric covered. The rudder had a horn balance and these horizontal and vertical flying surfaces both used combined servo trim-tabs.

The Sturgeon's undercarriage was by far the strongest British unit yet manufactured and the powerplant was two Rolls-Royce two-stage, two-speed supercharged Merlin 140 engines. Each of these drove a 10ft (3.05m) diameter contra-rotating Rotol six-blade propeller with wooden blades (wood because it reduced interference for the Type 77 anti-surface vessel

Nothing like so handsome was the target-tug version of the Sturgeon, which to begin with had a much extended nose shown here. This was the version, however, which took the type into service. The example shown is VR371, the second prototype Mk.2. *Shorts*

[ASV] Rebecca IV radar scanner in the nose). Radiators were placed beneath the engines and in the wing leading edge and full internal fuel totalled 410 gallons (1,864 litres), but another 180 gallon (818 litre) tank could go in the bomb-bay. The crew was made up of the pilot, navigator and radio-operator. Two 0.5in (12.7mm) machine-guns were mounted in the lower nose, eight rocket projectiles would go under each wing and one 1,000lb (454kg) bomb, two 500lb (227kg) bombs or four 250lb (113kg) depth charges could be loaded into the small weapons-bay. Alternatively one F.24 and two F.52 cameras could be carried.

The complex arrangement of the Sturgeon airframe's contra-rotating propellers and wing folding is shown beautifully by this view. Although the bomber was abandoned, these features and an arrestor hook were carried through into the target tug Mk.2. *Shorts*

30 Supermarine B.12/36

Supermarine B.12/36

Type: Six-Seat Heavy Bomber

Powerplant: Four 1,330hp (992kW) Bristol Hercules HE.1.SM air-cooled radial engines

Span: 97ft 0in (29.57m)

Length: 73ft 6in (22.40m)

Gross Wing Area: 1,358sq.ft (126.3m^2)

Maximum Weight (at 11 November 1938): 44,000lb (19,958kg); maximum overload 59,000lb (26,762kg)

Maximum Speed (estimate at 11 November 1938): 330mph (531km/h) at 17,000ft (5,182m)

Rate of Climb: Not available

Service Ceiling (estimate at 11 November 1938): 32,000ft (9,745m)

Armament: 8 x 0.303in (7.7mm) machine-guns; 29 x 250lb (113kg) or 27 x 500lb (227kg) or 7 x 2,000lb (907kg) bombs

This model depicts the Bristol Hercules-powered Supermarine Type 317 bomber with twin fins.

The aircraft behind the development of the Short S.36 in Chapter 28, the Stirling, resulted from a Specification issued in 1936 for a heavy bomber. This was called B.12/36 but the Stirling was not the only design for which prototypes were ordered against this document. Supermarine was asked to build two examples of its Type 316 proposal and the reason why they never flew is unique in this book – enemy action.

B.12/36, dated 15 July 1936, had requested a bomb load of 8,000lb (3,629kg) to be carried over a range of 3,000 miles (4,827km) or a maximum load of 14,000lb (6,350kg) over 2,000 miles (3,218km). The aircraft would cruise at a speed at least 230mph (370km/h) at 15,000ft (4,572m) and the service ceiling had to be at least 28,000ft (8,534m). The two Supermarine prototypes were ordered in 1937 under Contract 605350/37 and given serials L6889 and L6990. At this stage the aircraft's powerplant was interchangeable between the Bristol Hercules and Rolls-Royce Merlin and in January 1937 the project was revised to introduce an increase in wing area from the original 1,240sq.ft (115.3sq.m) to meet the Specification's landing requirements. In addition, twin fins and rudders were now adopted and the revised project was renumbered Type 317. The air- and liquid-cooled engines could be used without alteration except to the nacelles and cowling but in July the Chief of the Air Staff decided that the firm should now concentrate on the Hercules-powered Type 317 and abandon the Merlin-engined variant (which by this time had been called the Type 318). The mock-up was officially assessed on 12 August 1937. Revised

data submitted on 11 November 1938 indicated a range with the 8,000lb (3,629kg) bomb load on board of 3,680 miles (5,920km).

The value and status of the project was appraised in an Air Ministry memo of 21 July 1937. The death of Supermarine's famous designer R.J. Mitchell had: "...introduced a certain degree of risk into the production of this type." (the 316 was the last design Mitchell worked on before his tragic death in early 1937 and it was his successor Joe Smith who had to try and take the bomber through to fruition). However, the "importance of this four-engined heavy bomber was enhanced by the fact that other countries, namely the USA, Germany and France, were making use of the type". The Air Staff considered the aircraft to be of outstanding importance "...and think that it will become the main heavy bomber type in the near future". The Air Staff also regarded the manufacture of the 317 on a large scale to be of vital importance and it was essential that every possible step should be taken to ensure that no undue delay should occur in obtaining four-engine heavy bombers in production. Unfortunately, the project did experience some delay, in part of course through Supermarine's vital preoccupation with the Spitfire. In fact, work on the Type 317 was actually cancelled by a Contracts letter sent out in September 1939, but by 11 March 1940 the firm had resumed its efforts to complete the prototypes.

Sadly, on 26 September 1940 the Woolston factory where the two 317s were being constructed was raided by the German Luftwaffe and the part-assembled fuselages were damaged beyond repair. This was a mortal blow and the prototype order was cancelled on 25 November, although the programme was at least one full year behind schedule anyway. This left the Stirling (which had originally been intended to be an insurance against the failure of the Supermarine prototypes), and then the Handley Page Halifax and Avro Lancaster, to fill the RAF's four-engine bomber requirements. In truth, Supermarine had enough to do with perfecting so many versions of its Spitfire and Seafire.

Image showing the forward fuselage of the Type 317 under construction in the Supermarine works in spring 1939.

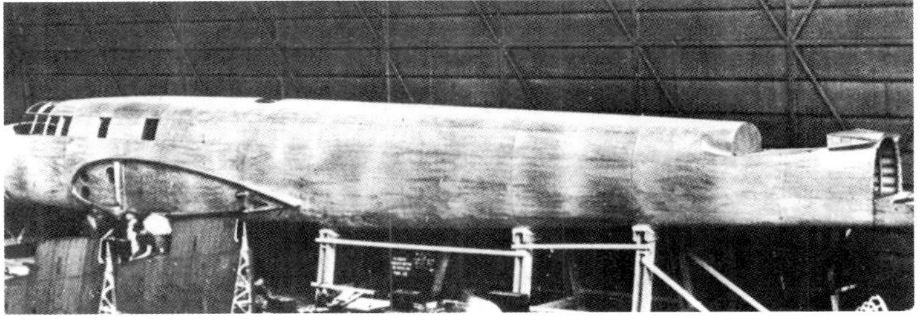

Now skinned, the prototype's fuselage sits on trestles in the summer of 1940.

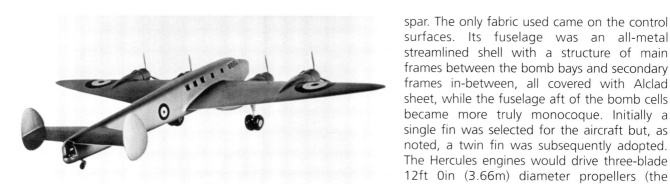

This model depicts the Bristol Hercules-powered Supermarine Type 317 bomber with twin fins.

Structure

The Type 317 had a single spar wing built in light alloy with stressed skin covering and the aircraft's bombs were to be slung in a single layer in the fuselage and in the wing aft of the spar. The only fabric used came on the control surfaces. Its fuselage was an all-metal streamlined shell with a structure of main frames between the bomb bays and secondary frames in-between, all covered with Alclad sheet, while the fuselage aft of the bomb cells became more truly monocoque. Initially a single fin was selected for the aircraft but, as noted, a twin fin was subsequently adopted. The Hercules engines would drive three-blade 12ft 0in (3.66m) diameter propellers (the 1,100hp (820kW) Merlins on the Type 318 were to have had 12ft 6in (3.81m] diameter propellers). Fuel tanks served as part of the wing leading edge structure (total internal fuel for the Hercules variant was 2,290 gallons (10,412 litres)) and the undercarriage had side-by-side twin main wheels to reduce the space required for their retraction. Production aircraft were to have had interchangeable nose and tail turrets with fixed transparent cupolas and accommodating either two or four Browning machine-guns, and there was also a retractable lower mid-turret for two more Brownings.

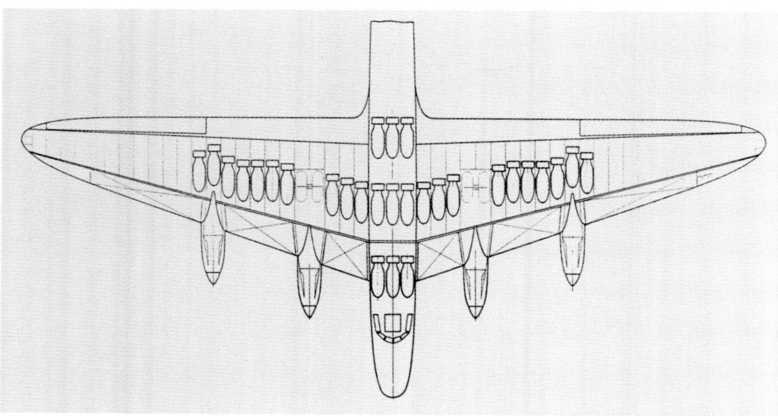

Above: Plan view of the original Type 316 proposal with Merlin engines showing how twenty-nine 250lb (113kg) bombs were to have been carried.

Below: General arrangement drawing of the Supermarine Type 317 (B.12/36) in its final prototype form. As originally proposed the design had a single fin.

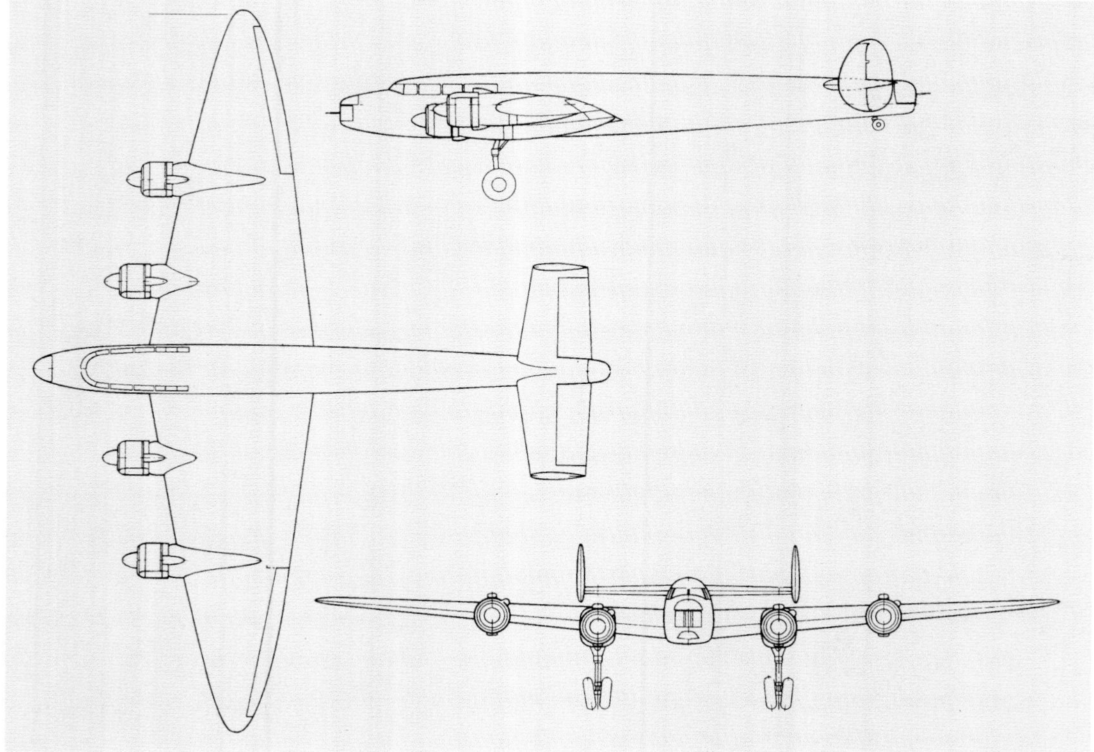

31 Supermarine 322 'Dumbo'

Supermarine 322 'Dumbo'

Type: Three-Seat Naval Torpedo/Dive Bomber

Powerplant: First prototype one 1,300hp (969kW) Rolls-Royce Merlin 30 liquid-cooled inline engine, Second prototype one 1,640hp (1,223kW)) Merlin 32

Span: 50ft 0in (15.24m)

Length: 40ft 0in (12.19m)

Gross Wing Area: 319.5sq.ft (29.7m²)

Maximum Weight (design figure): 12,000lb (5,443kg)

Maximum Speed: 279mph (449km/h) at 4,000ft (1,219m)

Rate of Climb: Unknown

Service Ceiling: Not available

Armament: 2 x 0.303in (7.7mm) machine-guns; 3 x 500lb (227kg), 6 x 250lb (113kg) bombs or 1 x torpedo

The subject of this chapter presents another feature which has never been common in the history of aviation, a variable-incidence wing. This is designed to have its angle of incidence adjustable in flight, thereby providing an aircraft with good low speed characteristics while reducing its take-off and landing distances. The idea actually goes back to before the start of the First World War and was patented by George Boginoff, an inventor from Bulgaria, in May 1912. Although designed to an official specification for an operational torpedo bomber, the Supermarine 322 'Dumbo' described here was fitted with a variable-incidence wing and was never intended for production, so it has to be considered as a pure research aeroplane.

Model of the Bristol proposal to Specification S.24/37, which was to have been powered by the same firm's Taurus engine. It is shown here with a wheeled undercarriage and carrying bombs under the wing and fuselage. *The late Jim Oughton*

Bristol's model in the alternative floatplane configuration with a torpedo under the fuselage. *The late Jim Oughton*

Specification S.24/37 of 6 January 1938 asked for a carrier-based torpedo bomber, dive-bomber and reconnaissance aircraft all within a single airframe. Its maximum all-up weight with a mix of bombs or a single 1,500lb (680kg) torpedo had to be 10,500lb (4,763kg), a cruising speed of not less than 185mph (298km/h) was desired and the folded span for ship stowage was

not to exceed 18ft (5.49m), while spread it was to be no more than 50ft (15.24m). An alternative float undercarriage for use in sheltered waters was to be provided in the proposal but this did not have to be constructed as a prototype, the maximum length for the ship-plane being 40ft (12.19m) and for the floatplane 44ft (13.41m) (the floatplane requirement was later cancelled). Companies who submitted designs included Fairey and Supermarine and the latter's Type 322 was to be powered by a Rolls-Royce Exe engine (the Exe was eventually abandoned and substituted by a Rolls-Royce Merlin) and it had the novel feature of a variable-incidence wing with slots and flaps and which could also be folded. This, however, prevented the use of a retractable undercarriage because it would not be possible to house landing gear in the wings (and retraction into the fuselage was also difficult), but that did not really matter since S.24/37 did not specify any extreme performance figures anyway. The Type 322 was one of the first designs produced by Joseph Smith, Supermarine's chief designer, without any input from his predecessor R.J. Mitchell.

At the S.24/37 Tender Design Conference held on 31 March 1938 it was agreed that a prototype contract should be placed with Fairey, and in due course production orders also followed for the aeroplane which became the Barracuda, the prototype flying for the first time on 7 December 1940. It was also agreed that Supermarine's design was too experimental, but then in April 1939 an order was placed (Contract 976687/38) for two examples of the Type 322 and these received the serials R1810 and R1815. The aircraft was given the nickname 'Dumbo' and the objective was to test the variable-incidence wing as part of a general research programme. However, the outbreak of war delayed the design and construction process which held back the first Type 322's first flight until 6 February 1943.

One of the benefits to a single-engine landplane from a variable-incidence wing, and particularly to a carrier-based aircraft, was that it would provide a better forward view for the pilot over his nose-mounted engine – with a fixed-incidence wing the nose would rise just at the critical moment of touchdown and blot out a large arc of forward view. A high wing was chosen for the Type 322 since this provided the simplest arrangement to operate the variable incidence (and also a good downwards view). The design of the incidence-changing mechanism on the aircraft was quite simple – the wing pivoted on the front spar and the incidence was changed by two screw jacks which connected the rear spar to the fuselage. A bonus was that this arrangement did not present any serious worries in regard to extra weight, but the first prototype was built almost entirely in wood since it was considered that this would be quicker for producing a prototype at a time when light alloys were in short supply.

To achieve a high maximum lift coefficient the wing was fitted with slots and flaps, and their combination with the variable-incidence wing required some wind tunnel testing to be performed by RAE Farnborough to ensure there were no serious aerodynamic problems. To obtain the desired high lift Supermarine decided to use full-span slots and part-span slotted flaps. In order to ensure that tip stalling did not occur, the slat of the outer slot was arranged such that the stall occurred four degrees later than the stall behind the inboard slats. Initially the prototype had plain ailerons but it was found that these did not enable full use to be made of the very high lift coefficient available, and so slotted ailerons were subsequently fitted which gave good results. During the design process it was thought at one stage that a variable-incidence tailplane would also be necessary to ensure tail-stalling did not occur, but it fact it was found that the change of incidence between wing and tailplane affected by the change in wing angle actually provided trim in the right direction.

When the wing's incidence was changed it automatically operated the slotted flaps to provide the desired relative angular movement

This image of R1810 shows the variable-incidence wing in the fully down position. The propeller is also without its spinner.

R1810 at rest with its wing in the 'normal' flying position. Had a fixed wing been in use the long nose would certainly have blocked the pilot's view for landing.

between wing and flap – when only a small angle of incidence was being used then only a small amount of flap was required, but at higher angles the flap angle would increase progressively (but not at a constant rate). At 2° of incidence the flap angle was zero, at 8° the flap would be set at 25°, at 12° the figure was 52°, and at 15° the flap would move to 60°. These relative angles were found suitable for both take-offs and landings, but early flight testing revealed rather higher maximum lift coefficients than had been predicted in the wind tunnel. For example with the engine turned off and the aircraft at a weight of 10,000lb (4,536kg), slots fully open and the wing set at 15° the maximum lift coefficient was 2.65. With the wing at 16° and its slats locked the figure was 2.03, and then with the engine running slots open and the wing setting 16° it became 3.9. These three figures for coefficient corresponded to a stalling speeds of 68mph (109km/h), 78mph (126km/h) and 57mph (92km/h) respectively. The stall was preceded by a lateral twitching on the ailerons and at low wing angles the stall was gentle, but at the 15° setting the right wing would drop sharply. It was also found that flying the aircraft in rough weather was quite heavy going.

R1810 arrived at RAE from Vickers by air on 24 November 1944 to begin its variable wing investigation programme. This found that when flying at 75mph (121km/h) the 322's ailerons were light and effective but the rudder was very light which made it quite ineffective. Consequently, in yaw the aeroplane would oscillate slightly and it would pitch fairly strongly in a phugoid motion which was continuous. During take-off trials made at various angles of wing incidence, with the tail held down during the run, the main wheels would always leave the ground first, and when the tailwheel finally left the ground the 322 would climb very steeply. Landing trials were made with the wing set at 10° and then at 15°, the latter providing an excellent view for the pilot with the fuselage's very nose-down attitude although the smaller angle still provided a very good view out. At the smaller angle a landing was simple and straightforward, but at 15° the task became quite difficult, in part because of poor longitudinal control and poor rudder control; at that setting it was also not possible to make a baulked landing.

On 22 June 1945 R1810 caught fire on its port side after glycol had begun to leak internally and pilot Capt Eric Brown and his two scientist passengers had to make a quick return to Farnborough since the flames would spread quickly around a wooden airframe. Fortunately, back on the ground the fire was rapidly extinguished and the aircraft suffered damage only around its nose, but it was not to be repaired. R1810 was returned to Vickers to go into temporary storage on 28 July, and on 1 July 1948 authority was given for 'reducing to produce' (scrap), the engine (and possibly the airframe) having been despatched to Wrigley Ltd at Belper on 20 June.

The Type 322 record cards provide few details for the careers of the two aircraft and the first flight date for the second example R1815 is unrecorded, but the airframe had its engine installed on 6 May 1943. Its record card gives no further information until 28 June 1946 when the aircraft was at Vickers, Hursley Park, for "flight trials". It is understood that the second machine was used by Supermarine until 1947 as a low speed chase plane for the

A lovely photograph of the first Supermarine Type 322 'Dumbo' R1810, which shows how relatively sleek the aircraft was, despite its chunky fixed undercarriage and large main wheels. *Phil Butler*

A view of R1815, the second 322. Note the slightly shorter tailwheel fitting. *Phil Butler*

In terms of production orders and squadron service the winning S.24/37 design was Fairey's Barracuda. This example, P9791, is seen at RAE Farnborough in 1943 performing a take-off with RATOG equipment.

firm's Attacker jet fighter, when the low speed part of that aircraft's flight envelope was being explored. For the task R1815 was eventually based at Supermarine's new flight test centre at Chilbolton and this proved to be its last home. On 5 February 1948 the engine was removed and sent to No.1 MPRD (Metal Produce Recovery Depot) at Cowley as scrap, and on 27 January 1949 the airframe was sold to R.J Coley at Hounslow.

Despite having a fixed undercarriage, the second 322 prototype with duralumin wings and fitted with the same Merlin 32 engine as the Barracuda Mk.II actually flew substantially faster than its rival from Fairey, at 279mph (449km/h) compared to the Fairey aircraft's 240mph (386km/h). Overall the two Type 322 airframes provided some fascinating and very promising data but the end of the war and the advent of jet-powered flight (with no engine in front of the pilot) removed some of the need for a variable-incidence wing. However, one of the few types built and flown with this feature was the American Vought F8U Crusader supersonic jet fighter flown in the 1950s and this aircraft stayed in service for over three decades.

Structure

The first 322 was built almost entirely in wood and the second airframe had duralumin wings, although the two-spar wing was really of composite construction. It had a front spar and webs of light alloy and then ribs made in spruce, and on the first machine the covering was in spruce but on the second in Alclad. The control surfaces were also plywood covered and the wing had automatic full-span leading edge slats together with trailing-edge landing flaps. All of this had to be accommodated within a folding wing and in addition 65 gallon (296 litre) fuel tanks made in Alclad formed the nose portion of each side of the wing centre section. The fuselage was built around four spruce longerons with frames of spruce and plywood and a covering in plywood. Most unusually, the tailplane had no spars – the structure was actually a shell assembled from spruce ribs and diagonal planking. The semi-cantilever undercarriage had a narrow wheel track (just 6ft 4in (1.93m)), a four-blade propeller was fitted and one Browning machine gun was to go into the wing and another on a flexible mounting in the rear cockpit, but these were never fitted. It is also thought that the type probably never flew with a torpedo or any bomb load.

32 Supermarine Spiteful and Seafang

Supermarine Spiteful F.Mk.XIV

Type: Single-Seat Fighter

Powerplant: One Rolls-Royce Griffon 69 liquid-cooled inline engine developing 2,375hp (1,771kW) at 1,250ft (381m)

Span: 35ft 0in (10.67m)

Length: 32ft 11in (10.03m)

Gross Wing Area: 210sq.ft (19.5m^2)

Normal Weight: 9,950lb (4,513kg), Overload with 180 gallon (818 litre) tank 11,400lb (5,171kg)

Maximum Speed at Normal Weight: 409mph (658km/h) at sea level, 483mph (777km/h) at 21,000ft (6,401m)

Maximum Permissible Diving Speed: 525mph (845km/h) at 10,000ft (3,048m)

Maximum Rate of Climb at Normal Weight: 4,890ft/min (1,490m/min) at 2,000ft (610m)

Service Ceiling: 42,000ft (12,802m)

Armament: 4 x 20mm cannon; provision for 2 x 1,000lb (454kg) bombs or 4 x 300lb (136kg) rocket projectiles, two under each wing

Supermarine Seafang F.Mk.32

Type: Single-Seat Fighter

Powerplant: One Rolls-Royce Griffon 89 liquid-cooled inline engine developing 2,350hp (1,752kW) at 1,250ft (381m)

Span: 35ft 0in (10.67m)

Length: 34ft 1in (10.39m)

Gross Wing Area: 210sq.ft (19.5m^2)

Normal All-Up Weight: 10,450lb (4,740kg)

Maximum Speed: 475mph (764km/h) at 21,000ft (6,401mm)

Rate of Climb: 4,630ft/min (1,411m/min) at 2,000ft (610m)

Service Ceiling: 41,000ft (12,497m)

Armament: As for Spiteful

Throughout the Second World War, Supermarine continually improved and developed its Spitfire and Seafire family of fighters to match the enemy's developments in fighters. New and more powerful engines were introduced which required changes to the airframe and tail assembly, more powerful gun armaments were installed and so on, with the result that by the end of the war the fighter's performance and destructive power, and particularly its speed, were far in excess of the Spitfire that flew in the Battle of Britain in 1940. A constant presence throughout, however, was that famous elliptical wing first designed by the late R.J. Mitchell. With the Spiteful, and its naval version the Seafang, Mitchell's successor Joe Smith finally replaced this with a tapered laminar flow wing.

The theory behind the laminar flow wing was that the boundary layer transition point would be moved further aft on the wing surface so that the point where turbulent airflow started was delayed, thereby reducing drag. The boundary layer is the layer of air adjacent to the aircraft's surface which has zero velocity at the surface itself, going up to freestream velocity (the speed at which the air is moving over the aircraft) at its outer edge. A thin 'laminar flow' boundary layer would produce less skin friction drag than a thicker or turbulent layer and the principal benefits were expected to be increased performance, the avoidance of compressibility effects and an improved rolling manoeuvrability from the resulting smaller span and wing area. In the middle war years compressibility was a growing problem caused by shock waves building up as aircraft flew ever nearer to the speed of sound. In April 1944 for example, Sqn Ldr A.F. Martindale flying Spitfire F.Mk.IX EN409 in some very high speed dive experiments reached a speed of over 600mph (965km/h) after a dive from 40,000ft (12,192m) to 27,000ft (8,230m). During this event the propeller came adrift and the aircraft's structure was badly strained but, after a 20 mile (32km) glide and by exercising great skill, Martindale was able to return to Farnborough. Later, in another aircraft Martindale dived from above 36,000ft (10,973m) to over 600mph (965km/h) and the engine supercharger burst. This time he crash landed in a wood but survived. High speed flight was dangerous!

The new wing was discussed at Supermarine's Hursley Park base on 19 November 1942 by Messrs Irving and Thomas from RAE and Messrs Smith, Alan Clifton, Mansbridge and Taylor from the firm. Unlike the Spitfire's elliptical wing this was straight tapered (two tapers) and the provisional dimensions were span 35ft (10.67m) and area 210sq.ft (19.53sq.m). The thickness/chord ratio was 13% over the inner 70in (178cm) of the semi-span and then tapered to 8% at the tip, and at the meeting it was agreed that the firm should now go ahead with the full design of the wing and aileron. As such the resulting Spiteful came to be regarded as the first 'thin wing' aircraft and the following month it was agreed that a four 20mm cannon armament should go into the new wing. The first pair of wings was expected to be ready in about eight months and Supermarine was initially instructed to build three Mk.VIII Spitfires with the new wing as prototypes. The National Physical Laboratory helped with the development work and wind tunnel testing (which at RAE and the NPL was considerable) and the wing's construction was certainly more straightforward than the Spitfire's elliptical shape. However, to the designer the laminar flow wing presented problems. A thin wing had to be made much heavier than a thick so that it could bear the loads in flight, there was little space inside for fuel and guns, and from the production point of view it demanded great accuracy of manufacture coupled with a much improved surface finish.

The first true Spiteful prototype was NN664, which in predominantly natural metal finish is pictured here standing at Boscombe Down on 29 June 1945. *Phil Butler*

The design and construction of the new fighter (eventually named Spiteful) was covered by Specification F.1/43 issued to Supermarine on 17 May 1943, and at this stage the type was basically a Spitfire Mk.VIII fuselage coupled with the new 'Type 371' wing (the Type number was originally given to just the wing, but later to the complete aircraft). The powerplant was to be a Rolls-Royce Merlin or Griffon with contra-rotating propeller which meant the wing must also fit the Griffon-powered Spitfire Mk.21; if possible, it was also be made to fold so that the Fleet Air Arm could use it. A maximum 525mph (845km/h) EAS, associated with a Mach number of 0.83, was to be used as a basis for the wing strength and stiffness calculations. Such was the optimism for the new design that by 1 October 1943 there were proposals to switch production at the huge Castle Bromwich factory to Mk.VIII Spitfires fitted with the laminar flow wing by August 1944. Plans for putting together production schedules, however, were hampered by a lack of available skilled draughtsmen and other labour, which was critical since real care was needed to ensure that the wing was manufactured accurately with such a very smooth surface. In the event, no Merlin-powered aircraft actually flew with the laminar flow surface, but it was to be mid-1944 before Supermarine agreed to forget the Merlin version. The presence of the Merlin explains why the first Spiteful was the Griffon Mk.XIV, the direct equivalent to the Spitfire XIV – lower mark numbers had been left vacant for Merlin-powered versions.

Contract Acft/2329 was issued on 4 February 1943 for three prototype Spitefuls, serials NN660, NN664 and NN667. However, NN660 was to be a hybrid prototype (a Spitfire Mk.XIV with the old-style canopy and fitted with the new wing) and it was first flown by Supermarine chief test pilot Jeffrey Quill on 30 June 1944. In fact Supermarine was criticised for taking so long to get the first aircraft flying. The direct Spitfire equivalent was the Mk.XIV and NN660 soon proved to be comfortably faster than the Spit, but not as fast as had first been hoped. Sadly, this prototype was lost along with its pilot Frank Furlong on 13 September during a flight from the High Post test airfield in Wiltshire. Furlong had been performing a mock dog-fight with a Spitfire XIV and during a manoeuvre he pulled a high level of *g* and the Spiteful flicked onto its back, Furlong hitting the ground near the airfield before he could recover. The cause was never established but it is thought that the ailerons may have jammed momentarily, something that was experienced later by Quill in NN664 at a higher and safer altitude.

In December 1944 the firm was criticised again by the Ministry over the programme's slow progress, N.E. Rowe informing Smith that it was his "personal job" to ensure that the second aircraft flew soon. In fact Quill flew NN664, the first true full standard prototype, on 8 January 1945. Flight testing soon revealed problems with 'snatching' of the ailerons and a wing would drop prior to the stall, and under high *g* there was also a pronounced flick at the stall (overall the stall was not as pleasant as the Spitfire's). Flights with the wing covered with wool tufts revealed that the area ahead of the ailerons was stalling before the rest. On the Spitfire the stall started at the wing root and worked its way along the wing to the tips, but it was found that the laminar flow wing did the opposite with the stall appearing to begin at the tips and moving inwards. Another problem was the difficulty in keeping the wing surface very smooth and clean – splashes of mud or dead insects could provoke turbulent flow in the boundary layer which automatically destroyed the laminar flow and cut the speed.

Much of the company test flying in NN664 was performed by Navy pilot Lt Patrick Shea-Simmonds who had been seconded to the firm. He too found that the aircraft performed well at high speed and was pleasant to fly, but that its low speed handling was inferior to the Spitfire. Originally NN664 had a standard Spitfire F.Mk.21 tailplane with elevators and rudder covered in fabric, but later this was enlarged to the standard Spiteful tailplane with far more area. This aeroplane was also used for other modifications to try and cure some of the faults – reduced span ailerons, modified wing sections near the ailerons, and beading on the aileron trailing edge. The redesigned and enlarged tail surfaces subsequently fitted to this aircraft and production machines did improve the low speed handling characteristics and made them more pleasant for the pilot, but they would also bring a drop in top speed which resulted in a performance not much better than late mark Spitfires. NN664 arrived at Boscombe Down for its official flight trials in June 1945, and both Quill and Shea-Simmonds flew the Spiteful at the RAE Farnborough 'At Home' exhibition and display held in late October 1945.

This page and next: The first production Supermarine Spiteful was RB515, and the aircraft is shown here on test in a series of air-to-air views. The pilot is Patrick Shea-Simmonds. *Phil Butler*

Charles Brown's skill in using cloud and landscape for his subjects is shown to the full with this gorgeous shot of Spiteful RB515 taken on 27 July 1945.
RAF Museum

The third aircraft NN667 introduced a longer 'low drag' air intake directly behind the airscrew, but it still suffered from the problems that affected the earlier Spitefuls. Fitted with an 11ft (3.35m) diameter five-bladed Rotol Hydraulic variable-pitch propeller, NN667 was at Boscombe between 1 February and 6 June 1946 but its engineering and maintenance appraisal was not encouraging. The report stated that the aircraft was generally considered "below average" with a bad cockpit layout and too much time required for routine operations such as refuelling and rearming. In summary it was thought that the Spiteful would be difficult to service and maintain. In an unpainted condition, NN667 made a surprise appearance in 1947 at the Marham flood relief display.

Contract Acft/1877 covered a large order for Spitefuls and Spitfires. The first seventeen were built as Spiteful Mk.XIVs (RB515 to RB525, RB527 to RB531, and RB535) but the rest were subsequently cancelled. The combination of Griffon 69, short air intake and five-blade Rotol airscrew was called the Spiteful F.Mk.XIV, while aircraft with Griffon 89s or 90s and a six-blade contra-rotating propeller were to be F.Mk.XVs. It is thought that all of the RB serials appeared as Mk.XIVs, and no photos are known to exist showing a Mk.XV. The Griffon 69 with its two-stage supercharger differed very little from the Spitfire's Griffon 61, the main difference being that the 69 was modified to operate at a maximum 25lb/sq.in boost when using 150 grade fuel (when using 100 Octane fuel the boost had to be restricted to 18lb/sq.in by fitting the appropriate throttle stops). RB515 made its maiden flight on 2 April 1945 with the original F.21 Spitfire tailplane and a Griffon 69, but after three more flights the larger tail was fitted. As such it flew much better with improvements to the low speed lateral control near the stall and enhanced directional stability. On production Spitefuls the clean stall (preceded by lateral pecking of the wings and then a very sharp port wing drop) occurred at 109mph (175km/h), and with everything down at 101mph (163km/h).

On 28 September 1945 RB515 suffered an engine failure at 30,000ft (9,144m) altitude but the pilot, Shea-Simmonds, found the aircraft handled quite well as a glider and he was able to make a wheels-up landing at Farnborough. Saving the aircraft allowed the engineers to find the problem (the first-stage supercharger had disintegrated) and the pilot was awarded the King's Commendation for Valuable Service in the Air. With relatively little damage RB515 was repaired and flew again. With the possibility that the fighter-bomber role might prove to be the Spiteful's salvation, RB516 was to be tested by A&AEE in this form from April 1946. In the meantime RB517 was used at Boscombe for engine cooling and performance testing, RB518 was used for propeller development, RB519, RB520 and RB521 for general testing, and RB523 to clear the armament installation. On 23 August 1945 the Air Ministry told Supermarine that the Spiteful was to be dropped from the fighter programme other than as a fighter bomber. Eventually interest in the type died and it never entered RAF service. Plans were raised again briefly in November 1945 to equip one Spiteful fighter squadron for trials (replacing Spitfire 22s) but these were soon dropped and in the end just the seventeen examples were delivered (plus the two prototypes) before production ended in December 1945 (the original plans had called for 88 deliveries to be made in 1945 and 248 in 1946). Thirteen Spitefuls were sold for scrap on 8 July 1948.

On 9 August 1948 Supermarine reported on a programme of propeller tests made with RB518 fitted with a Griffon 101 engine with two stage three speed supercharger and flown at a weight of 8,600lb (3,901kg). As such the type was designated F.Mk.16 and was the sole example. It had a Seafang-type windscreen

Production Spiteful RB517 with five-blade propeller seen at rest. The tapered laminar flow wing is well shown.

This view of of RB518 shows the air intake position moved to underneath the nose – the long intake from directly behind the spinner on RB517 and other Spitefuls has gone. RB518 was the only Spiteful F.Mk.16.

Fitted with a five-bladed propeller and a Griffon 101 engine, RB518 eventually qualified as Britain's fastest piston-engined aircraft.

and hood plus the original Spiteful air intake and tests were carried out with this aircraft to compare the level speed performance when fitted with an 11ft 0in (3.35m) diameter wide chord NACA 16-section propeller and with a double wedge section propeller of similar diameter. The tests were confined to the measurement, over a range of heights, of level speed performance in FS gear, but the double wedge propeller tests had to be concluded prematurely after RB518 was forced to land with its undercarriage retracted. It was found that the double wedge propeller gave a small gain in level speed (3 to 4mph (4.8 to 6.4km/h) below full throttle height - FTH) and possibly an increase in full throttle height of up to 1,500ft (457m). The NACA propeller had a FTH of 33,600ft (10,241m) with a speed at that height of 487mph (784km/h); the double wedge figures were 35,100ft (10,698m) and 494mph (795km/h), and at 33,600ft (10,241m) the latter's speed was 490mph (788km/h). Such speeds did not do the engine much good, but 494mph (795km/h) was a record for a British piston aircraft. RB518 was subsequently dismantled.

In early October 1943 Supermarine had also begun looking at fitting the laminar flow wing to the Seafire Mk.XV, but the idea of a naval version received no official backing until the Type 396 Seafang was described by Specification N.5/45 of 17 July 1945. This document outlined a prototype based on the Spiteful and its folded width was not to exceed 27ft (8.23m) and folded height 13ft (3.96m). An arrestor hook was to be fitted, hydraulically-operated wing folding was introduced, the powerplant was one Griffon 85 or 87 engine and besides the four 20mm Hispanos the aircraft would carry bombs or rocket projectiles. Production Spiteful RB520 was fitted just with a sting-type arrestor hook as an interim Seafang prototype and first flew as such early in 1945. Supermarine conducted all of the early flight trials on this aeroplane before it was made available for collection by the Navy on 22 September 1945, but it was not actually collected until 13 January 1947, and then it was struck off charge. The 'hooked' Spiteful was first shown to the public at a display of new naval aircraft staged by the Admiralty at Heston on 2 October 1945.

Contract Acft/5176/C.23(c) was placed on 12 March 1945 for two full Type 396 Seafang F.Mk.XXXII (Mk.32) prototypes, VB893 and VB895 with Griffon 89s and contra-rotating propellers. The airframes were to be built at Hursley Park and VB895 made its first flight from there in early 1946, arriving at A&AEE Boscombe Down on 30 June. Information on VB893 is scarce. It was apparently 'Ready' at Vickers on 3 December 1946 and may have gone to A&AEE later that month, but nothing else is known. There is no MAP history card for it and the aircraft remains a mystery. Jeffrey Quill demonstrated VB895 at the Farnborough event staged to show off British aerodynamic achievement on 27 to 30 June 1946, and a Seafang 32 (and a Seafire 47) also attended the 7th SBAC Display and Show at Radlett during the week ending 14 September. There it was revealed that the new fighter could carry 180 gallons (818 litres) of external fuel, and that it had a rather longer take-off run than the Seafire 47, but during its flying display the Seafang demonstrated that it had exceptional aileron control. On 21 August 1946 Supermarine test pilot Lt Cdr Mike J. Lithgow (who had replaced Shea-Simmonds in early 1946) demonstrated the Seafang to Dutch, French and American naval officers during a visit to Valkenburg in Holland, but the fighter was not to win any export orders.

VB895 was used from 1 May 1947 to conduct deck landing trials at an all-up-weight of 9,870lb (4,477kg). Lithgow was the pilot and he reported flap settings of 76° for landing and 30° for take-off. To start with, approximately forty-five simulated trial landings were carried out at Chilbolton and at RNAS Ford. The engine-off stalling speed was 89 knots (102mph/164km/h) ASI, at which speed there was a certain amount of elevator and general buffeting, commencement of general aileron snatching, and a high rate of descent. The aileron snatching, however, did not seem to be much in evidence when actually landing (it was thought due to ground effect). The spring tab elevator and long stroke oleo legs were both considered by Lithgow to be essential for deck landing, the former being very effective in reducing the otherwise large stick forces involved in manipulating the flaps, and the latter to eliminate bounce and absorb the shock of the necessarily rather heavy landing.

Seafang VB895 was displayed at the Farnborough Exhibition of late June 1946. Spiteful RB522 was also shown there, although this particular photograph does not appear to have been taken at Farnborough.

Magnificent views of Spiteful RB523 being demonstrated for the cameraman. The aircraft has light grey undersides. Note the wing shape, and the 20mm guns in the wings. *The late Jim Oughton*

| Spiteful RB520 was fitted with a sting-type arrestor hook to serve as an interim prototype for the navalised Seafang.

The prototype Seafang was actually VB895, which first flew after VG471. It received a Griffon 89 with contra-rotating propellers.

The aircraft was first landed aboard HMS *Illustrious* on 21 May and went on to complete eight landings without incident. The view of the deck was generally excellent and Lithgow found that it was possible to make the final approach, for the last 200 yards (183m), from dead astern. The approach speed of 95 knots (109mph/175km/h) felt "quite comfortable", the only criticism being the over-light aileron control with no self-centring tendency, a feature of the Spiteful family generally. Lithgow also compared the equivalent airspeeds of the Seafang and the Seafire FR.Mk.47, the former having a leading edge pitot and the latter an underwing pitot head. Although the position error correction figures were not very accurate, the Seafire had an approach speed of 77 knots (89mph/143km/h) ASI (=89 knots (102mph/164km/h) EAS), compared to the Seafang's 95 knots (109mph/175km/h) ASI (=91 knots (105mph/169km/h) EAS). Overall, it was felt that there was little more than a few knots difference in the two approach speeds. On receiving the 'cut' signal, the Seafang sat down on the deck extremely well with no float whatsoever, and using take-off flap and +18lb/sq.in boost pressure the take-off was "easy and straightforward". In general Lithgow considered that the Seafang was a good deck landing aircraft, mainly owing to the good view and lack of float on cutting the throttle. A few months later Lithgow succeeded Jeffrey Quill as chief test pilot, while VB895 was used later to test a 170 gallon (773 litre) drop tank that was shaped like a torpedo. When the aircraft was flying at 10,000ft (3,048m) having this tank aboard reduced the speed from 373mph (600km/h) to 360mph (579km/h).

Contract Acft/1877 also covered 150 production Seafangs in the serial range VG471 to VG679, but in the end only 16 were built and all apparently as F.Mk.31s (which had a Griffon 61 with Rotol five-blade propeller). In fact the Spiteful order was cancelled on 2 May 1945 right at the end of the war, and the Seafang order was placed on 7 May so the latter was actually a reinstatement, and materials and components rendered surplus by the Spiteful cancellation were to be absorbed where possible in the Seafang series. However, only the first nine Seafangs, up to VG479, were delivered as complete aeroplanes, the remaining seven being delivered in a dismantled form. The last example left the manufacturers in 1947.

VG471, without wing folding and fitted with a five-blade propeller, made its first flight and then arrived at RAE Farnborough for arresting proofing trials (the latter on 15 January 1946) both before VB895 had first flown. However, the aircraft failed these trials initially because the rudder skin wrinkled during off-centre arrests, and they were not actually passed until 30 April. Compared to the earlier Spiteful VG471 introduced another 3°of dihedral and more rounded leading edges to its wing (items which were eventually added to later examples of the landplane) but the Seafang's subsequent official deck landing trials left the impression that the Seafire 47 was the better aircraft. The contra-rotating propeller and the wide undercarriage did make the take-off easier than in a Seafire Mk.46 with non-contra-rotating propellers and there were no torque effects. In the air the controls were beautifully light and effective at normal speeds but Captain Eric Brown described the Seafang's stall as

Seafang VG471 banks away from the camera to present some underside detail. Note the large wide-span radiators.

vicious. In the end the Navy decided against putting the new type into service, instead acquiring the final marks of Seafire, an order for FR.Mk.47's being placed on 8 April 1946. It appears that the Seafang Mk.31 was indeed generally inferior to the Seafire 47 in terms of deck operations and the 47 also performed better at high altitude than had been expected.

However, the Seafang was employed on numerous test and research programmes. VB895 was at Boscombe Down between May 1948 and May 1949 for gun and weapon firing. However, on 18 May 1948, during ground firing trials for the Supermarine Attacker jet fighter's guns there was an explosion in the gun bay which seriously damaged VB895's port mainplane. Ventilators had to be fitted to ensure that in future the gun gasses were cleared out and these had intakes below the wings and exits above. Mk.31 VG475 fitted with Mk.32 contra-rotating propellers had a pitot comb unit attached on the inboard wing trailing edge (which required the span of the ailerons to be reduced by 15in (38.1cm)) to allow it to compare the drag coefficient relative to the Mach number. For the task this Seafang had its guns removed and the rear fuel tank replaced by cameras. As such it was test flown by John Derry who on 23 June 1947 performed several dives in the aircraft, including one from 27,000ft (8,230m) to a speed of 400mph (644km/h) ASI at 20,000ft (6,096m) and Mach 0.77. On this dive violent pitching began at Mach 0.75 in the form of a high-frequency phugoid (which was recorded by the cameras) and it proved quite impossible to hold the stick steady. However, this did not occur in later dives to 450mph (724km/h) at 10,000ft (3,048m) and 480mph (772km/h) at just 1,000ft (305m), which confirmed that the phenomenon was related to a specific Mach number only. The cause was traced to the wake apparatus fitted to the airframe and once corrections had been made the Seafang was dived to Mach 0.83 without trouble.

For comparison, pictures of VG471 with five-bladed propeller taken on the ground (in March 1946) and also in the air. Note the guard just ahead of the tailwheel to prevent it from catching an arrestor wire.

In 1947 VG474 was used to flight test a Servodyne-assisted aileron system which proved to be excellent and improved the aircraft's rate of roll at medium speeds considerably. However, at 450mph (724km/h) speed the results were inferior to the Attacker jet fighter's spring tab arrangement (which on the Attacker's ailerons was the only difference to the Seafang's standard balance tabs). In July 1948 VG474 fitted with Attacker-type ailerons was flown by Capt Brown, and he was able to report near perfection in lateral control.

A form of the Spiteful laminar flow wing was subsequently used on the firm's first jet fighter, the Attacker already mentioned, which also became the Navy's first jet fighter. Despite their faults, the Spiteful and Seafang were primarily defeated in their attempt to enter service by the arrival of the jet fighter – the airscrew-driven fighter's time was almost over! These two types, however, remain the ultimate development of the Spitfire, and the Spiteful is still one of the fasted piston aircraft ever to have flown.

Structure

The Spiteful airframe used metal monocoque construction throughout, with stressed skin covering. Its fuselage was redesigned from the Spitfire and had more of a humped-back appearance while the laminar flow wing had two spars. The Spiteful pilot's seat was more reclined than in the Spitfire and the view over the nose was improved. One permanent weakness of the Spitfire and Seafire had been their narrow track undercarriage but the Spiteful and Seafang introduced a wide track landing gear, although during taxying this did tend to make the aircraft wander off course. For its planned carrier operations the Seafang had hydraulically-operated upward-folding outer wings (in fact really just the tips) plus powered ailerons. Spiteful's normal fuel capacity was 178 gallons (809 litres), but a 90 gallon (409 litre) or 180 gallon (818 litre) drop tank could be fitted without reduction in military load. Early Spitefuls could carry only 118 gallons (537 litres) internally but a 60 gallon (273 litre) tank was later added in the rear fuselage. There was provision for RATOG gear.

In the end the Navy decided not to buy the Seafang, opting instead to have the latest marks of Seafire. This image shows FR.Mk.47 Seafires of 804 Squadron. *Phil Butler*

Close-up of the contra-rotating propeller used on some Spitefuls and Seafangs. Note the wide-track undercarriage.

Seafang FR.Mk.32, VB895, deck landing trials on HMS Illustrious, May 1947. Copyright *Richard Caruana*

33 Vickers 432

Vickers 432

Type: Single-Seat Twin-Engine High-Altitude Fighter

Powerplant: Two 1,520hp (1,133W) Rolls-Royce Merlin 61 liquid-cooled inline engines

Span: 56ft 10.5in (17.34m)

Length: 39ft 3in (11.96m)

Gross Wing Area: 450sq.ft (41.85m^2)

Maximum Weight: 19,721lb (8,945kg)

Rate of Climb: Unavailable (see text)

Maximum Speed achieved: 380mph (612km/h) at 15,000ft (4,572m)

Service Ceiling: Never established

Armament: 6 x 20mm Hispano cannon

The Type 432 was the last Vickers fighter to reach manufacture and flight test. Only two airframes were built and just one completed, and that flew a mere 29 times. The 432's story starts in 1939 when Specification F.6/39 was issued in April for a fast two seat fighter capable of a minimum 400mph (644km/h). In the meantime the Vickers design team led by Rex Pierson had been working on a proposal for a fighter with a single Vickers 40mm gun, a powerful cannon mounted in the extreme nose and which could be elevated to an angle of 45°, depressed 5° and trained 20° to either side. The complete installation was based on the theory of accurate single-shot firing – if the gunner kept the sight on the target, the predictor would automatically keep the gun pointing at it.

In July a brochure was prepared which covered the single 40mm fighter but which also had two layouts for a fixed gun fighter. A new specification, F.22/39, was raised for the 40mm version (now the called Type 414), but interest in the fixed gun designs continued. A contract (B.17894/39) for two 414 prototypes was awarded on 30 August (which were eventually given the serials R4236 and R4239), but on 15 April 1940 Pierson produced a brochure for a design to F.22/39 with eight 20mm Hispano cannon and two Rolls-Royce Griffon RG.2SM engines. Little structural work was done on the 414 before a new specification, F.16/40, was written for the 20mm cannon aircraft, which Vickers called the Type 420. A new brochure prepared in October showed a single fin and rudder for the first time, and by January 1941 the armament had been cut to six 20mm.

In January 1941 Pierson produced a brochure for a two-seat high altitude fighter which can be considered as the first layout for the Type 432. Work on the Type 414 was subsequently stopped and thoughts turned to fitting Merlin instead of Griffon engines. By mid May the new design had become a single-seat high altitude fighter with a pressure cabin 16ft 6in (5.03m) long with a 4ft 6in (1.37m) maximum diameter. The pilot was placed in the extreme nose and was covered by a hinged dome, and provision was now made to incorporate six 20mm Hispanos in the underbelly fairing. Vickers received an order (Contracts/Acft/1346 dated 9 September 1941) for two single-seat prototypes with serials DZ217 and DZ223 (these seem to have been allotted around the end of July 1941) and they were covered by a new specification F.7/41. The powerplant was to be two Merlin 61 engines and the first machine would have complete flying and engine instruments, oxygen and pressure cabin equipment, R/T and navigational facilities, with the second equipped

The Vickers Type 432 prototype DZ217 flies high above the clouds and shows off its unique wing shape. Test Flight 22 (11 November 1943) was partially devoted to photography and so this is the most likely date.

to full operational standard. The pressure cabin had to be capable of maintaining conditions appropriate to 25,000ft (7,620m) when flying above that height up to 42,000ft (12,801m), and its operation had to be automatic. Top speed would not be less than 415mph (668km/h) at 33,000ft (10,058m).

Construction of the first Type 432 was ongoing throughout 1942 in the experimental hangar at Foxwarren and it was agreed by the Ministry in April of that year that DZ223 should be kitted out with the required equipment to

Model of the Vickers Type 414 with its 40mm nose gun. Prototypes of this design were ordered but never built. *Joe Cherrie*

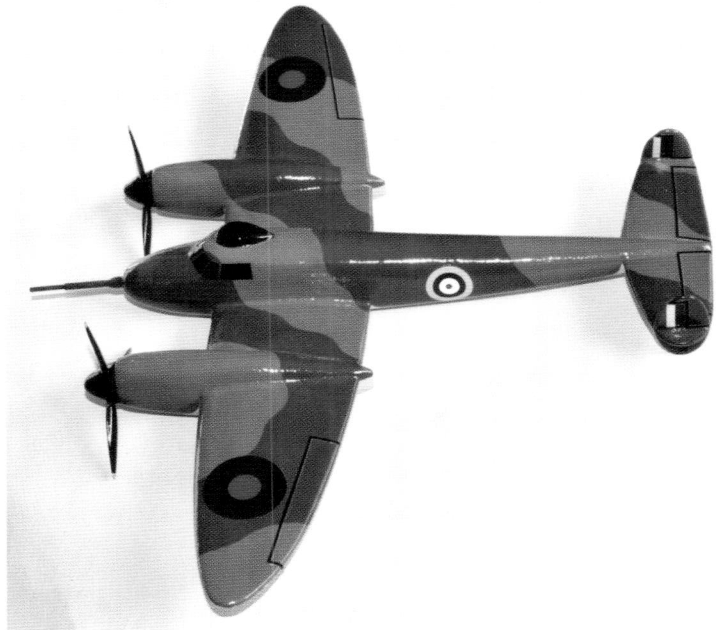

Three-quarter starboard front view of DZ217 on the hard standing, with a Vickers employee to provide an idea of the aircraft's size.

enable it to be tested as a two-seat night fighter. DZ217 was taken to Farnborough for taxying and initial flight, but this was delayed after the wing test specimen failed at the end of August under static load: it was not until 6 November that repeat load testing achieved a satisfactory result. Taxying trials took place on 20 December and now it was found that the machine was difficult to control directionally (the solution was to move the main chassis wheels backwards by 5 in (12.7cm)). Finally the Type 432 achieved its maiden flight on 24 December 1942 from Farnborough with Flt Lt Douglas Webster 'Tommy' Lucke in the cockpit. Just five days later, however, MAP informed Vickers that all work on DZ223 was cancelled, although some parts in manufacture could be completed and held as spares (the official confirmation of this move was sent in May 1943). The next four flights looked at general handling, stalling, temperature checks and retraction of the undercarriage. Ten flights had been completed by 19 February, after which new Westland type ailerons were fitted. The aircraft flew again on 14 March and the next six flights up to 1 May embraced aileron and elevator testing. On Flights 18 and 19, on 14 and 20 May 1943, the level speed performance was measured at heights from 5,000ft (1,524m) upwards at 5,000ft intervals. This was continued on Flight 21 (2 July) and it was on these sorties that engine 'cutting' was experienced (see below).

The Type 432 flew on just 29 occasions, between December 1942 and November 1944, and all bar one of these sorties was made with Lucke at the controls. Aileron overbalancing (which increased with speed) plus elevators that were heavy at all normal flying speeds were reported after the first flight, the latter being ineffective near the ground as shown by the aircraft's inability to make a three-point landing. Indeed, the difficulty in getting the tail down gave a landing distance that was far too high. The powerplant installations were satisfactory. Later flights showed that elevator control disappeared in steep turns under various ASI and *g*-load combinations. When first flown the aircraft had Irving-type balances and the overbalancing increased with speed, considerable force being required from the pilot to centralise the ailerons. Various alterations provided little or no improvement and as a result these balances were scrapped and substituted with the Westland type (which had proved successful on the Blackburn Firebrand naval fighter). These made the ailerons more effective and gave a rate of roll that was fairly good.

The early flights also revealed premature stalling of the wing centre section between the fuselage and nacelles (which corroborated earlier wind tunnel results) and also slow undercarriage retraction. Further tunnel testing showed that this early stall could be improved by extending the centre section leading edge by 15in (38cm) using built-on structure, thereby increasing the wing area by 6sq.ft (0.59m^2), but in fact this modification brought little improvement to the 432's flight characteristics. Juddering and the loss of control in tight turns occurred as before,

Side view of DZ217 which shows how the engine nacelles obscured the pilot's view to the side.

A three-quarter port angle photo which gives some more detail of the Merlin 61 engine nacelles.

although the pilot did report that the aircraft felt "smoother". Thanks to the aileron difficulties it was Flight 10 before Lucke could confirm that the 432 lacked lateral stability, and he declared that the aircraft needed to be "flown" all of the time and was "tricky" to fly and land.

Several attempts were made to climb the aircraft to an altitude of 30,000ft (9,252m), but on each occasion the engines would cut out at between 22,000 and 24,500ft (6,706 and 7,468m). On Flight 18 tests were started to establish the 432's level speed performance but during an attempted climb from 20,000 to 25,000ft (6,096 to 7,620m) the port engine revs began to surge violently at 24,000ft (7,315m), at which point the starboard revs also surged mildly; the same thing happened in either 'M' or 'S' boost positions. After the engines had cooled down another attempt was made but this time the port engine cut out completely at 24,500ft (7,468m). On later flights further efforts to reach 25,000ft (7,620m) produced more engine cutting, overall the aircraft's rate of climb was very slow and the engines just would not function above about 23,000ft (7,010m).

Subsequent analysis showed that the cooling on the Merlin 61s was inadequate for both the oil and the coolant. The radiator exit flaps were located forward of the landing flaps and the positive pressure generated by lowering the latter so reduced the cooling flow that very high temperatures were experienced in an 'engine on' approach. Also the fuel coolers were located in the rear of the engine nacelles and when these were in operation the all out level speed was reduced by 30mph (48km/h). Consequently, in October 1943 de Havilland Mosquito-type fuel coolers were fitted. As a result of these problems very little data was collected for the Type 432's performance. The maximum level speed

actually achieved (in May 1943) was 380mph at 15,000ft (612km/h at 4,572m) at an all-up weight of 17,700lb (8,029kg), which was some way off the design estimate of 435mph at 28,000ft (700km/h at 8,534m). However, 400mph (644km/h) was exceeded in a dive at which point the ailerons became solid.

Delays between flights were caused by various modifications and also through the burning out on two occasions of a Merlin engine (once as a result of radiator failure). On Flight 23 Lucke attempted a steep climb but due to the application of negative *g* at the top of the climb both engines cut at around 2,000ft (610m) and 130mph (209km/h) ASI. The port engine went first and almost simultaneously the machine inadvertently flicked over into a left hand and near vertical spin. Recovery was affected at 600 to 800ft (183 to 244m), although the aircraft showed no signs of recovery until the slipstream was available. The aircraft's persistent desire to stall or spin gave some nerve-wracking moments and Lucke's description of his recovery at low level did not indicate in any way just how close he was to the ground, and how much danger he was in. RAE Farnborough was never happy with the 432's spinning characteristics but proper spinning trials with the aircraft were never begun. The guns were never fitted either, and the pressure cabin not completed because in October 1943 a decision was made not to proceed with its installation.

Flight 25 was performed on 25 January 1944 by Sqn Ldr Longbottom who at the time was attached to Vickers to assist with test flying. He reported a strong tendency to swing to the left on take-off. By the time the throttles were open the load on the elevators was quite large but the tail came off the ground practically without using the elevator at all, although after that it was necessary to pull very hard on the stick to get the aircraft off the ground. In the air he found that the ailerons were overbalanced at 140mph (225km/h) ASI or less so that they stayed in the position to which they were disturbed. Above this speed they acquired a 'knife edge' in the central position, and if released would go immediately right across to one side or the other – usually to port. This effect became rapidly worse with increases of speed, and at 250mph (402km/h) ASI or above in bumpy conditions it frequently required the use of both hands on the stick to control the aircraft. However, at all speeds the ailerons were quite effective, and the rate of roll was quite good. At low speeds the rudder was quite effective with full power on, but with only a little power or none at all it was practically non-effective and had no feel at all. At high speeds the rudder was quite light at small angles, but became very heavy at large angles and was quite effective.

Longbottom added that the elevators were extremely heavy at all speeds but, if the pilot was able to move them, they were very effective at all normal speeds. The elevator trimmer was also very powerful. The change of trim with speed was very small indeed and this, combined with the power of the trimmer, and the apparent instability of the aircraft, made it quite impossible to trim the aircraft fore and aft. However, it appeared that the trim changed very slightly nose up with increase in speed. The inability to trim the aircraft also made it impossible to attempt phugoids (pitching the aircraft up into a climb and then down into a descent, accompanied by an increase in speed and then slowing down as it went 'uphill' and 'downhill'). In turns up to about 60° bank releasing the stick caused the aircraft to come out of the turn, and there did appear to be a tendency to tighten into the turn. With the rudder fixed good turns and recovery from them could be done on ailerons only, and also with rudder fixed the aircraft would bank without hesitation up to 90° on aileron only. He also found that the problems with the controls made landing the 432 difficult – the aircraft was held off at about 5ft (1.5m) from the ground with the power right off and with the stick pulled back with all the force that could be exerted on it. When it landed on its main wheels the tail wheel was still about 3 or 4 ft (0.9 to 1.2m) from the ground.

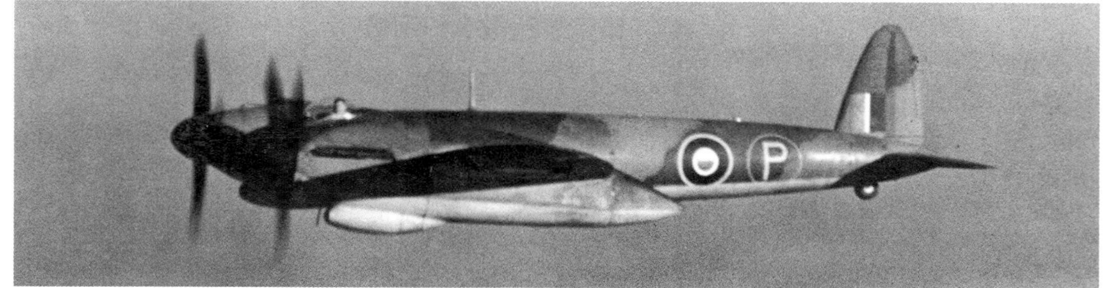

This is the second known air-to-air photograph of DZ217 and again was presumably made on 11 November 1943. If others were successfully taken then they have presumably and sadly been lost.

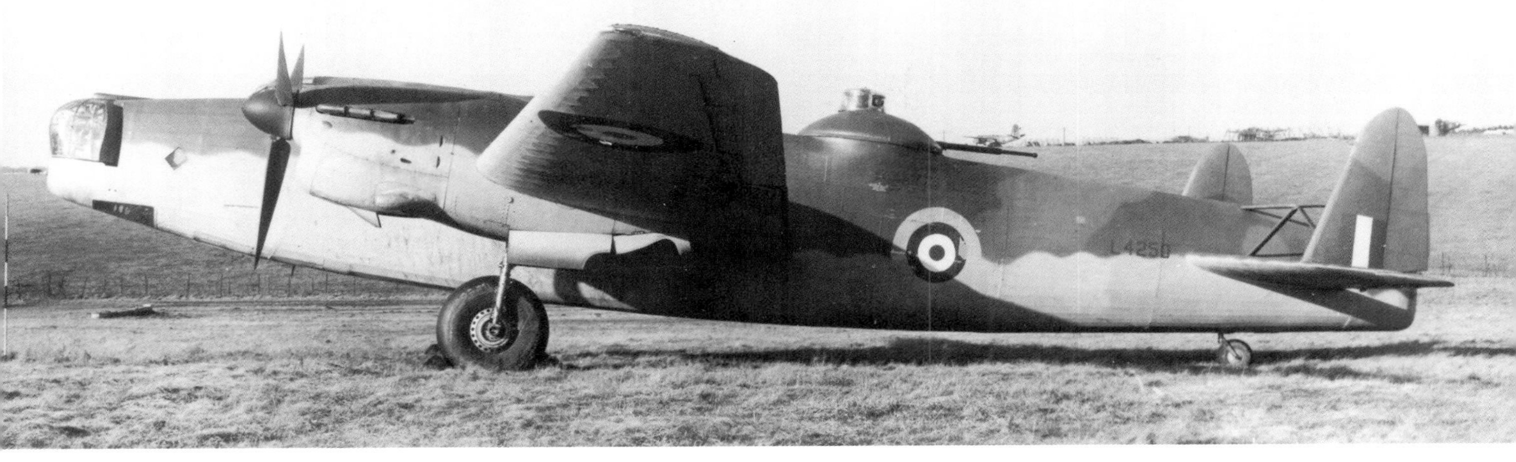

Wellington Mk.II prototype L4250 was fitted in 1941 with a 40mm cannon in the dorsal position to serve as a trials aeroplane for the weapon. Some trouble was experienced in flight with tail vibration and in due course a change was made to the twin-fin arrangement shown here. *Phil Butler*

Using the available flight data, on 31 January 1944 test pilot Mutt Summers was able to compile a report on the 432. The cockpit was described as roomy and comfortable but the operation of the canopy dome was considered to be unacceptable as a service proposition – in an emergency its jettison and the pilot's escape would be extremely difficult! There was insufficient rudder control to correct the swing to port on take-off with equal opening up of the engines, and towards the end of the take-off run a heavy rearward pressure was necessary on the stick to keep the tail from getting too high. The aircraft then flew itself off the ground nicely. The lack of positive longitudinal stability combined with the elevator problem made the initial climb unpleasant, but cruise flight was smooth and fairly quiet with a good forward view although the side view was restricted by the nacelles. The problems highlighted by Lucke and Longbottom were confirmed and at low speeds the 432 was under-ruddered which, in the event of losing an engine on take-off, or a single engine approach, was a hazard. At 185mph (298km/h) the application of full right rudder in straight and level flight saw the resulting bank and skid held easily on the ailerons – at 120mph (193km/h) full rudder could be applied either way without positive results. The stalling speed with everything down was 77mph (124km/h); with flaps and chassis up the 432 could be flown at 80mph (129km/h) but the stall was close. In the end little progress was made in solving the 432's numerous problems because towards the end of 1943 the decision was taken not to proceed further with the project. Three more flights (numbers 26 to 28) were made, however, between 28 February and 25 March 1944 in an attempt to assess the aerodynamic efficiency of DZ217's wing structure.

By autumn 1943 the Ministry of Aircraft Production had expressed its wish to close the F.7/41 contract by the end of the year. On 4 October a meeting was held at Burhill between Pierson and selected Ministry and RAE representatives to discuss any additional testing that could be completed where the results might be of general benefit. The measurement of the stalling speed and checking of tunnel test data by flight test were two areas that would be simple to arrange and so the proposal was agreed. However, discussions also began in regard to some extra flights to test the 40mm gun installation first mooted back in 1939. The Wellington Mk.II prototype L4250, first flown on 3 March 1939, had been converted to carry a 40mm cannon and its predictor installation (by now called the 'S' gun) and it was first flown with the weapon in October 1942, making Vickers the only company to take such armament on flight test. From the start of 1943 this aircraft was kept at RAE Farnborough but for seventeen months practically nothing was done with it. In early May 1944 arrangements were made to return DZ217 to Weybridge for a programme of flying and firing trials to be worked out, and in June orders were raised for an experimental 40mm power-operated turret for the fighter. By 5 October refitting DZ217 with an 'S' gun in a bow installation was nearly complete and only the coupling up and testing of the predictor, gyro rate gear and hydraulic equipment was required. In the end, however, the 432 flew just once more (Flight 29 on 26 November 1944) where it performed a speed against power trial to determine the drag curve. The final scrapping date is unknown, but the contract to break down DZ217 was not received by Vickers until 21 December 1945.

Since no real effort was ever made to correct the Type 432's faults it will never be known just how good this aircraft might have been. The long time taken over its development was critical because, by the time flight testing was

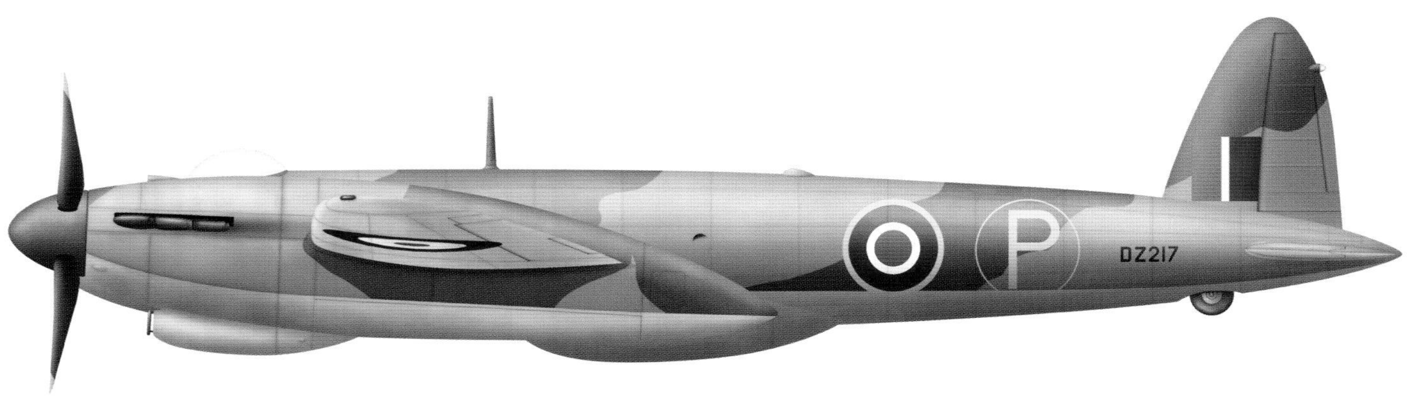

DZ217 was the only Vickers 432 to reach the flight-testing stage and spent much of its life in the hangar . *Chris-Sandham Bailey www.inkworm.com*

underway, many twin-engine fighter functions were soon to be, or already in the hands of, the de Havilland Mosquito in its numerous forms. The need for and value of a Type 432 had died. Vickers itself was also very busy with bomber work and never had the capacity to give any priority to its fighter and to solving its many in flight problems. Nevertheless, the Vickers 414/420/432 series was of great interest and supplied knowledge and experience in new areas of design, such as the 'lobster-claw' wing structure [below] and the fitting of heavy cannon and pressure cabins.

Structure

The Vickers Type 432 had low drag elliptical wings and a tail unit very like the Mosquito but, unlike that aircraft which used wood construction, the 432 was built in metal. The aircraft required a surface finish that had to be better than the fabric-covered geodetic structure used by Vickers' bomber aircraft and so a true stressed-skin construction with mostly duralumin skins was used throughout (the first Vickers aeroplane so built), although the control surfaces were finished in fabric. The ingenious method of manufacture used for the wing has long been a source of interest since it made use in the torsion box of what was termed 'lobster-claw' construction (with heavy-gauge skinning), although Vickers also described it as 'peapod construction'. The span-wise spar booms showed a cross-section shape of a lobster's claw and were accommodated in a thickened section provided in the skin. It was considered that this structure eliminated the need for ribs and spars, the thickened spanwise parts of the skin substituting the latter. The shell was made in two halves to facilitate manufacture, the halves being united at the leading and trailing edges by mechanical linkage using annular dowels clamping split bosses to provide a shear connection; the torsion box then had the rear control surfaces attached to it. The 'lobster-claw' structure coupled with flush riveting gave a very smooth wing surface.

Two Merlin 61 engines with two-stage two-speed superchargers were mounted in long nacelles which also housed the main undercarriage, and four-blade constant speed 11.5ft (3.5m) diameter feathering propellers were fitted. The radiators were buried in the wing between the fuselage and nacelles and the leading edge duct provided a ram air intake. The radiator wing intakes had to be modified after tunnel testing revealed bad premature stall between the fuselage and the nacelles. Flexible self-sealing fuel tanks were carried inside the outer planes, the wing structure providing unobstructed space for these tanks. The streamlined fuselage embraced closely spaced circular frames covered in flush-riveted skin, this method of attachment being employed throughout the aircraft to reduce skin friction drag. Built in two main sections the front portion housed the small pressure cabin while the rear fuselage was unpressurised. The fullest use was made of the skin strength around the cabin by fitting it in such a way that the skin became uniformly stressed by the pressure instead of being locally restrained when riveted to the hoop frames. Cabin pressurisation was achieved with two Rotol blowers, one being driven by each engine. The extreme tail end of the fuselage came as a further separate section with a short cone to carry the tail surfaces.

34 Vickers Windsor

Merlin Windsor

Type: Five-Seat Heavy Bomber

Powerplant: Four 1,750hp (1,305kW) Rolls-Royce Merlin 85 liquid-cooled inline engines, Production aircraft to have 1,850hp (kW) Merlin 100s

Span: 117ft 2in (35.71m)

Length: 76ft 10in (23.41m)

Gross Wing Area: 1,248sq.ft (116.1m^2)

Maximum Weight: NK136 72,000lb (32,659kg), production 77,000lb (34,927kg)

Maximum Speed: 360mph (579km/h) at 21,000ft (6,401m), 300mph (483km/h) at sea level

Rate of Climb: 960ft/min (293m/min) at sea level

Service Ceiling: 27,250ft (8,306m)

Armament: 4 x 20mm cannon (in NK136); 8,000lb (3,629kg) bombs, later 12,000lb (5,443kg)

Clyde Windsor Project

Type: Five-Seat Heavy Bomber

Powerplant: Four Rolls-Royce Clyde RCl.1.AC turboprop engines giving a combined 3,020hp (2,252kW) and 1,225lb (5.4kN) of thrust at sea level

Span: 117ft 2in (35.71m)

Length: 77ft 8in (23.67m)

Gross Wing Area: 1,248sq.ft (116.1 m^2)

Maximum Weight: 79,000lb (35,834kg), with auxiliary fuel 79,800lb (36,197kg)

Maximum Speed: 409mph (658km/h) at 28,000ft (8,534m)

Rate of Climb: 3,050ft/min (930m/min) at sea level

Service Ceiling: 37,000ft (11,278m)

Armament: 4 x 20mm cannon; 12,000lb (5,443kg) bombs

During the war Vickers-Armstrongs looked at a multitude of heavy bomber projects and proposals, but in the end the only new aircraft to appear after the Warwick (first flown in 1939) were the Windsor bomber prototypes. In 1941 the firm began work on a high altitude bomber against Specification B.5/41 of December 1941 powered by four Rolls-Royce Merlin engines, and in July 1942 prototypes DW506 and DW512 were ordered against Contract Acft/1153/C4(c). At the same time Vickers was also working on a twin-engine bomber replacement for its hugely successful Wellington. Later the two projects were merged and covered by a new Specification B.3/42 dated 8 December 1942. The removal of some weight limitations gave Vickers the freedom to blend the two requirements into one and the result was the Type 447 Windsor. This proved to be the last wartime type built at Weybridge, and the last to feature geodetic construction.

Specification B.3/42 called for four Merlin 61 engines, a take-off weight of 55,500lb (25,175kg) and a maximum speed for stressing of 350mph (563km/h) EAS. A relatively light load of eight 1,000lb (454kg) bombs was to be carried. New prototypes MP829 and MP832 were ordered under Contract SB.24954/C4(c)

A well-known view of the first Windsor prototype DW506 taken on its maiden flight. The shot just about shows the upward flexing of the outer wings under load.

but, since the basic structure was to be the same as the B.5/41 bomber, it was subsequently decided that prototypes DW506 and DW512 should be finished to B.3/42 standards. Contract 1153/C4(c) was accordingly modified and SB.24954 (with MP829 and MP832) was cancelled. The official Mock-Up Conference took place on 29 and 30 October 1942. However, as the development process moved forward the bomber's weight increased, and DW506 and DW512 were no longer representative of production aircraft, so three additional prototypes had to be added that would be fully representative of the specification, one (NK136) by amendment to contract dated 17 December 1942, and two more (NN670 and NN673) by amendment dated 15 February 1943. Consequently the final prototype line-up had two aircraft that were not representative and which would only serve to develop the structure and give flight experience, plus three more that were fully representative of the production aeroplane. In fact the first pair had to be limited to 55,000lb (24,948kg) all-up weight because they were too far advanced in their construction to allow some additional strengthening to be added that would have matched B.3/42's requirements. At some point between 11 September and 10 November 1943 the new bomber was named the Windsor B.Mk.1.

Designer Barnes Wallis' geodetic method of construction had been used for the earlier Wellesley, Wellington and Warwick. It employed a basket-weave framework of spirally crossing duralamin load-bearing

Model of the Vickers Windsor fitted with annular radiators. No photo is known to exist showing one of the prototypes from this angle, which reveals the slim high aspect ratio elliptical wing that made identification of the Windsor in the air quite easy.

Windsor prototype DW506 seen under construction in the Vickers Experimental Shop at Foxwarren.

members which then formed a lattice work structure with the members either in tension or compression. This gave a very strong and light airframe which was then covered in fabric. The structure used the principle that two geodetic arcs could be drawn to intersect on a streamlined surface in such a way that the torsional loads on each arc would cancel out that of the other. Wallis actually gave the term 'geodetic' to his airframes, to distinguish it from 'geodesic' which is the correct word for a line on a curved surface. The resulting structure had tremendous strength with any one of the stringers capable of supporting loads from the opposite side of the aircraft, a vital aspect if the aircraft received battle damage to one side. Despite such damage this load-bearing structure would as a whole still be intact, and there were cases during the war of Vickers aircraft getting home with large pieces of fuselage missing. The weakness of the geodetic form was its complex nature, which meant making changes to the physical shape and structure of the airframe was more difficult than for conventional forms.

The Windsor featured some novel wing geometry in that it was designed to have a defined droop so that when it came under load the wing became straight, theoretically improving its structural characteristics. For the wing Wallis arranged the geometrical pattern to suit the critical wing loadings (which had similarities to today's carbon fibre structures formed from directional tape laying). On the Windsor the geodetics ran across the outboard wing at an angle of 45° to provide torsional

Third prototype, serialled NK136, powered by four 1,635 horsepower (1,219 kW) Merlin 85 engines, armed with four 20mm guns in remote-controlled barbettes in rear of outer engine nacelles (a pair in each) aimed from the unarmed tail position. *Tim Brown*

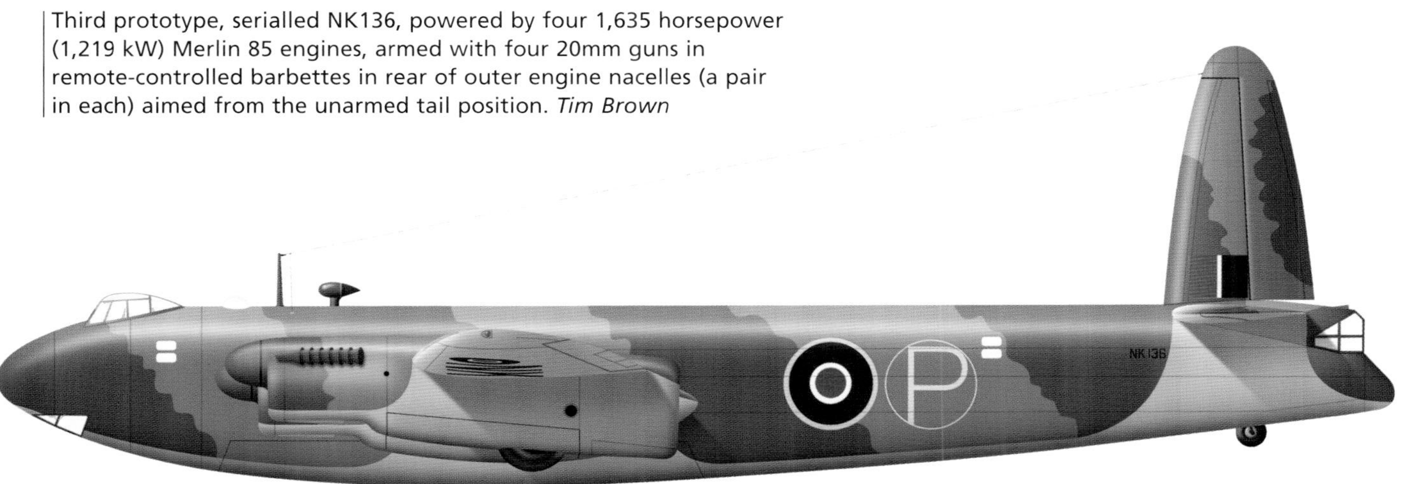

stiffness, while inboard they were set at 16° to the spanwise direction to absorb and control the heavy bending loads. Using this method removed the need for separate spars in the wing, which again offered a lightweight wing and also removed the potential for fatigue problems. However, on the earlier Wellington and Warwick the geodetic structure had been quite simple, but on the Windsor wing the geodetics required heavy back-to-back channels at the root and lighter single channels outboard, which introduced many different joints and meant that this simplicity was now lost.

DW506 pictured at Farnborough prior to its maiden flight, which took place on 23 October 1943 in the hands of Capt Joseph 'Mutt' Summers.

Another issue was that the fabric covering which had been adequate for the earlier bombers would not give a surface finish that was good enough for the Windsor's higher speeds. As a result Wallis developed a composite fabric covering that eventually (after some problems – see below) featured fine grade high tensile steel wires running through the fabric in the spanwise direction. These were then clamped to the structure at regular intervals and tensioned tight on the upper surface. Finally, one of the most curious features of the Windsor was its undercarriage, made up of four separate main legs – one per engine nacelle. At the design stage there was some opposition to this idea because of the potential high drag that it might create, but it did permit a light and neat and sufficiently strong undercarriage rather than having to have the much larger and heavier twin main gears used by the RAF's other heavy bombers. In the end, the four legs gave no perceptible effect to the aircraft's performance except when taxying. Care was necessary when taxying to ensure that the outer wheels did not go onto the grass on some of the narrower taxi ways, and for turning differential braking was used where the inner wheel was locked on the inside of a turn and the outboard wheel went into reverse.

The aircraft's defensive armament was the subject of much discussion. In August 1942 an arrangement was confirmed which had two fixed 0.303in (7.7mm) machine guns in the nose and two 20mm cannon in a turret at the rear of the fuselage. However, in February 1943 the tail turret was dispensed with and the vacated position re-used as a sighting and control station for two remote control barbettes, each with two rearward firing 20mm guns and to be mounted one to the rear of each outer engine nacelle. In 1944 Vickers Warwick prototype L9704 was used to test these rear nacelle mountings but with 0.5in (12.7mm) machine guns instead of 20mm cannon. Amidships beam guns were added to the Windsor in April 1944.

The three Windsors eventually completed were all constructed in the Vickers experimental hangar at Foxwarren under the control of George Edwards. DW506 with Merlin 65s first flew from Farnborough on 23 October 1943 with Vickers' chief test pilot Capt Joseph 'Mutt' Summers in control. The aircraft had been moved in sections by road to Farnborough and then re-assembled in a specially constructed hangar. This first aircraft lacked the remote control armament and was really just a flying test bed with ballast instead of guns.

During 1944 the prototype Vickers Warwick L9704 was used to test rear nacelle barbette mountings that housed a pair of 0.5in (12.7mm) machine guns.

The first Windsor on the runway at Farnborough waiting for permission to take-off in October 1943 – quite possibly for its maiden flight! Note the outer wing droop, the aircraft's large span, and of course the four legs of the main undercarriage.

A side angle of DW506. The very tall narrow-chord fin is well shown, and note the glazing around the end fuselage which originally was to have housed a gun turret.

This poor quality but unique photo is believed to show DW506 overshooting at Wisley.

On 29 December Summers issued a progress report describing the twenty hours of flying made on DW506 so far. A full analysis of control surface movements was yet to be carried out and trials had been flown at approximately 47,000lb (21,319kg) weight, which was well below the eventual all-up weight (the third prototype was built with a considerably stiffer fuselage which would eliminate this restriction). However, at this weight and with just 12lb boost the take-off run was straightforward and with little swing (which could be easily held on the rudder). It was not possible in the cockpit to tell that the undercarriage was in the slightest way unconventional and at this load it had good riding and damping characteristics. The tail came up easily, the aircraft flew itself off when ready and the initial climb was good. All controls were handled up to the aircraft's limiting speed of 300mph (483km/h) ASI but large rudder applications were not allowed above 240mph (386km/h) ASI due to fuselage restrictions. At speeds below 180mph (290km/h) the ailerons (which had had chord added to the trailing edges in order to increase the loads) were much too light and bordering on overbalance and they did not have positive self-centring. However, the controls were extremely effective giving an excellent rate of roll down to the stall. At 200mph (322km/h) ASI the overbalance tendency had disappeared and the pilot had an extremely nice positive and effective aileron with light stick loads, and at 300mph (483km/h) ASI they were a little heavier but still regarded as very good.

The rudder was light and effective at all speeds up to 240mph (386km/h) ASI and had good feel. There was no sign of overbalance or directional 'hunting', and in the event of an engine cutting the aircraft could be held easily on rudder alone and without excessive foot loads. With two engines feathered on the starboard side, the worst case, and the two port engines running at 2,850rpm and 12lb boost, the aircraft could be held down to a minimum speed of 150mph (241km/h) ASI without bank and 138mph (222km/h) ASI with 3° of bank. These speeds were with full trim tab and some foot load. Instrumentation of the rudder and spring tabs showed the main surface could only be applied to about 14° before the rudder felt solid – the aircraft was designed to allow 20° of rudder movement so more investigation was necessary on this control. Full rudder had been applied in level flight at 110mph (177km/h) ASI without any signs of fin stalling.

The elevators were nicely harmonised with the rudder and very powerful. They were light, positive and had good feel. Even at 250-260mph (402-418km/h) ASI the aircraft could be turned sharply in a vertical bank without undue effort, and during landing the control was light, easily handled and powerful without any unpleasant tendencies. The machine had a nice stall without any violent wing dropping tendencies from a straight stall. All controls were effective down to the stall, and the stalling speed with flaps and chassis up was 97mph (156km/h) ASI and with flaps and chassis down 84mph (135km/h) ASI. These figures were with the engines fully throttled and a slight tail shake gave good warning of the stall's approach. Under normal flight conditions the aircraft had small changes of trim, but any trim change due to the extension of the flaps and landing could easily be counteracted by stick movement. Change of trim with variation of power was not apparent until the engines were fully throttled, when a small nose down tendency was noticed. The trim change with the lowering of the chassis was nose down, and trim change with lowering of flaps slightly nose up. A baulked landing could be held easily on the controls while cutting an outboard engine during cruising conditions gave little swing and was easily held on the rudder. An inboard engine failure gave a small swing, but even if two engines were cut on one side at cruising power the resultant swing was easily handled by the rudder without heavy foot loads.

The approach to land was easy because of the small trim changes, nice feel of the controls and good view. The landing was simple, no rapid deceleration occurred when the throttles were fully closed and the stall was not sudden or violent. The elevator had ample power and travel at the CofGs so far used. The approach was made at 110mph (177km/h) with the final flatten out at about 105mph (169km/h) ASI. The brakes were good and could be used hard until near the end of the landing run. At slow speeds it had been possible to lift the tail without braking violently. Sadly, DW506 crashed on 2 March 1944 and was written off when being flown by Sqn Ldr English of RAE. After attempting to feather different engines, English was unable to un-feather the starboard inner engine and had to make a forced-landing at Grove aerodrome near Wantage. DW506 ran off the runway and into a ditch, the aircraft's back was broken and its flying career ended after 40 flights; fortunately no one was hurt and the cause was found to be a small piece of metal that had wedged into the fine pitch groove. Some of the airframe still found employment in the Windsor development programme. An outer wing (i.e. a fuel tank) had its vulnerability to gunfire assessed at Marston Excelsior's range at Fordhouses in Wolverhampton, while the rudder later found its way on to DW512. DW506's top speed had been measured at 317mph (510km/h) at 23,000ft (7,010m). Most of the prototype's flights had been performed by 'Mutt' Summers and Sqn Ldr M.V. Longbottom.

DW512 with Merlin 85s was first flown from Wisley by Summers and Longbottom on 10 February 1944, but again without armament (note: the 10 February date is given in a Vickers report but not in Summers' log book; other sources give 15 February). Although, basically the same as DW506 the second aircraft was heavier since it carried more equipment and some armour plating. Wg Cdr R.J. Falk, chief test pilot at RAE, flew both Windsors at Farnborough in February 1944 for brief handling trials. In general he liked the aircraft but reported an unpleasant oscillation throughout the fuselage, which he thought was not due to instability but rather to a lack of rigidity in the fuselage.

Views showing the wreckage of DW506 after the aircraft had left the runway at Grove on 2 March 1944. Salvage work is taking place and the rudder was one part that was to fly again, on DW512.

DW512 pictured in August 1944. It had made its first flight in February. Like its predecessor it lacked armament, but had some armour plating.

Later, during a trial dive with DW512 it was noticed that the upper wing fabric was ballooning, and over further flights the fabric began to deform. This worrying problem reached a head when the aircraft was hit during another dive by a bird and the impact was sufficient to remove 10sq.ft (0.93sq.m) of fabric. This flaw had also begun to appear on DW506's fabric before it was lost, and the subsequent deterioration affected the Windsor's stall characteristics quite badly. In due course new glass cloth-backed fabric was applied to DW512's upper wings and at the same time the tailplane incidence was changed (and DW506's rudder was attached). (Note. The metallised fabric and four main undercarriage legs had previously featured in the Vickers-Armstrong submission made against Specification B.1/39 [Chapter Five] and indeed had collectively been the prime reasons for that proposal's rejection. The Air Ministry team assessing the B.1/39 tenders correctly foresaw the fabric problems that would come to pass with the Windsor).

The second aircraft performed most of the Windsor aerodynamic test flying. For example on 21 November 1944 it took off from Wisley with a flight comb fitted to the rear of the wing on the inner section near the fuselage to check the wing flow. After the fabric had been polished it was flown again with this fitting on 26 November, but the gain in top speed was just 3-4mph (5-6.5km/h) and not as much as had been expected. Another problem discovered by flight testing was vibration with the bomb doors open. DW512 was grounded in November 1945 after the Windsor programme's cancellation and it was put up for disposal by HQ No. 43 Group on 28 June 1946.

The third and final Windsor, NK136, flies with its rear outer engine nacelle cannon barbettes faired over to permit aerodynamic drag measurements to be made. At this stage the gun mounts were still not ready for installation. *Phil Butler*

The experimental barbette armament was to be installed in NK136 and as such the aircraft was designated Type 461. NK136, again powered by Merlin 85s and much closer to the production standard, first flew on 18 July 1944 (apparently by Mutt Summers and without weight restrictions), but the remote-controlled barbette guns were not ready and were not in place until January 1945. They were used for firing trials both on the ground at Pembrey and Angle and in the air over Lyme Bay at different heights and speeds. NK136 arrived at Pembrey on 21 April and had its tail pointed out to sea and jacked up to keep it static. Firing commenced soon afterwards, all four guns were fired for the first time on 27 April, and on the last day (the 30th) all four were fired at angles of up to 45° in elevation and 45° in azimuth. On 3 May NK136 was flown to Angle and parked on the cliff edge, again with its tail pointing out to sea to permit extended tests with horizontal and depression systems. Air firing trials carried out from Wisley and flown over Lyme Bay began on 29 May, the aircraft being piloted by Sqn Ldr Keating. DW512 was flown as a camera platform and this is the only known occasion when both surviving Windsors flew in close proximity to one another. Further trials took place over Lyme Bay on 12 June but both flights had problems with the guns jamming.

The barbettes did raise some weight issues with the aircraft's CofG and the single pilot cockpit was also controversial because some felt that the Windsor's complexity required a second pilot. In addition, if the pilot was injured, access to his seat by another crewmember was near impossible because of the narrow cockpit, which had room for only the one seat. Consequently, in August 1944 drawings were produced showing a new Windsor nose which had a canopy similar to the Avro Lancaster's (the all-round view out from the original cockpit was described as outstanding). By 17 September 1944 the three prototypes had completed 133 flights in all, many at altitudes above 20,000ft (6,096m) and up to 31,000ft (9,449m) and with no unusual effects experienced. Elevator control on both 'DW's was normal down to -45°C, but it was found on NK136 that the elevators began to stiffen up considerably at low temperatures until at -20°C they were almost immovable. The cause was traced to contraction of the control rod guides.

In January 1945 Vickers designer Rex Pierson submitted a proposal for a Windsor powered by four Rolls-Royce RB.39 Clyde turboprop engines, a new concept with a jet engine and a propeller joined together. This powerplant was subsequently considered for production machines as the Type 601 Windsor

Three-view drawing of the Rolls-Royce Clyde turboprop-powered Windsor. Visibly the airframe was largely unchanged except for the engine nacelles. The rear nacelle guns were retained but the main undercarriage legs now had six-wheel bogies replacing the original single wheels, a new design at the time that was in the course of development.

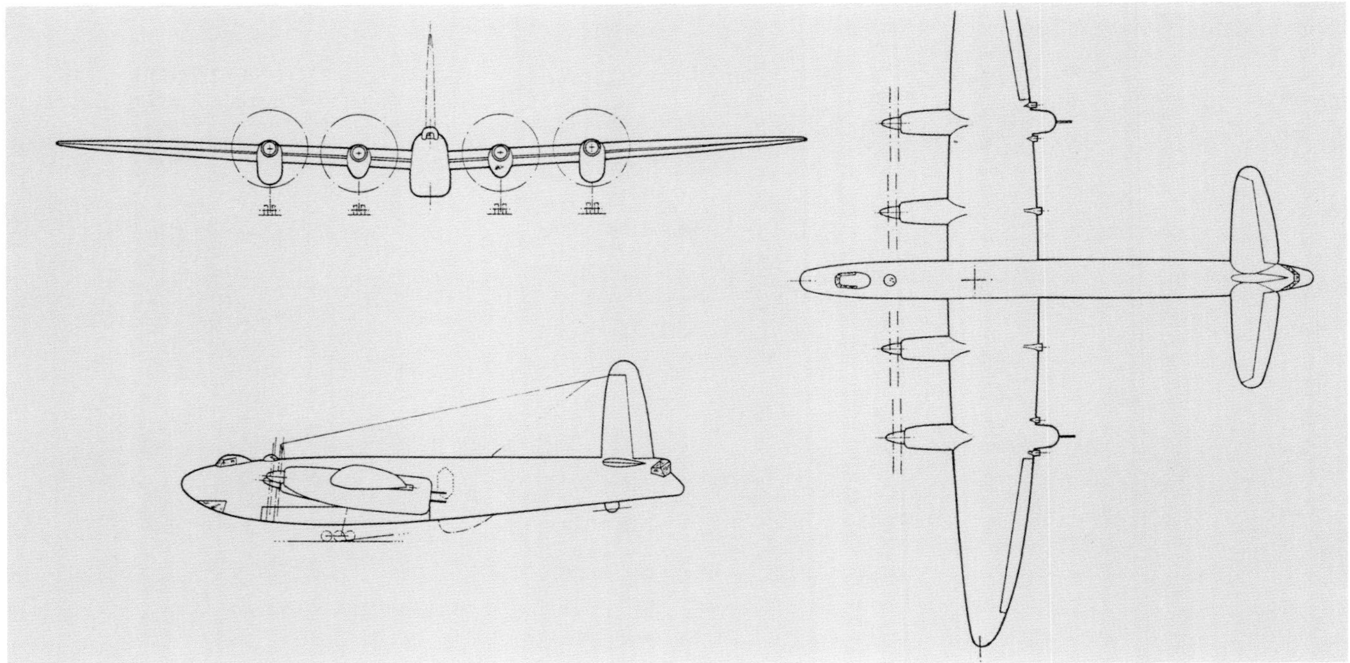

B Mk.II. The new version also had its four undercarriage legs fitted with six-wheel bogies and would carry 3,580gal (16,278lit) of internal fuel. The Clyde would have 12ft 0in (3.66m) diameter contra-rotating propellers if they were available, but it was estimated that the performance would be substantially the same with 13ft 3in (4.04m) diameter five-blade single rotation propellers should the former be unavailable.

A total of 300 production Type 483 Windsors was ordered by Contract Acft/2999 of 21 April 1943 with serials PE510-PE553, PE565-PE606, PE618-PE658, PE671-PE715, PE727-PE769, PE782-PE826 and PE839-PE878, all to be built at the Vickers works at Weybridge. Of the last two prototypes, which were classed as pre-production machines, NK670 was to have Merlin 85 engines and become the first long-range (4,000 miles (6,436km)) Windsor, and as such was to have been assessed at Boscombe Down. NN673 was to fly initially with Merlin 100s but it would later receive the Clyde as the Mk.II prototype. In June 1945 the first production aircraft were expected in July 1946 and to be followed by six deliveries per month, and at one stage back in 1944 it had been hoped that by mid-1947 as many as thirty squadrons might be equipped with the type, primarily for operations in the Japanese theatre. However, the end of the war changed everything. In fact the production order had been cut to 100 in November 1944, later the figure was reduced to 40 (and now all as Mk.IIs with Clyde engines), and then the decision to cancel all Windsor production was made at a Ministry meeting on 12 November 1945, leaving no other contracts apart from the prototypes. With the impending cancellation, on 26 November George Edwards wrote to the Ministry to suggest that fitting a Clyde into a prototype for research would be of considerable value to Vickers, but the conversion of prototypes to this engine was cancelled on 16 January 1946.

NK136 and its guns were shown to overseas representatives at Farnborough on 4 and 5 April 1945, and test pilot 'Tommy' Lucke demonstrated the aeroplane impressively at the German Aircraft Exhibition held at Farnborough on 29 and 30 October (demonstrations of several new British aircraft such as the Windsor, and the Martin-Baker M.B.5 in Chapter 21, were added to this event). Besides the weapon trials the third aircraft was used for a lot of general aerodynamic flying. At high altitudes NK136 was found to be some 25mph (40km/h) slower than the two earlier prototypes, primarily through a rise in weight but also from a rough surface finish. It also had its tailplane set at about 1° greater incidence than the first aircraft which Summers reported improved considerably the controllability of low speeds with full flap and chassis down. On more than

Views of NK136 taken outside the hangar at Wisley in 1945 after the nacelle gun mounts have each been fitted with two 20mm cannon. The barbette inspection ports are not in position. Note the partly open bomb doors and the rear fuselage sighting station.

one occasion the ever growing weight of the aircraft prompted thoughts towards fitting Rolls-Royce Griffon engines. After November 1945 NK136 was grounded until it was flown to Manby on 17 September 1946 for use by the Empire Air Armament School (EAAS) for ground instruction under the airframe number 6222M. It was scrapped at Manby in 1948. NN670 and NN673 were not flown. At the point of cancellation in March 1946 NN670 was almost complete (it was missing some of its radio equipment) and was being prepared for its maiden flight at Wisley, while the construction of NN673 was about half finished; both airframes were eventually reduced to produce.

There was a lot of discussion on just how suitable the Windsor would be for Pacific operations, but the end of the war halted any plans and it was to be the Avro Lincoln development of the Lancaster which entered production and served the RAF post-war. The Windsor was a handsome aeroplane, but accounts from the people involved indicate that its complex geodetic frame made it very difficult to construct. George Edwards described it as something of a freak, thanks to its four main undercarriages and how the wings would droop when the bomber was on the ground. However, on take-off the wings would come up to the level as they took the weight, and in fact they often went beyond the level taking the wing

Lovely photograph of NK136 seen airborne over Surrey with both 20mm barbettes set at extreme elevation.

from anhedral on the ground to dihedral in the air. On becoming airborne at maximum load the wing tips could rise as much as 4ft (1.22m), at the time an almost unheard of characteristic which took 'Tommy' Lucke and indeed most Windsor pilots a few flights to get used to. Vickers had plans for civilian airliner versions but these were never ordered. The Windsor is a fascinating aeroplane and was a pleasure to fly because it had no vices. Those company and service pilots who sampled the beast certainly seem to have liked it.

Close up of the off-centre annular radiators on the second Windsor DW512. The serial numerals '5' and '1' are just visible between the two Merlin nacelles.

Structure

The Windsor had a light alloy structure covered in a special pre-tensioned woven metallic fabric. The heavyweight version of this fabric only appeared on NK136, the early machines having a lighter form. The framed portions of the geodetically braced fuselage had tubular longerons and built-up open frames – on NK136 four longerons were used in the forward position and three in the mid and rear positions, but the early machines had just three all through (four longerons were required to prevent the airframe twisting in flight, which could have affected gun aiming). The geodetic structure was built of lipped channels so that the bottom panels formed a flat flooring below the bottom longerons, the space below being taken up by the bomb compartment with belly fairings fore and aft.

The mainplane was another geodetically braced structure and in planform was elliptically tapered, the inner wing extending from the fuselage centreline to the outboard side of the outer engine nacelles, and the outer planes from this point to the plated wingtips. The main spar consisted of single rectangular booms top and bottom, and the leading and trailing edge members were of light alloy square tabs. Again, for NK136 the inner and outer mainplanes, ailerons and tailplane were all strengthened. Each inner plane carried the three portions of split flaps while the outer planes provided space for the main fuel tanks and carried the ailerons which extended almost the entire length of the section. Production aircraft would have had an internal load of 3,580 gallons (16,278 litres) which is why the outer wing drooped so much when the aircraft was sitting on the ground. The ailerons had trimmer and balance tabs at the trailing edge. Both tailplane and fin used geodetic construction and had horn balanced elevators and rudder, which were provided with balance tab and trimmer tab.

The Merlin 85s with automatic two-speed superchargers each drove a four-blade Rotol hydraulic constant speed wooden propeller. On NK136 and DW512 these were housed in off-centre annular cowlings, but the Merlin 65s in DW506 had chin-type radiators. The pilot had a detachable hooding, the bomb-aimer's station was in the nose and the navigator and wireless operator were aft of the pilot. Only NK136 carried guns. The undercarriage track was 50ft (15.24m).

These rare photos provide close-up detail for DW506 and its engine nacelles (with chin radiators). Note the undernose glazing in the frontal view.

Close-up detail for the Windsor's massive and formidable barbette-mounted 20mm Hispano defensive cannon. Just how effective the weapons would have been in these rear nacelle positions is unknown, but any enemy fighter pilot would undoubtedly have approached from the rear with some trepidation.

The gentleman inspecting the barbette of NK136 is Mr 'Sammy' Walsh, who was the Vickers design engineer for armament installations.

35 Westland Welkin

Westland Welkin

Type: Single-Seat Twin-Engine High-Altitude Fighter

Powerplant: Welkin I: Two 1,690hp (1,260kW) Rolls-Royce Merlin 72/73 liquid-cooled inline engines fitted with two-speed two-stage superchargers. Alternative similar power Merlin 76/77 also fitted. Welkin II: Two Merlin 76/77

Span: 70ft 0in (21.34m)

Length: Welkin I 41ft 6in (12.65m), Welkin II 45ft 8.4in (13.93m)

Gross Wing Area: 460sq.ft (42.78m^2)

Maximum Weight: Welkin I: 19,775lb (8,970kg), Welkin II: 21,892lb (9,930kg)

Rate of Climb: Welkin I: 3,850ft/min (1,173m/min) at sea level, Welkin II: 2,650ft/min (808m/min) at sea level

Maximum Speed: Welkin I: 387mph (623km/h) at 26,000ft (7,925m), Welkin II: 346mph (557km/h) at 20,000ft (6,096m)

Service Ceiling: Welkin I: 44,000ft (13,411m), Welkin II: 41,000ft (12,497m)

Armament: 4 x 20mm Hispano cannon

In the late 1930s much effort worldwide went into the development of aeroplanes fitted with pressure cabins to permit them to fly at very high altitudes. Then, once war had broken out, the possibility of high altitude German aircraft making sorties over Britain put some urgency into the requirement for a new type that could intercept them – a high altitude fighter. Indeed, when Junkers Ju 86P aircraft did precisely this in 1940 and 1941 they were completely immune from attack because no RAF service type could get near to the heights at which they operated (over 40,000ft (12,192m)). Consequently, Specification F.4/40 was raised in 1940 for a Single Seat High Altitude Fighter fitted with a pressure cabin to maintain conditions appropriate to 25,000ft (7,620m) when the fighter was flying at heights above this up to at least 45,000ft (13,716m). Its maximum speed was to be in excess of 400mph (644km/h), the powerplant was two Rolls-Royce Merlin engines, and four 20mm cannon would be carried. In January 1941 Westland's P.14 project was chosen as the winning design proposal and two prototypes, DG558 and DG562, were ordered. The new fighter was named Welkin, an archaic English word which refers to the upper air in the sky or the heavens. The Westland design team was led by W.E.W 'Teddy' Petter.

DG558 with Merlin 61 engines first flew from its Yeovil birthplace on 1 November 1942 in the hands of Westland test pilot Harald Penrose. The flying programme, however, was hampered by several forced landings which in part were due to the aircraft not having feathering propellers. These made the engine overspeed even when it was switched off - once an engine had failed and had been shut down the propeller would windmill and the resulting overspeeding could eventually start a fire. DG558, which was itself force landed several times, was fitted with Merlin 77s in February 1943 but was badly damaged after another landing accident on 23 September. However, after repair the machine was used into 1945 for drop tank trials at Yeovil. DG562 first flew in March 1943, and on one occasion early in its career reached an altitude of 44,000ft (13,411m). After spending time at A&AEE in 1943 it flew until at least October

Side view of prototype Welkin DG558/G (G for Guard) taken in October 1942 just prior to its maiden flight.

DG558/G pictured on a test flight during January 1943. *Westland*

1945 on trials work with the manufacturers. DG558 and DG562 were allotted for disposal in October 1945 and January 1946 respectively.

On 13 May 1943 a fuselage mock-up for the P.14/2 project was officially examined. This was a two-seat day and night fighter development fitted with air interception radar and two prototypes were ordered during May. On 22 November F.9/43 was issued to cover the type – again the top speed was not to be less than 400mph (644km/h) at 25,000ft (7,620m), service ceiling not less than 42,000ft (12,802m), and

This ground shot of prototype DG558/G was also taken in January 1943. Note the four-bladed propellers.

Official Ministry views of the sole Welkin II prototype PF370 which show the aircraft's nose radome. *Westland*

PF370 is prepared for another flight. *Rolls-Royce*

four 20mm guns were carried. The Welkin II had a longer cabin to allow the pilot to be moved forward and an observer added facing aft, and a longer nose housed an AI.Mk.VIII radar scanner. The outer wings had increased dihedral (4.5° on the top surface rather than 3° on the Welkin I) and Contract SB.26569 of 29 April 1943 covered prototypes PF370 and PF376, although in the end only PF370 was completed after its conversion from Welkin I DX386. PF376 was cancelled, as was a third example RT661 ordered on 6 January 1944 also to SB.26569. PF370 flew for the first time on 23 October 1944 and was demonstrated by Penrose at the 1946 SBAC Show at Radlett, as such the only Welkin to be shown in public (the Welkin was on the Secret List until June 1945). Afterwards, with Class B marking P17, it was used by Westland for pressure cabin development, and later for a series of test flights for a UHF radio development programme that lasted until May 1950. By that time the aircraft had been re-serialled WE997 (to receive a second serial without major airframe changes was a very rare occurrence).

Test pilots Capt. Eric Brown and Westland's own Harald Penrose have described in print what the Welkin was like to fly. Brown, in his book *Wings of the Weird and Wonderful* (Hikoki) gives a quite in-depth report, while Penrose's account presents a wonderful picture of the very new experience that came with flying at such high altitudes. In *Air International* for August 1976 he explained that high flying was only permitted on the clearest days and he flew in radio silence except for the odd transmission to allow plotters to fix his position. Although

PF370 was the only Welkin to be displayed to the public, at the SBAC Show at Radlett on 12-13 September 1946. In this view PF370 is seen with Supermarine Spiteful RB515 behind, but no Spiteful attended the Radlett 1946 event, so just where this picture was taken is a mystery.

Westland Welkin I, DX318, 20 April 1944. *RAF Museum Hendon*

flying over the West Country he could see the Dee and Mersey estuaries to the north, or the hostile coast of Normandy to the east, all while inside a warm cabin with just the noise of the engines to keep him company. Up above was the vast emptiness of "the dark stratosphere" which few pilots had experienced before!

Detailed accounts in A&AEE Boscombe Down and Westland reports provide more information. By 9 April 1943 Westland had tested both de Havilland and Rotol propellers and found a better all-round performance with the Rotol, and as a result the firm wished to change to this propeller. However, a month later the de Havilland props had begun to show promise. A&AEE's report of 23 June noted that DG558 flying with de Havilland four-blade propellers at a take-off weight of 17,400lb (7,893kg) had achieved 383mph (616km/h) at 26,000ft (7,925m), whereas with Rotol 12ft 6in (3.81m) diameter propellers at a weight of 17,330lb (7,861kg) the figure was 375mph (603km/h) at 25,750ft (7,849m). Overall the climb and level performance with the de Havilland propellers was also better than the Rotol type. With the engines running at their combat rating the initial rate of climb increased from 3,700ft/min (1,128m/min) to 3,840ft/min (1,170m/min). The most marked increase in level speed took place at 40,000ft (12,192m), from 323mph (520km/h) to 351mph (565km/h), and at this height the helical tip speed of the propeller was approximately equal to the speed of sound. However, due to a lower than expected propeller efficiency and an increase in drag the Welkin's actual speeds fell below initial estimates; the full throttle level flight speed was in fact about 30mph (48km/h) below expectations.

DG558 went to Boscombe Down in April 1943 and on 6 June A&AEE reported that: "The aircraft is easy and straightforward to fly and take-off and landing present no difficulties." However, improvements needed to be made to the ailerons and elevators. In general the longitudinal behaviour was extremely safe but wandering on the climb added to the pilot's difficulty. Heavy shaking gave adequate

Three-quarter rear view of DG558/G. *Phil Butler*

warning of the approach of the true stall but behaviour of the stall was considered unsatisfactory. The prototype's maximum diving speed was 415mph (668km/h) ASI, but by the end of May Westland had encountered shock stall conditions on the outer wing. Penrose reported that in yawed dives (with some aileron applied) he suddenly experienced, at 270mph (434km/h) ASI at 35,000ft (10,668m), a heavy vibration of the wing which appeared to be of a dangerous character. He reduced speed and the vibration disappeared at 220mph (354km/h) ASI. The aircraft was not damaged.

Previously it had been agreed that 0.7, with an absolute maximum of 0.75, were the highest Mach numbers likely to be reached in practice, and a diving limitation of 460mph (740km/h) on the prototype and 480mph (772km/h) for production aircraft at 10,000ft (3,048m) had been fixed. It now appeared that the Welkin would accelerate at altitudes much more rapidly than had been anticipated and these Mach numbers would certainly be exceeded at altitude. It appeared from recorded data that a very high Mach number (0.87) was safe in straight dives, whereas 0.73 might lead to trouble in dives where aileron control was used. Petter suggested a limit in diving speed to Mach 0.7, which gave the following: 40,000ft (12,192m) – 230mph (370km/h), 30,000ft (9,144m) – 295mph (475km/h), 20,000ft (6,096m) – 365mph (587km/h) and 10,000ft (3,048m) – 440mph (708km/h).

The problem was the wing's high thickness/chord ratio. Between October 1943 and January 1944 production Welkin DX279 was at Boscombe for performance and handling trials. The aircraft had two Merlin 73 engines with 13ft (3.96m) diameter four-blade de Havilland Hydromatic non-feathering propellers, and the muzzles of its 20mm cannon were sealed with the ejection chutes open. In the course of these trials unusual characteristics appeared in both dives and recoveries at high Mach numbers. All dives were started with the aircraft trimmed for all-out level flight and the throttles were left open in the dives. In one dive which started at 35,000ft (10,668m), at about 32,000ft (9,754m) a fore and aft movement of the control column commenced which grew in intensity and amplitude and was accompanied by a pitching motion of the aircraft. The pilot was unable either to hold the control column steady or pull out of the dive. On reaching about 25,000ft (7,620m) the pitching and control column damped out and a normal recovery was made.

It was thought that these control abnormalities had occurred due to compressibility effects since they were only encountered at high Mach numbers. When the maximum attainable acceleration for any given speed-height condition was reached, a high speed stall occurred and the elevator became completely ineffective. Any further aftward movement of the control column merely caused buffeting from the tailplane. When the critical speed was reached in a dive without normal acceleration a fore and aft oscillation of the control column occurred accompanied by a pitching motion of the aircraft, and the elevator was again completely ineffective. This loss of longitudinal control persisted until a lower height was reached where the Mach number

Production Welkin I DX319. *Westland*

was less. A&AEE's pilots declared that these limitations would clearly handicap the aircraft to some extent in its role as a high altitude fighter, though it was probable that other twin-engine aircraft would also suffer in these respects to some extent.

Early A&AEE trials also revealed that the behaviour of the rudder in single-engined flight was unacceptable. Further development of this control was at the time ongoing and involved a form of spring rudder bias that dispensed with a trimming tab, but the report only dealt with the behaviour of the original rudder. When the aircraft was tested in single-engined flight it was found that on either engine at speeds below the cruising speed (i.e. below about 170mph (274km/h) ASI) very severe rudder oscillation occurred (the propeller control of the 'dead' engine was in positive coarse pitch). For this condition almost full rudder trim was necessary to relieve the footload and the oscillation only occurred when the trimmer tab was near its fully deflected position. As a first measure towards affecting a cure the travel of the rudder trim tab was reduced to about 2/3rds of its original value, a move which reduced the amplitude of the oscillation but did not eliminate it, but at speeds below 165mph (265km/h) ASI there was still a movement of about 1in (2.5cm) at the rudder bar which was unpleasant and unacceptable. When the speed was taken above 165mph (265km/h) the oscillation persisted and was difficult to stop.

After receiving modified ailerons DX327 was tested in February and March 1945 to re-determine the maximum diving speed. The aircraft had received a higher percent mass balancing of the ailerons (110% of the whole aileron) and spring tabs (120% mass balance of the spring tab), but in all other respects it was a standard Welkin. The results showed no aileron oscillation was present over the aircraft's speed range, but the aileron response had not improved. The results of high altitude diving tests showed that the longitudinal pitching, indicating the onset of compressibility trouble, started at a Mach number just above 0.65 as opposed to 0.70, the critical Mach number for early production aircraft such as DX279. At low airspeeds the aileron control force was very light. At the high end of the speed range (400mph (644km/h) ASI at 10,000ft (3,048m)) full aileron deflection could be obtained with a moderate stick force, and in dives up to 270mph (434km/h) ASI at 30,000ft (9,144m – Mach 0.63) the characteristics were similar to those at low altitude. At all conditions of height and speed the aileron effectiveness was poor and the rate of roll very slow. During dives it was found that the aircraft began pitching, due to compressibility effects, at speeds corresponding to a Mach number of 0.65, and the degree of pitching could not be checked by use of the elevator. The general effect of the onset of compressibility was to cause the aircraft to recover from the dive. In conclusion, the new ailerons were considered to be satisfactory throughout the speed and height range in so far there was no sign of aileron flutter, but a speed corresponding to a Mach number of 0.65 was considered to be the maximum safe diving limit. This represented an appreciable lowering of the Welkin's critical Mach number from the 0.7 figure for early production aeroplanes.

Air-to-air view of early production Welkin I DX281 in the original production colour scheme.

Between 20 September 1943 and 21 January 1944 intensive flying trials were conducted with DX278, DX280 and DX282, but on 24 October DX278 was burnt out after a forced landing and it was subsequently replaced by DX282. DX280 was also burnt out after a wheels-up landing on 11 December and it was not replaced before DX282 had crashed on take-off on 21 January 1944. The trials were suspended but enough had been done to reveal major troubles with engine surging and with the fuel system, problems with the riveting and cracking of the skin and with windscreen misting on the ground. It was not thought that there would be much difficulty in correcting any of these major faults, but the Welkin was an unusually complex aircraft (particularly in respect to its electronics for operating in and 'through' the pressure cabin) and so it required more than the normal amount of servicing. Although there was no inherent tendency to swing on take-off the Welkin was found to be sensitive to power differences at similar throttle settings. In addition, a mock combat held between a Welkin and a Mosquito Mk.IX at altitudes up to 35,000ft (10,668m) was not that successful because the Mosquito struggled with its performance at this height while the Welkin's compressibility problems limited the fighter when it tried to chase the Mosquito in a dive. It was observed that Westland's aircraft had very poor aileron control for the requirements of combat, but a trial against another Welkin made at 38,000-40,000ft (11,582-12,192m) did prove more fruitful and established that a Welkin could attack a heavy bomber, although a single-engined fighter would be able to outmanoeuvre it.

A further trial was performed with DX340, a production F.Mk.I fitted with a new Merlin that was eventually developed into the Marks 113 and 114 (RM.16.SM) for late version Mosquitoes. As such DX340 introduced beard type radiators of increased cooling area. All Merlins up to the 100-series had up-draught carburettors, but most of the 100-series had down-draught carburettors and so to fit this type into a Welkin the air intake had to be pushed out into the wing. This move displaced part of the radiator and the only place left was to put it under the engine itself. The airframe was taken directly off the production line and fitted with the new installation in a modification that entailed removing the lower front cowlings of the engine nacelles and placing a smooth fairing over part of the original arrangement. The radiator cooling area was increased and it is thought that another 450hp (336kW) was available from this modification. However, DX340 used standard propellers which were incapable of absorbing that much additional power. The new arrangement was tested at Yeovil but sadly no detailed reports appear to survive. It is known that the beard radiators made relatively little difference to the aircraft's handling and there was not much effect on performance. Top speed at height was unchanged because of compressibility, while at low level the top speed rose very slightly but the change was still marginal. What did improve was the rate of climb at height – *Jane's All the World's Aircraft* stated that in June 1945 DX340 had reached a speed of 398mph (640km/h) at 30,000ft (9,144m).

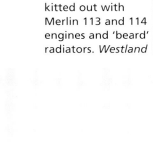

In 1945 DX340 was kitted out with Merlin 113 and 114 engines and 'beard' radiators. *Westland*

Close up of DX340's starboard engine beard radiator. *Westland*

In all the Welkin production run under Contract Acft/1350 embraced 67 F.Mk.Is delivered complete (DX278-DX295, DX308-DX349 and DX364-DX370) while the remaining 33 of the first production order (DX371-DX385, DX387-DX389, DX407-DX420 and NT623) were delivered without engines. Production began early in 1943 but the date of the first flight of the first example, DX278, is uncertain. However, a Ministry memorandum of 31 May 1943 noted that the first production aircraft was expected to fly that very day, so one can assume that 31 May or early June 1943 is pretty close. Plans to build another 700 were abandoned. There were also ideas to convert 60 Mk.Is into the radar-equipped two-seat Mk.II but this did not materialise either. In the meantime, due to the aircraft's weaknesses and that high flying enemy aircraft never really presented any problems over Britain, the RAF's interest in the Welkin died. Other factors were the superior performance and better manoeuvrability of the de Havilland Mosquito, and the shortfall in the Welkin's own performance against the original estimates. In the end most Welkins fitted with engines (to DX370) were delivered direct to store at No.18 Maintenance Unit (MU) at Dumfries, while engineless airframes (including NT623) found their way to No.5 MU at Kemble or to a Ministry of Aircraft Production site at Marwell Hall.

Completed Welkins lined up for delivery at Westland's grass airfield at Yeovil. The nearest example (on the left) is DX309. *Westland*

On 20 April 1944 the famous aviation photographer Charles Brown took a series of photos of DX318, some of which are shown here. *All Westland*

Some examples did manage to accumulate flight hours on test work. From 31 August 1944 DX287 was used for armament trials, in June 1944 DX314 was employed on gun-heating trials, and as noted earlier DX327 tested the modified flight controls in a programme that started on 20 February 1945; from 31 August 1944 DX333 was used on high altitude trials. On 5 May 1944 the Air Force's Fighter Interception Unit (FIU) at Wittering received DX286 and DX289 (coded ZQ-X and ZQ-B respectively). At Wittering they were used for trials to establish tactics and operational procedures until the effort was terminated on 10 July, both machines returning to Yeovil. Their FIU 'career' included DX289 making a landing at Acklington with an engine on fire, plus altitudes achieved of over 43,000ft (13,106m), while the pilots described the 19 minutes taken to reach 40,000ft (12,192m) as remarkable. The pilots also commented against the unnecessary weight carried as armour to protect the pilot, when at such altitudes it was highly unlikely that anything would fire at a Welkin from behind. The reduction in weight through its removal would have improved the type's performance.

In March 1945 DX328 went to RAE Farnborough for further trials to look at the problem of compressibility, and it continued flying until at least 12 March 1946. For a period DX330 was based at Rotol's Staverton airfield where from 10 November 1944 it was employed on propeller trials, and later in testing a Rotol blower for the pressure cabin. On 10 October 1945 the Welkin was declared 'obsolete' and on 29 November almost all of the stored aircraft were struck off charge and subsequently scrapped. The sole Welkin II PF370 kept the type in the air for a little longer, finally flying back to Yeovil in May 1950. PF370 is thought to have been scrapped in 1953/54. The Westland Welkin was for its time an ambitious and very advanced aeroplane, but its role and the need for it eventually disappeared. Nevertheless, it did fly higher than any previous British production aircraft and helped to uncover some of the secrets of compressibility. It also broke new ground in the development of pressure cabins which would become so important in the jet age, but the type never fired its guns in anger and quickly faded from the scene.

Structure

The Welkin had an all-metal stressed skin wing with a wide-span centre section plus two outer sections with detachable tips. A single main spar passed through the fuselage while a secondary spar within the centre section carried the flaps, which later were of the Fowler type: the metal Westland-Irvine ailerons each had a spring tab. The fuselage consisted of an oval structure built in two parts with the forward piece with the

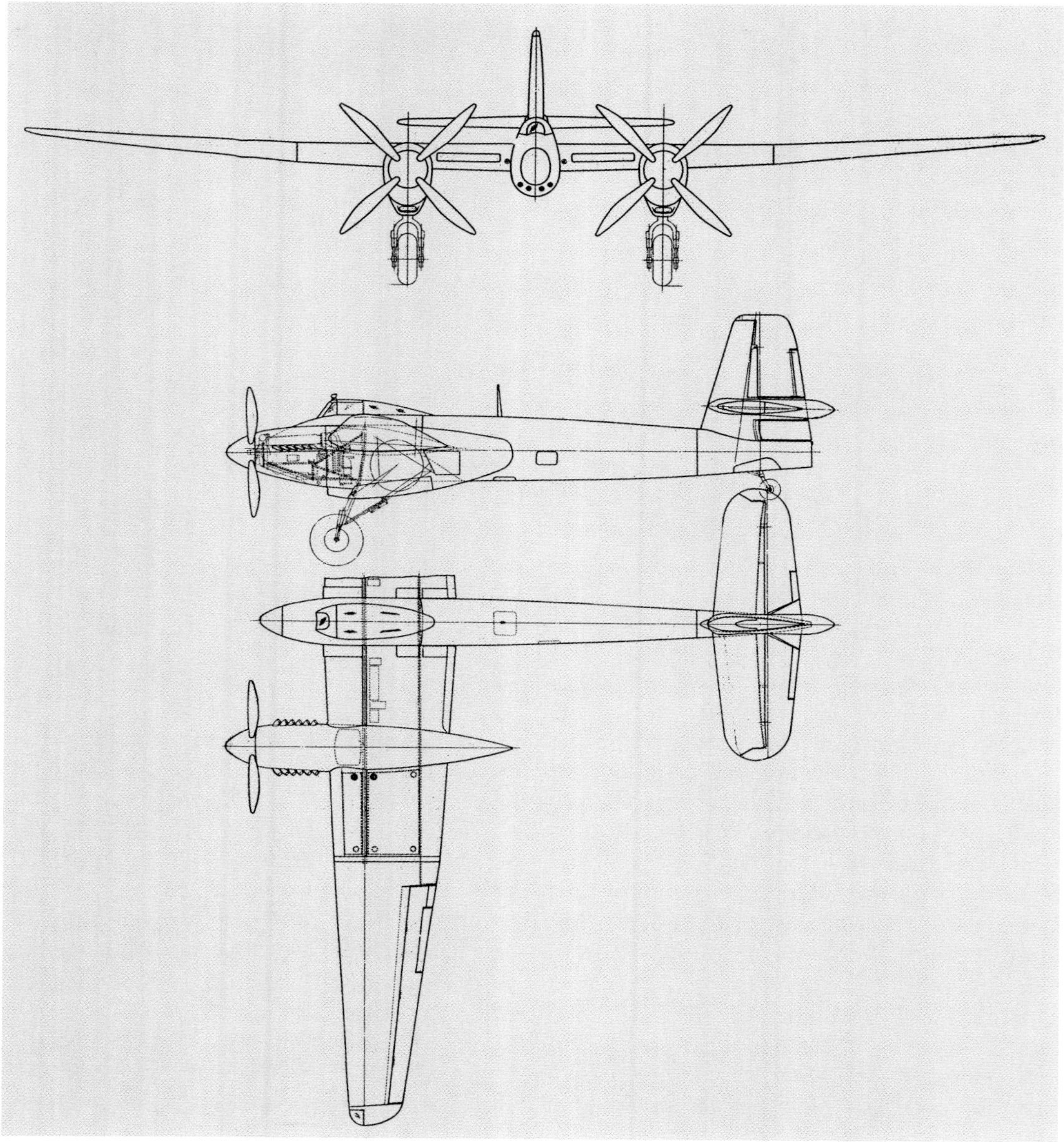

Original manufacturer's drawing of the single-seat Westland Welkin I which in fact shows an optional third pair of 20mm cannon mounted in the wing roots. *Westland*

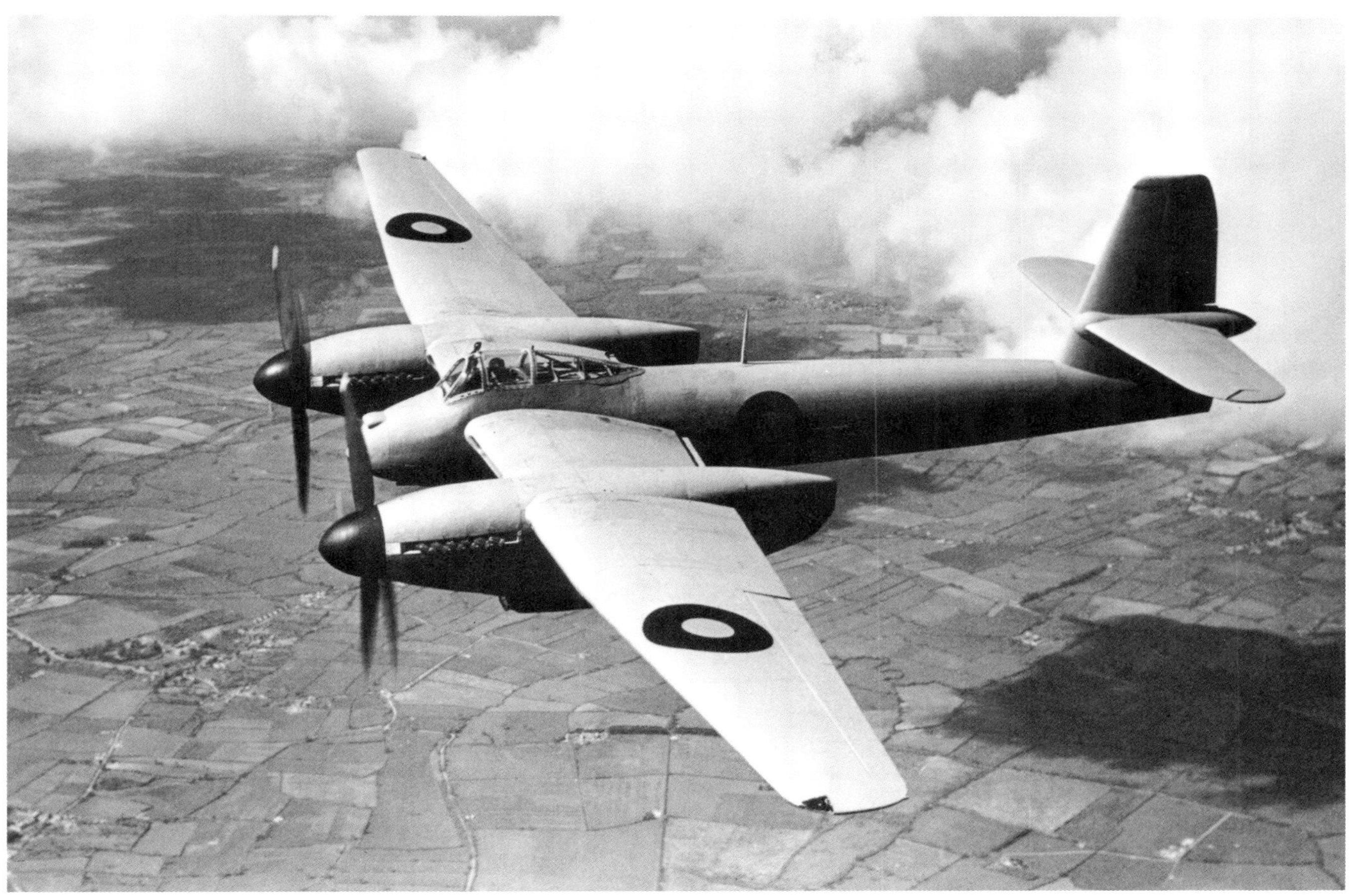

Westland Welkin I, DX318, 20 April 1944. *RAF Museum Hendon*

cabin built in duralumin. The pressurised cabin section, built as a separate unit in heavy gauge light alloy, was bullet-resisting and was bolted to the front face of the main wing spar and terminated with the steel armoured bulkhead. The rear fuselage was manufactured in magnesium alloy in a monocoque structure with longitudinally plated skins. To ensure good anti-spin qualities when flying at high altitude the cantilever tailplane was mounted about a third of the way up the fin which meant that the rudder had to be fitted in two sections above and below the tailplane; it was separated by a torpedo-shaped fillet. Both elevators and rudder used electrically operated trim tabs.

The cabin pressurisation was automatically regulated by a Westland control valve while another control automatically looked after the cabin heating, thereby removing the need for the pilot to wear special clothing – hot or cold air could be admitted at low level. A Rotol blower on the starboard Merlin was used to create the pressurization using air from a small intake in the starboard wing leading edge that passed through a Volkes filter to the blower. The pressure-resisting canopy and bullet-proof windscreen were double-skinned to permit warm air to be pumped between the two to stop icing up and misting. The problem of creating an effective seal between the sliding and fixed parts of the canopy was solved by a rubber gasket fitted around the periphery of the hood which inflated automatically when the cabin pressure was on, thereby creating the seal.

Power was supplied by two Merlin engines with two-speed two-stage superchargers. The starboard nacelle housed a Merlin 72 or 76 and the port a Merlin 73 or 77. Standard production aircraft had 12ft 6in (3.81m) diameter de Havilland four-blade constant-speed fully-feathering airscrews, the propellers rotating in the same direction. Radiators were placed in the wing centre section between the engine nacelles and the fuselage, the air being directed to them by a ducted leading edge entry while the flow at the trailing edge exit was controlled by the angular setting of the main landing flaps. Fuel was carried in four integral wing tanks – two 60 gallon (273 litre) forward and two 140 gallon (637 litre) main tanks just outboard of the nacelles – and a 79 gallon (359 litre) fuselage tank just behind the cockpit. There was provision for one 200 gallon (909 litre) drop tank under each wing and four 20mm guns were mounted in the fuselage beneath the cockpit.

Appendix One

One-Off Modifications to Production Aircraft: A Photographic Gallery

Although this book concentrates on prototypes and designs which did not enter production, during the war years there were many one-off or very short run modifications made to production type airframes which for a variety of reasons were not put into series manufacture. There is insufficient space to provide detailed coverage for these here, and they possibly do not justify a separate large-scale book for them either. Therefore, a selection of the more interesting examples has been assembled as this Appendix to ensure that some form of record is made and that they are not forgotten.

Modifications to standard airframes were usually carried out either for general research purposes or maybe to try out a specific feature applicable to a certain type of aircraft – for example the effects on the airflow from fitting a gun turret. A common change was the installation of alternative engines, either with production in mind or to test a new engine. Several of the wartime bomber types were used to test new or different engines – for example the Fairey Battle light bomber was flown with the company's own P.24 Monarch experimental piston engine and also with engines from several other manufacturers. Other examples of adapted production aeroplanes appear in the main text where they are associated with the subjects covered by individual chapters. However, modifications that were made after the war had ended, for example the use of Avro Lancaster bomber airframes as test beds for a variety of jet engines, are not included, and neither is the carriage of certain weaponry or the addition of small radars for which there was just a minimal change to an airframe's structure.

This Appendix gives nothing like a complete list but it will give the reader a flavour for the sort of work that was going on. Emphasis is given to types where a modification to a production aircraft was of particular interest, or where a version was flown as part of some production plans which in the event did not proceed. Their captions provide a certain amount of background information and the group of aircraft covered here make a fascinating collection, but there were many others and no doubt readers may offer alternative choices for types that should have been included.

Avro Lancaster

Two Avro Lancaster airframes, serials HK541 and SW244, were fitted with fuselage saddle tanks to provide the bomber with more range to allow it to perform operations in the Far East. The conversions were started in 1944 and both aircraft were flying in their new configuration by spring 1945. They made trips to the Indian and Pacific Ocean regions but the end of the war brought an end to the requirement and these aircraft were subsequently scrapped. This view shows HK541. *Peter Green*

An air-to-air view of Lancaster BI (Special) SW244 taken in June 1945 while flying with A&AEE. *Peter Green*

In addition two more Lancasters were kitted out as flying testbeds for early jet engines. In 1943 and 1944 respectively BT308 and LL735 (seen here) each had a MetroVick F.2 jet installed in the end of the fuselage with a dorsal air intake forward of the fins. *George Jenks, Avro Heritage*

Boulton Paul Defiant

The two-seat Boulton Paul Defiant was built as a turret fighter but one airframe, in fact the original prototype K8310, was reconfigured as a single-seat aircraft with the turret removed and flight-tested as such in August 1940. It was intended to serve as an unarmed flying demonstrator for a fixed-gun development of the Defiant which Boulton Paul called the P.94. This would have had twelve 0.303in (7.7mm) Browning machine guns with six in each side of the wing centre section. However, the new version was never ordered, the Air Ministry's rejection of the project being recorded on 26 September 1940. The first image shows the machine unpainted, the second following the application of full livery. *Peter Green, Boulton Paul Association via Les Whitehouse*

Bristol Beaufighter

Several modifications were made to Bristol's very successful twin-engine Beaufighter. In 1940 R2268 was fitted with a wide span tailplane and twin rudders in an attempt to enhance the aircraft's stability, but after some test work RAE at Farnborough was able to advise Bristol that this would not provide an improvement. Tail flutter was also experienced because the fins were now lined up with the airscrew wash. *Airbus*

R2274 was fitted with a standard Boulton Paul Defiant dorsal turret with four 0.303in (7.7mm) machines guns, in which form it was called the Beaufighter Mk.V (the guns could not be fired). When the turret was rotated in flight it did not affect the aircraft's control but the idea was not pursued. The picture was taken at Boscombe Down in May 1941. *Airbus*

Finally T3177 was fitted with Rolls-Royce Griffon engines, four-blade propellers and semi-annular cowlings and was flight tested at Rolls-Royce's Hucknall airfield. *Airbus*

De Havilland Mosquito

Another type considered for fitting with a turret was the de Havilland Mosquito, although in this case a dummy only was flown on W4050. The picture was taken in August 1941 and the additional drag produced by the installation brought a substantial drop in speed but gave no problems to the aircraft's handling. *BAE SYSTEMS*

During the middle war years the argument of bolting a common powerplant on to as many types of aeroplane as possible was seen as a useful step in helping production and maintenance. Between 3 November 1943 and 1 February 1944 DD723 was test flown with Avro Lancaster-type power units and it was found that these made no difference to the aircraft's speed against the standard Rolls-Royce Merlin nacelles, but there was a slight drop in the rate of climb. *Rolls-Royce Heritage*

Gloster Meteor

With its wing-mounted nacelles the Gloster Meteor proved suitable for testing a variety of different jet engines after the war. In its early days it also flew with several alternative power units, but the most distinct difference was seen in the installation of MetroVick F.2 axial engines in DG204/G, which used underslung nacelles rather than the mid-position fittings seen on all other Meteors. The aircraft flew in this form on 13 November 1943, but was lost on 4 January 1944 when it disintegrated at altitude after an engine compressor had burst. The pilot (Sqn Ldr Davie) was killed.

Hawker Typhoon and Tempest

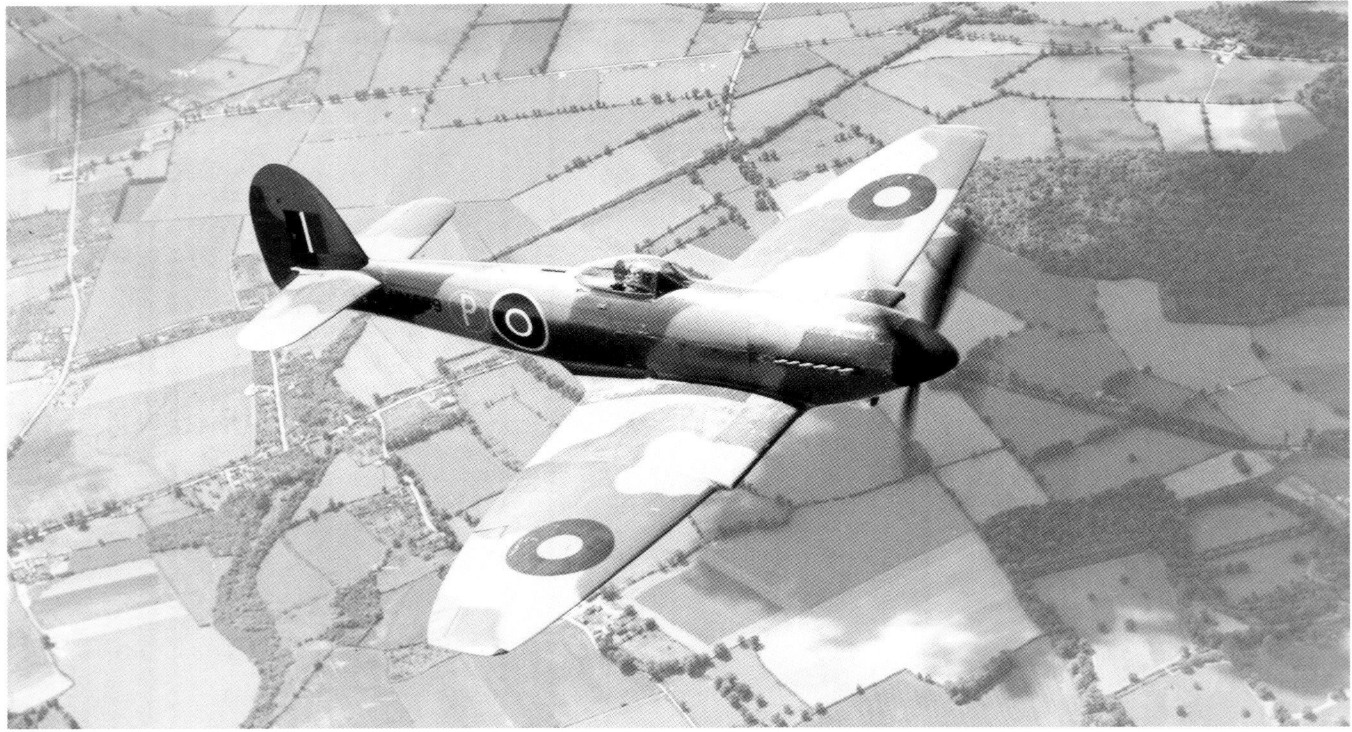

Although the Hawker Tempest was put into production in several versions only one example of the attractive Mk.1 with wing mounted radiators was flown. The Mk.V with chin radiator became the first standard variant.

Two Tempests (EJ518 and NV768 in 1944, the latter pictured) and a Hawker Typhoon (R8694 in 1942/43) were fitted with annular radiators in an attempt to reduce the overheating problems associated with their Napier Sabre engines. All aircraft were fitted with four-blade propellers and, although not adopted for the fighters, Napier's decision to adopt a ducted spinner for its later Naiad turboprop engine resulted from the intensive programme of flight testing carried out on these installations.

Typhoon R8694 fitted with its experimental annular radiator. *Peter Green*

Hawker Fury

It was intended that production Hawker Furies for the RAF would be powered by the Napier Sabre VII engine in the form flown by prototypes LA610 and VP207 after the war was over, but the programme was eventually cancelled (the Navy's Sea Fury was powered by the Bristol Centaurus). However, when it was first flown on 27 November 1944 LA610 had a Rolls-Royce Griffon in place with contra-rotating propeller and annular radiator beneath. This very distinct configuration was not selected for production.

Short Sunderland/Seaford

In late 1941 an upgrade of the Short Sunderland flying boat began with the introduction of Bristol Hercules engines as the Mk.IV, as a type to operate in the Pacific theatre. Two prototypes MZ269 and MZ271 and forty production aircraft were ordered. Changes to the airframe were minimal but included a slightly longer and wider hull, a new planing bottom, a bigger fin and a larger tail, and a powerful defensive armament. MZ269 first flew on 30 August 1944 and the upgrade was renamed the Seaford GR.Mk.1, but with the close of the war in the Pacific there was no need to continue the programme. Only eight production Seafords were completed and most were converted for civilian use while other production airframes were finished as Solent airliners or cancelled. The type was listed on the strength of 201 Squadron during March and April 1946 and the picture shows production Solent NJ205 in July 1946.

Vickers Wellington

Between 1942 and 1945 Vickers Wellington Z8570 flew with several different Whittle and Rolls-Royce jet engines mounted in the very end of its fuselage, and this machine was subsequently joined by W5389 (flown 1943 to 1946) and W5518 (1944 to 1948) on similar trials programmes. The picture shows the modifications made to W5518/G (G for Guard). *Phil Butler*

A quite large number of high altitude bomber variants of the Wellington were produced which featured a different nose with a pressure cabin to permit the aircraft to fly at these greater heights. Examples reached 109 Squadron in 1942 but they were on strength from only March to July of that year. The picture shows Mk.VI W5798 on 12 February 1942. *Phil Butler*

An early high altitude Wellington was Mk.V R3299.

Westland Lysander

K6127, the original prototype of the Westland Lysander army co-operation aircraft, was heavily modified with a Delanne wing as the Westland P.12. This involved fitting an extra wing as an enlarged tailplane with end-plate fins and rudders. The theory behind the Delanne was to introduce a second wing having 50% of the area of the mainplane, and both wings would act as lifting surfaces. The idea was to give the aircraft a large range of CofG and the designer, French aerodynamicist Maurice Delanne, acquired a patent to cover it. This particular modification was also an experiment to covert the Lysander into a turret-armed night-fighter with a four-gun power-operated tail turret, but only the prototype was test flown. The first flight was made on 27 July 1941 and the photos are dated 17 February 1942. In the air the aircraft proved very stable.

P
K6127

P
K6127

Glossary

A&AEE Aeroplane & Armament Experimental Establishment, Martlesham Heath (until August 1939) and Boscombe Down.

AI Air Interception (radar).

AMC Air Materiel Command (USA).

Anhedral Downward slope of wing from root to tip.

Angle of Attack The angle at which the wing is inclined relative to the airflow.

Angle of Incidence Angle between the chord line of the wing and the fore and aft datum line of the fuselage.

ASI Airspeed Indicated.

Aspect Ratio Ratio of wingspan to mean chord, calculated by dividing the square of the span by the wing area.

ASV Anti-Surface Vessel (radar).

AVM Air Vice Marshal.

AWA Armstrong Whitworth Aviation.

Capt Captain.

CAS Chief of the Air Staff [UK Air Ministry post].

Cdr Commander.

CinC Commander in Chief.

Chord Distance between centres of curvature of wing leading and trailing edges when measured parallel to the longitudinal axis.

CofG Centre of gravity.

CRD Controller of Research and Development (MAP post).

CS(A) Controller of Supplies (Air).

Dihedral Upward slope of wing from root to tip.

DTD Director of Technical Development (MAP post).

EAS Equivalent Airspeed (rectified airspeed with a compressibility correction).

ETPS Empire Test Pilots' School at Farnborough.

Flt Lt Flight Lieutenant.

FS Fully Supercharged.

g Acceleration due to the earth's gravity. In other words if a pilot takes an aircraft through a 3-g turn he will weigh three times his normal weight.

Gp Capt Group Captain.

Gross Weight Usually signifies maximum weight with internal fuel plus all equipment/weapons aboard, but not external drop tanks.

Lt Lieutenant.

MAEE Marine Aircraft Experimental Establishment.

MAP Ministry of Aircraft Production – created in May 1940 to relieve the Air Ministry of its role of procuring aircraft and the equipment and supplies associated with them. Functions transferred to the Ministry of Supply in 1946.

MoS Ministry of Supply – created August 1939 to provide stores used by the RAF (and Army and Navy).

NACA National Advisory Committee for Aeronautics (USA).

MS Medium Supercharged.

MU Maintenance Unit.

nm Nautical mile.

OR Operational Requirement.

RAE Royal Aircraft Establishment, Farnborough.

RAeS Royal Aeronautical Society.

RAF Royal Air Force.

RATOG Rocket-Assisted Take-Off Gear.

RNAS Royal Naval Air Station.

rpm revolutions per minute.

RTO Resident Technical Officer.

SBAC Society of British Aircraft Constructors.

sl sea level.

Sqn Ldr Squadron Leader.

TRE Telecommunications Research Establishment, Malvern (became RRE – Radar Research Establishment in 1953, Royal Radar Establishment in 957).

USAAF United States Army Air Forces.

Wg Cdr Wing Commander.

Finally, a note about the 'B' Condition marks allocated to some of the aeroplanes in this work. On 17 October 1940 a letter was sent by an official working for the Director of Technical Development at MAP to the Resident Technical Officer (a Ministry representative permanently based at a factory) at each aircraft manufacturer. Titled *Colouring and Marking of Private Venture Aircraft* it was designed to remove some uncertainty that had previously existed as to whether Private Venture aircraft were to be treated as 'Civil Aircraft' or as 'Prototype Service Aircraft'. It had now been agreed that they should be painted in the manner appropriate to a prototype aircraft with upper surfaces camouflaged, undersurfaces yellow, red, white and blue roundels on the sides of the fuselage and the undersurface of the wings, and red, white and blue stripes on the fin or fins.

In addition, since no service registration marking was allotted to private venture aircraft a substitute was necessary. This was to comprise a letter followed by four figures, for example – A-0232 – with the letter to be used one that had been allocated to a specific firm under what was termed 'B' conditions. The first figure was to be 0, but the remaining figures were at the disposal of the firm subject to the following limitations:

(a). figures 0 and 1 were not to be used.

(b). the first aircraft numbered would therefore be 0222 and thereafter in sequence.

A dash would go between the letter and first figure, but as can be seen in some photos this did not always appear when the mark was painted on certain airframes. These requirements did not apply to aircraft with civil registrations – they were painted and marked as civil aeroplanes.

The reason for the allocation of the numbers in the sequence decreed was to ensure that no combination of numbers would duplicate the then current RAF serial numbers. The purpose for this arrangement was also to make the aircraft's identity during wartime conditions sound more like a normal service serial or civil registration, thereby (hopefully) drawing less attention to an experimental type. This wartime numerical system remained in use until 29 January 1946, although by then it was also being used for the test flying of refurbished ex-RAF aircraft as well as new prototypes.

Bibliography and Source Notes

Although the coverage of each individual type in a book like this is really the equivalent to a magazine article, a great deal of primary source material still needed to be consulted, namely original documents held by National Archives (especially Boscombe Down and company flight reports) and in museums and company heritage centres. The archive collections of individuals listed in the Acknowledgements were an important source, the FlightGlobal Archive website www.flightglobal.com/pdfarchive/index.html was most valuable for finding contemporary reports, and the aviation pages of John Dell (*Dinger's Aviation Pages*) provided some splendid snippets of information. The most important secondary source books and articles were as follows (the *Aeromilitaria* items in particular present really well researched and deeply studied material):-

A Co-Operative Challenger: Flight, 15 April 1943.

Aircraft for the Royal Air Force: Michael J.F. Bowyer; Faber and Faber, 1980.

Back to the Biplane: The 'Slip-Wing' and the Hurricane: Ken Ellis; *Air Enthusiast* 107, Sept/Oct 2003.

Blackburn B.20, B.40 and B.44: Phil Butler; *Aeromilitaria,* Summer 2007.

Boulton Paul Aircraft since 1915: Alec Brew; Putnam, 1993.

The British Aircraft Specifications File: K. J. Meekcoms & E. B. Morgan; Air-Britain, 1994.

British Research and Development Aircraft: Ray Sturtivant; Haynes Publishing, 1990.

British Secret Projects: Fighters & Bombers 1935-1950: Tony Buttler; Midland Publishing, 2004.

Folland Fo.108 – Specification 43/37 (The Frightful): Phil Butler; *Aeromilitaria,* Autumn 2006.

Gloster F.5/34: Phil Butler; *Aeromilitaria,* Autumn 2008.

Gloster F.9/37: Potentially Powerful Punch: Roger Dennis; *Aeroplane,* February 2006.

Handley-Page Aircraft since 1907: C. H. Barnes; Putnam, 1976.

The Hawker Tornado: Phil Butler; *Aeromilitaria,* Winter 2009.

The Hawker Typhoon and Tempest: Francis K. Mason; Aston Publications, 1988.

Jet Pioneers: Gloster and the Birth of the Jet Age: Tim Kershaw; Sutton Publishing, 2004.

Miles Aircraft since 1925: Don L Brown; Putnam, 1970.

Miles M.39B mods: Graham K. Gates; Letter in *Aeroplane Monthly*, July 1991.

Nothing Ventured.... (Folland Fo.108): Philip Jarrett; *Aeroplane Monthly,* June 1991.

Nothing Ventured.... (Hawker Hotspur): Philip Jarrett; *Aeroplane Monthly,* May 1991.

Nothing Ventured.... (Hillson Bi-Mono): Philip Jarrett; *Aeroplane Monthly,* April 1990.

Nothing Ventured.... (Miles M.20): Philip Jarrett; *Aeroplane Monthly,* January 1992.

The RAF in the Bomber Offensive Against Germany: Volume 1 – Pre-War Evolution of Bomber Command 1917 to 1939: Ministry of Defence Air Historical Branch Draft Narrative.

The Saro A.37 'Shrimp': Phil Butler; *Aeromilitaria,* Summer 2010.

Saunders and Saro Aircraft since 1917: Peter London; Putnam, 1988.

Seafang: E.B. Morgan and C. Burnet: *Aeroplane Monthly,* January 1978.

The Secret Years: Flight Testing at Boscombe Down 1939-1945: Tim Mason; Hikoki, 2010.

Shorts Aircraft since 1900: C H Barnes; Putnam, 1967.

Short Shetland: Flight, 17 May 1945.

The Short Shetland: Phil Butler; *Aeromilitaria,* Summer 2010.

Spiteful: E.B. Morgan and C. Burnet: *Aeroplane Monthly,* December 1977.

Spiteful and Seafang: Francois Prins; *FlyPast,* September 1986.

A Spitfire Too Far: The Supermarine Spiteful: Dr Alfred Price; *Aeroplane,* July 2001.

Sturgeon: Target-Tug Extraordinaire: Tony Buttler; Ad Hoc Publications, 2009.

Supermarine Aircraft since 1914: C F Andrews & E B Morgan; Putnam 1981.

The Tandem Monoplane: George H. Miles; *Flight,* 27 April 1944.

Test Pilots: The Story of British Test Flying 1903-1984: Don Middleton; Collins Willow, 1985.

Variable Incidence: Flight magazine, 25 April 1946.

Vickers Aircraft since 1908: C F Andrews and E B Morgan; Putnam.

Vickers Windsor: Forgotten Heavyweight: Francois Prins; *FlyPast,* May 1985.

The Vickers Windsor: Phil Butler; *Aeromilitaria*, Autumn 2010.

The Westland Welkin: Phil Butler; *Aeromilitaria,* Spring 2010.

Wings of the Weird and Wonderful: Capt. Eric 'Winkle' Brown; Hikoki, 2010.

Index

INDEX OF AIRCRAFT

INDEX OF PEOPLE

INDEX OF PEOPLE continued...